The Persistence of Allegory

The Persistence of Allegory

Drama and Neoclassicism from Shakespeare to Wagner

JANE K. BROWN

PENN

University of Pennsylvania Press

Philadelphia

10 9 8 7 6 5 4 3 2 1

Published by
University of Pennsylvania Press
Philadelphia, Pennsylvania 19104-4112

Library of Congress Cataloging-in-Publication Data

Brown, Jane K., 1943–
    The persistence of allegory : drama and neoclassicism from Shakespeare to Wagner /
Jane K. Brown.
        p. cm
    Includes bibliographical references and index.
    ISBN-13: 978-0-8122-3966-9
    ISBN-10: 0-8122-3966-0
    1. European drama—History and criticism.   2. Neoclassicism (Literature)—Europe.
I. Title.
PN1811.B76 2006
                                                                    2006042173

Frontispiece: Andrea Mantegna, *Minerva Chasing the Vices from the Garden of Virtue.*
© Réunion des Musées Nationaux/Art Resource, Paris.

For my mothers, Gertrude and Hermione

Gestaltung, Umgestaltung,

Des ewigen Sinnes ewige Unterhaltung.

Contents

Preface

In today's climate of culture studies and globalism, some explanation for a book focused on the forms of the European literary past seems to be in order. The short answer is that synthesizing our knowledge of the history of drama in Europe since the Renaissance changes unreflected assumptions into which we all relapse from our immediate specialties and that are widespread outside the academy. A more reflected relation to what seems obvious to us and closest to home might, by alienating our tradition, make it more understandable in the global context within which our disciplines now aspire to understand it.

The longer answer comes from the circumstances surrounding the genesis of the book. My training and early career were in German Baroque and eighteenth century, especially Goethe. When I moved to the English Department at the University of Colorado in 1979 to keep my family together, I was writing a book on *Faust* and found myself teaching Shakespeare. I soon learned that my German Romantic take on the Renaissance led to equally vehement, but contradictory, reactions: either that there is no allegory in Shakespeare or that allegory and Shakespeare's medieval roots are old hat. As I learned more about Shakespeare, about Ben Jonson as a writer of masques, and about their Spanish contemporary, Pedro Calderón de la Barca (also necessary to understand *Faust*), I decided my next book would be about allegorical drama—"The Other Drama" I wanted to call it.

The area has in fact been well studied, but the people who study its different parts don't talk much to one another. Despite the establishment of comparative literature as a discipline more than a generation ago, non-German scholars interested in Benjamin on allegory do not read German Baroque drama (nor indeed do most German scholars interested in Benjamin, nor do scholars of seventeenth-century drama in other European traditions), nor do they read Calderón, despite Benjamin's strong emphasis on him, much less the obscurer eighteenth-century texts, the "Haupt- und Staatsaktionen," to which he points. Nor do they read these people next to the great French dramatists or, with rare exceptions, English dramatists of the century, let alone their great Dutch contemporary, Joost van den Vondel. In the last decade or so scholars have become more interested in opera, but opera in the seventeenth and even eighteenth centuries is, for all practical purposes, an entirely separate field from drama. I was soon learning all kinds of information that was surprising to friends, students, and colleagues in adjacent specialties, even when it was familiar to specialists. And so arose my central thesis: the history of European drama is a unity, and it is necessary to read it across the boundaries of languages and subgenres.

In the process I learned there really was no "other drama." Given the prejudices of Goethe and his friends, for whom French neoclassicism was the Antichrist, I had assumed that my "other drama" was allegorical and neoclassical drama mimetic. Writing this book, I learned that both kinds emerged from the same primal soup, from Western Europe's repeated efforts to reinvent itself by returning to classical antiquity. The last thing I had in mind at the start was to rewrite the history of neoclassicism, but that is precisely what this book proposes—that we think of neoclassicism not as a single movement, but as a wave of interrelated movements that sometimes further and sometimes retard one another. Now I was really not writing about allegorical drama, but about all European drama from Shakespeare to Wagner.

To be sure, this is not a comprehensive synthetic history of European drama; instead I trace the development by its evolving skeleton. I am interested in the forms that underlie and enable the conventions of European drama. Others might call the goal structuralist, but I would prefer to think of it as morphological in Goethe's sense of the word. The coverage is broad but selective; I have not shied away from synthesizing information any specialist would know, yet I have tried to avoid what nonspecialists will already take for granted, such as demonstrating the structural richness and psychological insight of Shakespeare or Racine. I have tried instead to introduce the materials from a point of view less obvious to most readers, and I have often turned to dramatists of great interest who are less well known, at least in my cultural context, than they deserve. I hope that by repositioning the familiar dramatists in an "other" seventeenth- and eighteenth-century context, both dramatists and context will gain in depth.

I also hope that readers will come to share my view of the subliminal unity of European drama since the late Middle Ages across national and historical boundaries, and even across the boundaries of different arts. I have no wish to undo generations of careful and important work analyzing the distinctions among different forms of theater art and understanding the relation of those forms to historical and cultural circumstances, but rather hope the distinctions will take on richer meaning when understood as variations from a constant underlying possibility. Even more, I hope readers will appreciate the unexpected historical and formal diversity of both neoclassicism and allegory that I have tried to make visible. Both phenomena must be understood historically, not as fixed categories. While under certain circumstances it is useful to think about allegory as a static mode in the still-helpful terms of Angus Fletcher, it is also necessary to understand it as a phenomenon that varies historically and generically. It is possible to use the term "allegory" about such different figures as Shakespeare, Claude Lorrain, Goethe, or even Ibsen without leveling them to a simplified understanding of medieval allegory. It also means that all texts should be read, to different extents for different texts, allegorically, whether dramas, operas, narratives of whatever sort, not just certain kinds of arcane novels and a historically and generically specified subset of dramatic works called morality play or masque. And conversely, there is a real historical basis for allegorical reading that validates it as more than just the preference of a particular kind of reader.

This work has benefited from the generosity of more people than I can name here. First, I must thank above all my former colleagues at the University of Colorado, especially but not only Everly Fleischer, Elissa Guralnick, Jim Kincaid, Paul Levitt, and Ruth Widmann. There was nothing obvious about hiring me in an English Department or letting me teach the Renaissance; I appreciate both the imagination and tolerance that provided me such a constructive working environment for nine years and hope the department felt it received some adequate return. Second, I am grateful to all the students at Colorado, Washington, Munich, and Tübingen who have joined me in exploring new, sometimes rather arcane, areas over the last twenty years. Third, I owe an enormous debt to my colleagues at Washington and elsewhere who supported this work for so many years with opportunities to teach this material, letters of recommendation, and generous research leaves. The work was supported at different times by the University of Washington Royalty Research Fund, the Walter Chapin Simpson Humanities Center at the University of Washington, and a year-long fellowship from the National Endowment for the Humanities; I am deeply grateful to all of these institutions.

Part of Chapter 4 is adapted from "Double Plotting in Shakespeare's Comedies: The Case of *Twelfth Night*," in *Aesthetic Illusion: Theoretical and Historical Approaches*, ed. Frederick Burwick and Walter Pape (Berlin: de

Gruyter, 1990), 313–23. Parts of Chapter 7 are adapted from "The Queen of the Night and the Crisis of Allegory in *The Magic Flute*," *Goethe Yearbook* 8 (1996): 142–56; "Der Drang zum Gesang: On Goethe's Dramatic Form," *Goethe Yearbook* 10 (2001): 115–24; and "The Theatrical Practice of Weimar Classicism," in *The Literature of Weimar Classicism: Camden House History of German Literature*, vol. 7, ed. Simon Richter (Rochester: Camden House, 2005), 139–66. I am grateful to the various editors for permission to reuse the material here.

I have received significant help and encouragement on this project from old and new friends; I am especially grateful to Dieter Borchmeyer, Cyrus Hamlin, Fred Hauptman, Meredith Lee, Simon Richter, Jerome Singerman, and Humphrey Wine for inspiration, for suggestions, and also for their long-term faith in the project. Finally, the loving support and interest from my family have been of more value than they realize—my children have inspired me with their superior knowledge of Spanish and Dutch, two of the languages I had to learn for the work. My husband, Marshall, is, as probably most readers of this book will already know, a colleague, editor, and mentor of the first order, and the book is more accurate, better informed, more ambitious, and better written for his generous labor. Indeed, it is unimaginable without his interest, stimulation, resistance, and assistance at every step of the way—and for his forty years of loving companionship.

Chapter 1

Introduction

I take as my epigraph the frontispiece to this book, Andrea Mantegna's *Minerva Chasing the Vices from the Garden of Virtue* (1502), which depicts Minerva expelling ugly personifications of the vices from the bower of learning. Designed for the Studiolo of Isabella d'Este, it represents humanist classicizing wisdom expelling the vice of medievalism from the realm of learning, and neoclassicism expelling personification allegory from the stage of European representation, as will become clearer below. The program thereby expressed was to be fulfilled in the course of the next 350 years: allegorical representation on canvas and in literature was to yield to ever more realistic imitation of nature, that classical mimesis at the heart of Aristotle's *Poetics* and celebrated with such penetration in Erich Auerbach's *Mimesis*. In drama, the particular topic of this study, accurate imitation of nature is understood to triumph in the drama of Elizabethan England and the psychological dramas of French Classicism, both in different fashions the result of the neoclassicists' recovery of Aristotelian poetics.

But Mantegna's painting can be read in this fashion only if it is understood still to be operating allegorically, despite its highly developed realistic representation of the human figure. Of course personification allegory persisted in painting into the eighteenth century, and even as an archaism in public art of the nineteenth and twentieth centuries. The persistence of comparable representation in drama is the thesis of this study. To be sure, the language for discussing drama shifted rapidly from allegorical to mimetic representation when Aristotle was assimilated into the Latin grammatical tradition in the sixteenth century. Since the time of Scaliger and Castelvetro, the most influential of the Italian neoclassicists in the later sixteenth century, the *Poetics* has provided the inescapable vocabulary for analyzing drama. Even today college anthologies of drama are likely to begin with an introduction to Aristotle, and the neoclassical focus on character is nearly universal outside the academy. But dramatic practice is learned at least as much from plays seen and read as from treatises, and it adjusted to the new norms only gradually. For a mode of representation is like a language: European dramatists had not only to learn to represent mimetically, but also not to carry over vocabulary and syntax from their older allegorical "language." Thus the critical vocabulary for drama emerged abruptly in the Renaissance, but dramatic practice evolved more slowly.[1] Indeed, with the advent of the illusionist stage in the late sixteenth and seventeenth centuries, new allegorical forms such as masque and opera began to flourish, morality with its personified virtues and vices entered a heightened development in Germany and Spain, but commercial drama accommodated to it only relatively late. During this period the apparently competing forms actually enriched one another.

While some individuals adjusted more rapidly than others, for the culture the process took until well into the eighteenth century. It proceeded at different rates in different regions, social strata, areas of cultural expression, and genres. Even when drama was no longer explicitly religious, it still alluded to phenomena allegorically with reference to common religious and cosmological views. Furthermore, in the natural inertia of things, rhetorics of representation, like other cultural practices, persist—often in the popular arena—long after they cease to be current and have lost their original meaning. This lag was particularly visible in the delayed shift to mimetic representation in opera, but it occurred widely in other forms of drama as well. No sooner was the development substantially complete than some farsighted dramatists, Goethe primary among them, recognized the cultural wealth about to be lost and mounted an effort to recover the older tradition: much of the peculiarity of his *Faust* can be explained in these terms. Even in his wake there were efforts, mainly in Germany, to recover allegory as a viable representational mode for drama in, for example, Wagner's Festspiele in Bayreuth and Hugo von Hofmannsthal's in Salzburg. Yet when Walter Benjamin returned to the theory of allegory on the stage in the 1920s he reinvented something quite new and different.

The kind of gradualist narrative I propose here has long been in effect for descriptions of developments in the sixteenth and early seventeenth centuries, perhaps most thoroughly and eloquently for England, where the emergence of Shakespeare from the clumsiness of the preceding generation left so much to explain. No serious student of Shakespeare would deny that there are still elements of medieval patterns of thought and representation at work in the plays; although some would deny such elements much place in their current approaches to the plays, most would regard them as hulls still clinging to a more modern kernel, and essentially all would reject the designation "allegorical" to characterize them. But these elements are less often denied than ignored. Shakespeare is, after all, such a convincing representer of character and society that all else can be comfortably overlooked. Thus

Harold Bloom subtitles his popular Shakespeare book "The Invention of the Human" and begins, "Literary character before Shakespeare is relatively unchanging . . . In Shakespeare, characters develop rather than unfold, and they develop because they reconceive themselves" (Bloom, *Shakespeare* xvii). Between the cultural materialism of much recent scholarship in the English Renaissance and the rear guard of those who consider Shakespeare above all a dramatist of character—this includes many in and virtually everyone outside of the academy (just look at the director's notes for any production)—there is little space left for those who see a plurality of discourses operating in the plays.[2] The historical difference and apparent inaccessibility of the great dramatists of the seventeenth century such as Calderón, Corneille, and Racine, similarly, are ritually acknowledged, but discussion of them always proceeds in terms of characters, as if they were only important for their psychological realism. This priority accorded to psychological mimesis is, as I will show below, entangled with the heritage of neoclassicism.

There are also generic questions at stake. Today the term "drama" tends to be reserved for the play staged or filmed about psychologically believable people. Even where stage practice is antirealistic or absurd, as in the plays of Samuel Beckett, intriguing, convincing characters drive the play and the audience's reaction to it. Both the scholarly canon and the curriculum relegate the allegorical tradition in drama— mystery play, morality play, court masque, and opera—to secondary status, as mere precursors to modern drama (which "begins" with Shakespeare and Corneille's tragedies of passion) or as the purview of nonliterary disciplines. Stephen Orgel, who has done more than any other modern scholar to make English court masque accessible and comprehensible to the current generation, asserts that it is simply an accident of time that the modern reader takes masque to be a form of drama (*Ben Jonson: The Complete Masques* 1). But only a thoroughgoing Aristotelian would insist that drama (actually tragedy) is the imitation of human action. Orgel himself has helpfully identified a competing Platonist poetics in the Renaissance that would justify precisely the creation of admirable illusions as the proper province of drama in his introduction to *Inigo Jones: The Theatre of the Stuart Court*. And in fact the history of European drama is not just a chain of Aristotelian plays, but the mutual interaction of many different forms—at the turn of the nineteenth century Goethe was still writing court masques as well as verse tragedies, tragicomedies, farces, and libretti. The dramas of Metastasio were performed as both stage plays and operas in the eighteenth century.[3] I want to show how reading all the possibilities together changes our understanding of the more narrowly defined traditions of drama.

Such a version of the history of European drama is not only more gradualist than has been the norm, but also less linear. I will focus here on the eddies of literary history: not where it flows forward smoothly but the places where it stubbornly holds back or even seems to reverse itself. In general terms dramatic representation became steadily more mimetic from the sixteenth to the nineteenth century. But if some of its greatest moments in the seventeenth century are startling advances in psychological representation, some of its other greatest moments are allegories of exquisite sophistication. At other times, even in the late eighteenth and early nineteenth century, only recovering allegorical modalities enables us to make sense of major works that clearly appealed to their age and to us, such as Goethe's *Faust* or Mozart's *Die Zauberflöte (The Magic Flute)*.

Structurally, these eddies arise from naming the beginning and end points of the historical development with the conceptual abstractions "allegory" and "mimesis." Basically I follow the terminology of Angus Fletcher in *Allegory: The Theory of a Symbolic Mode*, which is still for me the most helpful conceptualization of allegorical practice. It is understandable that the eighteenth and nineteenth centuries needed to discredit allegory in their struggles to establish the validity of material reality as object of investigation and as legitimate principle of causality. From our different historical perspective we can afford to readmit the term, even to the sacred precincts of Shakespeare criticism, where the recent use of "emblem" (for example, Belsey, *The Subject of Tragedy*, or Daly, "Shakespeare and the Emblem") is a poor substitute, since it more properly refers to the particular marriage of allegorical image and text popular in the seventeenth century. "Mimesis" is the term Fletcher, drawing on Auerbach, opposes to allegory. It is particularly appropriate in my context because it is Aristotle's term, and Aristotle was the name attached to the neoclassical thrust that ultimately drove allegory from the European stage. It is also appropriate in that the common objection that allegorical drama is not really "dramatic" refers to its lack of probability and its lack of a structured plot with suspense: probability and plot are the two central categories of Aristotle's *Poetics*. By confronting allegory and mimesis I intend to keep the focus on the tension between dramatic practice and Aristotelian (which I will also use as a cover term for neo-Aristotelian) theory. Indeed although Fletcher claims to derive his categories from Coleridge, his chapters overlap with Aristotle's rubrics for discussing tragedy—(in Fletcher's order) character, diction, plot, causality, thought. Causality is the underlying and driving concept of the *Poetics*, even though it is not one of Aristotle's categories; Fletcher substitutes it here for Aristotle's spectacle, and like most moderns, silently ignores the role of song, Aristotle's sixth rubric. Fletcher's last chapter on psychoanalytic analogues to allegory returns to character and causality—the most important aspects of Aristotle for the moderns—joined together. The very organization of his book bears witness to the continuing and profound impact of Aristotle on our thinking even about non-Aristotelian genres.

By using attributes instead of simply the designations "medieval" and "modern" I intend, of course, to characterize the different modes of representation. The terms chosen can be aligned with a tension within Greek epistemology between Plato and Aristotle, as I shall do in the next chapter. They can also be aligned with the cautiously elaborated distinction between Judeo-Christian and classical representation drawn by Erich Auerbach in *Mimesis*. The Judeo-Christian side tends to parataxis, abrupt shifts, stylistic mixture, and what one might call a vertical line of vision—movement along the axis natural-supernatural, whether in plotting or in explanation. On the classical side we find a tendency to precise designation of syntactic relations, connection, clear distinction—indeed hierarchy—of styles, and a horizontal line of vision—an interest in temporal and causal relations more consistently within the natural sphere. Auerbach's distinction is an important model for what I have in mind in choosing the term "mimesis." "Allegory" for the opposing term I have adopted from Goethe's usage in *Faust, Part II*, where he works against his own previous denigration of allegory in favor of symbol, almost as if he knew that Coleridge was to give to his distinction a currency that unfortunately still endures.[4]

But of course both "mimesis" and "allegory" are notoriously shifty terms. Allegory already extended in antiquity over a range of meanings from metaphor and simile through irony and sarcasm to riddle, proverb, and allusion,[5] while the recent major "theories" of it are really phenomenologies determined to a large extent by a particular group of texts of interest to the author.[6] Treating allegory and mimesis as a dyad is intended to neutralize their instability: where their precise meaning is unclear they can still be understood in terms of their mutual difference.[7] Mimesis is "realistic," it "imitates" what is natural and materially real. Allegory, by contrast, represents something other than what it appears to claim (from the Greek "allos" = other). In mimetic representation one knows what one is looking at, assuming one can recognize the outlines, so to speak, but in allegory either the name or the ontological level must always be changed. By allegory I understand, basically, a mode of representation which renders the supernatural visible, by mimesis a mode which imitates the natural, what is already visible.

The terms thus refer both to modes of representation and objects of representation.[8] Practitioners of mimetic representation represent the objects of material reality, while allegorists depict something other than what they really mean. Their objects of representation are normally invisible, either because they are abstract (for example, Faith or the soul), because they are supernatural and invisible in the world (angels, the devil), or because they are politically too dangerous to represent directly. This particular distinction of the objects of representation is valid for allegory and mimesis in drama from the sixteenth to nineteenth centuries; I would not assert it without qualification for other forms of allegory, particularly not for classical and medieval allegory.

Like many oppositional pairs, allegory and mimesis necessarily implicate one another. There can be no allegory without a mimetic component, for mimesis is required to represent any semblance of existence. As visual representation in Europe became more mimetic during the Renaissance with the discovery of perspective,[9] so too allegorical beings such as virtues and vices also began to look more like representations of real humans. Thus while we may say without hesitation that Caravaggio's work is more mimetic than the fantasies of Bosch, Bosch's creatures presuppose his sophisticated capacity to represent surface, space, volume, the human form, and all the other elements that he must alienate to make us understand them allegorically. Indeed allegory is characterized not by its abstraction but by its concreteness,[10] by making ideas material in sometimes disturbing ways. Nor does mimetic art or drama represent only the visible. Any representation in which we can identify a discursive element is to some limited extent allegorical.[11] The texts I will discuss all operate between the two modes, for the terms refer to asymptotes, to abstractions that delimit the possibilities of representation open to dramatists.

This construct is intended to apply exclusively to drama. The overwhelming proportion of the scholarly discussion of allegory, ancient and modern, has to do with narrative.[12] Although allegory was originally invoked in antiquity to legitimate fictions, beginning with the Homeric poems, apparently the sacral content of ancient drama was so obvious that it did not require allegorical justification. Only in the late Middle Ages does allegory emerge as an important concept in drama. Just about the same time, at the turn of the fifteenth century, with the rediscovery of Aristotle's *Poetics* and the discovery of scientific perspective, the standard of mimesis in painting and poetry is suddenly raised. Figural representation ceases to have the force of literal truth, and the relation between allegory and mimesis becomes a problem. This tension continues to generate vital texts in various dramatic genres until the end of the eighteenth century, and *Faust* marks its last surge. After Goethe there are efforts, often significant ones, to revive the tradition of allegorical drama—Wagner's *Ring* is the greatest of them—but the fact of conscious revival marks the death of the tradition. From the mid-nineteenth century on, with the first stirrings of modernism in the narrower sense, the opposition between allegory and mimesis ceases to be productive, as both allegory and mimesis are seen to be the imposition of meaning by a subject in the face of the incommensurable materiality of the world. Art henceforth needs to be freed from both.

The shift from allegorical toward mimetic representation in drama corresponds to the advancing secularization of European culture. The point is obvious if we consider that the explicitly allegorical forms of drama—religious drama, school drama, masque, to a large extent opera—have died out with church and court, the institutions they served. The intimate connection of the shift to secularization also arises logically from what Fletcher identifies as "kosmos" (70–146). Without embedding in some perceived cosmic order, Fletcher argues, there can be no allegory, which always refers to a fixed, communally accepted context. Indeed, the connection to secularization is part of the standard view: Honig attributes the demise of allegory to the Renaissance adoption of classicism and secularization, which results in the "growth of realism" (*Dark Conceit*, 38–39), and Tuve sees allegory in rapid decline after the efflorescence of secular allegory in Spenser, though she realizes with regard at least to the seventeenth century that "it is never safe to conclude . . . that allegory had died and no one knew where it was buried" (218).

But secularization was also a gradual process, and remained incomplete even in the early nineteenth century. As structures of universal belief broke down in the seventeenth and eighteenth centuries, the primary reference point of explanation became centered in the individual rather than in the cosmos. For this reason E. R. Curtius called allegorical drama "theocentric" and mimetic drama "anthropocentric" (142). The older allegorical mode of representation, in which the supernatural was rendered visible, was less suited to the Enlightenment's internalized grounding of significance, and gradually gave way to more mimetic modes of representation, in which nature and material objects represented themselves, not aspects of an invisible supernatural order. Instead of representing some function of the soul as conceived by the church, dramatic characters came to represent particular human beings. With this shift the representation of a modern interiorized subject became possible, but again, only gradually. The sense that the self dwells inside the body was already implicit in classical and medieval views, but introspection took the form only of moral evaluation. In Shakespeare introspection broadens its scope to include motivation, but still tends to take place in specially designated monologues, in which the self is seen from a bird's-eye perspective.[13] Only very gradually does the represented self become so interiorized even to the speaking subject that it can articulate motivations of which it is no

Figure 1. Lucas Cranach the Elder, *Judith with the Head of Holofernes*. The Metropolitan Museum of Art, Rogers Fund, 1911. (11.15.)

longer aware: Rousseau identified this possibility in the eighteenth century. Although the great neoclassical commentaries on Aristotle shifted his focus from plot to character, the first appearance of an interiorized self in drama is unclear, because we as post-Rousseauist critics have such a well-developed sense of the interior subject that we tend to see it even where it has not been intentionally represented. But identifying the first appearances of the interior subject is less important than seeing both the shifts and the increasing self-consciousness of its representation in our period.

Secularization generated considerable anxiety both in its own terms and also with regard to representation; these anxieties persist up to the demise of the allegorical tradition in the nineteenth century, but they are especially easy to identify in the earlier stages.[14] As brief examples, consider the painters of the German Reformation. Cranach and Dürer helped to import the new Italian style into the more conservative and less secularized provincial society north of the Alps. This modern, more mimetic, style celebrated the nude body, especially the female body. In the older German context, only personified vices had been painted nude; now nudity was to be seen positively. Hence the sudden popularity of Adam and Eve and Susannah and the Elders as pictorial motifs, for both allow the painter to paint naked bodies yet acknowledge the sinfulness attributed to them by the religious tradition in the embarrassment of the figures. This ambivalence was inherent in virtually all representations of women since, until the Renaissance, females represented in European painting were basically either figures from religious history or personified virtues or vices. Now all of Cranach's women, from Eve to Judith to Venus as the personification of luxury, even when fully clothed, appear slightly embarrassed or dangerous—or both—as they peer at the spectator through narrowed eyes. If Cranach had to paint—or wanted to paint—women who were not saints, then they had to be the embodiment of sin—the allegorical tradition left no other alternative.[15] Their embarrassment reflects their uncomfortable transitional status.

"Allegory" and "mimesis" are shifty terms also because they are historically conditioned, for allegory operates differently at different times.[16] Medieval mystery plays and most medieval painting involved the figures primarily of biblical narrative and saints' lives. In the Christian morality tradition of the sixteenth and seventeenth centuries allegory refers mainly to the projection of moral and ethical qualities onto visible figures who accompany the main figure. Yet another language of allegory emerges in Renaissance Italy in the arguments of the neoplatonist syncretists, who map Christian meaning onto classical myth. By the seventeenth century, emblem, which combines word and pictorial image in specified ways, becomes the dominant allegorical mode, only to yield in

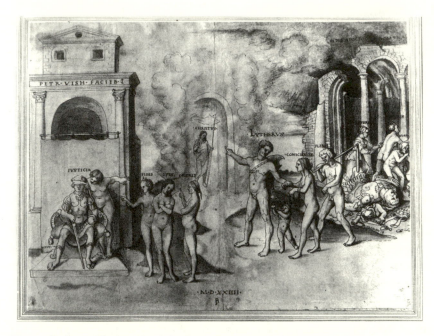

Figure 2. Peter Vischer, *Symbolic Representation of the Reformation*. Stiftung
Weimarer Klassik und Kunstsammlungen, Goethe Nationalmuseum, Weimar.

turn in the eighteenth to allegory understood simply as personification.[17]
In its later forms, in the eighteenth and nineteenth centuries, allegory
also included romans à clef, in which one figure stood in for another
equally or perhaps even more real figure—a late and trivial development, when the material had gained such ascendancy over the spiritual
that it could usurp the place of the supernatural in allegory. Mimesis is
equally variable: it refers to a range of representational modes from the
neoclassical imitation of idealized nature to the accurate imitation of
evanescent detail or even atmosphere represented by Naturalism and
Impressionism at the end of the nineteenth century.[18] Nevertheless
through these historical transformations there remains the common underlying distinction that mimesis represents visible nature, allegory renders the supernatural (or what is left of it) visible.

Historical development in allegory can be discerned even during the
Renaissance. An extreme and unusually obvious example may be found
in *Symbolic Representation of the Reformation* (1524, watercolor drawing,
Goethe House, Weimar), by Peter Vischer (ca. 1460–1529), a minor
German artist of the Reformation. Luther, having toppled papacy and
driven out its accompanying vices, all labeled, leads newly freed Con-

science and the People toward Justice and points toward Christ, approaching from the rear center. The allegory is obvious and strictly traditional; the figures are either concretely embodied abstractions or figures from religious history. Yet the style is modern—Italianate architectural forms and classicizing nudes. Justice is clothed in Roman armor, while the others imitate classical sculpture. More important, all the figures, including Luther, are nudes, and the vices are not uglified. In effect, the older Christian allegorical mode (typical, for example, of morality drama) has been translated into the forms in which myth was represented by Renaissance artists. What Vischer did here feels very odd, even today, because this particular combination of two representational languages did not become common.

Andrea Mantegna's *Minerva Chasing the Vices from the Garden of Virtue* offers a less extreme but more complicated array of representational modes.[19] In the pond in the foreground the traditional vices are represented in late medieval style as ugly, deformed, and labeled, with three of the cardinal virtues floating on high in a mandorla of clouds. But other aspects of vice and virtue are represented in the forms of classical mythology: the centaur in the pond, satyrs, and insect-winged putti, an evil Venus on the back of the centaur, pursued by Minerva and, presumably, Diana.[20] Finally, there are ad hoc allegories and grotesques: the maiden running next to Diana (perhaps Chastity,[21] an embodied idea like the medieval vices, but unlabeled; classicizing in form, but without mythological attributes), the mother of virtue as a human olive tree on the left, the putti with owls' heads who aid Minerva in the background. Christian, classical, and modern, Mantegna thus operates in three different allegorical "languages" simultaneously.

The same layering of allegorical idioms is still occasionally visible even in the second half of the seventeenth century, as for example in Guido Cagnacci's (1603–63) *Martha Rebuking Mary for Her Vanity* (after 1660, Norton Simon Museum). Across the bottom a half-nude Mary lies sprawled with her torn-off jewels about her while Martha kneels before her and remonstrates. Above this historical representation hovers an angel driving away a flying demon, the abstract or personified version of virtue banishing vice, as if to explain the meaning of the historical scene just below it. In the doorway on the right stand two women, ad hoc allegories of the particular virtue and particular vice at issue, but they are identifiable as Contrition only by the pot of ointment and Vanity by the irritation on her face. While everything is rendered in the now typical mimetic style solidified by Guercino, Caravaggio, and Reni, the painting reiterates its statement through three different types of figures.

These idioms are reflected in Mantegna's painting in the scroll wrapped around the olive tree in the left foreground, which states its

Figure 3. Guido Cagnacci, *Martha Rebuking Mary for Her Vanity*. Norton Simon Art Foundation, Pasadena.

message in Latin, Greek, and Hebrew. The simultaneous presence of the three languages of divine revelation represents the typical syncretism of Renaissance humanism as we also find it, for example, in similar triple labels in the garden of Erasmus's dialogue, "The Religious Banquet." While all three languages are those of divine revelation, nevertheless Greek and Hebrew carry special significance in Erasmus's dialogue, for they are the new and unusual languages. Latin, as the language in which the entire dialogue is written, constitutes the "background" of ordinary reality. In parallel fashion, the medieval allegories in Mantegna are the foil to the new iconography of the mythological figures and the classicizing grotesques, while in Cagnacci, 150 years later, the historical differences have been almost forgotten. But whatever the relative value placed on the different forms of allegory, in all these artists there are visual discourses equivalent to historically different languages, and thus different kinds of allegory. Although the Italian classicizing style, which I would compare to the early stages of neoclassicism, ultimately won the day, just as it did in literature, these paintings reveal the same transition that will be visible, for example, in Bale's *King Johan,* a play where the surface neoclassicism has not yet obscured the allegory. But we will see the underlying allegory also well into the seventeenth century—in Shakespeare, in Claude Lorrain, and in the development of tragicomedy and opera.

It is clear that sometime in the seventeenth century the capacity of the intellectual vanguard in Europe to appreciate and feel itself represented by allegorical drama began to wane sharply. The language for this secularization of style, which we call neoclassicism, emerged from the rediscovery and reinterpretation of Aristotle's *Poetics* that had begun in the sixteenth century.[22] But, like allegory, neoclassicism too is plural, and even contradictory. It is common to equate neoclassicism (or "Classicism" as it is often called in French scholarship) with neo-Aristotelianism, but in fact it encompasses classicizing impulses that also include imitation of classical comedy, Senecanism, perspectivist stage sets, court masque, opera, and the imitation of Greek tragedy, which really began with Racine and flowered only more than a century later in German Classicism. One might even consider morality drama, with its prosopopoeia derived ultimately from Prudentius's fourth-century imitation of classical epic, as the earliest neoclassical impulse in European drama. While all attempted to recover the practice and dramatic form of antiquity, these forms developed in different directions in response to the prevailing allegorical mode of representation and frequently clashed with one another, to create numerous historical eddies and backwaters. Aristotle and the classical dramatic models obviously militated in favor of mimesis, while prosopopoeia in morality, perspectivist stage sets, and the invention of opera contributed to a flourishing of allegory. Thus opera emerged from the efforts of the Florentine Academy to recover the performance mode of Greek tragedy yet was the object of unremitting hostility by neoclassicists in the eighteenth century. The interference among these different modes of neoclassicism is a major theme in the book that follows.

As the few examples from Renaissance painting have already shown, there is a cognate issue in the visual arts, so I will begin with a parallel exploration of the Italian landscape painter Claude Lorrain and his lengthy reception through the nineteenth century. In order to clarify this development the argument will focus first on the complexity of the neoclassical impulses that arose with the Renaissance, then on the persistence of allegorical representation in areas where it is often denied or marginalized in drama, including Shakespeare, court masque, opera, and Racine. Then I will address the elaboration of allegorical representation in drama in the seventeenth century in Spain and Germany. In the eighteenth century the issue will be the tension between an apparently unconscious continuance

of formal structures that presuppose allegorical thinking in an age that regarded such patterns with, at best, deep ambivalence. The argument
ends, finally, with the renewed self-consciousness toward allegory at the
end of the eighteenth century, with the efforts to recover it, and the end
of the continuous allegorical tradition in drama. Each chapter will simultaneously focus on a different classical revival in order to clarify the historical richness of the term neoclassicism.

Chapter 2

Claude's Allegories and Literary Neoclassicism

> *From where I stood I watched them recede in the frame of the roadway, between the Moorish house and the Lombardy poplar. Then the little sedan . . . spurted up the shining road, which one could make out narrowing to a thread of gold in the soft mist where hill after hill made beauty of distance, and where there was simply no saying what miracle might happen.*
>
> —*Nabokov,* Pnin *190*

Like neoclassicism, the paintings of Claude Lorrain (1604/5–82), the most popular landscape painter of the seventeenth century, have remained sacrosanct preserves of mimetic representation. In painting the term is "Classicism," but both terms identify the same stylistic intent, namely mimesis—the accurate representation of reality understood not as the particular but as the typical or general, and defined for both by Aristotle's *Poetics*. In painting, the position was first publicly articulated by Giovanni Pietro Bellori in 1672 but actually was formulated and practiced much earlier (Panofsky, *Idea* vii); it is still the operative theory in Sir Joshua Reynolds's *Discourses on Art* (1776–90). According to this theory, which remained dominant well into the nineteenth century, the painter imitated nature, but not slavishly; instead his images combined the best details of their type to form the "beau idéal," the perfection of which nature is capable but which it never achieves in any single example. Claude's classicizing landscapes were famed in their time for their "truth to nature" and are regarded today as precise evocations of the atmosphere or mood of a landscape in the same way that Shakespeare, Corneille, and Racine are understood to represent with uncanny genius the human passions. Despite their recognizable elements of convention and idealization, most critics nevertheless deny Claude's paintings any conceptual or even narrative meaning.[1] In parallel fashion drama of the seventeenth century, beginning with the mature Shakespeare and continuing with Corneille and

Racine, is normally regarded as preeminently drama of character rather than of idea or theme. Both are thus the supreme manifestations of the triumph of Aristotelian mimetic style over the thematic religious and mythological allegory prevalent in the morality drama and court masque, on the one hand, and religious painting, on the other, that they superseded. Behind the formal conventionality of Claude and Racine equally there breathes a power of direct feeling, in essence a psychology, that is the real raison d'être of both.

As a prelude to the discussion of drama, this investigation of Claude's representational mode will show concretely how even this most classicist of painters is full of allegorical moments that correspond closely in structure, style, and theme to those identifiable in drama of the period: time, character, pastoralism, myth, and theatricality can be shown to function identically to our expectations for seventeenth-century drama. And as scholars have recovered an allegorical literary culture in the seventeenth century, to be sure more focused on Germany and Spain than on England or France, art historians have identified allegorical representation in seventeenth-century portraiture and still life.[2] Furthermore, Claude's painting stands in the same relation to work of the preceding century as that of the dramatists to their predecessors of the century before. On the surface, the older allegorical languages of painting familiar from the Middle Ages and Renaissance seem entirely absent: at most a few mythological or biblical figures wander through his landscapes, often so small as to seem secondary even to the decorative shepherds for which he is notorious. But beneath the surface lie similarities to more explicit allegories. The epigraph reveals, finally, the remarkable persistence of this ambiguous mode of mimesis, when even in the twentieth century so self-conscious an allegorist as Vladimir Nabokov can end his ironic self-portrait, *Pnin*, with an obvious evocation of Claude.

Until the mid-nineteenth century, Claude's name was synonymous with landscape painting in Europe. Although he never maintained a large workshop like Rubens or Rembrandt, his avidly collected paintings became the models not only for representation, but altogether for the perception of landscape. The eighteenth-century English park is to a large extent modeled on Claude's work, so that his paintings became a reality imitated by nature.[3] The success of Ruskin's attack on him in *Modern Painters* (1843–60) reflects partly the stifling multitude of mediocre Claude imitations cluttering collections by 1800 and partly the increasingly materialist understanding of imitation as the century progressed.[4] In Claude's own day landscape painting had just emerged as a recognized genre in Italy, almost a century after the Low Countries, where it was part of the same secularizing development that also resulted in genre and still-life painting (see Gombrich, "The Renaissance Theory of

Art and the Rise of Landscape," and Lagerlöf, *Ideal Landscape* 4–17). As an import from northern Europe it was the appropriate specialization for transalpine artists living in Rome, including such eminences as Claude and Poussin. Like still life (another northern genre), it was perceived in Renaissance art theory as restrictedly mimetic (Gombrich, "The Renaissance Theory of Art and the Rise of Landscape" 115–16). Claude's paintings are among the first to make the human figures and therefore the narrative aspects of the painting, whether religious or secular, secondary to the representation of nature (cf. Gombrich, "The Renaissance Theory of Art and the Rise of Landscape" 108). By opening the door to a true absence of plot, they represent a major advance in the mimetic tradition;[5] hence it is especially important if they reveal even residual allegories.

I first survey the obvious allegories in Claude with the techniques of literary hermeneutics, next reflect on the ways in which they became invisible to viewers from the late eighteenth century on, and then close with an analysis of Ruskin's condemnation of Claude in *Modern Painters*. Ruskin demonstrates the inability of the nineteenth century to deal with the seventeenth century's typical mixing of allegorical and mimetic modes in both painting and literature. Claude is thus an excellent test case for identifying the allegories behind even the most apparently mimetic aspects of neoclassicism.

Time

Claude was famous as the painter of sunrises and sunsets, as the representer of time through light, an assertion already routine among his friends (Russell, *Claude Lorrain* 417–33). Explicit allegories of time are natural to the seventeenth century, and he himself described his pair now hanging in Munich, *Landscape with Abraham Expelling Hagar* and *Landscape with the Angel Appearing to Hagar* (LV 173 and 174) as: "Abraham et Agar qui est le soleil Leuan [levant]" and "L'Ange qui montre la fontaine a Agar que rapresente apres midy" (Röthlisberger and Cecchi, *Tout l'oeuvre peint de Claude Lorrain* 14).[6] The words "est" and "rapresente" are important here: they suggest that Claude regarded time as somehow the "meaning," not just the subject, of the paintings. Indeed, the first depicts an early morning departure, a common theme in Claude, as Abraham sends Hagar and Ishmael from his house into the desert. He directs them not into the populated depths of the painting where the sun rises, but across the foreground to the hills, presumably on into its pendant (he commonly painted his landscapes in pairs), which depicts the desert and was intended to hang to its right, as it now does. The double sense of beginning—of the day and of the journey—is

Figure 4. Claude Lorrain, *Landscape with Abraham Expelling Hagar.* Bayerische Staatsgemäldesammlungen, Alte Pinakothek, Munich.

enhanced by the Edenic aspect of the painting. Amid lush greenery herds graze peacefully, scattered at great distances from the tiny herdsmen on the right. The noble Roman architecture also makes the sense of beginning in the painting historical and general as well as local and individual. Yet the painting is full of ruins. Abraham and Sarah live not in patriarchal tents, but, like many Italians of the seventeenth century, in the remains of once greater buildings. As in Virgilian pastoral, with which Claude's painting is frequently connected, human time has no absolute beginning.[7] Instead a gentle continuity of time is expressed by the juxtaposition of ruin, continuing life, and new day. Virgil is himself an intensely nostalgic writer, especially in the *Eclogues* and *Aeneid* VIII, and Hagar suffers the same fate as the banished shepherds in the *Eclogues*—exile from the fruitful civilized world into a strange desert. Thus both ruins and pastoral landscape express nostalgia for a golden past that one has missed—perhaps by a hair's breadth, perhaps by millennia. Using allegory not as a convention but as a language capable of great specificity, Claude, then, portrays this departure as a loss rather than a new beginning.

Hagar leaves civilization for nature, but nature does not always signify loss in Claude or even in this painting (consider the rising sun); the allegory is specified by the relation of the figures to the sun. Claude painted numerous departures from harbors, mostly in the 1640s; they

Figure 5. Claude Lorrain, *Landscape with an Imaginary View of Tivoli*. The Samuel Courtauld Trust, Courtauld Institute of Art Gallery, London.

commonly signify the beginning of a journey into a world protected by God, associated with the rising sun.[8] The religious significance of the sun depends not only on prevalent neoplatonist interpretations of the sun as the representation of divinity, but also on its position at the vanishing point of the perspective. This position is typical in Claude's paintings. The sun enables us to see the landscape by illuminating it and by organizing it: as the origin of both light and understanding it is divine. *Landscape with an Imaginary View of Tivoli* (LV 67, Courtauld Institute, London), where the dome of St. Peter's glitters on the horizon just beneath the setting sun, renders the religious significance of the sun explicit. Small wonder that Claude's paintings were heavily patronized by the princes of the church, for the worldview of the Counter-Reformation is made visible in their most basic construction.[9]

Once perspective is recognized as an allegorical signifier, the direction of movement in *Abraham Expelling Hagar* can be read more precisely. In the seaports the beams of the rising sun mark the path from

Figure 6. Claude Lorrain, *Seaport with the Embarkation of the Queen of Sheba.*
National Gallery, London.

the foreground through the open mouth of the harbor and the boats
can only move from the harbor directly into the ordering light, as for
example in London's *Seaport with the Embarkation of St. Ursula* (LV 54) or
Seaport with the Embarkation of the Queen of Sheba (LV 114). But Hagar sets
off on foot, not in a sheltering ship of the church. Furthermore, she
heads *across* the painting, and *across* the path marked by the rising sun.
Her departure is not an embarkation, but an expulsion, and Claude
specifies the difference in concrete visual terms. If departure can mean
gain or loss, depending on the signs with which it is combined, there is
not only a unique mood to each of Claude's paintings, as Kitson has argued (*The Art of Claude Lorrain* 5), but a unique meaning as well. Allegorical reading thus goes beyond that based on detailed allusions to
texts or on the specifically narrative elements; it depends also on elements of style. Claude's allegories have a semantic dimension and operate in the same way as literary allegories.

Symmetry connects the pendant, *Landscape with Hagar, Ishmael and
the Angel,* or the late afternoon sun, to the first painting, as so often in
Claude's pairs. From the opposed outer edges of each a tree leans in-

Figure 7. Claude Lorrain, *Landscape with Hagar, Ishmael and the Angel.*
Bayerische Staatsgemäldesammlungen, Alte Pinakothek, Munich.

ward. Ahead of the tree in *Abraham Expelling Hagar* is the house of Abraham; in the second painting the house is replaced by a large vertical
natural mass that closes the edge of the painting in similar fashion. The
mountains on the right of the first painting recur here on the left; so
similar are the high dome and the weathered mesa-like formation that
we seem only to have walked around them to the other side. Corresponding to the tree-covered protuberance just in front of them and to
the left in the first painting is a bare natural arch in the second. A receding prospect of water and mountains fills the backgrounds of both,
but again it seems as if we had simply walked some distance to the right
from the first painting so that the mountainous spine separating two
bodies of water is now on our left—as if we had made the same journey
within the paintings as our literal stepping to the second painting on
the right. Such correspondence between our world and that of the
paintings affirms their meaning for us, while the correspondences between the paintings invite specific interpretation. Various signs are associated with the stated difference between morning and afternoon.
Wild animals replace peaceful herds and the only humans are Hagar
and Ishmael. The noble temple gives way to natural rock, and the lush

vegetation—especially the hillock covered with trees—to bare rock. The difference is between Eden and the desert. And yet the oppositions are not extreme. This desert landscape is still green, and still slightly populated. There is a sail on the sea in the background; the natural rock arch is remarkably square, as if it were the remains of an ancient gateway; and just ahead of it, almost in the center of the painting, what looks like a ruined bridgehead corresponds to the intact bridge in the first painting. Like *Abraham Expelling Hagar* this painting does not allow even a distant past to be entirely forgotten in the present, so that morning and evening have visible counterparts in the morning and evening of history.

But if morning is associated with expulsion, afternoon is associated with rescue, for the elderly Abraham has been replaced by the young angel. If in the morning Hagar must depart, in the evening she in effect returns home, not to her literal home, but to her figurative, in religious terms "true," home in the safety of God. Now the light in the painting comes not from the rear but from the right, the direction in which the angel (and, one notes retrospectively, Abraham) points with the left hand. But the angel does not really direct Hagar to look at the sun; he directs her with his right hand to look at the fountain springing beneath the rock in the center foreground. This spring is almost the last thing the observer notices in the painting, because, as critics never tire of remarking, the eye is immediately drawn to the horizon in Claude's paintings (for example, Kitson, *The Art of Claude Lorrain* 7; Barrell, *The Idea of Landscape* 8; Paulson, *Literary Landscape* 48). Only when the angel's understated gesture is recognized as deliberate do the spring and the end of the story reveal themselves. The light and perspective do not lead to meaning in the depths of the painting, as in *Abraham Expelling Hagar* or in the seaports—not because order does not ultimately reside with God, but because God is saving Hagar in the world by sending her water in the desert. It is still afternoon, not quite evening, not yet time for her to leave the world for the arms of God. The language of gesture points toward universal history, not toward individual character.

View of La Crescenza (LV 118, New York) offers an allegory compressed in the manner typical of seventeenth-century literary emblem. On the surface it would seem the most extreme version of Claude's mimeticism because of its similarity to two of his drawings of the same villa, apparently from nature, one of which is labeled "La Crecensia" (Russell, *Claude Lorrain* 161; Kitson also asserts Claude was sketching in the area again in the early 1660s, *Liber Veritatis* 126). Because the painting lacks the trees that usually frame the foreground in Claude landscapes, Kitson suggests that the painting itself "almost gives the impression of having been executed from nature" (*Liber Veritatis* 127).[10] But even the

Figure 8. Claude Lorrain, *View of La Crescenza*. The Metropolitan Museum of Art, Purchase, The Annenberg Fund Inc. Gift (1978.205), New York.

historical evidence suggests that the painting represents light and time more than the particular building. It is uncertain who commissioned the painting, or indeed, whether it was commissioned at all (Russell, *Claude Lorrain* 161–62); seventeenth- and eighteenth-century portraits of buildings were commissioned by their owners, but neither of the possible patrons could have owned La Crescenza. Hence the public, and probably therefore primary, purpose of this picture was not to represent the building as it was. The overwhelming impression from this rather small painting is of rich golden light—the trees lit from the right rear shine bright gold and the right face of the building is warmly lit. Highlights invite the viewer to follow the path of the light, as in the seaports, but here they do not lead to the horizon or to the vanishing point. This painting is unique in Claude's oeuvre in affording only the tiniest view of the distant prospect (one hill visible just to the right of the villa).[11] Instead the path begun from the golden treetop to the right facade of the villa leads out of the picture, whence the late afternoon sun still shines brightly but invisibly to us. The painting thus moves the viewer's eye from the visible to the invisible; this is the movement of allegorical interpretation. And the invisible sun toward which the eye is drawn lights up and gives meaning to the visible world. In that sense the allegory is the same Christian allegory of the sun as in the seaports, but now divested of the narrative elements implied by the journey of life.

Time is also at issue. The warm low light evokes late afternoon, while the gold of the leaves evokes autumn. Once again the painting engages us in an allegorical move from the visible—space—to the invisible—time. In the absence of both figures and distant prospect, our attention moves to the four trees in the foreground. Each is lit—or has changed, for it is ambiguous whether the color signifies time of day or time of year—to a different degree. The tree at the right is darkest (or greenest), the next to the left is brightest (most golden), and the last two show different intermediate degrees of color. Thus not in schematic order but with a certain staged naturalness, the full range of possibilities of temporal change is rendered visible. This allegory of mutability is hardly original; indeed, it is to be found almost everywhere in seventeenth-century literature and art. But that is precisely the point: that Claude's paintings still participate in this discursive allegorical tradition.

Claude and the Tradition of Allegorical Painting

It was necessary to read the two Munich paintings as a material unity in order to comprehend the full extent of their allegory. The apparent identity of the hills at the right/left sides of the paintings connects and separates them both literally and figuratively, as if one painting were divided in two to enhance the opposed meanings of each half. Considered as one painting, with the hills superimposed, the structure is in fact familiar from narrative painting of the Middle Ages, in which the same figure appears in different life stages in different fields of the painting, or in diptych panels. Claude has, as a mimetic representer, separated the different points of time into separate paintings, but the ready connectibility of the two reveals the older allegorical structure beneath the surface.

The allegorical structure is even closer to that of the French Renaissance, as is evident from comparison to *The Emperor Augustus and the Sibyl of the Tiber*, painted around 1580 by Antoine Caron (1521–99), court painter to Henry III of France.[12] The painting, now in Paris, memorializes a court fête at which Queen Catherine de Medici watches the king perform the role of Augustus in *Octavien et les Sibylles*, a mystery play known to have been performed repeatedly in sixteenth-century France. The sibyl, clothed in blue, points out to Augustus the deity whom he should adore, the Virgin and child visible in the mandorla at the upper right. The fountain running oil is the miracle that proves the power of the new god. Between the foreground of this dramatic scene and the miraculous revelation of the Virgin is a large midground filled with

Figure 9. Antoine Caron, *The Emperor Augustus and the Sibyl of the Tiber.*
© Réunion des Musées Nationaux/Art Resource, Paris.

various examples of fantastic classicizing architecture and a bit of the
Paris skyline, all inhabited by visitors and members of the court participating in the fête and its associated tournament. The allegorical court
celebration and the painting assimilate the king of France to the Roman
emperor. This allegory in turn rests openly on the older religious allegory embodied in the mystery play, partly secularized but not completely out of touch with its religious roots. While Claude may never
have seen this painting, it is typical of allegorical representations in the
generation that preceded him (Ehrmann, *Antoine Caron* 131), and its
structure underlies essentially all of his paintings—a foreground with
figures disposed theatrically in a structured setting (either colossal
buildings, framing vegetation or both), a midground with some striking
architectural monument or group (sometimes many) and with often
large numbers of tiny figures going about their business, and finally the
light in the background, often the sun itself. Claude is obviously much
more mimetic, especially in his enchantingly full midgrounds, where
not only a striking ruin but also innumerable buildings or cities dotted
through the landscape, a rich natural setting, a bridge with travelers,

Figure 10. Claude Lorrain, *Landscape with Apollo and the Muses.* © National Gallery of Scotland, Edinburgh.

and bodies of water speckled with tiny white sails replace Caron's evenly scattered monuments. Yet the seaports tend to have at least a few figures in the foreground who are looking directly toward the sun, and in the late *View of Delphi with a Procession* (LV 182, Chicago) the foreground figures walk toward the temple shining on the hill, and some of them point. Even a very early pastoral (LV 18, Duke of Portland) has a cowherd pointing to the sun. It is a far cry from sibyl and king to shepherd and shepherdess, but the structure is the same.

Indeed, the underlying allegory can be more or less evident, as in the Munich Claudes. Even without knowing the title of the second, it is not difficult to identify Hagar and the angel: the child clearly suffers, the overturned bottle indicates the cause of the suffering, the angel pointing to the spring indicates the solution. In the first painting however, without knowing the title one could not be certain that the woman and child are to set out on their own; perhaps she just carries the burden because the man is old. Mary and Joseph are consistently represented with this age difference and they travel together. Nor could one know that the child is the old man's own, nor that the route will not take them over the bridge and down to the sea. Compared to the first, the second is stripped down—take away the facade of the building and you have a vertical wall of rock; take away the trees and you have a bare rock arch;

change the time of day and the mountaintops are bare rock. In this world everything is seen more clearly, and divinity no longer appears in symbolic form: instead of the sun there is a visible angel. In this respect the second painting is more allegorical, the first more mimetic.

Mythological representation enters relatively late into Claude's oeuvre and is generally understood as a kind of effort to "keep up with Poussin," that is, to move his landscape paintings from the bottom of the classicist hierarchy of genres to the top by making them historical or allegorical. The Edinburgh *Parnassus* of 1652 (LV 126) demonstrates how self-consciously Claude enters into such allegorical representation. The color values of frame and subject are reversed, so that the magnificent land-scape prospect in the right half of the painting and the river god in the right foreground are brightly lit and the white swans show up by con-trast in the dark left foreground, while the ostensible subjects of the painting—Apollo and the Muses—are obscured and Pegasus creating the spring of Helicon is virtually invisible. These different areas of light are also different modes of representation. The landscape is, though ide-alizing, mimetic. The river god and the swans are emblems, standard signs for something else, in this case the river and poetry or art. Apollo, the Muses, and Pegasus are myths. Both myths and emblems are forms of allegorical representation, but they are not identical; emblems are more abstract, more explicitly semiotic, and, in the seventeenth century, more modern. The obscurity of the mythological figures is, then, directly cor-related to their antiquity as a mode of representation; the emblems are somewhat better in Claude's terms, but the clearest of all is the unalle-gorized landscape. A parallel argument can be made about *The Sermon on the Mount* (LV 138) in the Frick Collection in New York. The brightest light, which emanates from the horizon of the splendid background, is blocked by the dark mountain upon which a tiny Christ and his disciples sit in obscurity. In effect the religious allegory blocks our access to the ideal nature in the depths of the painting. Here is one explanation for the tininess and apparent irrelevance of the biblical or mythological fig-ures in Claude: like the mythological figures in the *Parnassus* they be-long to an older, more obscure mode of representation. By obscuring the fashionable mythological figures the *Parnassus* in effect appears to critique the emerging classicism for its ambivalence about breaking its ties to allegory.

Character

Character is such an obvious category in Aristotelian dramatic theory that it is often forgotten that until the mid-sixteenth century character was communicated in drama not mimetically but allegorically, that is, by

Figure 11. Claude Lorrain, *Landscape with Psyche and the Palace of Cupid*. National Gallery, London.

the personage carrying a name that revealed his or her "character." In morality play characters have abstract names like "Hypocrisy," "Wealth," "Understanding." But into the eighteenth century, long after the advent of Aristotelianism, figures still have speaking names like Sir Toby Belch, Thorowgood, Surface. Similarly in painting, identity was first represented allegorically by a figure's clothing or often even a label. Mimeticism enters with expressiveness of face and gesture. Claude is considered at best a marginally adequate painter of figures, and his figures are unusually small in proportion to his landscapes, especially compared to Poussin. Both qualities derive ultimately from his allegorical conception of character.

Consider, for example, *Landscape with Psyche and the Palace of Cupid* (LV 162) in London. A leading Claude interpreter makes character central by saying the painting is intended "to evoke Psyche's grief after Cupid had abandoned her because, in defiance of his command, she had gazed on him in the night" (Kitson, *Liber Veritatis* 154; the narrative here is Book V of Apuleius's *Golden Ass*). But the painting might just as well show Psyche earlier, when she worries about whether she was truly married to a monster as her sisters claimed (full analysis of the possibilities in Wine, *Poetic Landscape* 52–55). Indeed the painting is full of disorienting phenomena. It is unusual for Claude to have a solitary figure in the foreground and to place a building at the center rather than to one side of the painting.[13] More striking is the relation of the single figure to the light and to the perspective. The sun is present in the sky, just to the left of the castle; this is much more obvious in the LV drawing, where rays emanate from the sun just as they do in the seaports. But there is no path from the foreground to the sun, and Psyche looks neither at the sun nor at the vanishing point of the perspective, which would be behind the castle. Instead she gazes across the painting to the right, which is rather dark; it is difficult to tell whether she looks out to sea, into the dark trees, or at the ground. The uncertainty is increased by the diffusion of the light. Despite the visible presence of the sun, its light organizes neither the picture nor Psyche's view of the world: it is not recognizable as the source of light and understanding. Nor does the perspective in the painting enable her to see the truth as it does for the figures in the foreground of the harbor scenes, as well as for the spectators. Thus Psyche's position with regard to landscape, sun, and perspective all manifest inner uncertainty. Since Apuleius's tale is an allegory of how the soul (Psyche) finds its way to divinity (at the end she is carried up to heaven) through Love (Cupid), the uncertainty that Claude represents is the central theme of the story. Perhaps this is why Psyche's figure is "curiously bulky for this phase of Claude's career" (Kitson, *Liber Veritatis* 154). Even so, the clumsiness of her figure is the only thing

Figure 12. Claude Lorrain, *Coast View with the Trojan Women Setting Fire to Their Fleet.* The Metropolitan Museum of Art, Fletcher Fund, 1955 (55.119). Photograph, all rights reserved, The Metropolitan Museum of Art.

about Psyche herself that reflects her spiritual state, while all the other aspects are projected onto her relation to the world of the painting. Indeed, Tom Lubbock thoughtfully remarks that Psyche's very "extraneousness" in the painting represents her "own unhappy situation" ("Claude's Extras" 22). Caron similarly evokes the virtue of Henry III by representing his spatial relation to the sibyl and the Virgin. The literary parallel to this is character representation in morality drama, where figures are accompanied by their attributes represented externally, or in medieval epic, where being lost in a forest may represent confusion of the soul, as in Dante.

Such projection is typical in Claude's narrative paintings and is related to their astonishing absence of affect, despite the fact that their figures are clearly within the Italian tradition. Occasionally peasants flee in terror (from brigands [LV 3, 34] or from a battle [LV 27, 73, 173]), but normally Claude's figures are in repose, even when the situation calls for excitement. The women setting fire to the Trojan fleet (LV 71) in New York, for example, stroll calmly from ship to ship as if nothing were wrong; their passion is displaced onto the steaming volcano in the right background. A related puzzling aspect of Claude is that his figures are always so tiny in proportion to the landscape—consistently smaller than in Claude's own record drawings of the paintings in the *Liber Veritatis*. Both of these puzzles are explained by the allegorical representation just demonstrated in *Psyche*.[14] Allegory, representing as it does a theocentric universe, has little interest in representing emotion other than fear of damnation; character is an ethical category. Thus morality play projects a figure's virtues and vices onto concrete figures. Claude, however, evokes not virtues and vices, but Psyche's epistemological state or the mood of the Trojan women. This concern with affect can only arise in the anthropocentric world of a secularized post-Renaissance culture. Claude uses the old technique to represent a new mode of being in the world. Seventeenth-century painters like Caravaggio, who expressed affect strictly mimetically, were decried by contemporaries for their naturalism. Claude's move to the opposite extreme of projecting it onto the landscape manifests in another way the period's considerable ambivalence toward its powerful new technique of representation and its own commitment to secularization.

Allegory and Theme

It is easy to connect a term like "theme" to allegory but harder to know if it can properly be applied to painting, where, in the case of Claude at least, the preferred expression is "subject." Furthermore, Claude has at most three subjects, and they are all interrelated: journeying (his "single great subject" according to Russell, *Claude Lorrain* 83), pastoral (the single most common title given to his paintings), and classical myths. The current tendency to name all the paintings "Landscape with . . ." reveals the assumption that the subjects have no specific significance, that they are not themes in the literary sense. Nevertheless, they can be shown to function with the same degree of specificity as literary motifs, and are, therefore subject to interpretation, always, of course, within the prevailing tension between allegory and mimesis.

More than a quarter of Claude's oeuvre involves journeys by water. The relation of figures to the light and, usually, perspective as well, tends to make these into departures on the journey of life. The occasional ends of sea journeys involve appropriate, often subtle adjustments—the light is diffused for the problematic arrival of Cleopatra (LV 63) in Paris or for that of Aeneas at Pallanteum (Anglesey Abbey, LV 185); when Ulysses returns Chryseis to her father (the cause of the great quarrel in the *Iliad*, Paris, LV 80) a ship blocks the sun. But Claude depicts other journeys as well, the generally popular Flight into Egypt (the most frequent), Mercury stealing the cattle of Apollo (with Mercury always running off), the rape of Europa (always just before the departure into

Figure 13. Claude Lorrain, *Seaport with Ulysses Restituting Chryseis to Her Father Chryses.* © Réunion des Musées Nationaux/Art Resource, Paris.

the water), and two processions (to be understood as pilgrimages?) to Delphi. Furthermore, virtually all of his paintings with no more title than "pastoral" have either a river leading to the sea or, more commonly, a bridge and road with travelers heading into the distance; water in the background is regularly dotted with sails. The rare representations of violence in Claude are disruptions of the means of journeying— battles on bridges (LV 27, 34, 137) or the Trojan women attacking their own ships (LV 71). The human world of Claude's midgrounds and backgrounds is always underway amid the much slower progress of the natural world through time. The universality of the motif in Claude justifies its generalized religious interpretation, but also dilutes its significance by its very generality.

Journeying is constitutive to the pastoral. Behind Virgil's *Eclogues* looms the expulsion of peasants from Italy as their land is awarded to Augustus's veterans, and the cycle not only celebrates the luck of those who remain in their shady paradise but also laments the losses of farms and love (in 9 and 10). The initially refreshing pastoral shade becomes at the end harmful to fruit ("nocent et frugibus umbrae," 10.76), so that even the fortunate shepherds must abandon their sunny paradise, at least for the night and possibly forever. It is, of course, obvious that Claude is a pastoral painter—except for the seaports, his paintings routinely have a herdsman and a few animals somewhere, often as a frame in the foreground that actually dwarfs the historical figures and makes the title subject difficult to identify (especially with the motif of the Flight into Egypt, for example, LV 60, 104, 110). Claude must separate the journeys from the act of herding, since without the verbal element a shepherd on the road would be indistinguishable from a shepherd going about his normal business. But the journeying opens the paintings to Virgil's insecurity. Virgil's shepherds are driven out as a result of war, which also threatens the pastoral realm; so too in Claude violence occasionally enters the pastoral world. In the *Liber Veritatis* there are two scenes with brigands (3, 34), two battles on a bridge (27, 137), St. George killing the dragon (73), and the Trojan women setting fire to their ships (71).[15] Additional pictures involve hunting (24, 37, 180) and, in Claude's last painting, Ascanius shooting the stag of Rhea Sylvia, the wanton act that releases the final spasm of violence in the *Aeneid*. Other paintings suggest violence hovering in wait just beyond the moment portrayed, like the war that will break loose on the death of the stag: Europa and the bull (LV 111, 136, 144), the golden calf (LV 129, 148), Diana and Actaeon (LV 57). The most astonishing is Jupiter and Callisto (LV 76): Jupiter appears in the form of Diana, so the picture shows two young women sitting calmly together—only the title gives any hint of the violence to come (Callisto will be seduced, changed into a bear and hunted to death). No affect is portrayed in any of these scenes, except for the haste of the peasants to escape. Violence is present, then, as in Virgil. Tasso and Guarini, in the sixteenth century, readily admit violence into their pastorals, but Shakespeare already returns to the Virgilian balance, as in *As You Like It*, where the lines between violent court and gentle pastoral are clearly drawn. Increasingly in the seventeenth century the pastoral is purged of violence to become the conventional locus amoenus of the eighteenth-century idyll, as in Watteau and Geßner. Claude's pastoral, in which violence is largely repressed but still lurking, corresponds exactly to the state of literary development. The background of violence seems more real than the pastoral, so that the pastoral represents the real by exclusion. Thus allegory represents not only the invisible, but also, by implication, the repressed visible normally the purview of mimesis.

Claude's use of myth feeds on the same tensions. Both Virgil and Ovid, the two main sources of Claude's classical images, deal with metamorphosis or transformation and were routinely read allegorically in

Christian Europe.[16] Claude prefers myths of transformation, in particular ones involving Apollo, Mercury, or Diana.[17] The three divinities
regularly appear in pastoral settings in Ovid—Apollo and Mercury as
herdsmen, Diana as huntress—where they are unlikely to call attention
to themselves as supernatural, and Claude represents the moments just
before the transformation (excepting only *Landscape with the Metamorphosis of the Apulian Shepherd*, LV 142). The tendency suggests, of course,
a will to mimesis and avoidance of allegory. The three are, however, popular in the seventeenth century precisely because they are the most as-
similable to the Christian myth. Apollo is the god of the myriad
Orpheus operas; in Monteverdi's (1607) he is the father who brings his
repentant son into heaven. Mercury is the most important divine mediator in Renaissance neoplatonism, and is as such a placeholder for the
Son. Diana, similarly, embodies for the Renaissance the purity and grace
of the Divine One conceived as feminine: in Shakespeare, for example,
she normally signifies divine grace. And in Claude, too, she appears preserving her purity (LV 57) or as mediatrix in the invented episode of
Cephalus and Procris reunited by Diana (LV 91, 163). In LV 76, in
which the Diana sitting with Callisto must be read to be Jupiter disguised as Diana, Diana is not a figure but a cipher, in effect an allegory
of an allegory. The myth Claude painted most frequently is Ovid's rendition (*Metamorphoses* 2.676–707) of Mercury stealing the cattle of Apollo
(LV 92, 128, 135, 152, 170) and bribing Battus to conceal the theft (LV
131, 159). The appeal seems to be the pastoral element: Mercury drives
the cattle while Apollo pipes. But Claude's representations eventually
extend to the conclusion of the tale (that Ovid leaves out), when Mercury makes peace with Apollo by giving him the first lyre. The painting
that corresponds to LV 135 (Holkham Hall) shows a lyre at Apollo's
feet, suggesting that Claude was aware of the end of the myth.[18] And in
his last treatment of the pair he shows Mercury presenting the lyre to
Apollo (LV 192), resolving the feud that had occupied him for so long.
Ultimately the realistic herdsman Mercury becomes the inventor of the
lyre, the allegorical midwife of poetry: Claude gives meaning to the
scene he had represented so many times. Here, then, is a drive toward
allegory that balances, if not counterbalances, the drive toward mimesis
registered in the avoidance of transformation.

Theatricality and Self-Consciousness

"All the world's a stage" is a central metaphor for the seventeenth century's self-consciousness about representation. Not only is an important
history of the time called *Theatrum mundi*, but the fact that theater itself

Figure 14. Rembrandt, *Holy Family with Curtain*. Staatliche Museen Kassel, Schloß Wilhelmshöhe.

becomes a constant play-within-the-play (*Hamlet*, for example, or Corneille's *L'Illusion comique*) has spawned a substantial critical literature of metatheater and metadrama around it (for example, Calderwood, *Shakespearean Metadrama*). The open painted curtain, found as early as Raphael's *Sistine Madonna* (1514, Dresden) is widespread in seventeenth-century Dutch painting. Although such curtains apparently represent real curtains that protected paintings in the period (and thus artistic self-consciousness but not necessarily theater), in Rembrandt's *Holy Family* (1646, Kassel) the painted frame of the painting behind Rembrandt's painted curtain strongly resembles a proscenium arch. Equally important is the common scenic structure in Rembrandt in which the figures, often elaborately costumed as in the many self-portraits and portraits of Saskia, seem conscious of being watched.[19] There is surely substantial self-consciousness, if not outright irony, when Rembrandt casts himself as the Prodigal Son and Saskia as his trollop (1635, Dresden). The easy combination of mimesis and allegory in Renaissance painting can be rescued only as self-conscious playacting.

Claude's theatricality addresses the same issue, with less irony. Indeed, a common complaint about Claude is the staginess of his scenes and the inevitable trees that frame one side of the pastorals as "coulisse"; a few scholars have written in passing about the similarity of especially the seaports to stage backdrops of the period, and Marcel Röthlisberger has referred to the paintings as "ideal stages" ("Das Enigma der über-längerten Figuren in Claudes Spätwerk" 98).[20] These are important insights, and they deserve more than passing notice, for it is typical in Claude that a specific stage space is set aside for the figures. In *Abraham Expelling Hagar* the figural space is enclosed by a low rock wall facing into a gully just behind it, while the figures in *Hagar and the Angel* stand on higher ground bounded in front by large rocks (in the LV drawing the difference in height is much more obvious). Claude's paintings always have their own internal frame, consisting usually of a dark line across the foreground, a tree on one side, a hill and/or some significant architectural structure on the other, with the deep space of the painting somewhere in between. The framing is varied richly and occasionally violated to startling effect, as in *Psyche and the Palace of Cupid,* where the earliest drawing had the building on the left.[21] Many paintings include spectators, even artists sketching (for example, LV 24, 44, 130), but more commonly, and more emphatically allegorically, such dramatic scenes are ignored by other figures (usually shepherds or travelers in Claude's enchantingly busy and well-populated midgrounds): those who do not recognize that all the world's a stage miss the miraculous occurrence right under their noses. This lesson is especially apparent in the various Flights into Egypt, and was already found in Caron, although Claude's foreground figures rarely receive so explicit a lesson as Caron's.[22]

The theatrical theme appears most explicitly in *Landscape with St. George Killing the Dragon* (LV 73, Hartford), where St. George fights the dragon on a raised tongue of ground; the figures too close to the action flee, but others watch the spectacle comfortably from a bank above. The permeability of the boundary between stage and house (figures flee from the "stage" to the "boxes") is a large and important topic in the period (think of the interruptions to the play of the mechanicals in *A Midsummer Night's Dream*), but occurs in Claude only here. The proscenium arch spread over Europe's stages in the seventeenth century; the relation of audience to stage had, therefore, only just changed. Even in Claude the permeability of the boundary marks the allegorical relation of theater to human life in the period.[23] But it also marks the self-consciousness of classicism. In the words of Erwin Panofsky, "Classicistic art can be defined as a classicism that has become conscious of its own nature after a past no longer classical and within an environment no longer classical" (*Idea* 107). Like his literary contemporaries, as we shall see in subsequent chapters, Claude is fully aware of his competing stances.

Figure 15. Claude Lorrain, *Landscape with St. George Killing the Dragon.*
Wadsworth Atheneum Museum of Art, Hartford, Conn. The Ella Gallup
Sumner and Mary Catlin Sumner Collection Fund.

The End of Allegory

It is easy to register the disappearance of this awareness among Claude's
later admirers. Consider, for example, LV 122 and LV 82. In the 1770s
they were identified in John Boydell's *A Collection of Prints Engraved after
the Most Capital Paintings in England* (1769–72; vol. 2, plates 59 and 60;
reproduced Russell, *Claude Lorrain* 60 and 65) as the *Rise* and *Decline of
the Roman Empire.* Since ruins routinely emblematized mutability and the
vanity of earthly existence for the seventeenth century, Boydell's titles
state what no contemporary of Claude would ever have needed to articulate (cf. Russell, *Claude Lorrain* 81–96). In an effusive review of the volume
published in 1772 ("Englische Kupferstiche," *Gesamtausgabe* 16:23–25),
the young Goethe elaborates the allegory suggested by the titles, but actually devotes more attention to the literal time of day than to its allegorical significance, the time of history. His stance reflects the shift that had
taken place in the course of the seventeenth and eighteenth centuries
that gave the mimetic priority over the allegorical mode of representation, and that led to today's less allegorical titles, *Seacoast with the Landing*

of Aeneas in Italy and *Pastoral Landscape with the Arch of Titus,* and to Kitson's (I think incorrect) argument that "a romantic historical theme of this kind" belongs "rather to the age of Gibbon than to the 17th century" (*Liber Veritatis* 104). Goethe thus registers both an important moment of transition, and also the reason for Claude's enormous popularity in the eighteenth and early nineteenth centuries: he satisfied the modern need for a clear mimetic representation of the real world and also the older one for that representation to have a coherent significance in a world-historical or universal context. Today the argument needs to be made for the relevance of allegory—rather than mimesis— to classicism (and literary neoclassicism).

Allegory was, to be sure, still used in "public," government-commissioned painting and statuary, and also in court masques in the eighteenth century. But in more private forms of art, including landscape, allegory was avoided (Lagerlöf, *Ideal Landscape* 2–4). Boydell's commentator sees allegory in only two of the eight Claudes included in the collection, and having registered the allegory he hastens to add, "Claude was never a more faithful imitator of nature than in this picture" (*A Collection of Prints* 2:15), while his discussion of Poussin's "Shepherds in Arcadia" implies that allegory is positively distasteful.[24] The prevailing category for praise of landscape even in Diderot's *Salons* is "truth," as in his typical praise of Vernet for "La vérité la plus parfaite" (*Oeuvres esthétiques* 581). Despite the high status of allegorical (= historical) painting in the hierarchy of genres in classical art theory, allegory was no longer a normal mode of reading painting in the late eighteenth century. Goethe's effusions signal that the allegorical significance of the paintings was no longer obvious, that it had to be figured out. Thus, it could be argued, his descriptions register a willed act of memory—the owl of Minerva flies only at dusk.

Allegory in the Nineteenth Century

Henceforth all reaction to Claude took explicit account of his allegory, either by focusing on it or by denying it. In the *Discourses on Art* (delivered 1769–90) Reynolds refers repeatedly to Claude as an obvious model for emulation. Indeed Hazlitt reports Reynolds to have said "there would be another Raphael before there was another Claude" (cited Jack, *Keats and the Mirror of Art* 67). His special quality among the great landscape painters, according to Reynolds, is that "he conducts us to the tranquillity of Arcadian scenes and fairy land" (*Discourses on Art* 208). The reference to fairy land is later echoed by Goethe, who notes that Claude revels in "[das] Feenhaft-Architektonische" (565) and Keats, whose verse epistle "To J. H. Reynolds, Esq." evokes Claude's *Enchanted Castle* (*Psyche and the Palace of Cupid*) as a magic castle inhabited by fairies (cf. Jack, *Keats and the Mirror of Art* 127–30). In contrast to these three, Constable admired Claude for his naturalness. The tension also appears among his imitators. Claude's influence pervades all landscape painting in the nineteenth century, and not just that of explicit Claude imitators, of which there were still many (cf. Röthlisberger, *Im Licht von Claude Lorrain*) but even that of painters whom we think of as looking forward and setting new styles. I have chosen somewhat arbitrarily Caspar David Friedrich (1774–1840), Paul Cézanne (1839–1906) and Claude Monet (1840–1926) from many possible examples to show how the framing so crucial in creating allegorical meaning becomes a touchstone for escaping the entire allegorical tradition and its concomitant self-consciousness.

Friedrich, the representative painter of German Romanticism, takes the staginess of the seventeenth century to an extreme. The most typical Friedrich landscape has figures in the foreground, small or large, looking into the painting with their backs to the observer. By following their line of vision the observer is led to the proper goal of observation (often the rising moon rather than Claude's sun). Both the object of observation and the act of observation are more openly thematized than in Claude, where attention is always pulled back and forth between the light in the depths of the painting and the historical event depicted elsewhere. Friedrich also works with the same generalized elements of religious allegory as Claude—light in the sky, heading off to sea, ships, religious buildings. But again he is more obvious; where Claude's *Imaginary View of Tivoli* has a tiny dome of St. Peter's visible on the horizon just beneath the setting sun, Friedrich typically has larger, more readily visible church towers toward which his figures gaze intently, as in, for example, *On the Sailboat* (1818–19, St. Petersburg) or *Sisters on the Harbor-View Terrace* (ca. 1820, St. Petersburg). Or the viewer sits in the ruins of a church window, or a cross dominates the fore- or midground, giving meaning to the landscape beyond (*The Cross in the Mountains* [1807–8, Dresden] or *Morning in the Riesengebirge* [1810–11, Berlin]). If anything, Friedrich makes Claude's allegories more explicit.

Yet Friedrich also critiques the entrapment in allegory. The very intentness of vision calls the validity of the allegories into question—if they are so clear, why must they be repeated with such intensity? The framing in his drawings and paintings of windows is often hyperbolic. *Window Looking over the Park* (ca. 1806–11 or 1835–37, St. Petersburg), for example, divides readily into Claude's typical three planes, here represented by the inside of the room, the midground with buildings and trees, and the background of empty sky. It also displays the same vanishing-point perspective as in Claude's harbors, where, too, the foreground is the human realm. But here the perspective is determined primarily by the window

Figure 16. Caspar David Friedrich, *Window Looking over the Park*. The State Hermitage Museum, St. Petersburg.

frame, and corroborated secondarily by the positioning of the buildings in the midground. Thus it arises from a human grid imposed on nature. At the same time the absence of humans in both foreground and midground, almost unheard of in Claude, creates a painful discontinuity between the human perspective imposed mechanistically by the window lattice and the natural world outside. And there is no sun at the vanishing point of the perspective, just the evenly diffused light of the unmarked sky, even though the illumination on the window sill shows that the light does enter from the vanishing point. This evident source of light, combined with the tall, pointing poplar on the right (traditionally the positive side, and echoed here by the taller of the house plants on the window ledge) shows that Friedrich is still in contact with the tradition that light represents divine transcendence. But transcendence is not visible as in Claude: whatever it is that the tall poplar points to is blocked from view by the closed shutter at the top of the window, by the very human perspective that orders the view and renders it meaningful. Even the symbolic emphasis on height on the right is at least partly an artifact of the human activity that placed the taller plant on the right side of the window ledge. Friedrich's allegories are not truths resident in the landscape, but structures imposed on it by human consciousness. Claude's self-consciousness balances the allegorical and the natural; Friedrich's more extreme version reveals their incompatibility.

Claude lost standing precipitously in the wake of Ruskin's *Modern Painters* at midcentury. Ruskin's hostility to Claude is complicated but shows the ultimate ascendance of the mimetic mode. His explicit purpose in writing *Modern Painters* was to rescue the reputation of Joseph Turner, who had, in Ruskin's view, died unappreciated. The choice of Claude as the foil against whose vices all Turner's virtues were to shine testifies to the stature that Claude still enjoyed in 1840. While claiming but little knowledge of Claude (*Modern Painters* 1:266), Ruskin nevertheless makes him stand for the limitations of all previous landscape painters: the spectacular passage on how only Turner painted the full glories of clouds, for example, is repeatedly punctuated with "Has Claude given this?" (*Modern Painters* 1:263–64). But it was not Claude's stature alone that drew Ruskin's wrath. Ruskin consistently prefers the sublime to the Arcadian, vigor to repose, mountain gloom and mountain glory to distant crests fading into the mist, plenitude to the generalizing ideal, time and change to slow calm, narrative plot to contemplative overview. Above all, however, Ruskin rejects Claude for inadequate imitation—in direct opposition to Constable and, to some extent, in opposition to his own idol Turner, whose admiration for Claude is well documented. At the heart of *Modern Painters* lies Ruskin's detailed scientific description

of the natural phenomena of landscape and his passionate demand that
they be rendered without error. The nature to be reproduced by the
painter is "material nature" (*Modern Painters* 3:279): "The duty of an
artist is not only to address and awaken, but to *guide* the imagination;
and there is no safe guidance but that of simple concurrence with
fact. . . . This is still the only question for the artist, or for us:—'Is it a
fact? Are things really so?' " (*Modern Painters* 3:133). Ruskin's central criterion is mimetic capacity, and by that criterion Claude fails miserably.

But the situation is not quite that simple. Although Ruskin works with
the opposition between allegorical and mimetic representation, he does
not see Claude as being allegorical—symbolic, he would have called it—
where he fails to be mimetic. He recognizes symbolic representation as
the mode of the Middle Ages, but it ceases for him at the end of the
fourteenth century with the appearance of blue sky in European art,
precisely the quality that Claude brought to its apex. Ruskin loves the religious simplicity, the innocence, and above all the unself-consciousness
of the Middle Ages. As a result, he attacks Claude from both sides. Not
only is he inaccurate—read: insufficiently mimetic—but he also misses
the deep truth of the biblical situations he represents. Claude's representation of Moses and the burning bush (LV 161), with the burning
bush inconspicuously off to one side, evokes as much indignation (*Modern Painters* 3:320–21) as supposed errors in drawing (ibid.).[25] Furthermore, Ruskin argues, quite convincingly, that Claude's representation of
landscape derives more from the landscape conventions of the Florentine Pre-Raphaelites (Ghirlandaio is his prime example; *Modern Painters*
3:322 and 4:1–2 and plate 18) than from correct observation of nature.
Why should this use of an incorrect convention anger Ruskin in Claude
but not in Ghirlandaio? Because in Ghirlandaio the religious subject is
at the center; his conventionality keeps the focus on the religious truth
and not on the misleading imitation of the world.[26]

Ruskin hates not the symbolic or allegorical mode, but rather the
transition period in which mimesis was used to expound the values of
the older period: he abhors the High Renaissance (except for the Venetian School, most of the time) and above all the Baroque. The mimesis
practiced by Renaissance and seventeenth-century artists is evil because
it is seductive without being either sincere or truthful. By representing
biblical figures not exactly as they were described in the Bible, but in
richer and contemporary settings, for example, painters misled their innocent viewers, "darkened faith" (*Modern Painters* 3:49), and ultimately
discredited Catholicism. (Evangelicals had the wisdom to turn away, but
they threw out the baby with the bath water: *Modern Painters* 3:55.) Truth
resides for Ruskin in two apparently opposite places: in the sincere language of the New Testament and in scientific fact. A perfect blending of

Figure 17. Paul Cézanne, *Le Lac d'Annecy*. The Samuel Courtauld Trust, Courtauld Institute of Art Gallery, London.

these two kinds of truth is attainable in the nineteenth century, but at no time previously. Evidently he saw in Claude precisely the duality this chapter has tried to establish: typically for his age, Claude represented both mimetically and allegorically. Ruskin saw clearly that this was true of the entire period of what we might call the extended Renaissance—the fifteenth through the eighteenth centuries. Furthermore, by the 1840s Ruskin could raise the question of reviving the allegorical representation of the Middle Ages. For him now the mimetic tradition is dominant and obvious; the task is to infuse back into it the religious truth driven out by the self-conscious and hence insincere mimesis of the Renaissance. But what must be revived is dead. Ruskin reveals how the allegorical mode had finally succumbed to the mimetic mode.

Or at least, so Ruskin believed. Yet even the Impressionists still had to struggle to break out of Claude's structure. Cézanne, for example, reproduces typical Claude landscapes in two well-known paintings in the Courtauld Institute—*La Montagne Sainte-Victoire* (ca. 1887) and *Le Lac d'Annecy* (1896)—with foreground trees on the side, a large expanse of land or water ending in a mountainous skyline, and a soft blue sky that melts into

Figure 18.   Claude Monet, *Antibes*. The Samuel Courtauld Trust, Courtauld Institute of Art Gallery, London.

the landscape. But in both paintings the mountains swell up to close off the background and collapse the painting into a flat plane. Any invitation to transcendence still implied by Claude's structure has been effaced. Beyond similar structural parallels to Claude, Monet's *Antibes* (1888, also in the Courtauld Institute) contains several specific allusions to him in the sails that fleck the water and especially in the angled tree in the foreground. It is also tempting to consider the rich blues here and in Cézanne an allusion to Claude, before the Impressionists the greatest painter of natural blue in the tradition. Above all, Monet has in common with Claude that he is a painter of light, as much so in this painting as anywhere in his oeuvre. And yet this painting does not feel like a Claude; rather than imitate it breaks away. The tree neither frames the painting (it is too far from the edge) nor is it the center, as it is occasionally in Claude to focus attention on figures. Indeed it disrupts the foreground altogether because it extends beyond the top edge and breaks the frame. At the same time the front piece of ground, on which we as observers stand to look at the sea, has been perilously narrowed in comparison to the foreground framing strip in Claude. The lack of frame combined with the characteristic Impressionist flatness effectively brackets the observer and the whole idea of observation out of the painting—there is no interest in giving the observer a place to stand or in evoking any particular mood or emotional response. Nature is simply there. Having discovered the interior subject modern culture has redefined true mimesis as its exclusion.

But of course to demand such strict mimesis in painting as Monet does is to create a structure that must be read allegorically. Monet confronts us with the dilemma that Ruskin avoided by expecting a revival of allegory, namely that there can be no completely mimetic representation any more than there can be completely allegorical representation. Without mimesis there can be nothing to see and interpret, and similarly without allegoresis there can be no knowledge of what is seen. Classicism is not the triumph of mimesis but rather the perfect balance of mimesis and allegory.

Chapter 3

Secular Tragedy: Neoclassicism in the Sixteenth Century

People are only productive in poetry and art for as long as they are still religious.

—*Goethe*[1]

"Perfect balance" evokes, of course, the classical—and classicist—ideal. But the literary analysis corresponding to the overview of the issue from the standpoint of Claude the idealist encounters the vagaries of history and involves less balance than dialectical interaction. For literary neoclassicism in the sixteenth century involved three strands, each equally modern in the period and each representative of a different revival of classical culture: the Aristotelianism based on the recovery of Aristotle's poetics, Renaissance neoplatonism, and the indigenous tradition of morality play. They are so intertwined in the late Renaissance that my dissection will inevitably look artificial, but the separation is necessary to clarify what follows.[2] Aristotelianism correlated primarily with increased mimesis and the morality tradition by and large with enhanced allegory. Renaissance neoplatonism was more ambiguous. On the one hand it reveled in the arcane allegory that has made it a domain of enthusiasts still often regarded with suspicion; on the other hand neoplatonist thinking about poetry blended so intimately with early Aristotelianism that it distorted the understanding of mimesis in odd directions. The following discussion outlines the important characteristic aspects of each and at the same time identifies their historical specificity in the late Renaissance, the beginning point of the larger argument. I will then examine how they work together and against each other in the earliest two flowerings of secular drama in Europe, Shakespeare's history plays and Italian pastoral.

Morality

Morality drama represents, as I am about to argue, the earliest form of neoclassicism in the extended sense. Early modern secular drama is generally understood to emerge beside and in part out of religious drama, that is mystery and morality play, in the sixteenth century, with ample acknowledgment of a no-man's-land of some fifty years of experimental hybrids between the two. For the history of allegory, the distinction between mystery and morality, fairly constant under varying terminology throughout Europe, is important. Mystery play refers to texts based on Christian narrative, whether biblical or hagiographic; it includes therefore mystery plays, passion plays, miracle plays. Mystery is the older of the two forms and seems to have developed from medieval tropes, ornaments, and elaborations of particular parts of the Mass. It operates in a mode we would now call mythic, but that was in its own day considered more or less historical. Morality refers to didactic religious dramas not specifically based on Christian mythology; it centers either on personification allegories or, especially in its later development, historical figures. As a result it tends to include martyr drama (as distinct from the lives of saints who perform miracles). Its most famous and typical exemplar is one of the earliest, the late fifteenth-century English *Everyman*. School drama, whether Protestant or Catholic, is morality drama. Spanish Corpus Christi drama (*auto sacramental*), a seventeenth-century phenomenon, is morality, although English Corpus Christi plays (fifteenth century) are mysteries.

It is not obvious to begin the history of neoclassicism with morality, but there are good reasons to do so. First, the conventions of morality drama derive from Prudentius's *Psychomachia*, a fourth-century epic describing the allegorical battle between the vices and the virtues.[3] Prudentius draws on the conventions of classical epic, like Milton filling the golden bowls of the classics with Christian content, and represents perhaps the earliest of a series of medieval classical revivals. Second, the forms of drama more commonly called neoclassical continue, as we shall see, to draw directly on the conventions of morality into the nineteenth century. While there is no direct evidence to suggest that the earliest writers of morality drama saw their form as particularly classical, the plays were often a vehicle for Humanist polemics, as for example, *The Marriage of Wit and Science*, circa 1570. These are the preliminary bases for my revised taxonomy; the ultimate justification will be the coherence of the larger narrative it enables.

Morality's recourse to a form derived from the classics resulted in important differences from the mystery plays and Corpus Christi cycles based on biblical narrative and saints' lives that immediately preceded it in the late fifteenth and early sixteenth centuries. First of all, it was more secular than its predecessors in social terms. The separation of drama from the liturgy in the twelfth century had enhanced the church's traditional ambivalence toward acting, yet the feast of Corpus Christi (established 1264) came to be celebrated in the late fourteenth century, for reasons not fully understood, by the performance of plays by municipalities, particularly in England and Spain.[4] The church welcomed the development and remained a strong supporter of such drama until the Reformation in England, and through the seventeenth century in Spain and southern Germany. Whether the Reformation is seen as the result or as the cause of the conflict between a powerful Catholic church and centralizing national monarchies, religion was politics and religious drama was necessarily political. The static Catholic theology of the mysteries and English Corpus Christi cycles, which Protestants sought to ban with increasing success (Wickham, *Early English Stages* 1:112–16), was only passively political, but morality plays openly addressed theological controversies from both sides. So dangerous was the stage that it had to be brought under the control of the crown—in England in the course of the sixteenth century, as the right to maintain a company of players was increasingly restricted (by the end of the century to members of the immediate royal circle). In Spain and south Germany the stage was an important weapon of the Counter-Reformation in the following century. As the medium of mass communication to an audience of mixed levels of literacy it both shared in and was shaped by the struggle between religious and secular powers.

At the same time morality represents a shift to a professional theater. The mysteries had been performed first by clerics (in the church, where the distinction between liturgy and drama is often difficult to draw),[5] then by laymen as the municipal guilds took them over; but early in the fifteenth century traveling troupes of professional players, in England sponsored by one or another member of the landed aristocracy, were found all over the Continent, where they might or might not require aristocratic sponsorship. In Germany professional companies took their start from English troupes forced abroad by the occasional closings of the London theaters. Seventeenth-century Spanish Corpus Christi plays, moralities and not mysteries, were also performed by professional players. From the sixteenth century on, morality plays and their successors were also performed in schools by students.[6] Although its justification in the curriculum was preprofessional training for officials and priests, school drama frequently attained virtually professional status. London had its Boys Company in Shakespeare's time, while Jesuit school drama was the most important theatrical entertainment in Vienna before the court theater was established at the end of the seventeenth century.

This more secular drama had varied content, at least on the surface. Mystery plays are specifically connected to the liturgy, the Bible, or narratives of saints' lives; the Passion is often the central topic, at least by typological reference if not directly. Morality, by contrast, is homiletic, that is, it serves a function analogous to the sermon, with which it is closely related.[7] Where mystery draws its lessons from biblical narrative, morality constructs its own plot around the conflict of personified virtues and vices. In the fifteenth century the individual rather than the world was understood to be the locus of this struggle. In their focus on the figures and texts of Christian narrative, mysteries are as theocentric as any dramas in the European tradition. The cosmos and the totality of history are unities, and humanity is understood as a part of the larger structure. All nature is, so to speak, supernatural. Whatever interior existence individuals may have is relevant only in the context of the larger cosmos. Morality, however, takes the first step toward a more anthropocentric view, for now the issue is a single individual whose free will can jeopardize the possibility of salvation. In its new space for the individual we can recognize the secularization inherent in the Reformation, which, however hesitant, implies a different kind of allegory. In Prudentius the roots of the allegory in Christian narrative myth were explicit. Each of the six duels narrated in the *Psychomachia* has an explicit biblical parallel—the contest between Chastity and Lust, for example, is also that between Judith and Holofernes, while that of Humility versus Pride is also David against Goliath. Mystery plays likewise draw their lesson directly from the myth. Morality plays, by contrast, replace the figures of Judeo-Christian mythology with concrete figures whose metaphysical significance obliterates the historical status of myth. Because their material has no mythical status, moralities are more clearly presented not for their own sake, but for the sake of their meaning. They are, in this sense, though more secular, more allegorical than mystery drama. Secularity does not thus necessarily equate to increased mimesis.

Furthermore, both mystery and morality seem to have been open to elements from a popular tradition of clowning (well documented first in the sixteenth century, as Robert Weimann's *Shakespeare and the Popular Tradition* magisterially establishes); the allegorical tendency of morality requires special justification for what in mystery can pass as heightened mimesis. The fall of the morality hero is brought about by a head devil, the "Vice," supervising subsidiary figures, or Vices, who operate chiefly through deception. These entertaining Vices connected early on with the clown figures from the popular tradition to establish the tradition of the comic villain, or the villain who, like Iago or Goethe's Mephistopheles, attracts a disproportionate share of audience attention. In Shakespeare the clown and the Vice are mostly kept separate, but the common collapsing of minor Vice roles into that of the clown in stage adaptations, like that of the servant Fabian into Feste in *Twelfth Night*, shows how readily we accept the connection. Seventeenth-century Jesuit school dramas and Corpus Christi plays also depend on deception for their central plot complications. In his somewhat surprised assertion that the clown in early eighteenth-century German popular drama retains an aura of evil, Walter Benjamin still registers this relationship (*Ursprung des deutschen Trauerspiels* 133–36, although the phenomenon is not peculiar to German baroque tragedy, as Benjamin implies). But if the Vices' deception and disguise, which derive ultimately from the serpent of biblical narrative, are both the essence of theatricality and by definition evil, theater is in a difficult moral position, as the ambivalence of both Catholic and Protestant churches toward it confirms. Only by revealing its deceit—the basic pattern of morality play—can the theater legitimate itself. In his path-breaking book on late medieval drama, *The Play Called Corpus Christi*, V. A. Kolve emphasizes the dangers of blasphemy in overly mimetic representation in mystery play; by the sixteenth century the issue was more generally the moral problematics of mimesis itself, an issue that continued to preoccupy the great dramatists of the seventeenth century, as Jonas Barish demonstrates in *The Antitheatrical Prejudice*. In *Othello*, to take only the most extreme example in Shakespeare, Iago's constant lying and staging of little plays—with no positive clown to offset him—has so discredited all language and theatrical action, that the only avenue left Othello to assert his moral integrity is suicide, a drastic action that removes him entirely from the web of language and plot. This implicit moral imperative not to be too mimetic develops into the self-consciousness of its own theatricality so characteristic of European theater, particularly in the seventeenth century.

The earliest extant morality plays date from the twelfth century in Germany, but the typical focus of the morality on a single, if generalized, individual emerges in England only in the fifteenth century. The earliest and best known of these, *Everyman* (ca. 1485), reveals the basic structure of stripping away and restoration that characterizes such texts. Confronted with the first call of Death, Everyman is abandoned by Fellowship, Kindred, and Goods; Good Deeds is too weak to help him. This is Everyman's fall, for Goods tells him, "My condition is man's soul to kill" (Hazlitt, *A Select Collection of Old English Plays* 2:119). However, Knowledge comes to Everyman's aid, and teaches him to heal Good Deeds and to summon new helpers: the Five Wits, Beauty, Strength, and Discretion. But when Everyman must actually enter the grave his new friends also forsake him, excepting only Good Deeds. The latter however is sufficient to save him, as both Everyman and the audience are reassured by an angel and the Doctor, the play's in-house interpreter. With the occasional later variant on the Continent that the central figure is not saved but damned, as in the Dr. Faust or the Don Juan plots, this plot structure of fall and salvation through divine assistance is paradigmatic for the morality and its descendants. The more common version is slightly more elaborate, as for example in *Lusty Juventus*, from the middle of the sixteenth century. In this play Youth initially allies himself with Good Counsel and Knowledge, but soon falls prey to Hypocrisy, who has been set on him by Satan himself. Under the name of Friendship, Hypocrisy worms his way into Youth's confidence, then introduces him to Fellowship and Abominable Living. Eventually Youth repents through the efforts of Good Counsel and is welcomed back into the fold by God's Promises. This becomes the norm: the Fall is conceived as an event in the life of each individual instead of in biblical history.

If *Everyman* seems to preempt all possible morality plays because it is so schematic, the development of morality in fact drives toward historical particularity. Morality abstracts the history of salvation from biblical history (represented in the mystery cycles) to the history of the individual. This is a movement of generalization, on the one hand, but also of particularization in that it deals with the individual rather than mythology. In the English plays *Lusty Juventus, Interlude of Youth* (1554), and *Mundus et Infans* (1522), for example, the late fifteenth-century Everyman is particularized into Youth and the focus is concomitantly narrowed from religion to education, though the Vices still tend to be chosen from among the traditional seven deadly sins. But some moralities, especially school dramas, apply the same structure to errors other than the sins codified by the church. *The Four Elements* (1519) and *The Marriage of Wit and Science* (ca. 1570), for example, address the virtues and vices of students; the place of God or some leading virtue is taken by figures like Reason or Nature, so that the morality serves the Humanist program. A more striking example is the application to the virtues of a ruler in John Skelton's *Magnyfycence* (1515–18, pub. 1533). The play follows the familiar structure. King Magnyfycence places his servants Felicity and Liberty under the jurisdiction of Measure, but Measure loses control after Fancy, under the name of Largesse, wins Magnyfycence's confidence with a forged letter of recommendation. The court is given over to a pack of Vices directed by Counterfeit Countenance. Their names are Crafty Conveyance, Cloaked Collusion, Courtly Abusion (the alliteration becomes typical) and Folly. Measure is dismissed, Liberty set loose, and Felicity disappears. Adversity and Poverty, followed by Despair and Mischief, succeed the triumph of the Vices, but Good Hope leads Redress, Circumspection, and Perseverance to the rescue, and Fancy's initial forgery is revealed. The multitude of nuanced vices and virtues and the combination of moral and political categories make this plot both more particular and more elaborate than those of the other plays referred to. Yet it is difficult to separate the political allegory from the allegory of salvation, for the analogy between the two is seamless. On the one hand, Free Will is king of the realm of the soul and the qualities of a good king are the qualities of a good person. But the reverse is also true: the qualities of a good person are also the qualities of a good king. Magnyfycence is Everyman as well as king. From here it is no great distance to plays that mixed abstract and historical figures, of which the most important is John Bale's *King Johan* (probably 1536–37, revised 1561), to Norton and Sackville's Senecan tragedy *Gorboduc* (1561), which maintains the structure of morality while eliminating most of the personified abstractions, and to Shakespeare's histories.[8] Indeed, the recurrent plots and structures of morality will concern us into the nineteenth century.

Aristotelianism

If morality constitutes a pressure toward allegory, Aristotelianism impels drama toward mimesis. In common usage Aristotelianism is synonymous with neoclassicism generally, but my argument requires it to be identified in more specific terms, for it constitutes a body of terminology so well developed that it rapidly came to dominate all European discourse on drama. The *Poetics* became known belatedly in the West only through a defective thirteenth-century Latin summary (based on Averroës' twelfth-century Arabic commentary) that did not discuss Aristotle's central concept of imitation. But after the fall of Byzantium in 1453 the Greek text came to light and was translated into Latin in 1498. Alessandro Pazzi's 1536 edition of the Greek text with Latin translation, reprinted twelve times in the sixteenth century, unleashed a flood of commentaries and imitations beginning in 1548 in Italy.[9] Within a century of the first appearance of the *Poetics* in Renaissance Europe, Aristotle had become the leading theoretician of drama, and through his influence tragedy had become its preeminent form. But Aristotelians actually read the *Poetics* through the filter, so to speak, of Horace's *Ars poetica* (*Epistola ad Pisones*, a poem of 476 lines from the first century B.C.). Horace's summary of his own views on writing poetry, based on familiarity with Aristotle's text, was readily accessible to scholars in sixteenth-century Italy, who initially assimilated the rediscovered Aristotle to the more familiar text of Horace with little sense for their differences, a trend that persisted in the following two centuries (see Weinberg, *A History of Literary Criticism in the Italian Renaissance* ch. 4). While Aristotle was analyzed and interpreted at length, quick tags to support generalizations came from Horace. In the late eighteenth century commentaries shifted the focus from writing to interpreting tragedy. Despite continuing careful attention to the *Poetics* in the nineteenth century—by figures like Goethe, Schiller, Coleridge, and Hegel—and through the twentieth, the common understanding of its import is still profoundly shaped by the seventeenth-century interpretation of him. This impact is best explored for our purposes in the categories of probability or verisimilitude, the social context of drama, the relation of plot and character, metaphor and causality.

Probability enters Aristotelianism in conjunction with the foundational term "mimesis," or imitation, in the *Poetics*. It has been agreed by the entire tradition of Aristotle interpretation (with the exception of the occasional Renaissance syncretist) that mimesis excluded the possibility of symbolic or allegorical representation.[10] Despite occasional references to imitation of persons and objects, Aristotle focuses on the imitation of action (1449b 37–1450b 4), and indeed, idealized action. His nature is not simply the world of phenomena, but also the generalized ideal, and because it is teleological, the universal norm can always be deduced from the specific phenomenon. Because poetry deals in universal truths, Aristotle claims, the poet should represent not what has actually happened, but what might have happened because it was either probable or necessary (1451a 36–1451b 8). Nevertheless, as the word "probable" suggests, Aristotle also places great value on the real: the *Poetics* evinces little interest in myth or the supernatural. Probability rests on both experience grounded in nature and on Aristotle's firm faith in causality: the plot must be organized, he says, such that everything happens according to necessity or probability (1452a 17–19). Probability therefore combines elements of the real (experience) with the ideal (general). From this fundamental faith in natural law it was but a step to the strong normative tendencies of neoclassical thought and to its harsh rejection of the supernatural.[11]

Through the influence of the *Ars poetica*, where the object of imitation is human reality and character rather than idealized human actions, probability is superseded by verisimilitude, a standard more tied to the real. Neoclassicists distorted Aristotle's imitation beyond recognition in increasingly literal-minded discussions of the ubiquitous term "verisimilitude." By the seventeenth century Aristotle's observation that tragedies normally represented a single action that took place in no more than one cycle of the sun had crystallized into the three unities of action, place, and time. Tragedies could have no subplots; the action had to take place, if not all in the same room, then in the same building or at most city, and its scope could not exceed twenty-four hours. The rules were consistently in the name of verisimilitude, from René Rapin in 1674—"unless there be the Unity of Place, of Time, and of the Action in

Horat. Art. Poet.

Scribendi recte sapere est et principium et fons,

Figure 19. Frontispiece to Gottsched's *Critische Dichtkunst* (1751).

the great poems, there can be no verisimility" (Adams and Hathaway, *Dramatic Essays* 123) to Gottsched in 1751—"how is it probable that you should see evening fall several times on the stage, and yet remain seated in one place without eating, drinking or sleeping?" (Gottsched, *Critische Dichtkunst* 614). Similar literal-mindedness prevailed with regard to myth and the supernatural. Hence Saint-Evremond attacks both rules and classical drama in general because of their dependence on interactions with the gods, in whom, of course, no one believes any more. Drama should present only "purely natural but extraordinary things" (Adams and Hathaway, *Dramatic Essays* 112), for the superstition that ruled on the Greek stage was destructive (Adams and Hathaway, *Dramatic Essays* 113). Whatever probability and verisimilitude meant for Aristotle or Horace, for the neo-Aristotelians they became associated with Enlightenment secularism.

At the same time, the objects of imitation were distorted as well. So obvious had mimesis become in the seventeenth and eighteenth centuries—everyone cited Aristotle on poetry as the imitation of human action—that it came to mean almost anything. Gottsched's chapter on imitation claims only to distinguish three general types of imitation—descriptive, dramatic, and narrative. In effect, imitation means genre. But if so, then the object of imitation becomes fluid, so that Gottsched can speak of imitation of human action, of humans, and of natural things almost interchangeably (for example, Gottsched, *Critische Dichtkunst* 97–98). Horace urged the poet to cultivate his talent through copying Greek models (*Ars poetica* 268–69)—where Aristotle sought common practice and norms, Horace sought examples. Here too Gottsched follows, so that imitation is also a category of becoming a poet (100–101, 127), and poetry as the imitation of action is introduced in the context of training poets, a subject on which Gottsched regretfully notes that Aristotle did not discourse (97). Hence the frontispiece to his treatise represents Apollo and the Muses on a stage, whose work is transmitted to humanity in the book carried downward by Mercury to human figures, still on the stage of Greece, before an easel at which a diagram is being explained to classical figures who turn to face the audience below them, which appears to consist of modern Romans. These in turn transmit the lesson of the stage to the spectator, referring it also to the library pointed out by a figure to the left. Closest to us in this chain of transmission a figure, presumably Horace, seated on the works of Homer, writes in a book labeled "Ars poet." "Knowledge is the basis and source of correct writing" asserts Gottsched's epigraph (from Horace): not Aristotle's general knowledge of human action, but knowledge of the particular historical tradition of classical literature. This slippage will open the door to allegory for centuries to come.

If Aristotle's context for poetry was nature and human knowledge, Horace's and in his wake the neo-Aristotelians' is society, for an imitator of poetic models is part of a tradition, a community existing in history. Horace is interested in poets as those who distinguish between public and private rights, that is, as lawgivers (*Ars poetica* 396–99); genre is a matter of social function and role, and the poet's identity depends on embracing these socially determined norms (179–250), so that obscene language is improper because of the specific classes who would be offended by it (248–50). As a result taste and decorum become central concepts in neoclassical poetics, and, furthermore, poetry takes on a clearer moral function: "Poets aim at giving either profit or delight" ("Aut prodesse volunt aut delectare poetae"), as it is formulated in the most famous line of the *Ars poetica* (333). Horace's precepts for the chorus to side with the good characters (196) indicate which of the two is more important. Aristotle routinely assumed that his audience made moral judgments, but his own judgments of the outcome of plots were based on whether they aroused pity and fear (1452b 30–1453a 7), while Horace expects his poet to articulate the moral judgments of the leaders of his society. In *Reflections on the Poetics of Aristotle* of 1674 Rapin assimilates Aristotle to Horace: "'Tis true, delight is the end poetry aims at, but not the principal end, as others pretend. In effect, poetry being an art, ought to be profitable by the quality of its own nature, and by the essential subordination that all arts should have to polity, whose end in general is the public good. This is the judgment of Aristotle, and of Horace, his chief interpreter" (Adams and Hathaway, *Dramatic Essays* 122). Saint-Evremond criticizes Attic tragedy for "excessive rousing of fear and pity" and making "the stage a school of fright and compassion at which one learned to be frightened at all perils and to grieve at all misfortunes" (Adams and Hathaway, *Dramatic Essays* 113). While the tenor of the essay is to validate modern drama over that of antiquity, Saint-Evremond nevertheless ends by citing Horace on pleasure and utility (Adams and Hathaway, *Dramatic Essays* 117): Aristotle has been reduced to Horace.

The fact that Horace's poet speaks from a specific historical position rather than Aristotle's universal one introduces two basic tensions into Aristotelianism. For the teleologist Aristotle, tradition serves only to tell whether a phenomenon has reached its ultimate stage of development, but for Horace tradition is a storehouse of forms that might be continued by imitation or even revived. In discussing individual words, for example, Horace shows greater interest than Aristotle in words that are, or are becoming, obsolete, and also in coining words (46–72). Aristotelians thus inherited both the eternal verities of Aristotle's teleology and Horace's historicist awareness of temporality, a contradiction that later erupted in the Quarrel of Ancients and Moderns at the end of the seventeenth century. There is also a tension between Aristotle's focus on nature as ordering principle, virtually a divinity, on the one hand, and Horace's on society on the other. Horace's view of culture is considerably more anthropocentric than Aristotle's, for its values are all grounded within the human community. This duality within Aristotelianism opens it to the larger tension between anthropocentric mimetic drama and theocentric allegorical drama. Hence neoclassical dramatic practice is often less mimetic—and oddly enough in this respect more Aristotelian—than its largely Horatian theory would seem to allow.

Although Aristotle clearly subordinates character to plot, he says enough about character for it to be substantially reinterpreted in the sixteenth and seventeenth centuries. He has no interest in figures with the absolute qualities represented by allegory: his preferred heroes are neither particularly good nor bad, but simply prone to err. His term *hamartia*, the "tragic flaw" of our current vocabulary, meant "missing the target," and whether its import was moral or epistemological is not clear. Aristotle mostly discusses the relationship between virtue and outcome—whether one's lot goes from good to bad or bad to good. The purpose of the plot is to effect by means of fear and pity the "catharsis," or purging of these emotions, but to whom they belong is not specified. Aristotle only asserts, somewhat mysteriously, that catharsis should arise from the structure of the plot and not from the staging—and therefore presumably not even from the pathetic performance of the actors. Unity is explicitly a category of structure (not of imitation as later on) and is not guaranteed by the focus of all episodes on the same character (1451a 15). Similarly, Aristotle's other famous terms—reversal, discovery, and deus ex machina—identify typical moments or impulses in the plot and have nothing to do with the characters. What the characters know and feel is relevant only in the framework of an ordered perspicuous plot.

Aristotelianism reversed this priority. Horace uses the term character only in reference to the poet, and while he touches gracefully in passing on most of Aristotle's categories of plot, the only one that really interests him is unity, which becomes homogeneity and consistency (119–27). Lacking his guidance, Aristotelians redefined character, taking off from analyses of catharsis, where Renaissance commentators again encountered Aristotle with no explicit Latin mediation. These discussions introduce extensive analyses of characters, the effect of the passions of the characters on the spectator, and finally the character of the spectator. The sixteenth and seventeenth centuries tended to think the characters were purified, while Corneille ("Discours de la Tragédie," *Oeuvres Complètes* 831) and then Lessing ("Hamburgische Dramaturgie," *Gesammelte Werke* 2:649) thought rather the audience. Goethe turned against this whole

tradition and understood catharsis to be the aesthetic closure and autonomy of the drama ("Nachlese zu Aristoteles' Poetik," *Gesamtausgabe*
15:897–900). In Rapin fear and pity take on a more interesting and
modern function as well: "Tragedy cannot be delightful to the spectator
unless he become sensible to all that is represented; he must enter into
all the different thoughts of the actors, interest himself in the adventures, fear, hope, afflict himself, and rejoice with them. The theatre is
dull and languid when it ceases to produce these motions in the soul of
those that stand by" (Adams and Hathaway, *Dramatic Essays* 124–25). In
this more extended view of character both the characters and the spectator possess souls which constitute an interior space worthy of exploration. Aristotelian critics, with different degrees of enthusiasm, declare
love, with its interior and secret motivations, to be the proper subject for
modern tragedy, as opposed to the more public love of glory thematized
by the ancients. Racine defends his Nero with the assertion: "Nero is
here in the privacy of his family" ("Néron est ici dans son particulier et
dans sa famille," preface to *Britannicus, Oeuvres Complètes* 385). Tragedy
thus can now deal with private vice and virtue.

This shift to the primacy of character over plot will make it possible
within sixty years to legitimate tragedies about the middle class, entirely
about the private realm. Interiorized character reached a kind of apotheosis in nineteenth-century criticism—one thinks of A. C. Bradley—and
also remained the primary category of dramatic criticism in the twentieth. Robert Heilman, for example, writing in 1960, still asserted, "*tragedy*
should be used only to describe the situation in which the divided human being faces basic conflicts, perhaps rationally insoluble, of obliga-
tions and passions; makes choices, for good or for evil; errs knowingly or
involuntarily; accepts consequences; comes into a new larger awareness;
suffers or dies, yet with a larger wisdom."[12] Tragedy, in this view, takes
place within the individual ("the divided human being"), not between
the individual and the surrounding social or moral cosmos. It is entirely
and exclusively anthropocentric. Even a critic so devoted to allegory as
Edwin Honig (*Seizures of Honor* 2) can fall into this pit. It remains to be
seen how the postmodern attack on the subject will affect this heritage
of neoclassicism.

Aristotle's discussion of the "means" of imitation (thought, language,
spectacle, and music), is shorter than his discussion of its objects, and
this brevity has also been influential. For fuller discussion of thought
Aristotle refers readers to the *Rhetoric*. Because thought mostly involves
statements made by the characters, neoclassical critics tended to subordinate it to the growing category of character. Music and spectacle receive
the least attention from Aristotle and also from his neoclassical followers (except when they were attacking opera), presumably because the

latter at least focused more on drama as text rather than as performance. Corneille says explicitly, "Aristotle wants the well made tragedy to be beautiful and able to please without the assistance of actors and apart from its performance" ("Discours des trois Unités," *Oeuvres Complètes* 843; "Aristote veut que la tragédie bien faite soit belle et capable de plaire sans le secours des comédiens, et hors de la représentation"). But precisely music and staging were to become dominant elements of allegorical drama as it developed in the sixteenth and seventeenth centuries, particularly in masque and opera, which, as will appear below, derive from different strands of neoclassicism. Aristotle's final category, language, is the most interesting in this regard. The only trope he discusses at length is metaphor, which always articulates both tenor and vehicle, both sign and meaning. In Aristotle's formulation the clarity of this relationship is the prime concern. Allegory, by contrast, fuses sign and meaning into one term. Thus mimetic and allegorical dramaturgies can be distinguished to some extent by their preference for or avoidance of metaphor as characteristic trope.[13] As we will see below, the incidence of metaphor in Shakespeare increases where the dramaturgy is otherwise more mimetic. Because the aspects of drama that lend themselves to a nonmimetic dramaturgy are barely discussed by Aristotle, they lacked both critical status and developed terminology, both of which surely contributed to the eventual invisibility of allegorical drama.

Beneath the proliferation of terms in the *Poetics* lies Aristotle's most characteristic category, causality, the strongest affinity of the seventeenth century for Aristotle. Since he is a teleologist, causality is for him innate and too obvious to require articulation. It is implicit, however, in his invocation of probability. It also appears in the *Poetics* in his albeit limited interest in character, for characters enact, bring into being, and thereby "cause" the action on which tragedy depends. Categories of interior subjectivity or motivation are not required to see the characters as the cause of the action, for Aristotle is less interested in why characters act than simply that they do act. Universal norms adequately take the place of motivation; hence for Aristotle the appearance of a deus ex machina must seem as probable as the behavior of any other character. However, as the grounding of meaning and causality shifts at the end of the Renaissance from external system to internal individual, the causality of character is transformed into motivation. Causality moves inside the character, becomes obscure and therefore the object of interpretation, just as in science the laws of natural causality recede behind the phenomenon and must be inferred through a process of induction and abstraction. During the eighteenth century this obscurity will increase and become a primary focus of literary attention. Since, however, it is in the nature of allegorical drama for identity and meaning to be visible, as visibility became equated with superficiality, allegory has yet another reason to seem outmoded.[14]

Neoplatonism

It is remarkable that a single text, even one as intelligent as Aristotle's, could wield such influence, especially in the midst of the Renaissance revival of Platonism, for Aristotle's views on poetry were in many respects opposed to those of his teacher. But Plato had expressed himself, despite some famous utterances on divine inspiration (*Phaedrus* 245a, 265b and *Ion* 534), with notorious hostility toward poets, particularly in the *Republic*, where he denied them a role in the ideal state (*Rep* II, 377–83; III, 386–92; X, 595–607. Cf. *Phaedrus* 248e, where poets are ranked low on the scale of souls, between mystery priests and artisans; or *Timaeus* 19d, where they are a "tribe of imitators"). So powerful was his attack that Plato enters Renaissance poetics basically only in the context of defenses of poetry, which modulate into Horatian language and peter out toward the end of the sixteenth century, leaving the field of poetics to Aristotle and Horace (Weinberg, *A History of Literary Criticism in the Italian Renaissance* 1:293–96 and 345–48). Nevertheless, there is a theory of poetry, implicit in Plato as in allegorical dramatic practice, which became what Bernard Weinberg characterizes as a "κοινή of Platonic ideas, present universally but unspecifically in the minds of men" (1:345).[15] Even heavily Platonist discourse was readily intertwined with Aristotle's critical language. The central tenet, for example, of Platonist poetics, the evocation of wonder, was consistently but uncomfortably attributed to Aristotle, who had, to be sure, asserted the need for the marvelous in tragedy (1460a 12), but had then spent the remainder of the paragraph taking it back.[16]

A locus classicus for such blending is Sidney's *Apologie for Poetrie*, with its constant references to Plato. It is full of Weinberg's Platonist κοινή. The poet is prophet, and poetry is philosophy and even religion; the Old Testament is claimed as a poetic text. In direct contradiction to Aristotle all philosophy is claimed to be poetry, whether or not it is in verse. The probable is irrelevant, for poetry is to "borrow nothing of what is, hath been, or shall be" (Sidney, *An Apologie for Poetrie* 11). Rather the function of poetry, a rhetorical one, is to raise the mind to contemplation of goodness and perfection, "the everlasting beautie to be seene by the eyes of the minde" (7); it is "by knowledge to lift up the mind from the dungeon of the body to the enioying his owne divine essence" (13). At the same time, Sidney echoes the leading neo-Aristotelians of his day in his concern for the unities (51–52), and for the training of the poet. More than once he invokes Aristotle on imitation, most strikingly in combination with the neoplatonist terminology for representation as "figuring forth," a formulation that emphasizes the gap between text and meaning rather than their closeness:[17] "Poesie therefore is an arte of imitation, for so *Aristotle* termeth it in his word *Mimesis*, that is to say, a representing, counterfetting, or figuring foorth: to speak metaphorically, a speaking picture: with this end, to teach and delight" (10). The sentence moves with breathtaking speed from Aristotle to Plato to Horace (profit and delight).

Sidney's syncretism explicitly supports a poetics of allegory in its defense of poetry against the charge of lying—the heart of any Platonist discussion of poetry—on the grounds that it is "allegorically and figurativelie written" (Sidney, *An Apologie for Poetrie* 39). But Sidney seems to claim that even classicizing, Aristotelian poetry is allegorical, since his definition of mimesis shares Plato's validation of the invisible figurative over the literal and thereby subverts imitation into Platonist translation from one level of discourse to another. His phrase "speaking picture" was already used to justify allegorical drama in the earliest discussions surrounding the introduction of plays to celebrate Corpus Christi at the end of the fourteenth century (Kolve, *The Play Called Corpus Christi* 5–6). Sidney repeatedly reads characters as embodiments of particular virtues and vices (12, 18, 21), just as they function in the morality dramas that were only beginning to die out in England. Precisely at the moment where Sidney imitates Aristotle most closely by drawing his examples from classical texts, he deviates furthest from him by insisting that poetic characters must be purely good or bad, not mixed, as Aristotle had claimed for the hero of tragedy (18–21, no mixing on 21). When he asserts that Aristotle forbade comedies that "styrre laughter in sinfull things" (56) the assimilation of classical and Christian views is complete. In Aristotle's name an essentially religious, allegorical view of drama is developed. Sidney's readiness to operate in both Platonist and Aristotelian modes is especially typical of Elizabethan drama, where elements of allegorical religious drama and of classicizing mimetic drama openly rub shoulders.

Neoplatonism is not confined to poetics. Compelling arguments have been advanced by historians of art, music, and literature that there was widespread literacy in neoplatonist myths and imagery in the sixteenth and seventeenth centuries (for example, Wind, *Pagan Mysteries*; Yates, *Giordano Bruno and the Hermetic Tradition*; Gombrich, "Botticelli's Mythologies"; Tomlinson, *Metaphysical Song*; Panofsky, *Idea*). These had proliferated and their correspondences to Christianity had been worked out in arcane fashion by Renaissance Humanists like Ficino and his student Pico della Mirandola. The intricacies need not concern us here: since Christianity had absorbed substantial elements of neoplatonism in late antiquity, the plots of their basic myths already have much in common. Where Christianity is concerned with achieving harmony between the soul and God's law, neoplatonist myths focus on reconciling particular divinities such as Apollo and Bacchus or Diana and Venus or Pan and Proteus. The last—the one and the many—is the most general, and in this form, or renamed as spirit and world, it is readily recognizable as essentially identical to the basic Christian plot.

It is more important therefore, to identify a specific neoplatonist rhetoric than the specific myths.[18] For the purposes of the texts addressed below it is important to be sensitive primarily to the thematics of love and its relationship to the good-beautiful-true as it is developed in the *Symposium* and the *Phaedrus*. Love appears frequently in the language and imagery of pleasure and virtue, also expressed as love and chastity. These are most frequently associated with the figures of Hercules, Venus, and Diana (and therefore the moon). It also appears, equally importantly, in the thematics of the eye and the way in which the eye of the beloved reflects beauty and truth back into the eye of the lover. In this context light imagery of all sorts, especially sun and stars, always evokes neoplatonist tremors.

We move now to early examples of the encounter among the different neoclassicisms.

Pastoral

Pastoral drama represents the first example of the Aristotelian classical impulse that is not direct imitation of particular plays. Its popularity was established by the first major monuments of neoclassicism in European drama, Tasso's *Aminta* of 1573 and Guarini's *Il pastor fido* (The Faithful Shepherd, 1590), which owed a great deal to Tasso's play. Considering that they are the earliest attempts to apply Aristotle to drama, it is not surprising that they were hard to categorize. In a certain sense, the term pastoral simply begs the question of genre in classical terms, but a controversy surrounding *Il pastor fido* that attached pastoral firmly to tragicomedy shows that classical terminology had become fully ascendant. The term tragicomedy had originated, apparently as a joke, with Plautus's prologue to his *Amphitryon*, but an appropriate term became necessary for the early Protestant school dramatists in the sixteenth century as they assimilated their (mostly Latin) dramatizations of biblical narrative to the form of Terentian comedy, the more fully developed version of which we shall see below in Bidermann; it only emerged from a welter of similar terms as the standard term for plays that mixed tragic and comic elements in the seventeenth century.[19] More important than the term is precisely what combination of elements these pastoral dramas represent.

The birth of pastoral drama is normally traced back to Poliziano's *La favola d'Orfeo* of 1480. This brief dramatization of the myth of Orpheus was written in honor of Cardinal Gonzaga and contains at its center a long speech in his praise that has nothing to do with its plot. It is for all practical purposes an elaboration of Italian court masque, which tended to be a series of tableaux vivants, with some musical accompaniment, whose effect depended on elaborate staging and machinery rather than on plot. So sketchy and disconnected are the elements of the *Orfeo* that its eighteenth-century editor felt compelled to insert some additional characters and speeches to make the plot easier to follow. The basic structure of Poliziano's spectacle depends on the structure of the myth of Orpheus, but set into an explicitly pastoral landscape. This myth was central for Renaissance neoplatonists: the cliché that the text is a mystery play on a pagan theme reflects the general awareness that the neoplatonist theology of love makes sense of a text that is almost as much rite as play.[20] It is, therefore, neoclassical in the neoplatonist sense, but not Aristotelian.

Tasso's *Aminta* and Guarini's *Il pastor fido* about a hundred years later build on Poliziano's rudimentary classicism. As Richard Cody has shown, *Aminta* is a specifically neoplatonist allegory about pleasure and virtue, the difference between lower and higher love, and the function of art (*The Landscape of the Mind* 44–78). Its plotting, however, is more complex than Poliziano's allegory. Myth yields to a romantic love plot with a happy ending—though, because the lovers have no interfering parents, not one derived from Latin comedy. It seems rather to be a romanticized version of the Hippolytos plot, with the gender roles reversed and the rage that characterizes Phaedra eliminated: Cupid intends to take revenge on the shepherdess Sylvia, who prefers to worship only Diana. Both she and her lover Aminta are reported in acts 3 and 4 by the typical messenger figures of classical tragedy to have died violent deaths— Sylvia has been eaten by a wolf and Aminta battered to pieces (like Hippolytos) after jumping off a cliff. The reports of these deaths turn out to be false. There is choral commentary at the end of each act and the chorus also participates in the action in the last three acts in the fashion of a Greek chorus. The neoplatonism of *Il pastor fido* appears less in the structure of the plot than in occasional images, the most important being blindness: a game of blindman's buff plays on the neoplatonist motif of the blindness of love.[21] Guarini is both freer and more heavy-handed in his use of classical dramatic models like chorus and messengers. Notable, however, is his use of several motifs (slightly adjusted) from *Oedipus*—a plague sent as punishment from the gods, a child separated from his family in infancy because of a threatening oracle, a father who almost kills his son, the son's identity confirmed by a shepherd who saved him from destruction. Two facts here suggest that Guarini, like Tasso, seeks to write a specifically Aristotelian drama—that

Oedipus was Aristotle's model drama, and that the discovery is accompanied by several references to a cradle, one of the specific motifs listed by Aristotle as appropriate confirmation of identity in the *Poetics*. Both of these influential texts thus blend Aristotle and Plato in a fashion comparable to Sidney's *Apologie for Poetrie*.

Nevertheless the focus in both dramas on love relationships with happy endings separates them distinctly from classical tragedy. It has been argued that the end of *Il pastor fido* derives from Terence's *Andria*, where the newly discovered son replaces the unsuitable but previously betrothed one to make the play end with a happy wedding (again with a gender reversal from the source). But the basic elements of Latin comedy are toned down considerably—the clever servant who conducts the action is reduced to the courtesan Corisca, who plots against, rather than for, the main characters, and who fails to achieve her ends; the irate fathers who control their children's lives in Latin comedy are supplanted also by Corisca (and they are entirely absent in Tasso). The pressure for a happy ending evidently derives from somewhere other than Latin comedy.

The solution to this problem comes from the Christian language of the *Aminta*: the hero suffers "martyrdom" (3.2.269 and 270) at the report of Silvia's death, Silvia "repents" her cruelty (4.1.119), and, we are told, Aminta's "fall" from the cliff was "fortunate" (5.1.38). Seen in these terms, the plot centers actually on Silvia, who commits the sin of cruelty in her repeated rejections of the constant Aminta even after he has saved her from a brutal satyr; after she learns of his presumed suicide (in response to her reported death) she repents, wants to atone by collecting his remains, and is overjoyed to discover that a bush broke his fall. If Aminta reaps the reward of constant love, the audience is shown in considerably more detail that the proper role of woman is not permanent chastity, but to be entwined about her man. As Daphne tries to persuade Silvia to love Aminta in the first scene, she invokes, among other images, the vine twining around her husband the tree "with so many repeated embraces" ("con quanti iterati abbracciamenti," 1.1.152); at the end Elpine reports that Aminta now lies in Silvia's tight embrace (5.1.126). And in between, in the only scene where the hero and heroine actually appear together onstage, Aminta unties the naked Silvia from the tree to which the satyr has bound her. The bestial satyr literalizes the image of the vine bound to the tree, while Aminta, with his pure love (he averts his eyes as he frees her) and sacrifice of his life—fortunately not accepted—enables her to fulfill the purer, figurative meaning of the image of chaste married love. Despite its neoplatonism the play is thus a secularized morality.[22]

In the more complicated plot of *Il pastor fido* (with its two love affairs to be sorted out, as in Terence's *Andria*), the morality plot is more decisively articulated. Unlike *Aminta*, where the satyr is an incarnation of lust, but not a tempter to it, *Il pastor fido* has a true Vice. The sin of lust brought on the ancestral curse that drives the plot, and the courtesan Corisca tries to tempt the heroine Amarilli to the sin of lust, and when that fails to jealousy. Corisca tricks Amarilli into descending (that is, "falling") into a cave where she is caught with her virtuous lover Mirtillo, similarly tricked, and condemned to death as an adulteress. They are saved because Mirtillo, now stylized as the faithful or good shepherd, insists on being sacrificed in her place. His readiness to sacrifice himself despite his innocence proves, after his true identity is revealed, that he was the husband chosen for Amarilli by the oracle (and not his younger brother as had been assumed). At the end the pair even forgive Corisca, cementing the virtues of constancy, purity, and pity. Almost a century later Pedro Calderón de la Barca adapted this play without difficulty as a Corpus Christi morality, with Amarilli as the human soul and Mirtillo as Christ. The combination of morality with Latin comedy, called "Christian Terence" in sixteenth-century Italian school drama, resulted in a kind of serious comedy. With no real conflict between the classical and Christian elements, as the name suggests, both could be acknowledged. The courtier and classicist Guarini, however, was willing to acknowledge only his secular and classical roots; as a result, when challenged about the happy ending, he defended it exclusively in terms of classical categories.[23] Even so, Guarini's terminology should not blind us to the fact that comedy in these pastorals still has at least as much to do with divine comedy as with Latin comedy: the pressure for the happy end in pastoral arises from the encounter of classical tragic form with the structure of morality.

Representation in *Il pastor fido* varies from one scene to the next according to the dramatic subgenre on which Guarini was drawing at the moment. It contains scenes of pastoral lament and narrative (for example, act 1 and the first scene of act 2) as in the *Aminta*, but at times the action is allegorical in the manner of morality, as when both Mirtillo and Amarilli "fall" by descending into the cave (3.7 and 8) or when Silvio accidentally shoots Dorinda, repents his hatred of her and atones by caring for her. The fact that Silvio falls in love as the result of shooting an arrow (onstage), rather than being shot with one as the mythological imagery would lead one to expect, shows how complicated representation in the play becomes through the juxtaposition of so many different modes—the reversal suggests a deliberate dislocation of representation. Related to the morality allegories are several emblematic scenes. In 2.2 and 3 Silvio's exaggerated chastity is represented by his preference for his dog over the shepherdess Dorinda, who holds the dog ransom for a kiss from Silvio; in 3.1 Amarilli playing blindman's buff represents the blindness of love. In 2.6 a satyr binds Corisca to a tree in a parody of the binding of Silvia in *Aminta*; by tearing herself free she makes visible her distance from the Platonic concept of love as the force for ultimate unity. But the play also contains scenes with the heightened rhetoric of Senecan and Greek tragedy, as well as the simple verisimilitude of comic intrigue, as when Corisca pries after the secret of Amarilli's love in 2.5. In 4.5 Amarilli debates her innocence with Nicander in a stichomythic exchange typical of both Greek and Senecan tragedy. The epistemological problem here, whether Amarilli can ever prove the innocence of her intentions, is central to Euripides' *Hippolytos*, where Hippolytos can summon as witnesses to his innocence only the columns of the house, which of course cannot speak. Hippolytos dies because he cannot mount a convincing defense, but Amarilli lives: as she says right after their exchange, her innocence is known in heaven.

The omniscient god of the morality tradition opens the possibility of salvation. More important, Amarilli's hidden sense of her own innocence, incommunicable though it may be, takes on an existence in the world and effectiveness that Hippolytos's never can. It now becomes possible, as Amarilli had already said to Nicander, to see the invisible heart with the eyes of the mind ("Con gli occhi de la mente il cor si vede," 4.5.94). The debate of Aristotelian tragedy combines with the neoplatonist tag (the eyes of the mind) and the god of morality to produce a modern subject—feelings buried within the heart that nevertheless are acknowledged and taken seriously as agents in the real world. Such rhetoric lends all the other evocations of mood in the play a validity that carries them beyond the conventions of courtly pastoral rhetoric. Here is a hint of the psychological depth that became the ultimate hallmark of Aristotelian mimesis in drama. It makes more sense now that these plays were so popular in the seventeenth century: evidently they represented the current state of the European subject in compelling fashion.

Shakespeare's Histories

Thus three disparate classical revivals or neoclassicisms come together in the late Renaissance through a common concern for the representation of truth on the stage and a common modernity. Their earliest interaction still viable on the stage today is the Shakespearean history play. Elizabethan drama is generally agreed to be an amalgam of the late medieval tradition of mystery and morality drama with Latin comedy and Latin tragedy under the immediate influence of sixteenth-century Italian imitations of the latter. The last century saw the recovery of Shakespeare's medieval heritage in terms of both forms and themes in the work of scholars like Willard Farnham, E. M. W. Tillyard, Irving

Ribner, David Bevington, Glynne Wickham, and Anne Righter Barton. While this work has contributed enormously to understanding the origins and development of Shakespeare's dramatic practice, it has not effected any real change in the neoclassical critical language and focus on character that still dominates much of the discussion. The stakes here can be illustrated by a few quotations from introductions to *King John* by two of its best scholars, Irving Ribner and E. A. J. Honigmann in the Pelican (1962) and Arden (1954) editions, respectively. While both recognize the play's roots in morality, they take it for granted that Shakespeare's play belongs to a new generation and is therefore accessible through the standard neo-Aristotelian critical vocabulary (emphasized in the quotes below). Ribner, for example, asserts: "As a *tragedy*, it is interesting for its conception of a *hero* frustrated by a *sin* which he *repents* but cannot cancel, doomed to destruction by his commitment to *evil* means in *striving* for *great* ends" and "[the play] asserts also that a nation can be united only when a king has *learned to subordinate his personal desires* to the good of his country" (Ribner 18). Honigmann uses similar language: "Recreating the *essential* John, Shakespeare has, however, violated facts again and again, subordinating dates and like details to the *truth of character*, the *credibility* of climaxes" (Honigmann 31). While they are surely right that the play works at a hitherto unachieved level of mimesis, their Aristotelianism can only stumble over the implausibility of characters like the child prince Arthur, and the difficulty of identifying the hero or heroes—for Ribner John and the Bastard, for Honigmann John and Arthur—with the further difficulty that John is an essentially unsavory hero. Such problems follow legitimately on the assumption that the play's Gestalt is determined by its mimesis of human actions; if, however, *King John* is understood as an experiment in blending dramaturgies, the problems become opportunities to examine the interaction of Aristotelian, Platonist, and morality modes to create a more sophisticated allegorical dramaturgy rather than a mimetic one. In other words, the allegorical component is not simply a remnant of the medieval heritage absorbed and transformed into mimesis, but it was instead part of the development toward a heightened allegory whose results are visible in the later seventeenth century.

Both scholars must also defend the unity of the plot against the various defects that emerge from their unarticulated neoclassical assumptions. In the play John attempts to keep the throne to protect England from the destabilizing effect of a child king, even though his young nephew Arthur has the stronger legal claim. In the first act he defies a French challenge on behalf of Arthur and the latter's mother Constance, and in the second act after an indecisive battle makes peace with France by agreeing to marry his niece Blanch to the dauphin of France (and keep Arthur out of the succession). At the request of Constance in the third act the papal legate Cardinal Pandulph pressures France to break this new pact, and in the ensuing battle the English are victorious and Arthur is captured; Pandulph incites the French to invade England. In the fourth act John orders his noble Hubert to blind Arthur, but Arthur pleads successfully, flees his prison and dies in a fall from the walls. As John's other followers learn of the child's death, they abandon John, who repents. In the last act John submits formally to the pope's legate and receives his crown now in obedience to Rome. In return Pandulph goes to call off the French invasion, but the French refuse since they have been joined by so many English nobles opposed to John. Fortune intervenes: the French are defeated by a fluke storm, John is poisoned, the repentant nobles return to their first loyalty and John's son Henry is named king. Like all of Shakespeare's histories and many of his tragedies, the play has far too many events for a good Aristotelian plot, but more problematic is that the dispute over the crown has four parties with different interests (John, France, the papacy, Arthur). As they keep betraying one another the plot is both repetitive and chaotic: the audience never knows who to root for. The issue is complicated by the bastard son of Richard Coeur de Lion, to whom much of the first act is devoted, who has a major set piece in the second act, and then unaccountably turns into a secondary figure. At the same time John's attitude toward his cause and his followers' attitude toward him shift dramatically and unaccountably between the third and fourth acts, and then veer again as John dies. But if the play is read as an allegory all of the incoherence vanishes: I begin by analyzing the play as a morality, then consider the ways in which it calls morality dramaturgy into question, and draws on neoplatonist and neo-Aristotelian gestures to create a new kind of allegorical drama.

The relation to morality can best be observed in the differences between Shakespeare's *King John* (1594–96) and John Bale's morality play on the same material, *King Johan*, written sometime between 1538 and 1560.[24] Although the play was not published until 1833 and Shakespeare cannot be assumed to have known it, the line of development from *King Johan* to *King John* is illuminating, for *King Johan* is a hybrid between morality and history. It presents John's humiliation by the church and his subsequent poisoning at Swinstead Abbey (very like the end of Shakespeare's play), but apart from John himself most of the characters are allegorical: he defends a widow named Englande, and his persecutors from the church are Vices with names like Sedition, Dissimulation, and Usurped Power. The name changing, disguising, and lying of the morality tradition are taken to such extremes that even the Vices have trouble recognizing one another. But morality shades into

TABLE 1. PARALLEL SYNOPSES OF BALE AND SHAKESPEARE ON KING JOHN

King Johan	King John	Common Plot
I. John hears plea of England	I. a) John refuses claim on behalf of Arthur b) John confers identity on the Bastard	King as Judge
John berates Nobility, Clergy, Civil Order on mistreatment of England	II. John defends his city against French attack and his realm against a destabilizing child king by betrothal of Lewis and Blanch	John working for the good of England
The Vices introduce themselves and make plots; they are all associated with the church	III. Constance rages; Pandulph incites war against England and incites French invasion	Treachery inspired by church
II. John's supporters desert him at the behest of the Vices	IV. Arthur prevents his own blinding; Arthur and Elinor die; John is deserted	John deserted by his supporters
John delivers his crown; he cannot punish treason	V. John submits to Pandulph; Pandulph cannot stop Lewis; French treason revealed; John retires	King is subjected to church and loses his power
John is poisoned and then vindicated	John is poisoned; Henry is recognized as new king	King is murdered; Kingship is vindicated

history when Usurped Power turns out also to be the pope, and when Sedition and Private Wealth also take on the names of Stephen Langton (Archbishop of Canterbury), and Cardinal Pandulph respectively. Their double identities are a problem and connect to the considerable discussion in the play of metaphors used and of the reliability of language. After John's murder Veritas clears up all misunderstandings, not only those within the plot, but also those of historians. John was a traditional villain in English history: one of Bale's goals is to rehabilitate him as a hero of the Reformation *avant la lettre* because he resisted the church. This political issue is certainly still alive in Shakespeare's version, but more important for us are the concerns to establish truth. Bale takes us beyond a simple truth opposed to the deceits of the devil to the more complex question of establishing historical truth in a welter of competing representations.

The basic similarity of the two plays can be read from the parallel synopses in Table 1. In the common plot description in the right-hand column the paradigmatic morality plot is readily visible: a central figure innocent or at least unaware of his sin is beset by plotting Vices; he falls and is deserted by his natural supporters; he repents and is restored to divine favor—here posthumously vindicated. Shakespeare's play is actually closer to the morality paradigm than Bale's in that John himself is not merely the dupe of the Vice Usurped Power, as in Bale, but actually succumbs to the sin embodied in that name. The treachery and betrayal typical of morality Vices are the central activities: as a usurper John has been faithless to his nephew, but all of the main and secondary characters break promises or cynically deceive.[25] When Fortune fails both sides as their armies and supplies are lost in act 5, it is almost ironic, for the treachery of fortune scarcely compares with that of the humans. The actions in Shakespeare are little more developed than the actions called for in Bale's rather stiff morality, and they are always symbolic—kneeling, falling, taking or dropping hands.[26] The options for a history play in the 1590s were not by nature so limited. In *The Troublesome Raigne of King John,* a play of 1591 so close to Shakespeare's *King John* that it is disputed whether it is a source or a bad quarto, more action is depicted onstage than in Shakespeare's play and it is presented in more detailed, mimetic terms.[27] Either the compiler of the bad quarto felt Shakespeare's handling to be insufficiently mimetic, or—as seems more likely to me—Shakespeare deliberately stylized a more mimetic treatment of the material to reveal its underlying allegorical structure.

If the play is an allegory, then the Bastard and John represent illegitimacy in different ways. Philip gains the honor of being Richard's son through the stain of illegitimate birth, John pays for the glory of kingship by accepting the stain of usurpation: this parallel explains why the first act is devoted to the Bastard rather than to John, and suggests a continued meditation on the relative truth of the older and more modern (mimetic) modes of representation. Philip's normal designation, "the Bastard," makes him personify the illegitimacy of the central power and the initial focus on him transforms the tension between honor and bastardy explicitly into the moral conflict between virtue and vice. If King John is a historical example of illegitimate power, the Bastard is the concrete personification of it typical of morality. Not only are the two parallel, but the one is an allegorical version of the other. Later in the play the Bastard not only acts on John's behalf, as his messenger and then general, but he also acts as John should have acted, for example when he kills Austria in act 3 and especially when he kneels to the new, legitimate child-king at the end. In that gesture of reverence the Bastard repairs John's earlier failure to kneel to the child Arthur; such atonement is the proper end to the morality play. It becomes typical for Shakespeare, especially in the mature comedies (see below, Chapter 4), to organize his plays around parallel plots, one of which is more mimetic, the other more allegorical, but it will not always be the case that the allegorical hero will end better off than the mimetic one, as is here the case.

In fact, Shakespeare plays the two modes against each other even within the Bastard, who functions sometimes more and sometimes less allegorically. In the last few acts he functions more mimetically—what Ribner calls more heroically—as a participant in the historical action, but in act 1, as we have seen, he operates entirely with categories like honor and dishonor (virtue and vice). In Robert Weimann's analysis of the Shakespearean clown's wavering between dramatic modes, direct addresses to the audience from the front of the stage are characterized as more popular, withdrawal into the frame of stage action as more illusionist (*Shakespeare and the Popular Tradition in the Theater* 224–37). Similar variation prevails here, probably because the morality had already absorbed significant elements of what Weimann calls the popular tradition, so that allegory and popular style are aligned. Philip's abuse of Austria in acts 2 and 3 is particularly similar to the low language of the Vices in Bale, but his most interesting speech is that on commodity at the end of act 2. He means by commodity self-interested dissimulation, precisely the most common Vice of the morality tradition; there is one named Commodity in Bale, but the figure recurs constantly also under the name Hypocrisy. However, Philip speaks not as Dissimulation or Commodity here; he speaks about a personified Commodity, as if he were describing the Vice in an old play. Here we see mimetic dramaturgy meeting but not suppressing allegorical dramaturgy. Although the Bastard does not personify Commodity, as the king's bastard he does personify the tarnished honor characteristic of all the figures in the play. Less given by the theological system and created ad hoc for the particular social situation, this quasi personification is a typical step in the adaptation of allegory to a more secular society and leads toward the seventeenth-century cultivation of emblem.

The morality model is even called into question in the play's repeated failures to make God's will visible in the welter of history. In act 1 King John, supposedly God's representative in the realm, cannot actually determine the truth of the Faulconbridge brothers' claims, but only strike a compromise by severing material wealth from honor. When such claims escalate in act 2 to the contest between the brother kings of England and France for the English throne, they and the citizens of Angiers leave the decision to God, who refuses to speak through their indecisive battle. Historical particularity seems to triumph over allegory. The two queens, Elinor and Constance, repeat the indecisiveness in an ugly war of words. Here too the power of allegory seems to break down, since the figure most concerned with legitimacy in this act is Constance, whose constancy is ugly and repetitious hysteria. Like the mother of the Bastard, she besmirches the honor of Arthur's otherwise apparently legitimate claim to the throne. Cardinal Pandulph reopens the question of who speaks for God in act 3. In the ensuing battle England wins decisively, but John is excommunicated, so that a split decision replaces compromise. If Pandulph's appearance seemed at first the direct intervention of God in response to Constance's prayer, he undermines his own status as divine messenger by encouraging Philip to break his newly sworn faith, then loses it entirely when England wins the battle. In the contest in act 4 between Arthur and Hubert over whether Arthur must be blinded, Hubert succumbs without giving any reason, while Arthur pleads only in personal terms, invoking neither God nor right but mercy. Although Arthur finally dies not as a direct result of John's command but through his own attempts to escape, John nevertheless suffers the consequences of his wish to kill his nephew; from the moment Arthur's death legitimates John's claim to the throne, sanctioned now even by Pandulph and the church, John loses the loyalty of his nobles and his power. Ultimately John, Lewis and Pandulph all lose. But in the process most of the old dishonor and confusion are eliminated, and the final tableau shows the Bastard kneeling before Prince Henry, to whom the stain of Constance's hysteria and treason (her association with France and with Austria, the killer of Richard I) does not attach. This resolution does not follow logically on the preceding events; instead, divine purity descends into a repentant world that has recognized its own sinfulness and loss of direction, as both John and his nobles have by the end of the act; it is an uncomfortable and abrupt assertion of the old morality structure after repeated questioning of the inclination of divinity to intervene in the world of history. If the ethical values of the morality model seem weak here, they at least enable some kind of order to be imposed on the real details of history.

In this respect Shakespeare has actually extended the morality plot from its original religious significance to question the validity of any language, not just that of the Vice. Fidelity already appears as a problem of language in the opening lines, as Elinor comments on Chatillion's language, "A strange beginning: 'borrowed majesty'!" (1.1.5), the more so since the words "say" and "speak" appear in lines one and two. "Borrowed majesty" suggests the discrepancy between name or "title" (1.1.13) and identity that recurs in the scene's later concern for usurpation. The fidelity or validity of language is central to the much longer confrontation between the Bastard and his half-brother Robert that occupies most of act 1. The judgment John must render, whether Philip is the son of

Faulconbridge or the bastard of King Richard, turns on two conflicts between word and fact: first between a written will and the "fact" of Philip's birth six weeks too early, and second between the (albeit false) assertion of the mother and Philip's close resemblance to Richard. In both cases language, aligned with material wealth, conflicts with identity (recognized visually), which is aligned with the more abstract wealth of honor. When Philip is officially declared Richard's bastard, the visual takes precedence over the verbal, and with it idea over ordinary reality: this is the value system of allegorical drama. Morality is legible to its spectators because what is seen takes priority over what is said by the Vices. Shakespeare expands that guarantee, and thereby the reach of allegory, to a secular context.

The blinding of Arthur extends the reading as it introduces another dramatic style into the equation. Of all the figures in the play, Arthur and Hubert seem least related to the morality pattern. Hubert represents the power of the personal and individual—it is he who suggests the marriage of the rival thrones in act 2, and Melun's personal respect for Hubert prompts his own betrayal of Lewis to the English lords in act 5. The blinding scene is the one place in the play Shakespeare reaches back to the earlier, less allegorical, mystery tradition: in pleading for his eyes Arthur refers to his innocence, to an angel coming to him, and to a lamb in quick succession (4.1.64, 68, and 79), all motifs in the Brome Abraham and Isaac play (Honigmann, *King John* lxxi). Shakespeare not only uses the mystery tradition to shape exclusively historical material, but does so with thematic significance, for Arthur is rescued here not by an angel, but by his own words—the locus of presence has moved to human language.

The importance of eyes in this scene also engages neoplatonist allegory. The Bastard's angelic gesture directing our gaze to the child-king in the final scene offers a clue to Hubert's significance: Hubert spares specifically Arthur's eyes, the Platonic agents of higher knowledge. Even Hubert's eyes will ultimately determine the truth of his proceeding, for Arthur says, "Nay, [the shame of your proceeding] perchance will sparkle in your eyes" (4.1.112–14). Arthur's eyes offer the ultimate testimony to his innocence—

> The iron of itself, though heat red-hot,
> Approaching near these eyes, would drink my tears,
> And quench [his] fiery indignation
> Even in the matter of mine innocence. (4.1.61–64)

Because eyes both perceive truth and simultaneously mirror it, they offer a window out of the world into an ideal innocence and purity rather like the young prince at the end. Blanch in act 2 represents the same phenomenon. Associated with pure whiteness by her name, she is described by Hubert as beauty, virtue, and birth—not far from the Platonic triad of the good, the beautiful, and the true. Lewis accepts her with the typical Platonist paradoxes of the period:

> I do, my lord, and in her eye I find
> A wonder, or a wondrous miracle,
> The shadow of myself form'd in her eye,
> Which being but the shadow of your son,
> Becomes a sun and makes your son a shadow.
> I do protest I never lov'd myself
> Till now infixed I beheld myself
> Drawn in the flattering table of her eye. (2.1.496–503)

Here again the eye is not only agent of perception, but a miraculous mirror in which one sees one's true self while the material self is reduced to shadow. Blanch offered a moment of peace, soon disrupted by Pandulph, as the salvation of Arthur might also have brought peace to John's troubled realm. That Prince Henry knows how to give thanks only with tears at the end (5.7.109) connects him to this Platonist imagery of the eye. Behind the tangled confusion of word and action there is a validating higher truth, but it is secularized and Platonized, thus much harder to see than the Christian truth sought after by the historical characters in the play. The confrontation of the Christian allegory with the mimetic historical component is resolved by introducing what from Shakespeare's perspective must have seemed a more modern form of allegory, Renaissance Platonism.[28]

This secularization weakens the most obvious sign of the morality tradition the play had absorbed, its prosopopoeia. Although Arthur is spared by Hubert, he still dies as he tries to escape: he is destroyed by John's unspeakable wish and John suffers the guilt of Arthur's death even though neither he nor Hubert actually touches the child—and it seems right that he does. But if John's wish, rather than his act, can kill Arthur and eliminate him from the play, how much more evanescent is allegory than in the earlier moralities, which portray psychic forces at work only explicitly and literally in action. Blanch too is an evanescent allegory; it is much more difficult to drive the embodiments of divine grace off the morality stage, where they persist with puritan zeal in their efforts to save the hero. At the same time, in *King John* allegory spreads to action and detail in ways far beyond morality personification. The penultimate scene of the play, a gratuitous recognition scene between Hubert and the Bastard, contains its most modern version of allegory.

Bale has a few scenes in the middle of his play in which the Vices recognize one another only with difficulty; Shakespeare tosses one in, with no obvious plot function, just at the end. Although both Hubert and the Bastard have functioned as sometime Vices, by the end of the play they have emerged as the only possible carriers of truth to emerge from John's reign. Their inability to recognize one another is the final instance of the difficulty of knowing and identifying in the play; the darkness symbolizes the state of the kingdom around them. Here allegory is no longer a matter of concrete personification, but each and every detail becomes significant, as it will be in seventeenth-century emblems and in the moralities of Calderón fifty years after this play.

The way characters hover between modes often results in yet another new form of allegory. Blanch suddenly becomes grace, peace, and truth as she is accepted by Lewis, and she evaporates from the play just as peace and truth do. Constance is clearly constant in her aim to place her son on the throne, but her constancy comes to seem more a vice than a virtue. When she and Elinor confront one another before Philip as the hysterical and the charming mother, these two historical figures suddenly turn into types between which Philip—like a morality hero— must choose. Pandulph is supposedly a historical figure, but his only activity is to instigate bad faith, just like any Vice. Similarly, Salisbury, repeatedly referred to as "noble," is little more than a personal name to identify Nobility, who is a character in Bale. Even Honigmann says, "Salisbury . . . almost personifies Nobility" (Honigmann, lxx), and speaks of the challenge to John coming from the "spirit of England" (Honigmann, lxxii; England is the first character to address John in Bale's morality). But this is not simply a matter of echoes. The central Vice of morality, Dissimulation or Hypocrisy, is absent except in the Bastard's description of Commodity, but in its place is the central determining action of betrayal. Allegory as personification is translated into allegory as action. A new form of allegory arises here out of the carefully managed encounter between dramatic modes. If the play is deliberately stylized in terms of morality, it nevertheless works with a mimetic dramatis personae and lays conspicuous emphasis on the most famous Platonist image of the period. It thus operates simultaneously with the three types of representations, all aspects of neoclassicism. As we have seen, the play does not simply mix the forms, but draws its own statement out of their interaction. The allegories in this play are important not because of where they came from but because of their bold exploration of the possibilities they open up and the ways that their synthesis necessarily changes the form of allegorical representation.

Chapter 4

Allegory and Passion: Latin Dramatic Forms in the Seventeenth Century

Shakespeare is rich in wondrous tropes that are based on personified abstractions and would not suit us at all, but are entirely appropriate for him because in his time all art was dominated by allegory.

—*Goethe*[1]

Aristotle's *Poetics* describe the practice of Athenian tragedy in the fifth century B.C., but sixteenth-century intellectuals were more likely to read Latin than Greek, and to read it better, even if they had studied Greek. As it became fashionable at sixteenth-century Italian courts to stage the occasional classical play, it was a Latin one, not Greek. Thus Seneca, Plautus, and Terence actually provided the Renaissance its primary direct experience of classical drama and had their own impact on the development of European drama independent of Aristotelianism. Because the tragedies of Lucius Annaeus Seneca (ca. 4 B.C.–A.D. 65) are above all exercises in the expression of affect, his influence joined that of Horace to drive neoclassicists even more toward a focus on character rather than plot. It would be hard to find a dramatist in the seventeenth century untouched by Seneca's influence, but I have chosen to discuss here Joost van den Vondel, the great Dutch dramatist of the period, and Racine because they embody most clearly the ways in which Seneca accommodates Aristotelian theory, and because they also avoid the supernatural aspect of Seneca that was a problem for Aristotelians. I have thus tried to make my test for allegorical dramaturgy in Senecan playwrights as rigorous as possible.

I will begin by examining Senecanism in relation to morality plot, character, and allegory, then consider the two Continental playwrights. Against this background I will then consider the complexity of Shakespeare further. His plays were not obviously mimetic for eighteenth-century neoclassicists, but eventually they staged compromise adaptations, such as Nahum Tate's *King Lear*, which ended with perfect poetic justice (the marriage of Cordelia and Edgar), or the much-clarified version of *Hamlet* proposed ironically by Goethe in *Wilhelm Meister's Apprenticeship* (1795–96) in his critique of late neoclassicism in Germany. The nineteenth century read Shakespeare primarily as a dramatist of character— the ultimate heritage of neoclassicism—now via Hegel: A. C. Bradley's *Shakespearean Tragedy* is the representative document. In effe_t, Shakespeare was assimilated to Racine, the great neoclassical student of character. Such readings made the Aristotelian aspects of Shakespeare's dramaturgy obvious, but obscured its allegorical aspects. The goal of this chapter is thus not to reevoke the wealth of mimetic detail and complex insights that has made Shakespeare and Racine dominate their national canons, nor is it to rehearse the traditional comparison between them. Instead it is to consider the relation of character and allegory and thus to reposition the figures generally recognized as the two great psychologists of the seventeenth century against dramatists less well known to us but of equal stature in their time and in their own national traditions. I am looking for the shared patterns.

Latin Form, Seneca, and Senecanism

Latin comedy impacted the serious drama of neoclassicism in four important ways. T. J. Baldwin has demonstrated in extenso in *Shakespere's Five-Act Structure* that the five-act structure in Renaissance and Baroque tragedy developed from discussions in Renaissance commentaries on Plautus and Terence and was applied only retroactively to Seneca. Stylistically Latin comedy made available a model of casual "realistic" language. The happy ending of romance in which the heroine's (or less commonly the hero's) identity is restored is standard in Latin comedy. It occurred also in some tragedies of Euripides, and the restoration of identity with an unhappy end was already present in *Oedipus*, but in Latin comedy it became the necessary convention. From there it passed into Renaissance comedy, pastoral, opera, and neoclassical tragedy. The other standard plot convention of Latin comedy was the action being run by the clever servant of the hero. In Shakespearean comedy the action is often managed by the heroine disguised as a clever servant, but the convention even enters into tragedy with Iago in *Othello*. Thus even if the impact of Latin comedy was diffuse, it affected form, style, and plot conventions.

Seneca's nine plays, mostly adaptations of Greek tragedies, largely on the model of Euripides, do not seem necessarily to have been written for stage performance in their day; nonetheless their influence was pervasive in the later sixteenth and seventeenth centuries.[2] In accord with

Seneca's stoicism, the plays portray a claustrophobic, hostile world, in which the protagonists are driven by some crime committed in the past (*Thyestes, Agamemmnon*) or a secret sin (*Phaedra*); in either case the underlying evil is revealed with the opening of doors at the end of the play to show the figures destroyed by its continuation or working out. The protagonists are characterized above all by the violence of their passions, which they constantly refer to as beings that can seize upon them at any time: the central trope is personification, though without allegory. Anger is the primary Senecan passion, and as a result revenge is the primary theme. The rage of Seneca's protagonists expands to fill the entire universe (Braden, *Renaissance Tragedy and the Senecan Tradition* chs. 1 and 2, esp. p. 48), and makes them become identical to their opponents. In the *Thyestes*, for example, Atreus finds assurance that his sons are not the illegitimate offspring of his brother by making Thyestes commit sins as egregious as his own. The fall of the protagonist brings not only his house, but the entire cosmos to destruction. Violent and bombastic language, energetic stichomythia, and vivid choral interludes to mourn the progress of the plot compensate for the absence of stage action. The messenger's speech inherited from Greek tragedy becomes especially gory, and often includes omens and other striking manifestations of the otherwise invisible supernatural. The exceptions are prologues spoken by ghosts in *Thyestes* and *Agamemnon*, which, however, had disproportionate influence in the seventeenth century, when ghosts, revenge, and bombast are sure signs of Seneca's presence. The most dependable formal sign of Senecanism is the presence of choruses at the ends of acts—the norm in Dutch and German Baroque tragedy—but it disappears rapidly in England or merges with allegorical dumb shows more closely related to the indigenous religious drama.

Seneca was readily assimilated into the Christian tradition. Like moralities, Senecan tragedies focus on the isolated individual; even where other characters seem to have important roles, the plays focus exclusively on a crime that is evoked in a series of disputations saturated with the proto-Christian vocabulary of sin, soul, guilt, punishment, good and evil. Seneca conspicuously lacks divine presence, but has instead ghosts, omens, and prominent laments on the absence of divine intervention to prevent the horrors that drive the plots. The failure to make God speak in *King John*, for example, is the Senecan obverse of God's presence in morality. Although Senecanism is generally identified with the centrality of the revenge motif, and especially with violence in both language and action, some of these elements can be multiply determined in the Renaissance. Thus some of the representation of anger derives, in England at least, from the ranting Herod in the mystery plays, but becomes perceived as Senecan (Braden, *Renaissance Tragedy and the Senecan Tradition*

180). It also feeds in from the theme of martyrdom, important in some medieval saints' lives but especially widespread in seventeenth-century school drama. Usually written by the professor of rhetoric (in Latin) for performance by students as practice in public speaking, school dramas still had to accommodate the schools' religious programs—in the sixteenth century first among Humanists, Protestant and Catholic alike, and in the seventeenth century increasingly among the Jesuits, to demonstrate the power of Providence. As in a morality play the martyr is typically tempted to avoid martyrdom, so that his or her sufferings constitute triumph over sin and lead to salvation; this paradoxical union of punishment and salvation constitutes the specifically Baroque form of morality drama. Nevertheless, since the plays were also exercises in Latin rhetoric and oral delivery, Senecan horror mingles readily with the sufferings of the martyr, and martyr drama sometimes slides into tragedy when its focus becomes partly secular. This was especially the case in Protestant parts of Germany in the seventeenth century, where the plays were written and performed in German, still usually by students. Such are the Baroque tragedies of Andreas Gryphius and Daniel Caspar von Lohenstein. Andreas Gryphius's *Carolus Stuardus*, for example, celebrates the recently martyred English king from the Protestant point of view. Such plays are intensely Senecan in their mourning rhetoric, rage, diction, and use of the chorus, yet are still unmistakably morality plays.

The overlap took place readily in part because Seneca's plays, contrary to Aristotelian assumptions, were so open to allegory. Grim personifications (Chaos, Grief, Sorrow, and Fear) and dismembered or independently functional body parts abound in the rhetoric of his hysterical protagonists. As the central doors at the back of the stage open in the last scene of a Seneca tragedy they reveal the hitherto invisible crime now concretely embodied. The Ghost-prologue in the *Thyestes* begins by remembering the banquet on human flesh that Tantalus offered the gods; during the play that feast becomes a figure of speech, and at the end literal reality, as Atreus shows the heads of Thyestes' children, whose flesh Thyestes has just consumed. The same happens to the destructive power of Phaedra's love in the *Phaedra*, where the initial rhetoric of destruction is literally realized as the queen stabs herself over her stepson's dismembered corpse. When Oedipus announces his departure at the end of his play in company with Disease, Plague, Corruption, and Pain, the reader is hard put not to visualize the presence of these figures onstage. As a result, the influence of Seneca pulls in two directions simultaneously. On the one hand it enhances allegory, and on the other draws moralities into increased mimeticism, both from its pressure toward more secular subjects, but also from the tendency, especially strong in England, to represent much of the narrated violence onstage, an impulse that itself probably came from the strong tradition of the passion plays. While more or less pure morality plots persist on the stage in the seventeenth century, particularly in Spain and Catholic Germany, in the Protestant countries and even in France they are inevitably mixed to an almost indeterminable degree with Senecanism, which sometimes makes them seem more secular and mimetic, but paradoxically sometimes enhances their tendencies to allegory. As a result, Seneca enables morality to reinvent itself as tragedy.

Senecanism on the Continent: Racine and Vondel as Moralists

The term Senecan is appropriate for much European drama of the century: in Britain from *Gorboduc* (Norton and Sackville, 1561) to John Webster (ca. 1580–ca. 1632) and John Ford (1586–1639?), in France from Etienne Jodelle (1532–73) through Jean de Rotrou (1609–50) and Pierre Corneille (1606–84), and somewhat later in Germany with Andreas Gryphius (1616–64) and Daniel Caspar von Lohenstein (1635–83), all of whom are Senecan in the obvious ways. But the two who made the most creative use of the Senecan model and raised most clearly the issues surrounding its use were Jean Racine (1639–99) and Joost van den Vondel (1587–1679). I have chosen these two for several reasons. Racine has generally been considered to have adopted entirely the classical model of tragedy and to represent the acme of neoclassical decorum. Because he is one of the earliest of the great European dramatists to know Greek tragedy well in the original—the other was Vondel, who translated both Seneca and Sophocles—readers have also looked for the ways in which he is Aristotelian, rather than those in which he is not. Racine's connections to the allegorical tradition will be more telling than the more obvious ones of Corneille, who openly used the conventions of martyr drama even in *Polyeucte* and who has been more routinely compared (rather than contrasted) with Shakespeare. At issue in the following discussion is to show how even such high neoclassicists operate with allegorical dramaturgy, and my term "moralist" here is intended to evoke morality play as well as the more obvious sense of ethical interest, which no one would question in relation to either dramatist. Vondel is less well known today than Racine, but in his day he was widely respected, and especially influential in Germany, so that I juxtapose here the least and most forgotten major tragedians of their day. The comparison between the two makes it easier to clarify the tangled relations among Senecanism, Aristotelianism, and morality in these texts.

Although born a generation apart, Racine and Vondel followed comparable trajectories. Racine came from a Jansenist background, the puritanical anti-Jesuit movement of the French Counter-Reformation influential in the second half of the seventeenth century, and was educated at its center, Port-Royal, then at Paris under the supervision of Jansenist relatives. His devotion to literature and theater, which became a full commitment by 1663, seemed to break with the values of his upbringing, but in 1677 he renounced both the theater and his libertine lifestyle. For the remainder of his career, as courtier and royal historiographer, he appears to have been a model husband and devout Jansenist. After 1677 he wrote only two more plays, both on biblical themes for the girls' school at St. Cyr. Regardless of their classical purity it is thus appropriate to consider religious paradigms in his plays, and not just religious themes, which have of course been profoundly explored. Vondel came from an Anabaptist family in Antwerp driven by religious strife first to Cologne, where the poet was born in 1587, then in 1597 to Amsterdam, where he grew up and flourished. Unlike Racine, he was a hosiery merchant by day, an autodidact and occasional poet, whose dramatic talents developed relatively late. He wrote for a public stage, but it was the only public stage in the city and was run by the amalgamated literary societies of Amsterdam. It was thus more comparable in selectivity and intellectual aspirations to Racine's theatrical environment than to Shakespeare's. He became a Catholic in 1640, after which his plays became more biblical in subject matter. Unlike Racine, he never introduced the love plot into tragedy, and all of his plays are more openly martyr plays with an obvious affinity to morality drama. But his use of Seneca in his relation to the visual onstage seems more comparable to Racine's than anyone else's in the period, and hence of interest here. I will begin with Vondel, where the issues are easier to see, then consider the more complex case of Racine's classical form, his relation to morality plot structure and its tension with the elements of Latin drama, and finally the problem of the visual.

Let us turn to Vondel to confirm the continued presence of morality in Senecan form, and then to lay out the Aristotelian aspects of these plays, to the extent that they differ, especially with regard to plot structure. The alternation between long narrative or mourning speeches and stichomythia, the pathos, the themes of disaster and revenge, the destructive violence of the world, the severity of God are all obviously Senecan. Indeed, Vondel sits halfway between the Senecan rage that pervades Stuart tragedy in England and the pathos of the German tragedies of Gryphius and Lohenstein so famously characterized by Walter Benjamin as "mourning" plays. Nevertheless, Vondel's plays are still openly moralities: of his thirty dramas, fourteen are on biblical themes (primarily Old Testament), while the remainder (except for seven translations from the Latin or Greek) treat more secular subjects in morality patterns or as explicit martyr dramas. As in England in the sixteenth century, drama was religious politics, for Vondel's Holland was a hotbed of controversy among Puritans, moderate Protestants, and Catholics; indeed, Vondel first made his reputation as a dramatist through plays that were immediately banned and for which he was fined.[3] His *Maria Stuart* (1646), like Gryphius's *Carolus Stuardus* (prob. 1650), is an obvious example of a martyr drama speaking to the particular local situation. Vondel wrote it shortly after he had converted to Catholicism and it claims a space for Catholics in a hostile environment. Furthermore, while neoclassicism was clearly the new wave of the day, and the autodidact Vondel embraced it eagerly as soon as he learned about it, his audiences did not share the prejudice against the older forms of religious drama found at the more secularized and centralized French court (Aercke, *Gijsbrecht van Amstel* 15–17). Hence the morality model is not a suppressed subtext, but coexists comfortably with the more fashionable Senecan form.

Aristotelian deus ex machina and reversal also coexist in Vondel's eclectic vocabulary of plot gestures with no particular disruption. Deus ex machina and morality both depend after all on divine intervention. In aesthetic terms deus ex machina was a problem because it violated Horatian verisimilitude, and in political terms it engaged the problem of miracle, which divided Protestants from Catholics, and Puritans of whatever stripe from moderates. As a moderate Protestant who moved toward a tolerant Catholicism, Vondel was open to the deus ex machina, and seamlessly substituted it for the apotheosis or final divine judgment one would expect in earlier religious drama; good examples would be his *Maria Stuart* (1646) and *Zungchin* (1667). More interesting in this regard is Vondel's most famous play, *Gijsbrecht van Aemstel* of 1638. In a long Senecan prologue Gijsbrecht explains the prehistory of the play: tricked by a cunning cousin, Gijsbrecht, hereditary ruler of Amstel, was affiliated with an unsuccessful, but not totally unjustified rebellion. His efforts to mediate and to atone have all been rejected, but now in late December 1304 the enemy has suddenly lifted the siege of Amsterdam and pious Gijsbrecht is happy that God has finally made justice prevail. But the play itself shows the surprise penetration of Amsterdam by the enemy and its collapse in a plot obviously modeled on the fall of Troy in Book II of the *Aeneid*. The horrors of the brutal destruction are narrated by various characters at length; Gijsbrecht, his wife, and a few devoted followers flee in a ship to found a New Amsterdam on distant shores. The archangel Raphael appears at the end to order the future of the exiled protagonist and his family, and begins by telling him his cross is imposed by God. This is a Senecan martyr drama, but with a twist. Even though Gijsbrecht is a good and pious Christian, he suffers not for a religious ideal but for a national one. The ideology of the play is essentially that of the urban bourgeoisie: the highest values are the civic community and the marriage bond, and Gijsbrecht suffers at such length for trying to do the right thing by those for whom he is responsible. When the largely Senecan form suddenly gives way to the Aristotelian deus ex machina, the result is on the one hand salvation, but on the other, it is also a task that must and will be fulfilled, like those imposed by the gods who appear at the end of Euripides' plays. The play is openly religious and also secular.

In the less secular *Noach* (nevertheless identified as a tragedy [*Treurspel*]), the archangel Uriel appears at the end to condemn those who failed to listen to Noah's warnings and now repent too late. He seems less a deus ex machina than Divine Providence in morality meting out justice. And yet, in a morality it would be God himself who condemns, or Jesus, or the devil; here, however, it is a secondary messenger figure, the archangel who seems to function as the equivalent of a pagan deity—not God himself but a part or representative. The Aristotelian gesture serves a religious function quite foreign to it. The extreme example of this phenomenon comes in the tragedy *Lucifer*, in which archangels or falling angels narrate Lucifer's rebellion against God to one another in an extended teichoscopia on the ramparts of heaven. When Michael and Gabriel end by prophesying the coming of Jesus to redeem Adam, what in the other plays had been an amalgam of the Aristotelian and morality gesture of closure is here just more of what most of the play has consisted of: the god never has to descend in the machine, because the entire play takes place in heaven, which becomes, by default, also the world in which action can be seen. God himself never appears in the play. Indeed, the very logic of the Christian myth requires that the action be resolved by the ultimate God: the whole play becomes, in effect, the working of the deus ex machina, and the ultimate religious play becomes strikingly secular.

Racine's *Athalie* (1691) takes this development to its natural conclusion. The high priest, Joad, and his wife, Josabet, conduct a running argument through the play about faith versus doubt: Joad keeps identifying events as miracles that Josabet understands as natural. That miracles were visible as such only to the elect, and seemed natural to others was in accord with Jansenist theology, but in the context of the morality structure that underlies the play, the audience reasonably expects to see the supernatural with its own eyes. The plot centers on a nightmare recounted by Queen Athalie about how an innocent boy will kill her; the child turns out to be her own grandson, whom she had ordered murdered in his infancy to avenge the death of her father and to establish her own power. It turns out that the child has been raised secretly by the high priest and his wife; when the queen recognizes the figure from her dream helping in the temple and summons him, Joad hastens his plot to replace her with the lawful king. At the point of greatest tension, late in act 5, Joad has lured her into the temple with a minimal escort. When she demands the child, a curtain is pulled aside in a gesture rather like the revelation of Hermione in *Winter's Tale* to reveal him in his true identity, as the child she tried to murder. The deus ex machina is replaced by an earthly coup de theatre. In a strictly allegorical morality play divinity itself would be revealed at this point; but Racine's figure is the king, whose dramatic revelation deliberately claims for him the aura of divinity Louis XIV claimed for himself. This is mimesis, but mimesis of the deliberately stagy practice of allegory. The theater seems to be, in this reading, not something between allegory and mimesis, but their triumphant marriage.

In his earlier plays, too, Racine offers the prime example of the close partnership of neoclassical form with the Latin models and morality. He uses explicitly Greek sources; his prefaces regularly engage Aristotle's categories and the plays frequently invoke fear and pity; he is a master of reversal. Yet the plays are predominantly Senecan.[4] The typical rage and violence—the "juste corroux" of the seventeenth century—becomes an elaborate juxtaposition of passion and reason, focused on a central figure to generate what begins to look like modern psychological depth. At the same time the Senecan tendency to narrate the violent physical actions through a messenger, taken over in toto, facilitates their neoclassical decorum, which eschews almost all visible violence onstage. Seneca's claustrophobic world, finally, finds ideal formal expression in Racine's strict observance of the three unities. At the same time, the extreme concern for virtue, frequent confessions, and kneeling, and above all the strong sense of poetic justice, link these plays to morality.[5] Then, finally, the five-act structure and the central theme of love probably derive from Latin comedy; Greek and Latin tragedies rarely exhibit the love plot of French tragedy. The most prominent exception is Seneca's *Phaedra*, based on Euripides' *Hippolytus*, where the issue is love both forbidden and unrequited. The love theme moves toward the center of the stage occasionally in Shakespeare, most notably in *Romeo and Juliet*, but also in *Othello* and *Antony and Cleopatra*; for Corneille and especially Racine, it is regularly the heart of the plot. Thus *Andromaque* (1667) and *Britannicus* (1669) depend on the same plot as Shakespeare's problem comedy *Measure for Measure*, the heroine's choice between an unwanted powerful lover and the life of a beloved relative or the beloved himself. Others—*Alexandre le grand* (1665), *Mithridate* (1673), and *Iphigénie* (1674)—end happily for reunited lovers; in the last the happy figure is even in the title.[6] Even when Racine is at his most Senecan, as in *La*

Thébaïde, he has Créon propose to Antigone in the last act after all the younger men have been killed off.

Bajazet, a typical middle play (1672), offers a quick overview of the tensions present even for such a master of Senecan form as Racine. On the one hand it reflects the heightened level of mimesis in the period. His preface, like that of many mid-seventeenth-century plays, insists on the historical veracity of his text, even if Racine dispenses with the learned footnotes often found in his Dutch and German contemporaries. Racine was a serious and committed historian, both as a writer of history, and as a user of myth.[7] The preface also emphasizes that the episode is not just a history play, but also current events: the level of mimesis is thus substantially raised over Shakespeare's history plays. Although this is Racine's only play to deal with a contemporary event, the practice was not uncommon in Holland and Germany in the period.[8] The event is stylized in Senecan terms, and indeed seems an early version of *Phèdre*. Roxane, all-powerful mistress of the Turkish emperor Amurat, tries to persuade his younger brother, Bajazet, to marry her and seize the throne. Bajazet, however, loves Atalide, and neither is comfortable with the lies that diplomatic behavior with Roxane constantly requires of them. In the next-to-the-last scene a messenger reports how Roxane has Bajazet killed, which Amurat had already ordered her to do anyway, and is herself killed for her cruelty, along with the murderer of Bajazet. Like Seneca's Phaedra, Atalide stabs herself in the last scene. To be sure, the stoic Seneca sets reason or virtue above passion, but in Racine the concern for truthfulness outweighs the violence, as it never does in Seneca.

This positive desire for virtue reveals the underlying presence of the morality play. Its opposite is also present in the unremitting cruelty of Amurat and Roxane. Racine's secondary characters can often be characterized as villainous or virtuous: Néron, in *Britannicus*, is seen between his advisors for good (Burrhus) and evil (Narcisse). Other morality gestures in *Bajazet* are confession, kneeling to ask forgiveness, and atonement. Atalide's sin of jealousy—of Roxane, even though Atalide herself has enjoined Bajazet to accept the queen's love—precipitates the catastrophe, and in the final scene Atalide stabs herself to atone for her sin. Neoclassical poetic justice is the closure of morality, especially clearly in *La Thébaïde*, where Racine diverges from the plot of his Euripidean source, *The Phoenissae*, precisely at the end to close with Créon's iniquities, not with the expulsion of Oedipus that Racine criticizes in Euripides.

Yet other morality elements in *Bajazet* seem more problematic. Letters fly back and forth, but unlike those in Skelton's *Magnyfycence* and seventeenth-century morality and school drama, both in Germany and

Spain (see below, Chapter 5), they are neither forgeries nor temptations.[9] If this were a pure morality, the Vice would be Sultan Amurat, who never appears onstage. Although his vizier, Acomat, seems to mastermind the plot for Bajazet to supplant his older brother, Acomat's goal is more disinterested than to ensnare Bajazet in something evil; he wants to rescue himself and everyone else from Amurat's brutality. This mixed motivation blunts the distinctions between good and evil the play would otherwise seem to draw. The prominent gestures of begging forgiveness typical of morality are also strangely undermined. When Bajazet kneels to Roxane in 5.4 and confesses that he does not love her, it looks like a traditional gesture of atonement: but Roxane is a jealous woman, not God, and she denies him grace. The miraculous is naturalized throughout Racine, but here the morality model is deliberately, one almost feels maliciously, inverted. The implicit satire points covertly perhaps to the ascendancy of the court over the church and, by skewing the morality paradigm, contributes to the ascendancy of mimesis.

The tensions among different kinds of plots are more complex in *Iphigénie en Aulide* (1674), which takes Euripides as its primary source.[10] If we consider Agamemnon the central figure, the play can be read as a morality. At the beginning the king has already fallen. To preserve his stature among the Greeks and thus sustain his pride, he has agreed to Ulysse's ruse to summon Iphigénie to the camp under the pretext of marrying her to Achilles, but in fact to sacrifice her at the orders of the prophet Calchas. Agamemnon alternately repents and falls again until in 4.8, overcome with pity, he plots Iphigénie's escape. The plot fails, but the will was enough, and he is rewarded: Eriphile, a slave who foiled the escape out of jealousy, turns out to be another Iphigénie, sinful offspring of the same Helen (by Theseus) for whom the war is about to be fought, and the sacrifice really intended by the oracle. She stabs herself (offstage), everyone is reconciled, and the wind miraculously begins to blow. This is the trajectory of the morality hero. The Vices are Calchas, who insists on the sacrifice, Ulysse, who embroils Agamemnon in a web of deceit and betrayal of his family, and, finally, the entire Greek army pressing him onward in its eagerness for the war at Troy. His good angel is Iphigénie herself, forerunner of all the devoted daughters of eighteenth-century bourgeois tragedy. She alone understands the situation from Agamemnon's point of view, and even rejects offers of protection from both her lover and her mother. Pity for her drives Agamemnon to his final decision to save her and sacrifice his own reputation instead. But the play is also typical of Racine's Senecanism. Even with its outdoor setting, it is claustrophobic: the Greeks are trapped in Aulis, Iphigénie and Clytemnestre are trapped in the camp, and Agamemnon is trapped in his promise to sacrifice Iphigénie. Senecan rage abounds: while

Achilles in 5.2 and Clytemnestre in 5.4 offer obvious examples, even the angelic Iphigénie has her moments of jealous rage at Eriphile from the second act on.[11] The denouement consists of Ulysse's messenger's speech, in which the oracle's apparently arbitrary insistence upon the sacrifice of Iphigénie is finally explained. As always in Seneca, the play ends with the revelation of the hidden sin. Yet the happy ending emphasizes the pressure of Christian morality to point toward a redemption from sin absent in Seneca. Before the denouement Eriphile is also a negative principle, but less a Vice than a classical nemesis, as when she betrays Agamemnon's escape plot. It is not clear at first what divine framework grounds the moral struggle, since the priest Calchas seems such a threat, and perhaps even an opportunist. But when Eriphile is revealed to be the embodiment of Helen's sin, the necessary framework falls into place and the classical nemesis rescues the morality structure. If this solution is not fully convincing, that is precisely the point: morality demands a functioning divine framework, but Senecanism demands that the framework be in the process of collapse.

Racine tries to explain away such tensions in *Iphigénie* and justify its happy ending by invoking Aristotelian theory and Greek models in his preface. He justifies his addition of a second Iphigénie by appealing to Pausanias, whom he followed gratefully, he says, because Euripides' last-minute substitution of a hind for Iphigenia and his dea ex machina would be unbelievable to a contemporary audience.[12] As a result he was able to construct a perfectly unified plot: "Thus the denouement of the play is drawn from its very essence" ("Ainsi le dénouement de la pièce est tiré du fond même de la pièce," *Oeuvres complètes* 1:670). Otherwise, he claims to follow Euripides closely in representing the characters' emotions and uses the terms "imitation" (1:671) and "compassion and terror" (ibid.). But all is not well with this invocation of Aristotle, for Racine spends the remainder of the preface defending Euripides' *Alcestis*, another tragedy with a happy ending. Although Aristotle took Sophocles' *Oedipus the King* as the model tragedy and considered tragedies with happy endings possible but less obviously appropriate, Racine used Euripides' texts for his Greek model four times, and the first time he not only employed one with a happy ending, but felt constrained to defend another in his preface. The happy ending is, of course, virtually demanded by the underlying morality form: the invocation of Euripides covers for the entrenched practice that cannot be acknowledged.[13]

Racine skates quickly past French neoclassicism's real innovation on classical plotting, whether Senecan or Euripidean—the addition of the love story—to take pride in having used the love plot to suppress the improbable supernatural intervention at the end of Euripides' *Iphigenia*. In effect, coincidence has replaced the supernatural in the service of the underlying morality, and the love story functions as a secular cover, so to speak, for the forbidden religious structure. The assertion is supported by the inconsistency that the oracle requires a pure virgin at the beginning of the play, but at the end Eriphile, who has been burning with passion for Achille, is quite acceptable. The real goal is the purging of sin, and the love plot becomes an almost transparent layer over the morality plot. Paradoxically Greek tragedy and love tragedy are blended to keep the classical (Senecan and neo-Aristotelian) and morality traditions working together. In this context Agamemnon's constant changes of plan and the consequent constant reversal of situation for Iphigénie and the others represent less Aristotelian peripeties than the opposing pull of the two underlying modes. Thus it makes sense that Racine returned to religious drama at the end of his life. His are not unambiguously modern psychological tragedies, but troubled epistemological dramas seeking an appropriate form of expression.[14]

Shakespeare's Allegories: The Tragedies

Against this background of such obviously neoclassical dramatists as Vondel and Racine still engaged productively with the morality paradigm into the 1660s and 1670s, we can now return to the issue in Shakespeare, not as a question of how medieval or archaic a dramatist he was, but of how he made the historical tensions between the obvious Aristotelian, Senecan, and morality elements productive and was, as a result, a sophisticated allegorist. The discussion will inevitably lead beyond tragedy to the comedies and the issue of tragicomedy, because the notion of fixed dramatic genres is so problematic in Shakespeare, and then to the relation of allegory to narration and to the visual in seventeenth-century tragedy.

As an obviously Senecan tragedy based on classical history, *Julius Caesar* (1599) might reasonably be expected to be particularly self-consciousness about its fluid mixture of morality with classical structures.[15] Cassius is the morality Vice, most obviously when he outlines his plot to the audience: "Well, Brutus, thou art noble; yet I see / Thy honorable mettle may be wrought" (1.2.308–9). To be sure, he claims to address Brutus rather than the audience directly, but since Brutus is absent, this mimetic veneer is of the thinnest. He gloats and makes his evil intentions explicit (1.2.312–15), detailing how he will tempt Brutus into conspiracy, like Fancy in *Magnyfycence* and like Treason and Sedition in *King Johan*, "obscurely" (1.2.319) with forged letters. Like the Vices conspiring against the state in Skelton and Bale Cassius is surrounded by subordinates whose names mostly begin with the same letter (Casca, Cinna, M. Cimber). He is even associated with Satan as he paces the stormy streets baring his bosom to the thunder (1.3.49) and tempting the heavens (1.3.53). Nevertheless, Cassius is not simply sin personified, but suffers from envy, as Mark Antony says at the end (5.5.70); hence he emphasizes Caesar's ordinary human weakness in his first approach to Brutus, and Brutus takes care to avoid the appearance of wrath and envy in their conduct (2.1.164 and 178). Indeed, Cassius desires less to make Brutus guilty than to acquire his virtue as a moral shield for himself and the other conspirators—as Casca puts it, "O, he sits high in all the people's hearts; / And that which would appear offense in us, / His countenance, like richest alchymy, / Will change to virtue and to worthiness" (1.3.157–60). This change in motivation gives Cassius a mimetic surface unknown to the Vice, while the plot construction is still rooted in morality.

The common crux as to whether the play is really about Julius Caesar or about Brutus derives from this tension. Brutus is the morality hero who falls into sin by joining the conspiracy. Since he takes the decision in his enclosed orchard and casts Caesar as a serpent (2.1.14 and 32–34), his fall is marked as traditionally Christian. He fails to escape the conspiracy when Portia is prevented from hearing his confession, and her death signals to Brutus the end of his own earthly career: she was his good angel, unfortunately less persistent than Good Counsel earlier in the century. Late in the play Brutus becomes disillusioned with Cassius's dishonesty and avarice. Betrayed and deserted by the Vice, Brutus recognizes his isolation and approaching death as the just vengeance of heaven embodied in the ghost of Caesar. After his death he is, like King John both in Bale and in Shakespeare, restored to virtue by the closing pronouncements of Mark Antony and Octavius. The gesture is standard at the end of Shakespearean tragedy; in this fashion even the mature tragedies maintain the morality tradition. Caesar also falls, but nobly. "O, what a fall was there, my countrymen! / Then I, and you, and all of us fell down" (3.2.190–91), says Antony in his funeral oration, identifying not a morality fall into sin, but a fall brought on by fortune. The influence of the numerous Renaissance discussions of the fall of monarchs on the wheel of fortune upon Elizabethan drama is well known under the term *de casibus* tragedy and was the earliest form of Senecanism in England.[16] The moments around Caesar's death are marked by falling: the conspirators fall on their knees, Brutus twice exhorts them to "stoop" to bathe in Caesar's blood (3.1.105), Antony's servant falls at the feet of the conspirators. The contrast between Caesar's noble fall and the stooping of the conspirators underlines the sinfulness and the implicit morality context of the murder. In effect, the drama contrasts two different kinds of fall and thus two different dramatic models, *de casibus* tragedy and morality.

The morality elements shade increasingly into Senecanism. Caesar's ghost expresses not only the just vengeance of heaven, but also the translation of the morality into Senecan conventions, where ghosts and omens replace divine presence. Other Senecan elements in the play are the night of prodigies preceding Caesar's death, Brutus's speech on Conspiracy (2.1.77–85) and Mark Antony's apology to Caesar's corpse (3.1.155–275) with their violence and allusions to classical hells. But the plot is also more broadly Senecan; it does not focus exclusively on the question of Brutus's virtue, but shows the cynicism and evil prevalent throughout the entire social order. Caesar makes a show of rejecting the crown in order to establish his authority more firmly; although Antony is faithful to Caesar and uncovers the dishonest motivations of the conspirators, he callously proscribes his own relatives, betrays Lepidus, and is as callously crossed by Octavius (5.1.20). When Antony and Octavius confront Brutus and Cassius just before the battle (5.1), it is hard to decide which pair is uglier and less dignified. And between the two sides wavers the populace, always ready to follow whoever speaks last and to murder the opposition. This conflation of the political world characterized exclusively by evil and betrayal with the cosmos is typical of Senecan tragedy and quite the opposite of morality.[17] As in *King John*, the tension is made to serve the difficulty attached to knowing in the world of the play.

The historical details derived from Plutarch draw the play's Senecanism further from morality toward mimesis. All of the characters, even Cassius in the last two acts, are capable of a kind of self-reflection often narrated in Plutarch, but not conceivable in the morality tradition. Hence little of the stage action depends on the simple actions required to portray the sin and repentance of the main character. Brutus himself becomes a leader and decision maker among the conspirators; both this role and his ambivalent emotional relation to Cassius in the final acts exceed the limits of the morality plot and also most of the plot of *King John*. As a result, the interest in the play derives from the tension between the fall of a Brutus who virtuously renounces personal power and the Senecan society that denies the Christian Providence behind the social order. This more mimetic Brutus reinforces the role of the more archaic one: both represent the virtue of morality in the face of Senecan cynicism. Mimesis has been enlisted in the service of the older allegorical mode.

So deeply ingrained is morality structure in the general themes of Shakespeare's middle period plays from *Hamlet* to *Macbeth* that the emotional world of each is undergirded by one of the seven deadly sins, each associated with the virtue that opposed it and the gift of the Holy Spirit

TABLE 2. VIRTUES AND VICES IN SHAKESPEARE

Play	Vice	Gift	Virtue
Macbeth	Pride	Timor Dei	Humility
Othello	Envy	Pietas	Amity
King Lear	Wrath	Scientia	Temperance
Hamlet	Sloth	Fortitudo	Perseverance
Measure for Measure	Avarice	Consilium	Mercy
All's Well That Ends Well	Luxury/Lust	Intellectus	Chastity
Twelfth Night	Gluttony	Sapientia	Sobriety

that enabled one to overcome it.[18] This is not to say that the plays in question are only about a particular sin; while the basic organization of plot and imagery follow from the choice of sin, the elaborations far exceed the parameters of sixteenth-century homiletics. The issue is not that the plays should be reduced to moralities, but that Shakespeare's choice of sin functions rather like his the choice of subject (for example, Hamlet, Macbeth) to increase the variety of his material. Table 2 gives an overview.[19]

The chart is arrayed in the traditional order of ascending virtues—the highest virtues are represented by comedies and the lowest by tragedies. It is often asserted that Shakespeare's turn from tragedy to romance depended on a shift in prevailing fashions, but this chart implies an alternative possibility. Tragedy is the highest genre in neo-Aristotelian terms: the alignment of the highest virtues with increasingly romantic comedies suggests that the move to romance in the last plays had more to do with Shakespeare's own vision of drama as a mix in which Aristotelianism was but a single element, and a secondary one at that. It is obvious to any reader of Shakespeare that extensive references to lechery (lust, luxury) extend beyond All's Well. Luxury was, from antiquity on, the all-embracing sin.[20] In his emphasis on it, then, Shakespeare is neither individual nor specifically Elizabethan; lechery is sin generalized, and my point is that the plays are also more specific. It is noteworthy that Senecan rage is not the pervasive sin; in this respect the medieval tradition outweighs the neoclassical. While these plays resemble most seventeenth-century drama in dealing with good and evil in terms of reason and passion, they particularize passion in terms of the older allegorical tradition, for the chart suggests that all the middle plays are morality plays at bottom.

In the tragedies the system is straightforward:

- It is obvious to accuse Macbeth of pride and ambition; his moments of horror at the murder of Duncan—the dagger speech, his semiparalysis immediately after—and his horror at his and his wife's guilt at the end of the play can all be properly characterized as dread. Macbeth fails to achieve humility and attacks it in the meek Duncan, Banquo's and Macduff's innocent children, and Malcolm's purity. He himself cries, "Macbeth does murther sleep—the innocent sleep" (2.2.33); the phrase evokes the common image of Christian humility, "innocent sheep." Hence Malcolm's hope, as his army covers itself in tree branches, "the days are near at hand / That chambers will be safe" (5.4.1–2), for Macbeth threatens the very innocence and humility of nature.

- Iago is given the mimetic motivation of envy for Cassio's promotion to lieutenant in the first scene and his later suspicions of being cuckolded by Othello, but he is also envy personified. As such he incites Othello to mad jealousy, the specifically sexual form of envy. Piety appears in the play as pity, in Othello's tale of how the two fell in love (1.3.161 and 168) and in the lament Desdemona sings just before her death in memory of "poor Barbary" (4.3.33). The virtue of amity, associated also with benignity (Tuve, *Allegorical Imagery* 442), appears in the handkerchief, which has the magic power to make its owner "amiable" and able to command love (3.4.59); it appears again in Othello's greatness in the final scene—"one that lov'd not wisely but too well" (5.2.344), one who fought the "malignant" Turk (353), one who "was great of heart" (361).

- *King Lear* is full of anger—Lear's at his daughter, Gloucester's at Edgar, Edmund's at the world, Kent's at Oswald, Cornwall's at Kent and Gloucester, the impersonal rage of the storm. By contrast Albany controls his rage at his wife, and Cordelia exercises the ultimate discretion in her silence. Knowledge, the associated gift of the Holy Spirit, appears as the dominant theme of the play in the constant discussions of self-knowledge, blindness, and seeing.

- Hamlet's notorious inaction is clearly the central problem—sin—in the play. The medieval church associated sloth with melancholy and madness, Hamlet's other important qualities (Wittkower and Wittkower, *Born under Saturn* 102). Virtues of any sort are hard to find in *Hamlet*; nevertheless, Claudius criticizes Hamlet for excessive perseverance at 1.2.92–96. Magnificence, another term for the virtue of perseverance, is the state of kingliness, as also in Skelton's *Magnyfycence*. If Denmark lacks a proper king, Claudius overcompensates with the externals of kingship—*Hamlet* is the only Shakespearean tragedy with repeated court scenes and royal ceremonial, exaggerated in the cannons marking each toast of the king. Fortinbras, who was invented by Shakespeare and whose name suggests a transformation of the allegory, Fortitude, into the more modern speaking name of seventeenth-century comedy, drops into the play at the end indeed like a gift fallen from heaven. Like the other tragedies, *Hamlet* is not fully explained by this structure, but it does offer a phenomenology of a particular dyad of sin and virtue.

Shakespeare's major tragedies can thus be schematically described as morality plays in which the supernatural frame is suppressed or translated into Senecan ghosts: the religious framework disappears but the characteristic focus on the ethics of the central figure remains. Vices (often in extreme forms as in *Othello*) still drive the action by hypocrisy and/or playacting, but their malice is gratuitous and unmotivated (Cassius, Iago) or disproportionate to their energy (Edmund in *Lear*) or simply impenetrable and unreadable (the witches in *Macbeth*—but notice how the alliterative names of the Vices translate in their tag, "Fair is foul and foul is fair"). *Hamlet* is especially interesting in this regard, because the ghost as motivator of the action is obviously Senecan, and the ghost does not direct the action like a morality Vice. The more impenetrable the Vice becomes, the more he represents not evil or sin but the dangers of a world in which divine presence is no longer readily legible—a development already noted in Racine. As in *Julius Caesar* both the morality and Senecan modes acquire new significance through their juxtaposition. The power of Shakespearean tragedy derives not from superseding or suppressing an older tradition but from the enrichment of the allegorical tradition in its confrontation with the classical and mimetic traditions associated with the emergence of a more secular view of the world.

Nowhere is the productivity of this tension clearer than in *Coriolanus*. The skeleton of the plot derives from morality: in act 1 Coriolanus is accused of pride and exhibits it by ranting and forgetting the name of the person he wanted to save at Corioles (1.9.90). In a preliminary act of repentance he kneels to his mother in act 2 and appears in the gown of humility to be elected consul. The tribunes, as Vices, begin their deceit, and in 3.1 provoke Coriolanus to his real sin, wrath. Coriolanus fails in his ensuing public scene of repentance and is banished (falls). In act 4 he humbles himself by appearing in mean apparel to signify his repentance; this is, however, not full atonement, because it is a disguise to achieve revenge on the plebs. Coriolanus kneels to his mother in the last act in a scene saturated with the language of vice and virtue. Then the three women, all of whose names begin with V (three virtues, like the three Marys of the mystery tradition), kneel to him in the name of grace and turn him to mercy, so that he mediates with the enemy he has led to the gates and saves Rome. His wrath has been transformed into temperance by the appeal to grace. This is the morality hero making the standard

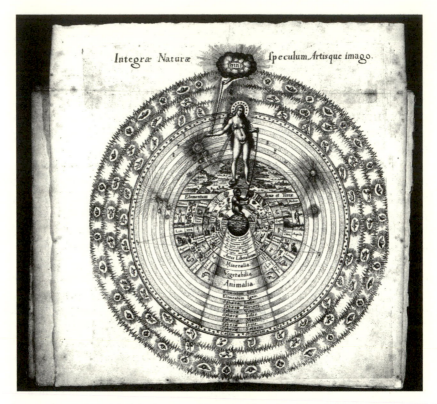

Figure 20. Robert Fludd, "Integrae Naturae Speculum" from *Utriusque cosmi . . . historia* (1617). Reproduced by permission of The Huntington Library, San Marino, California.

allegorical gestures of kneeling and the symbolical clothing of repentance. Yet this description omits important elements of the play. If Coriolanus is proud in his relations to the commons in act 1, he is modest about his military exploits and wants to reward kindness. While he kneels to his mother in act 2, he is nevertheless unwilling to appear in the gown of humility: he seems almost a textbook example of the mixed hero called for in Aristotle. His rage in act 3 is distinctly Senecan, for it drives him to revenge; his punishment is also typically Senecan in that it is political and takes place in the world. When Aufidius asks in act 4 whether it was pride (morality explanation) or defect of judgment (Aristotelian explanation) that led to Coriolanus's banishment from Rome (4.7.37–39), the tension between the two dramaturgies becomes explicit.

They and the play at first seem to achieve resolution in Aufidius's reference to nature (4.7.41): the "great creative Nature" of the romances is

Shakespeare's code word in the late plays for the neoplatonist synthesis that replaces the explicit divine presence of the morality tradition. This is precisely the presence evoked in 5.3, the climax at which the three V's transform Coriolanus's wrath into temperance. Coriolanus must choose between forging his own identity—a form of extreme individualism that follows on his rage—or returning to the bonds of state and kinship, here through the focus on mother and son characterized as "nature." Coriolanus formulates it first as a choice between his "rages and revenges" and their "colder reasons" (5.3.85)—between the Senecan mode and the judgment of morality. But coldness is otherwise associated in the scene with Valeria, whom Coriolanus addresses: "The moon of Rome, chaste as the icicle / That's curdied by the frost from purest snow / And hangs on Dian's temple—dear Valeria!" (5.3.65–67). In the comedies, most explicitly in *Comedy of Errors*, Diana is the goddess of grace who presides over the resolution, and she comes to this function from Renaissance neoplatonism.[21] Nature is the primary name for this figure, as we know, for example, from contemporary images like Robert Fludd's "Integrae Naturae Speculum," in which Nature, decorated with moon and stars (and thus also Diana) mediates directly between divinity and the human world. When the group first approaches Coriolanus, he hopes to break "all bond and privilege of nature" (5.3.25), and hears "Great Nature" cry to him not to deny their suit (5.3.33): he submits ultimately to the presence of his son and the extended appeal of his mother Volumnia, in effect, to "Great Nature."

As in *King John* the Christian context seems translated into the more secular neoplatonist terms, but here the resolution is less explicit. Though Coriolanus accedes to the natural and spares Rome, yet there can be no full resolution in the world—"Behold," he cries, "the heavens do ope, / The gods look down, and this unnatural scene / They laugh at" (5.3.183–85). By the time of *Coriolanus* it was forbidden to refer to God onstage, hence, we are told, the shift to pre-Christian settings, as in this play. But there is more at stake, for no morality God ever laughed at a sinner repenting. The play does not end with the restoration of the hero to grace; he returns with Aufidius to the Senecan world of political intrigue, where he is murdered. If *King John* showed Shakespeare experimenting with a synthesis of allegory and mimesis, and *Julius Caesar* showed him on the way to an effective blending of the two traditions, *Coriolanus* keeps the perspectives open and separate to create in the space between them a tragedy that is among Shakespeare's most neoclassical and simultaneously most in the morality tradition. Within this gap readers and spectators can disport themselves almost at will; as will appear below with Mozart's *Zauberflöte*, the gaps between discourses result in the perception of universality.

Shakespeare's Allegories: The Comedies

The case for a similar tension in Shakespeare's comedies between Aristotelian mimesis and classical models on the one hand and morality on the other is generally less obvious. Apparently it was more straightforward to assimilate morality to the demands of Aristotelian tragedy than to the structures of comedy, perhaps because the neoclassical focus on the tragic hero was already shaped by the experience of morality drama. But, as the chart above suggests, morality is certainly present. The main action of *Measure for Measure* is precipitated by the men's avarice: Angelo has abandoned Mariana because her dowry was lost and Claudio has delayed his marriage to Juliet in order not to lose her dowry.[22] As for Pompey the bawd, who gets money by selling women, avarice is intimately connected to lechery and its opposite, exaggerated chastity—Angelo insists on strict enforcement of the law yet lusts after Isabella; the Duke and Isabella wear the habits of monk and nun until they finally renounce such exaggerated chastity to agree on marriage. Avarice also appears in the pervasive imagery of coining, money, theft, and exchange. In a complicated multilevel morality plot Isabella both awakens Angelo from his avarice and lechery to mercy, and at the same time moves herself from excessive restraint and lack of sympathy with her brother's misfortune to committing a real deed of mercy—seeming to accede to Angelo and then forgiving him before she realizes her brother is still alive. Mercy is the code word of the final scene, and all the acts of mercy are made possible by the counsel of the Duke, who has spent most of the play giving advice to one character after another in the disguise of a friar and stage-managing the entire transition from avarice to mercy.

Lust and chastity make sense of the rather odd plot of *All's Well.* Its two Vices, Lavatch and Parolles, both make salacious speeches in act 1, and Parolles's witty exchange on virginity with Helena identifies the sin of the play as luxury or lust. The sin appears in more serious form when Helena demands Bertram in marriage without his consent: marriage without mutual love is a refined form of lust. Parolles's version of luxury is signified by the meaning of his French name: his lying is too luxuriant verbal behavior. Bertram is both lecherous with Diana and a liar when he abandons her. Helena, like the hero of a morality, eventually overcomes her lust for Bertram, first by winning him legally through her cure of the king with her father's medical knowledge, intellectus (intelligence, understanding), then by an elaborate act of penitence: she is declared dead and sets out on a pilgrimage. In Florence she takes on the name and place of Diana to win Bertram as her husband in deed, and thus to establish her own chastity. Parolles undergoes a parallel development: the soldiers tempt him to recover a lost drum, the objective correlative of his meaningless bombast, and trick him by speaking nonsense language. He returns chastened to the French court and is placed under the care of Lafew, leaving us with a chiastic interlingual pun: Parolles has become a man of few words. The end of the play shifts to neoplatonist allegory. Helena gives up her identity as the proverbial lecherous woman and takes on the name and identity of Diana, virgin goddess of the moon and a standard neoplatonist figure for chastity and truth. In the last scene she emerges from disguise as both the wise woman who can explain everything (intellectus), and as herself the meaning—Diana says "behold the meaning" as Helena enters (5.3.304). As Plato's truth itself she evokes the doubling language characteristic of wonder in Shakespeare as Bertram cries "Both, both" (5.3.308) and "I'll love her dearly, ever, ever dearly" (5.3.316). There is a strong temptation to believe still in this allegorical structure and enjoy the happy end, but also a pull to read Bertram's story mimetically and disbelieve his sudden conversion: the play's designation as a problem comedy reflects the doubleness of its bittersweet ending.

Twelfth Night, with its treatment of gluttony represents Shakespeare's most elegant exploitation of the tension between mimetic and allegorical dramaturgy.[23] The separation of its parallel plots revolving around Orsino on the one hand and Olivia on the other is extreme even for Shakespeare; although Orsino longs to marry Olivia the two appear together only in the final scene. Both immure themselves out of melancholy—Orsino from romantic love for Olivia, Olivia from familial love for her brother. Orsino's house is pervaded by his melancholy mood; in Olivia's house melancholy stalks the halls bodily in the person of Malvolio. Orsino listens to music, the metaphoric food of love (1.1.1), while Olivia's house is disturbed with raucous drinking songs and food is enjoyed literally by the gluttonous Sir Toby. Orsino's world is consistently presented in blank verse, Olivia's in prose until Viola imports verse. Typically Orsino's language is full of similes and metaphors; and equally typically, the language of Olivia's world is concrete and literal.[24] Orsino's plot is structured in terms of Latin comedy, in which the clever servant gains the master his beloved, while Olivia's is organized in terms of morality. Orsino's plot represents mimetically, Olivia's allegorically: the distinction adumbrated in the parallelism of John and the Bastard reaches its full development here.

Consider first the morality. Olivia's extravagant plan to mourn her brother for seven years is a form of gluttony, which is opposed by the cardinal virtue sobriety, also sometimes called simply Peace (signified by Olivia's name), the highest of the virtues. Her house has been occupied by its doorkeeper-Vices, her excessively sober steward Malvolio (ill will) and her gluttonous uncle Sir Toby Belch. Too much virtue, Shakespeare suggests in an incipient dialectic, is itself a vice. Viola rescues Olivia by persuading her to unveil, to lift the barrier between herself and the world: Olivia's repentance is brought about by Viola's poetic power. Ultimately Olivia marries Viola's twin, Sebastian, whose name means "that which awakens wonder." Her love of beauty is transformed into love of truth, precisely the effect of beauty described in Plato's *Phaedrus*, and Christian morality modulates into the Platonist myth of the soul. Sebastian then frees Olivia from the Vices Riot and Gluttony (Sir Toby and Sir Andrew) by his superior swordsmanship, while Maria, in a parallel action, reveals Malvolio's true ill will and drives him from the play. While Malvolio reads Maria's planted letter her co-conspirators keep hushing one another by saying "Peace." Thus the scene pits Peace against Ill-will; Peace wins and is freed from her prison to meet Orsino in the last scene. Maria is to marry Sir Toby at the end; as the parallel deliverer of Olivia she is the only figure who can control him. Thus the play shows Peace freed from Riot and Ill-will through the musical Viola and her twin brother, religious awe, and Maria, now unveiled, so to speak, as Mary mother of God: this is the Christmas message of the angels singing "peace on earth, good will to men" (Luke 2:13–14). Both Viola and Olivia begin by loving their brothers, both pursue husbands in the play, and both end by loving a restored brother—Viola discovers Sebastian, and Olivia welcomes Orsino as her brother (5.1.316–17). Romantic love turns out to be also the brotherly love of the Christmas message and the Platonist love of truth. There is nothing archaic or preachy about all this; indeed, in the figure of Malvolio the piety one might associate with morality play is satirized. Instead, *Twelfth Night* is an outstanding example of the modernization of morality into a highly particularized and up-to-date Christmas allegory.

Malvolio is clearly the most dangerous Vice in the play, but his gulling appears in its own terms as a travesty of the morality plot, in which deception and hypocrisy are central elements. Malvolio is plagued by the Vices of Riot (now Maria, Sir Toby, Feste), whom he first resists (2.3) but to whom he then succumbs (2.5) so that he eventually appears onstage dressed with absurd extravagance in yellow stockings and cross-gartered, his form of gluttony. As a result he is locked up in the dark, then rescued by the power of Olivia; nevertheless, he flees unrepentant. Typical morality gestures are the conspiracy of Maria, Sir Toby and others, the letter by which Malvolio is trapped, disguising (Maria writes in Olivia's hand, Feste plays Sir Topas the curate), betrayal and sitting in gloom. Feste compares himself to the Vice in the old play when he torments Malvolio (4.2). As in many Continental moralities or in Marlowe's *Dr. Faustus*, Malvolio is damned because he does not repent. Thus it is still within the framework of morality that we can find Toby and Maria, as the Vices in Malvolio's little travesty, nevertheless sympathetic, because Malvolio is a worse Vice yet. This embedding of the travesty within the "serious" morality gives the larger plot a degree of mimetic validity or "reality" that evokes a more complex emotional response than is typical of morality; the result is less a send-up of the older mode than its ultimate refinement.

The elaborate parallels between the plots begin with the anagrams connecting Malvolio, Viola, and Olivia. The first words of the play, "If music be the food of love," identify the metaphoric gluttony from which the twins will rescue the Duke. Viola plays the same role for Orsino as for Olivia: she transforms his melancholy love into a more valid living love through the wonder of her doubleness. This wonder is evoked by what Orsino calls "A natural perspective, that is and is not" (5.1.217), that joins what can and cannot be comprehended by the human mind, as the conclusion moves into the Platonist mode. But this plot is much more mimetic. Vice is not personified, and Orsino's name ("bearish") is suggestive rather than allegorical. Nevertheless, Viola's disguise connects even this part of the play to the morality tradition, for disguise is not typical of Latin comedy. Indeed, Viola turns the disguise tradition inside out, since she is a rescuing virtue, not a Vice. Nevertheless, her actions follow the common structure of the Vice's plot: introduction, disguise, winning the trust of the hero, revelation and betrayal. As Cesario Viola wins the hearts of Orsino and Olivia, both of whom trust her to do what is against her nature (woo Olivia), just as the morality hero trusts the Vice to lead him properly. In act 5 both feel betrayed—Orsino because he thinks Viola has married Olivia, Olivia because Viola denies it. The revelation of her true identity and of her twin, however, has more to do with the romance ending of Latin comedy than the exposure of the Vice, for it shows that her presence has worked for everyone's salvation rather than for their betrayal. By this interweaving of morality and classical modes Shakespeare has transformed disguise into a positive force.[25]

Hence Viola's delight in costume connects her to Feste, the only other character in the play to wear a disguise. Feste dons his when he plays the Vice to Malvolio. Yet he also enjoys his role. In 4.2 Feste plays a bewildering succession of older roles. As Sir Topas he is Chaucer's boring perfect knight. He alludes to the older Senecan and morality traditions with references to *Gorboduc* (4.2.14) and to the old Vice (4.2.124), and he parodies Malvolio's puritanism in sniffing out lechery (4.2.26) and calling him Satan (4.2.31). Finally, in the dialogue with himself as both Feste and Sir Topas, he becomes nothing but theatrical roles. Such arbitrary play keeps the comedy from being too mimetic, just as the conventions of mystery play did in their own time. In this scene disguise has expanded from its morality function of trickery (Malvolio is being gulled) to embrace play as a metaphor for drama itself, which is here and throughout the play a healing activity, not a destructive one. With this transformation of the morality's association of playacting and vice, Shakespeare mounts his own defense of poetry every bit as Platonist as Sidney's. In the spirit of Renaissance syncretism, the casting off of disguise leads to truth either way; truth is always revelation. Hence the seventeenth century's general preoccupation with the metaphor of the theater: all the world's a stage because playacting so perfectly connects the older and newer views of our place in the world.

Feste is a player in the broadest sense, for he is a musician and singer as well as an actor. In act 3 Viola meets him with his tabor by the church; in 2.3 he sings drinking songs for Toby and Andrew, and in the next scene he sings a melancholy ballad for Orsino. Feste and Viola ultimately embody what is most at issue for Shakespeare in the double dramaturgy of the play. These—the two disguised characters, the two singers—are until the last act the only figures who appear in the houses of both Orsino and Olivia. Shakespeare brings them together in the middle of the play (3.1) for a scene irrelevant to the plot, but central to the theme: the two discuss music and wordplay. Their first witty exchange on whether Feste lives by his tabor or by the church echoes Viola's twin association with music and religion. More important yet is the framed confrontation of the two wits, for these two live by manipulating and delivering words. Indeed Feste defines himself not as Olivia's fool, but as her "corruptor of words" (3.1.36). He means, of course, that he makes words take on new meanings. This is what poets do. It is also what Viola does. Both are always saying what they do and do not mean. Such linguistic doubleness is echoed throughout the play in twinned formulations like "Nothing that is so is so" (Feste, 4.1.8–9), "That that is is . . . for what is 'that' but 'that' and 'is' but 'is'?" (Feste, 4.2.14–16), or "A natural perspective, that is and is not" (Orsino about Viola, 5.1.217). The power of Viola, of poetry, of dramatic play is its capacity to say what is and is not simultaneously, to represent both literally and figuratively. Such language articulates Shakespeare's awareness that the opportunities opened by neoclassicism were not just mimesis, but a radically increased capacity to represent both literally and figuratively, both mimetically and allegorically. But the issue is not only to do both, but to make the two modes work together, to say what is ("mimetic") and what is not ("allegorical") simultaneously and to show their relationship.

Tragicomedy

The classical tradition seemed to draw a clear distinction between tragedy and comedy, but the pervasive underlying model of morality exerted great pressure for a happy ending, as we have already seen in both Italian pastoral and in French tragedy. Although Aristotle allowed for tragedies with happy endings, the common terminology in Elizabethan England made the designation tragedy or comedy depend primarily on the unhappy or happy outcome. Since, furthermore, the formal structures of Latin comedy penetrated tragedy as well as comedy, it is hardly surprising that tragicomedy posed a problem for discussion in the period, and has continued to trouble readers, especially of Shakespeare's so-called "problem comedies" (*Measure for Measure, All's Well That Ends Well, Troilus and Cressida*). In Vondel, as we have just seen, the issue was effectively suppressed into a form of tragedy that ended both happily and unhappily, often with recurrence to divine intervention, or, as in Racine, to coincidence as a more mimetic form of intervention. But *Troilus and Cressida*, written half a century earlier, indeed probably written in the same year as *Twelfth Night*, experiments with an alternative to what came to be the standard compromise, for it adjusts the balance of morality and Senecanism, allegory and mimesis in quite different fashion from its fellow Shakespearean problem comedies or from high neoclassical tragedy.

Like *Twelfth Night, Troilus* divides into two realms: Troy is focused on Troilus's lovesickness, which incapacitates him as it did Orsino, while the Greek camp has an extended clown plot with the gulling of both Ajax and Achilles as a way to cure its disorder. Aeneas trying to learn whether he is speaking with Agamemnon in 1.3 is remarkably similar to Viola seeking the lady of the house (1.5); foolish exchanges between Ajax and Achilles in 2.1 evoke Sir Toby and Sir Andrew; in 2.3 Achilles' conversation with Thersites sounds like Olivia's with Feste. Cressida is asked to unveil (3.2), just as Olivia was. Pandarus is a go-between, like Viola, and at the beginning of act 3, he encounters a servant with whom he exchanges quips about music as Viola does in the central scene with Feste. The two plots drift together in the fourth act with a duel, as in *Twelfth Night*,[26] and the worlds finally join onstage when the Trojans visit the Greeks in act 5. The linguistic doubling of *Twelfth Night* recurs in phrases like "brown and not brown" (1.2.96), "true and not true" (1.2.97), or "This is and is not Cressid!" (5.2.146), echoing Orsino's natural perspective that is and is not. Without its pervasive cynicism this least popular of Shakespeare's comedies would seem remarkably like the most popular.[27]

The Greek camp is largely the realm of morality. Ajax and Achilles embody its besetting disorder (identified by Ulysses in 1.3), which is variously seen in its component vices of pride, wrath, luxury, and sloth. Like Malvolio Ajax and Achilles are both Vices and morality heroes subject to the vices personified in Thersites and Patroclus—particularly in the last half of the play, where Patroclus is cast as Achilles' homosexual lover and where Thersites speaks incessantly of the devil of lechery. When Ulysses gulls Ajax and Achilles, he too plays the Vice, but, even more than Maria and Feste he intends to cure his victims of their vice, not to entrap them in it further. This plot thus shows most clearly how the simple reversal of purpose from the morality plot placed its allegorical dramaturgy in the service of neoclassical humor comedy to cure moral disorders.[28] Here is an unusual and readily visible link in the line from morality to what we might call "mimetic" comedy. Trickery is the staple of the comic plot already in Plautus and Terence, but in Roman comedy the purpose of trickery is to enable the young man to marry the right girl against his father's will; it has nothing to do with moral correction. The moral element enters not from the classical tradition, but from the allegorical Christian tradition.

The Trojan plot, like the Orsino plot, mixes mimetic and morality elements. Troilus's love affair with Cressida proceeds in essentially mimetic terms until he actually wins her. The wanton love play between Paris and Helena that precedes Troilus's first visit to Cressida concretizes the corruption at the center of the play, expressed most directly when Helen cries "This love will undo us all. O Cupid, Cupid, Cupid!" (3.1.110–11). The reduction of meaning to a single tableau and then to a single name, Cupid, transforms mimesis into emblem. Troilus meets Cressida in her orchard (as Brutus meets the conspirators), which Troilus compares to the Underworld (3.2.8–10). This encounter in the garden, like its original in Genesis, will bring not bliss but sin and death. No sooner has Cressida admitted her love than Troilus begins to fear that she will betray him (the traditional morality gesture) and angels become devils ("Fears make devils of cherubins," 3.2.69). In the ensuing discussion Troilus declares himself the embodiment of truth, while Cressida declares that she may be made the type of falsehood. No sooner does she arrive in the Greek camp than, with no obvious motivation, she plays the open wanton, gaily accepting the kisses of all the Greek leaders. When she betrays Troilus with Diomedes the scene is accompanied not only with Troilus's laments, but also with Thersites' commentary on the devil of lechery. The Troilus plot moves from mimesis through echoes of Genesis to full-scale allegory.

Decorum is a ubiquitous problem in *Troilus and Cressida*. Where everything is just right in *Twelfth Night* it seems all wrong in *Troilus and Cressida*. Its go-betweens, Pandarus and Thersites, hardly match Viola and Feste, either for charm, effectiveness, poetic ability, virtue, or appeal to audiences, and whoever depends on them for communication inevitably comes to grief. And however much dignity Aeneas preserves before Agamemnon, he hardly resembles Viola seeking to know to whom she speaks; without the presumed difference in gender the charm of the situation evaporates. If even Malvolio seems disproportionately punished to some twentieth-century readers, how much less appropriate is the transformation of heroes like Ajax and Achilles into buffoons with no historical justification on Shakespeare's part. Nor is the limited formal decorum of versification preserved. The distinction between prose and blank verse depends neither on world, as it does at first in *Twelfth Night*, nor on social level, as it normally does in Shakespearean comedy. While there is always some mixing in the comedies, the prosodic shifts in this play are positively promiscuous, starting in the first scene, where Troilus's elevated verse plays against the prose of Pandarus, his fellow townsman, social equal, and guardian of his beloved. *Twelfth Night* is probably extreme in Shakespearean comedy for the exclusion of bawdiness from the romance plot;[29] in *Troilus and Cressida*, by contrast, bawdiness begins with Pandarus's lewd prose in the first scene, comes to a focus in the wantonness of Paris and Helen, and takes over the entire play in the last act, as Thersites justly proclaims. At the end the two worlds come together but not in harmony. Despite the classical setting the romance ending, with its elaborate recognition inherited from Latin comedy, is replaced by betrayal; in the military plot gulling gives way to Senecan tragedy as Hector is brutally and dishonorably murdered. When Orsino refers to *Twelfth Night*'s natural perspective, that is and is not, he has before him two figures, Viola and Sebastian, dressed identically. When Troilus cries in the last act that the woman before him is and is not Cressida, the single figure before him embodies the failure to make distinctions that pervades the play. Such failures appear not only in indecorum, but also in the two great set pieces—Ulysses' famous speech on distinction and degree (1.3.73–137) and Hector's fruitless argument in favor of reason over passion in the Trojan council (2.2). However much either speaks in clichés of the period, the reason and order for which they speak is unquestionably more desirable than the enervating wantonness and promiscuity that pervade the play both thematically and structurally. Ulysses, who holds the Greek army together, and Hector, the great hope of Troy, are the only figures on either side with a genuine claim to dignity. It is typical of the play that these two voices are silenced, the one by disappearance and the other by death. If distinction brings salvation in *Twelfth Night*, its obliteration in *Troilus* brings death.

The lack of generic distinction has also brought death in a sense. At least some of the play's unpopularity is due not to its cynicism, but to the difficulty of classifying it. It begins as a romantic comedy but avoids the genre's signature conciliatory end. It slips in and out of the allegorical mechanisms of morality; its unremitting cynicism is revealed to be the oppressive atmosphere of Senecan tragedy when Troilus, the romantic love hero, becomes at the end the typical messenger of Senecan atrocities (5.10.11–31). It has been seen as a necessary preliminary experiment to *King Lear*, also as a romance with the happy ending unexpectedly withdrawn.[30] Both plays are actually unusual experiments in tragicomedy. The model that became established in Italy and then the rest of Europe was the apparent tragedy with the happy ending, most likely because this form accorded with the older practice of religious drama already in place. This is the model Shakespeare follows in the so-called "problem comedies" and romances, all of which are really tragicomedies in the Italian sense. But *Lear* and *Troilus* are romances that end unhappily. European culture has always resisted this particular mixing of genres, even though the morality model that seems to dictate the happy end of tragicomedy allowed on occasion for an unhappy end. But if the end of, say, *Dr. Faustus* or Tirso de Molina's *Don Juan* was unhappy for the hero, it did at least purify the world. But Hector's death is a pollution, not a purification. Indeed, the unhappy end of the much more successful *King Lear* was also resisted. Into the nineteenth century it was performed only in the adaptation of Nahum Tate, which ended with the marriage of Edgar and Cordelia. Ultimately *Lear* was recanonized under the rubric of tragedy. *Troilus* could not be because its mixing of different dramatic forms was so much bolder.

The discomfort with the classical barriers between comedy and tragedy was widespread in the Renaissance and seventeenth century, and will occupy us further below. For the moment it is important only to register that the apparent failure of Shakespeare's experiment in *Troilus and Cressida* signifies neither helplessness nor indifference to the rising interest in Aristotelianism. *Romeo and Juliet* demonstrates Shakespeare's capacity to write the kind of single-plotted romantic love tragedy that was to become the staple of French neoclassicism. It is equally clear from *The Tempest* that he could maintain with great finesse the Aristotelian unities of action, time, and place newly codified by sixteenth-century Italian commentators and still represent the correction of the sin of usurped power in a series of ingeniously unified plots. We witness in Shakespeare not the happy or fortuitous blending of different traditions to create a new form, but a systematic exploration of the possibilities and interactions of two different modes of representation.

Character and Allegory

Since personification allegory makes character visible by definition, it seems reasonable to attribute the increased complexity and the incipient interiority of character in seventeenth-century drama to the pressure exerted by the *Poetics* for mimesis and for mixed characters. The proposition seems too straightforward to deny, but I would like to identify some additional ways in which the layering of dramatic modes, allegorical and classical, makes its own contribution to the increasing sense of less and less penetrable selves. I begin with Vondel. As in Shakespeare's history plays and tragedies, Vondel's heroes are particularized: however much they act as standard morality heroes or martyrs, they take on historical individuality, even a kind of mimetic naturalism. Gijsbrecht von Aemstel is, to be sure, unjustly harassed by his enemies, and his city's fall stylized in terms of the *Aeneid*. Nevertheless, there is enough information about the pressures arising from consolidating political power and about Gijsbrecht's earlier participation in a coup attempt against his prince that the tormentors' point of view is also recognizably valid. As in *Julius Caesar* the reality of history becomes representable through the fuller indication of characters demanded by Aristotle.

The development is more striking in the late biblical play *Noach*. English mystery plays about Noah are famous for comic interchanges between the patriarch and his shrewish wife; this is one level of realism. But Vondel's Noah is more specific; he is regarded as a mad prophet of doom. Noah has been building his ark for a hundred years, and he delivers his warnings in ranting sermons against the sinfulness of the world typical of Baroque preachers like Abraham a Sancta Clara. His powerful opponent, the great prince of the East, sounds quite reasonable as he debates with him, and only gradually does it become clear that Noah is not hostile to all sexuality, as it at first seems, but only to polygamy. This mimetic complexity makes the characters more difficult to read, although in the end, the attribution of good and evil becomes clear. More problematic is the name of the prince's queen and favorite consort, "Urania." It means "heavenly" and Venus Urania embodied Plato's love of Truth and thus the harmony of the cosmos. It is so difficult to believe that she embodies lust that Noah's son leaves her and enters the ark only because his father insists. The sense of hidden danger in her character and the belief that people are too complex to be easily read depends here not on sophisticated mimesis, but on the misleading allegorical signal that name is character. The world is no longer so perspicuous and name is no longer necessarily character, any more than surface is. Yet complexity of character depends at this stage upon expectations inherited from the allegorical tradition: Noah should be a prophet, but seems insane, and Urania should be a positive figure. Here modern character depth emerges out of the play between allegorical and mimetic representation.

The mix of religious and classical forms in Vondel's *Lucifer* creates similar ambiguously secular characterization by projection. The fall of

Lucifer is obvious material for a morality play, yet who can be the tempter in a play about the fall of the devil? Perhaps this difficulty is what made Milton decide to frame the same material as an epic rather than as a drama. Vondel's solution is ingenious: he draws on the personification of passion in Senecan rhetoric and on the classical chorus. To be sure, Lucifer is displeased already with God's elevation of man early in act 2, but is not prepared to act decisively. In act 3 the angelic chorus divides into Luciferists and loyalists, who debate with one another and various of the higher staff of each side. Finally in the last scene of act 3 the Luciferists, with the aid of Lucifer's comrade Belzebub, persuade him to become their leader. So reluctant is he that he calls upon all present to bear witness to his unwillingness: "Prince Belzebub, bear witness, and ye, most royal lords, / Apolion, bear witness, bear witness, Prince Belial, / That I assume this burden under duress, / To defend God's kingdom, to forfend our destruction" ("Vorst Belzebub, getuig, en gij, doorluchtste Heren, / Apolion, getuig, getuig, Vorst Belial, / Dat ik, uit nood en dwang, dien last aanvaarden zal, / Tot voorstand von Gods Rijk, om ons bederf te keren," Vondel, *Volledige Dichtwerken* 370). So pathetic and exaggerated is the repeated cry "getuig" (bear witness) that we can only conclude that the performance is in some sense staged. Yet we are never shown Lucifer or his lieutenants trying to guide the chorus; evidently the chorus embodies Lucifer's own desires, and is both inside and outside him. The chorus is not the Vice, tempting the protagonist from outside, as Cassius does Brutus; Lucifer has already expressed the same feelings independently. They are both his self and not his self, an allegory of his divided self: not the personification allegory of morality but something new concocted out of a new use of the classical chorus that is, in this openly religious context, nothing short of astonishing.

In the case of Racine, there is, typically, more ambivalence. While meaning and intention are repeatedly attributed to the gods and to fate, in practice Racine also connects them to human passion and desire. In *Iphigénie* Agamemnon and Achille are really the slaves of their passion, not of the gods; the oracle only wants to punish illicit passion by destroying Helen's illegitimate daughter. God—or meaning—moves into hiding within the self. Motivation is particularly interesting in this context. In morality play and Seneca motivation is to a large extent exterior: the protagonist is prompted by a Vice (or good angel) or possessed by passion, which tends to be personified in Seneca. But in *Iphigénie* motivation is multiple. Agamemnon is driven both by the oracle (whose interests are represented by the "Vice" Ulysse), but also by his own drive for glory which does not come from outside. Similarly in *Phèdre* Hippolyte rejects his stepmother not only because of his love for virtue, but also because of his love for Aricie—the first could be personified in a morality play, but the second could not. The various lies in *Iphigénie* also make motivation more complex. The sacrifice of the heroine, for example, is first covered by the story that she is to marry Achille, while Eriphile covers her love for Achille with the story that she seeks to learn her parentage—in modern terms, her identity. In both cases the lie ultimately becomes true—Iphigénie does marry Achille and Eriphile does learn her parentage—and in each case the story engages the more personal, private aspect of the self. Taken together with the occasional language of innerness in the play, as when Iphigénie claims to have seen Eriphile's innermost thoughts ("le fond de vos pensées," *Oeuvres complètes* 697), the characters gain the appearance of modern interiority.

Nevertheless, this multiplied and even dishonest motivation has its own problems. Eriphile's story about seeking her parentage does express the essential truth about her; she dies because she is Iphigénie, illegitimate daughter of Helen—the fruit of lust—and not because she tried to interfere with her cousin's marriage to Achille. But in the case of Iphigénie, her true identity as the sacrificed daughter of Agamemnon, the reason she is remembered as a mythical character, is erased by her marriage to Achille, the naturalized cover story that comes to pass. She ceases to be the personification of sacrificed innocence and becomes instead an ordinary woman. Racine's play ends when it has destroyed the mythological tradition from which it drew its life. The substitution of coincidence for the deus ex machina marks the same phenomenon, the danger of neoclassicism's refusal to accept the supernatural. At the same time, the two women supplement one another. Eriphile is Iphigénie's shadow, the other Iphigénie who also loves Achille and is in fact her first cousin. At the beginning of the play Iphigénie wants nothing more than to help Eriphile; only in the course of the action do they separate definitively, and only when they have done so is their close relationship in blood and name revealed. United in one character they would represent the love-hate relationship of twentieth-century depth psychology. As Vondel does with Lucifer and the chorus, Racine, too, exploits the older allegorical structure to represent the tension between the self and its unknown other. But in Racine the role of the chorus is taken over by confidants, who can function not only, like the nurse in *Phèdre*, as a Vice urging the protagonist to sin, but also as this other self/not-self. Racine's psychology is modern for its time, and his modernity is based not on his classicizing, but on its marriage to the allegorical part of his plot. But how modern this interiority is judged to be depends on one's reading of the ambiguous presence of God's will in the world. Late in *Athalie* Joad asks Abner why Athalie unexpectedly freed him from prison: "By what miracle were you delivered?" ("Par quel miracle a-t-on obtenu votre

grâce?" *Oeuvres complètes* 934), as if the workings of her mind were dictated by God. And indeed, Abner answers, "Only God knows what passes
in this cruel heart" ("Dieu dans ce coeur cruel sait seul ce qui se passe,"
ibid.). Is God's knowledge the same as God's will? What is the difference
between God's will working within the self and a self that wills without
God, especially when God is, in Goldmann's influential formulation,
"hidden"? Allegory is not exclusively a bulwark against the anxiety of
secularization, but a part of it.

Allegory versus Narration

The final problem raised by Senecanism is a tension between narrating
and enacting that makes seventeenth-century drama seem static to many
spectators. Seneca largely avoids the ritual and symbolic actions typical
of Greek tragedy, like processions and prayers at altars or tombs. Instead, Seneca's dramas involve extensive descriptions, the famous messenger speeches that not only report, as in Greek tragedy, but overflow
with gruesome detail. It is largely due to the influence of Seneca that
drama emerged from the Renaissance primarily a matter of rhetoric.
The concrete objects that carry allegorical meaning in morality become
metaphors and, above all in Senecan rhetoric, similes. The normal verb
for attending a play in Elizabethan England was "hearing" rather than
"seeing" (Orgel, *The Illusion of Power* 16–17); and Latin drama was used
for rhetorical training in the schools. While Aristotle devoted a chapter
to distinguishing epic and tragedy, which he saw as neighboring genres,
Seneca modeled their close relationship. His are plays of telling and
hearing; seeing is only with the mind's eye. Indeed, no one is certain
whether Seneca's plays were ever written for staged performance. The
paucity of stage action in so much neoclassical drama thus belongs
partly to the Senecan heritage.

In this respect, Vondel is perhaps the most Senecan dramatist of the
century, even though he is less gloomy, violent and intolerant than most
of his contemporaries. He is above all a narrative dramatist. *Gijsbrecht
van Aemstel* contains vast amounts of action as Amsterdam is defended
and finally burned to the ground, but all of it is narrated. Vondel's preface identifies the striking similarities in plot between his play and Virgil's description of the betrayal and fall of Troy in the second book of
the *Aeneid*. Even though the play does not observe unity of place, it
moves from one location to another only to hear yet another extensive
narration of the action the spectator has just missed. It is almost as if
Vondel's six-beat rhymed couplets were not quite distinguished in his
mind from Virgil's hexameters. As in epic, the significance of figures
and their moral value is communicated in metaphors and similes. His

Lucifer is equally narrative; reading it feels in many respects like reading *Paradise Lost.* The huge battles among angels we hear so much about are all offstage. The same is true for Adam and Eve in Eden, who are described at compelling length in splendid poetry. Milton himself considered treating the material dramatically; Vondel tried his hand at epic on other topics.[31] This tendency is striking in his *Noach.* Vondel's texts lack stage directions, but the first scene makes clear that the ark is visible onstage. Nevertheless, the entire first scene of the second act consists of detailed descriptions of the structure by Noah's carpenter in response to a sequence of one-line questions from the great prince of the East. When God's storm finally breaks at the end of the play, every flash of lightning and crash of thunder onstage is also detailed by one or another character. Where the tradition of religious drama demands that the audience see certain things, Vondel's play has them described as well as seen.

Leo Spitzer's classic essay, "The 'Récit de Théramène,' " analyzes to similar effect the long report about the monster sent by Neptune to destroy Hippolyte in the fourth act of *Phèdre.* Spitzer focuses not on the epic aspect, but on the contemplative, analytic aspect of the characters seeing themselves seeing (Spitzer, "The 'Récit de Théramène' " 107), which thus becomes an ally to ethics in its constant, as Spitzer argues, typically Baroque struggle with passion.[32] The acquisition of knowledge through vision clearly belongs both to Renaissance neoplatonism and also to the visibility of lessons in allegorical drama. Nevertheless, the paradox remains that all of this seeing occurs only in the language, for the ears of the spectator. The spectator sees not the lessons, but characters seeing themselves with the mind's eye and learning the lesson— Spitzer argues, for example, that Phèdre sees herself stained with sin (Spitzer, "The 'Récit de Théramène' " 109). In effect, the characters become spectators of an imagined play-within-the-play that is an equivalent allegorical representation of their feelings, and we see its effect upon them. Their passionate response, their affect, now mimetically represented, replaces the lesson itself. Thematically, ethics triumphs, but representationally, the emphasis is rather on passion. The allegory may have been repressed by mimesis, but it hasn't gone away.

Racine's plays are the ultimate in Senecanism, not because of the plot or degree of violence, but formally, because the violence is not literally visible. Episodes like the blinding of Arthur in *King John* or of Lear have more in common with mystery or miracle plays, where physical violence could appear onstage; the most obvious example is the Wakefield *Herod the Great,* in which innocent children are slaughtered onstage, but violence also occurs in martyr plays, such as the Middle High German play of Saint Catherine.[33] In the terms of Norbert Elias, Baroque Senecan plays are more "civilized" for placing the violence behind the scenes, and of course also more courtly.[34] At the same time they are more obviously mimetic because the characters act according to the same secular code as their courtly audience, not according to a code prescribed by a visible religious mythology. Indeed, Seneca's supernatural elements, the omens and ghosts Shakespeare still used so freely, largely disappear in Racine's versions. Not only is violence placed behind the scenes, but with it the visuality upon which allegory depends. It is obvious that extreme classicism is not congenial to allegory as we have been discussing it; it is less obvious—but important—that it suppresses visuality.

Shakespeare, obviously, is very different in this regard, as is most English drama of the sixteenth and seventeenth centuries. Titus Andronicus loses a hand onstage, Macbeth's head is paraded on a spear, Lear goes mad, Gloucester loses his eyes.[35] Indeed, the tendency to visible violence onstage has led to the recent argument that English drama is least Senecan (in showing rather than telling) precisely in its most Senecan (gruesome) moments (Goldberg, "Going for Baroque"). But this difference from the Continental classicists agrees with the argument of this chapter that Shakespeare explores the tensions between morality and Senecanism, between showing and telling, with particular boldness. Examples of the tension between showing and telling occur all through Shakespeare. For instance, should Othello, who won Desdemona with his magnificent storytelling, believe what his friends tell him, or what Iago shows him in a series of adroitly staged plays-within-the-play? Senecan rhetoricity would seem to be associated with the positive, but duped figures, and the staginess of morality with the wiles of evil. Iago ends his role refusing ever to speak again (5.2.304), while Othello, in his last speech, tells a story, in which he enacts the last line as he tells it: "And smote him—thus" (5.2.356). In fact, Othello does not "enact" the last line in the play in the sense of acting it out, but in the sense of really stabbing himself. By punishing himself for his earlier error of judgment (Aristotelian *hamartia*) and sin of jealousy, Othello atones, and his literal death stands in for the redemption he would have received as a morality hero. As in Racine, the mimetic action becomes a metaphor for the older allegory. Ultimately the play reconciles narrative to enactment; the same truth—or the same lies—inhere in both kinds of drama.

It is thus striking that Shakespeare's last plays, the romances, contain both his most narrative and his most neoclassical plays. The last of these, *The Tempest*, observes the unities of time and more loosely of place, but does not resist the concrete parodic subplot typical of the comedies. The second scene contains two lengthy narrative expositions quite unusual for Shakespeare, one with Miranda and one with Ariel, both carefully marked. In the first Prospero worries about the length of the narrative and repeatedly asks Miranda if she is listening; in the second Prospero strictly limits Ariel's freedom of reply. But at the same time, the play begins with a tour de force of action in medias res—another unusual exposition for Shakespeare, this time extremely epic, but also staged. Later the play incorporates two masques—Ariel's moral banquet that teaches the Neapolitans not to be so greedy (3.3) and the marriage masque (4.1). If *Othello* seemed to be posing the question of whether narrating or enacting is better, *The Tempest* is serenely beyond questioning. It embraces all the possibilities in a rousing finale to Shakespeare's own magic show.

A final aspect of narration in drama that bears on the relation of mimesis to allegory is what I would call particularity. All forms of classical drama are more mimetic than morality drama because they deal with particular mythological and historical figures, not with generalized abstractions. However unrealistic Senecan drama may seem to us today, it was more representative of real details of seventeenth-century life than morality play. The narration enhanced its particularity by allowing space for specifics that cannot always be enacted and that cannot be readily noted. Vondel's *Gijsbrecht*, for example, tells us as much, or even more, about the heroism and nobility of the title figure in the narration than in what is shown onstage. Similarly in Racine's *Phèdre*, we learn who Thésée really is from the analysis of his character by Hippolyte and Théramène, not from his stage conduct. In *Noach* the ark, though sitting on the stage, is described at great length. The language probably allows us to see things beyond the capacity of the stage designer to represent; even if it could be represented in such detail, the spectator will only perceive it all by having it pointed out.

In Shakespeare, however, enhanced mimesis makes texts sometimes more rather than less allegorical. While Brutus and Cassius whisper together, in act 2 of *Julius Caesar*, for example, the other conspirators argue about where on the horizon the sun will rise (2.2.101–11). The world is as impenetrable here as in the dark night of *King John*:[36] no one knows anymore whence grace or salvation may be expected. The most important particularization of the allegory occurs in the central motif of Shakespeare's plots. In sixteenth-century moralities, the Vice tempts the hero to sin; in *Julius Caesar*, as in many Shakespearean tragedies, the Vice tempts the hero to murder. Brutus tempted by Cassius evokes Othello tempted by Iago, Macbeth by the witches, Hamlet by his father's ghost. In all of these plays the heroes murder grace in the person of an anointed king or a pure woman. But all sin violates divine grace; consistently to particularize the sin as murder is to specify, to make mimetic. In these plays, rather than narrate, Shakespeare has recourse to an enhanced form of allegory that engages both image and narrated detail, precisely the form of allegory that became fashionable at the turn of the seventeenth century under the name of emblem. It cannot be emphasized enough that Shakespeare's allegorizing is not conservative; it is part of the most interesting development in representation of the age.

Because Racine's stage and language are less visual, it is harder to find him being emblematic. The most striking example is the monster in *Phèdre*, which has much less explicit form than in Seneca's or Euripides' versions of the play. By being only a generic monster it expresses precisely the incomprehensibility of the evil that has emerged so unexpectedly from within Phèdre and has destroyed Hippolyte. Blindness and veiling play a similar role in *Iphigénie*. They are visual correlatives for the characters' general inability to penetrate the emotions and motivations of those about them except under the most extreme circumstances. Nevertheless, Racine avoids Shakespeare's precise imagistic language for marking particular situations. Yet he cannot escape something like an emblem at the end of *Iphigénie*. His typically neoclassical avoidance of the supernatural led to the revelation that Eriphile was the Iphigénie intended by the oracle in place of substituting a hind for Iphigénie. But however much Racine wants to rationalize the myth, he cannot erase it; the ending still carries its meaning only in our recognition of the extra substitution; like the monster in *Phèdre* Eriphile is an allegory for the suppressed supernatural. Not only violence, but allegory is, in effect, kept offstage. In Racine we see only real people, and their concrete allegorical existence is hidden behind a veil of incipient interiority. But offstage does not mean absent from the play. Lucien Goldmann grounds tragedy in Racine in the disappearance of God from the world in the wake of Cartesian rationalism, and Walter Benjamin makes an equivalent argument about the tragedies of the German Baroque; yet Seneca's ghosts and morality's God hover in the wings. Tragedy in this mode arises from what I have called the anxiety of secularization much more than from true Aristotelian practice. There is no pure neoclassicism.

Chapter 5

The Allegorical Idioms of the Illusionist Stage: Spectacle in the Seventeenth Century

> *Where there is chance, there is also room for the marvelous, even in modern drama. But even the mythic and ideal must be treated mimetically.*
>
> —*Fr. Schlegel*[1]

Aristotle has always claimed pride of place in our understanding of neo-classicism, but an equally great impulse toward mimesis in the Renaissance came from the revival of the Roman architectural treatise *De architectura* written by Marcus Vitruvius Pollio sometime in the first century B.C. It remained the primary authority on ancient architecture from the Renaissance through the eighteenth century. Three books of the treatise were devoted to theater design, with considerable attention paid to sight lines and stage structure; it also included a brief description of painted scenery and of machines for creating rapid set changes in the theater. A new attitude toward illusion on the stage followed from its reception, and the new perspectivist stage scenery created unprecedented standards of realism, first in Italy in the sixteenth century, and from there in England, Germany, France, and Spain in the early seventeenth. There is no need to argue whether the new scenery really advanced mimeticism on the stage more than Aristotelian material causality and psychological realism did; of crucial importance is that an early neoclassical impulse independent of neo-Aristotelianism or the literary page changed the practice of all drama. Initially Vitruvian stage illusion was favored for court spectaculars—masque and romance—and for Counter-Reformation morality—school drama and Spanish *autos sacramentales* (Corpus Christi dramas); only occasionally before the 1640s (and of course the 1660s in England) were the imitations of Latin comedy and the rapidly secularizing drama of the commercial stages in England, Spain, and even France performed on the new illusionist stage. Instead, the visual realism on the stage so essential to the naturalism of an Ibsen or a Shaw led first to a great flowering of allegorical drama. But it would be wrong to consider this in any way a detour in the history of drama.

These illusionist forms were not an arcane byway of drama, as we tend to treat them today, but a substantial portion of theatrical life. The courts for which masques were performed could be a large proportion of the population of a small state (25 percent of the town of Weimar worked for the court in the late eighteenth century); school dramas typically drew the general populace of a city as well as the resident court, while *autos sacramentales* were addressed to both a courtly and a popular audience.[2] Because they are understood to have different origins from the other forms of drama as well as from one another—morality from homiletics, masque from secular traditions of governmental pageantry and court mummings, and school drama from the curriculum in rhetoric—the subgenres tend to be studied in isolation. The Corpus Christi and school dramas of the period are generally understood to be allegorical, masques are thought of as theater of emblem or device, and commercial drama as mimetic; only the last is understood to be dramatic in the common usage of the word.[3]

Following a description of the Vitruvian revival, four themes will organize this survey of the different dramatic modes—masque, Spanish Corpus Christi drama, school drama, and some commercial drama—that came to share the techniques of the illusionist stage in the course of the first half of the seventeenth century. (Opera also belongs in this list, but will be treated separately in the next chapter.) First is its affinity with neoplatonism and its tension with Aristotelianism. Second is the essential identity of the different subgenres. Third is the elaboration of possible allegorical idioms that developed under the impact of neoclassicism, primarily mythology and contemporary reality; as allegory is secularized it becomes increasingly emblematic. Fourth is the problematic status of allegory that is no longer religious: this problem leads into the deepest anxieties arising from the early modern shift in religious and psychological paradigms.

In the interests of maintaining focus I have chosen examples primarily from masques of Ben Jonson, the Jesuit school drama of Jakob Bidermann, the Counter-Reformation morality plays and court spectaculars of Pedro Calderón de la Barca, and the work of his German contemporary, Andreas Gryphius, whose name may be familiar to the reader from Walter Benjamin's *Ursprung des deutschen Trauerspiels*. Benjamin's point is, famously, that German plays of the period, like those of their great Spanish contemporary, Calderón, are allegorical and categorically different from drama in the neoclassical tradition. The difference is, however, not categorical, but one of degree. Since these figures

and forms tend to be obscure to all but specialists, I preface the main argument with some background information.

Court masque emerged as a major genre in Italy, then had a short but
splendid career at the British court under the reigns of James I and
Charles I. In France it became assimilated to court opera during the
reign of Louis XIV; in Germany it was still practiced by the leading poets
of the age into the early nineteenth century. Between 1605 and 1631
Ben Jonson (1573–1637) wrote twenty-eight masques, mostly for Christmas celebrations at the court of James I, and mostly in collaboration
with Inigo Jones (1573–1651), who introduced illusionist staging into
England from Italy. The brief texts (often under three hundred lines) of
these learned masques structured entertainments of several hours of
music and dancing in which the audience participated, blending mumming and masquerade with the full didactic power of religious drama.[4]
Both Jonson and Jones considered themselves neoclassicists in the intellectual vanguard of their time, so that for them allegory was by no means
necessarily conservative.

The Jesuit school dramas of Jonson's contemporary Jakob Bidermann
(1578–1639), and of similar though less famous professors of rhetoric,
were performed annually by students for all the local notables—
members of the court, of the municipality, of the university, of the local
aristocracy—and the general populace. Productions included lavish
costumes, machinery, instantaneous scene changes, musical accompaniment, and even ballet interludes. In parts of south Germany such productions continued well into the eighteenth century.[5]

Like Jonson, Calderón (1600–1681) first established a reputation as a
leading author of plays for the public theater, an institution comparable
in many respects to the Elizabethan public theater, and in 1635 he succeeded Lope de Vega as court dramatist.[6] But after 1650 he wrote plays
only for the court and for the annual Corpus Christi celebrations in
Madrid and, occasionally, elsewhere. Calderón set the scenarios for the
lavishly staged *autos* himself; for the court he collaborated with the Italian stage designer and architect Cosme Lotti (1570?–1643), whose role
in Spanish stage history resembles that of Inigo Jones in England.[7]
Calderón's *autos* extinguished all competition and held the stage until
dramatic Corpus Christi celebrations were officially abolished in 1712.
His work was rediscovered in the early nineteenth century in Germany.
Thanks in large part to the efforts of Goethe, who considered him as important as Shakespeare, staged his plays, and promoted a complete translation into German, his status was largely restored in Europe, though he
has remained less visible in the United States.

The Spanish *corrales*, as the commercial stages were known, resem-
bled to a large extent the English open-air stage of the beginning of the

century in the 1620s and 1630s but made use of somewhat more elabo-rate machinery and sets. In England the example of court masque seems to have resulted in more lavish staging only of plays performed in-doors, as the late Shakespeare plays staged at Blackfriars indicate. Fur-thermore, there was a less rigid distinction between commercial and religious drama in Spain, so that it was not uncommon for popular *autos* to be adapted for the secular stage and vice versa; Calderón's popular *El mágico prodigioso* is a good example. There were also plays, like his *Devo-ción de la cruz*, that used the techniques of *auto*. Other early "secular" dramas of this sort include *Judas Macabeo, El purgatorio de San Patricio, Las cadenas del demonio* (in which the devil is a character), among many others. Calderón was not unique in this regard—the hero of Tirso de Molina's *El burlador de Sevilla* is carried off to hell at the end; his *El conde-nado por desconfiado* and Mira de Amescua's *El esclavo del demonio* are both moralities.

The Vitruvian Revival and Neoplatonist Poetics

Like Aristotelianism, Vitruvian staging emerged from the recovery and intense study of a classical text. The manuscript of Marcus Vitruvius Pol-lio's *De architectura* (first century A.D.) was discovered by Poggio Braccio-lini at St. Gall, first printed in 1486 then frequently reprinted, translated into the vernacular in 1521, and made the object of philological investi-gation and commentary from the 1530s on.[8] Book V of the *De architec-tura* discusses the use of scenery painted in perspective for the staging of plays, the changing of scenes, the formal differentiation of scenery by genre, construction and use of entrances and exits, use of machines and engines, use of thunder for divinity, and the public entertainment as a function of the ruler. The most important transmitters of Vitruvius for the stage were the widely influential architect Sebastiano Serlio (1475–1554), who produced the first published account of modern theatrical practice at the end of Book II of his *Tutte l'opere d'architettura, et prospetiva* (1537–75), and Nicola Sabbattini (1574–1654), whose *Pratica di fabricar scene e machine ne' teatri* (1638) became the standard handbook. The am-phitheatrical shape and tiered seating of Renaissance theaters (and in-deed the term "theater" itself) were based on classical models, though the pattern was later adjusted to accommodate the rectangular shape of the princes' halls in which much early court performance took place. In keeping with this classical provenance, the earliest Renaissance stage de-signers were architects, and into the eighteenth century stage design fo-cused primarily on architectural effects. Nevertheless, the line between architecture and painting was readily crossed in the Renaissance, and ac-cordingly concern for perspective—essentially the art of representing the three dimensions of architecture in the two of painting—was central to illusionist stage design from the beginning.

Both Serlio and Sabbattini begin their discussions with establishing the vanishing point on the stage, other questions of perspective, and the proper placement of the audience with respect to the stage. By 1560 in Italy the stage was a platform open on three sides to the audience with a fully developed proscenium frame designed individually for the particular performance; it was often covered by the curtain before the performance and thus considered part of the set itself, to complete the parallel to painting and the rediscovery of perspective there. By 1600 the new stage was often rather a box defined by an elaborate proscenium arch, although the term box set properly applies only from the late nineteenth century, when solid walls replaced painted cloths and wings. The front wall of this box was, of course, removed, and its depth artificially enhanced by the arts of perspective. Decorated shutters could be slid into place to close off or reveal parts of the stage behind them; the painted backcloth and the wings marking the side walls could be changed rapidly by means of machinery beneath the stage.[9] In the seventeenth century elaborate sets were the rule even for outdoor performances and school dramas. For each of Calderón's *autos* two special two-story carts were designed, ornamented, and equipped to his specifications with the same machinery as on the indoor stage. Devils rose and sank through trapdoors, ships sailed up to the stage, worlds sprang into being or disappeared as giant spheres opened and closed. Similar sets are called for in Jesuit school drama and also, though on a less lavish scale, German Baroque tragedy, which was a form of Protestant school drama.[10]

Although the new theory of the stage, like the new theory of the drama, was perceived as a classical revival, the two were at first largely independent, and assimilated to one another only with some difficulty in the course of the seventeenth century. Even in Dryden's day there was still complaining about too much spectacle on the dramatic stage, and the large amount of spectacle was one of the major grounds for the Aristotelian attacks on opera. In both England and Spain, illusionist staging began with collaboration between a local dramatist and an Italian-trained architect—Ben Jonson and Inigo Jones in England and Calderón and Cosme Lotti in Spain. Neither pair got along well, and the famous quarrel between Jonson and Jones has partly to do with the fact that Jonson was Aristotelian and Jones was not.[11] Despite the obviously enhanced mimetic impact of the new staging, Serlio conspicuously avoids Aristotelian rhetoric in his description of its effects:

Among all things made by hand of man few in my opinion bring greater contentment to the eye and satisfaction to the spirit than the unveiling to our view of a stage setting. Here the art of perspective gives us in a little space a view of superb palaces, vast temples, and houses of all kinds, and, both near and far, spacious squares, surrounded by various ornate buildings. There are long vistas of avenues with intersecting streets, triumphal arches, soaring columns, pyramids, obelisques, and a thousand other marvels, all enriched by innumerable lights . . . at times so skillfully placed that they seem like so many sparkling jewels—diamonds, rubies, sapphires, emeralds, and other gems.

Here the horned and lucent moon rises slowly—so slowly that the spectators have not been aware of any movement. In other scenes the sun rises, moves on its course, and at the end of the play is made to set with such skill that many spectators remain lost in wonder. With like skill gods are made to descend from the skies and planets to pass through the air. . . . Sometimes [in the interludes] one sees strange animal costumes worn by men and children who play, leap, and run, to the delighted wonder of the spectators. All these things are so satisfying to the eye and the spirit that nothing made by the art of man could seem more beautiful. (Hewitt, *Serlio, Sabbattini, Furttenbach* 24–25)

Lily Campbell associates this allusion to the rising and setting sun with the unity of time being advocated by Aristotelians, but the absence of any reference to Aristotle or to the unities is striking.[12] Wonder and satisfaction are the watchwords for both eye and spirit. Buildings, heavenly bodies and gods are equally valid objects of representation here, and the description moves without special demarcation from plays to intermezzi. The viewpoint is much more Platonist than Aristotelian.

What this means on stage is best illustrated by Tasso's *Aminta*, which has at first glance the most rudimentary of stage actions (in 3.2 Dafne keeps Aminta from committing suicide and Nerina shows Silvia's bloody veil to corroborate her mistaken report of Silvia's death). In Chapter 3 I emphasized its morality substructure; here I focus on its neoplatonist surface. Like Senecan drama *Aminta* is heavily narrative and consists largely of statements of feelings not specifically marked for the audience by the allegorical actions of morality, a few debates, and many reports of offstage action. Its neoplatonist dramaturgy depends on its *intermedii* (interludes), which are omitted in most publications, or at best relegated to an appendix. These consist in each case of a short speech spoken by a richly costumed god or chorus of deities that descended in the appropriate machinery with dramatic lighting effects.[13] In *The Landscape of the Mind* Richard Cody has demonstrated how, together with the Cupid and Venus of the prologue and epilogue, they outline the neoplatonist myth of Love reconciling the many and the one that undergirds the more realistic human events of the play itself. The *intermedii* are speaking pictures that identify for initiates to Platonism (essentially everyone at court) the secret or true meaning of the action otherwise being narrated: visual and verbal representation are separated into two complementary sequences. The action of the play as usually printed is itself allegorical in more abstract fashion than that of morality: the absence of action represents the invisibility of the encounters of the mind with beauty and truth that are represented in such Platonist mysteries.

It is widely agreed that the new staging was first used primarily for intermezzi and masques in the service of a poetics of wonder shared by all its poets.[14] The transition was not simple: as Stephen Orgel has shown, early audiences in England were uncomfortable with the scenes created by Inigo Jones while Italian visitors, who had seen such staging before, expressed great admiration for them (Jonson, *Complete Masques* 23; cf. Orgel, *Inigo Jones* 8–9). Nevertheless, once audiences did learn to see, the impact was substantial. As Orgel points out, on a perspectivist stage actions "begin necessarily to take on the quality of empirical data" (*Complete Masques* 28). The wonder the stage aroused was specifically the magical illusion of reality. It seems clear that people sensed the difference between the two kinds of neoclassical mimesis at work here, for in both masque and morality the dramatic interaction among characters took place on the stage platform or apron in front of the proscenium arch, while the space behind was reserved for illusionist wonders. Indeed, only in the eighteenth century did the actors move behind the proscenium arch (Laver, *Drama: Its Costume and Decor* 157). Thus a careful distinction was maintained between dramatic action and dramatic effect, which created a special space in the drama for spectacle and theme quite apart from plot. But as it became the norm, the realism of stage illusion blended with neoclassical verisimilitude. It has even been argued that the dominance of the three unities in France grew from the shift to the Italian illusionist aesthetic in the second and third decades of the seventeenth century, and verisimilitude came to mean that the spectator felt himself present at the action (Védier, *Origine et évolution de la dramaturgie néo-classique* 191). In the second half of the century Aristotelian commentators increasingly subordinated stage illusion, under the category of "spectacle" or "ornament," to furthering the action; in this function it was valued not for the capacity to evoke wonder, but for its realism and for maintaining unity of place (Campbell, *Scenes and Machines* 253–55). While some strand of pleasure in stage spectacle for its own sake clearly continued through the nineteenth century[15] and indeed into the present day with special effects in film, in the later seventeenth century the illusionist set became the norm for all stage drama and as such came to be understood in increasingly Aristotelian terms.

The new stage drew freely on indigenous practices of court ceremonial and religious drama that preceded the classical revival, and it transformed them into a more modern form of allegory. Mumming at courts in costume or disguise but with no theatrical action, pageantry for holidays, and royal entries with floats, stage carts, and even platform stages with machines for entrances from above or below the stage all date from the Middle Ages and account for the visual effects of most of the Shakespearean stage. Such activities enjoyed a great revival and elaboration in the Renaissance, beginning in fourteenth-century Italy.[16] Processions were the normal organizing pattern of the Italian court masque and were later absorbed into opera, where they remained essential parts of the plot through the late nineteenth century (think of the elephants in *Aida*). Older machines, such as those representing descending clouds or Glory remained popular and new ones—sea machines, heavenly bodies, flowing rivers and fountains, smoke, flames, wind, thunder, and rain—joined them. With the proliferation of machines and the advent of the proscenium arch, the stakes for allegory rose considerably. At first the proscenium arch was part of the stage set and designed specifically for each production: the allegorical figures painted on it contributed to the meaning of the dramatic representation, so that the allegory was no longer carried only by the figures onstage and their language, but by parallel representations in the proscenium frame and in the stage tableaus. With these added pictures allegory becomes emblem, the popular genre of the seventeenth century that tied a motto, epigram, and picture into a single unit. The framing presence of the proscenium arch contributed in and of itself to an increased sense that the stage representation was an image to be interpreted by the text.

Spectacle and Morality

Beneath the welter of images the sketchy plots of the spectacles written for Vitruvian staging are those of sixteenth-century moralities: a central figure is tempted by Vices, falls, and then either repents or is damned. Since many of these spectacles are school dramas, the fact is hardly surprising. Calderón's *autos*, of which he wrote two a year for decades, ring all possible changes on the plot—sometimes the protagonist is man (for example, *La vida es sueño*,[17] *La nave del mercader, Los encantos de la culpa*) or conceived in the feminine as human nature (for example, the heroines of *El divino Orfeo, El pastor fido*) with a plot that looks like a love story; sometimes the protagonist is a single personification (like Faith in *Psiquis y Cupido*), sometimes double (as in *El gran mercado del mundo*) or greatly multiplied (as in *El gran teatro del mundo*). The fall is often stylized in terms of eating an apple poisoned by the Vices, even if the ostensible subject comes from Greek mythology (for example, *El divino Orfeo, Andrómeda y Perseo*), but it can take other forms as well, such as literally handing over one's heart (*La nave del mercader*). Because *autos* were to celebrate the feast of Corpus Christi, a Christ figure—who can have such varied names as Moses (*La serpiente de metal*), Perseus (*Andrómeda y*

Perseo), Pilgrim (*El veneno y la triaca*), or Cedar Tree (*La humildad coron-ada de las plantas*)—normally effects salvation by means of the sacra-ment. Jakob Bidermann's *Cenodoxus* (1602), the best known of the German Jesuit school dramas of the period, seems slightly more modern because the hero, named for the sin to which he succumbs, is shown practicing the sins personified by the Vices and not just consorting with them as in the English moralities of the sixteenth century. Nevertheless the structure is the same, but on the negative model: Cenodoxus enters into sin, ignores adjurations to repent, and is damned. Examples of the negative pattern may also be found in Calderón's Malgenio in *El gran mercado del mundo* and in Baltasar in *La cena del rey Baltasar*. Even this brief survey suggests how much livelier and more particularized—mimetic—the richer costuming and stage effects enabled the plot to become.

More remarkable are the occasional traces of morality even in court masques, which often seem to lack plot entirely. Ben Jonson's *A Vision of Delight* has a Christian subtext, the adoration of the shepherds. The masque begins looking forward to spring (compare the complaints about winter in the older *Second Shepherds' Play*) in a night occupied by the evil phantasms who dance the first two antimasques (the entry and dance of grotesque or comic figures in English court masque, usually with minimal accompanying dialogue). The broad comedy of Fantasy corresponds roughly to the popular sheep-stealing episode in *Second Shepherds' Play*. Both end with the adoration of the king as light appears, spring comes, and a new age dawns, described appropriately in Jonson by Peace and Wonder. The morality plot appears in the text's assertion of divine order in a refractory world. Another masque, *Pleasure Recon-ciled to Virtue*, draws on the topos of Hercules choosing between Pleasure and Virtue, itself already a conflation of the Christian conflict between sin and salvation with a Ciceronian motif. The masque begins with Her-cules in the company of the Vice Comus, the sin of gluttony; after the first antimasque Hercules dismisses Comus and his brood in the name of Virtue. No sooner does he lie down to rest than he is attacked by pyg-mies, children of the earth and therefore of worldliness. By awakening to consciousness of his true self he drives them away, making it possible for Pleasure and Virtue, now reconciled, to celebrate. The Christian layer beneath the myth had originally legitimated its use in the period and continues to influence Jonson's elaboration of it. The first and most famous of Calderón's court spectaculars, *El mayor encanto amor* (Love the Greatest Enchantment), performed on the lake in the Buen Retiro park in 1635, dramatizes Ovid's version of the Ulysses and Circe episode in terms of the same choice between pleasure and virtue: Ulysses must come to consciousness of himself and assert his virtue by escaping the pleasurable toils of Circe's love. So close was this plot to that of morality, that Calderón reused the first and last acts, with relatively minor revisions, as an *auto sacramental* in 1645, *Los encantos de la culpa* (The Sorceries of Sin).[18]

Although Jonson was the most vocal Aristotelian in his generation when it came to commercial drama, his court masques are largely neoplatonist. *A Vision of Delight* is the most obvious example. Delight calls the audience "seers" (two syllables, l. 14), and Fantasy, too, emphasizes vision when she introduces the main dance:

> you cannot be
> Of such a true delight too free
>   Which who once saw would ever see;
> And if they could the object prize,
> Would, while it lasts, not think to rise,
>   But wish their bodies all were eyes. (*Complete Masques* 254)

Delight and Fantasy have the most lines during the antimasques; but when the real world of the street yields to the idealized bower of Zephyrus, Wonder takes over to guide the response of the audience to the "glories of the spring" (*Complete Masques* 252). After Fantasy's long and bawdy comic speech in rambunctious anapests in the antimasques, Wonder returns speaking decorous couplets. The heightening of delight to wonder by shifting vision from the real to the ideal that takes place here is the heart of Platonist poetics and underlies all of Jonson's masques.[19] Calderón's *autos sacramentales* also operate with neoplatonist allegories as they consistently move from the world to the revelation of divine presence in the sacrament. *El gran teatro del mundo* (The Great Theater of the World, ca. 1635) is paradigmatic—it begins with God calling forth the world and ends with the revelation of the Holy Sacrament in the open heavens. Many of Calderón's *autos* begin with the creation,[20] and all end with the wonder of the wafer, for the function of Corpus Christi drama was to celebrate the Holy Sacrament. By the seventeenth century the Platonist truth or mind was widely accepted as an analogy to the Christian God, and neoplatonist allegory could double for Christian. What was somewhat experimental in Shakespeare becomes, under the influence of the classical revival, the norm even for institutionalized Catholic drama.

In all of these kinds of text the visual effects heighten the sense of wonder when spheres and other shapes suddenly open to stage revelation, as happens repeatedly in Jonson's masques and Calderón's *autos*. Bidermann shows heavenly and earthly actions simultaneously at the climax of *Cenodoxus* to impressive effect: the soul of the hypocrite Cenodoxus is judged by Christ, while his body lies in state on earth but cries out as his soul is condemned. The humans onstage, who consider him saintly, do not understand the actions of the corpse, but the audience, which sees both, experiences divine revelation directly. Similar forms of spectacle underline the morality elements of Calderón's commercial plays. The best known of them, *La vida es sueño* (Life Is a Dream, 1636) begins with the spectacular fall of the heroine into the dark valley of worldly intrigue and sin, in which ultimately both she and the hero correctly choose between pleasure and virtue. In *El médico de su honra*, the lover Don Enrique actually begins the play with a spectacular fall from his horse described in a speech that evokes Lucifer's fall from heaven. The most extreme example is the end of *La devoción de la cruz*, where the heroine—who mistakenly chooses pleasure over virtue but then repents—is saved when the cross she embraces carries her upward out of her vengeful father's reach. A similar effect occurs in late Shakespeare. In the first two acts of *Antony and Cleopatra* Antony wavers between his Roman virtue and the pleasure that lies in the East. The simple choice is gradually complicated, so that Cleopatra/pleasure becomes love that ultimately transfigures the protagonists into an epiphany of beauty and truth. In a gesture rare in Shakespeare the dying Antony is literally hauled to the upper level of the stage (4.15), which is identified as Cleopatra's monument. This is hardly an apotheosis, given the discussion of his weight; nevertheless, what the spectator sees corresponds exactly to the transfiguration into a higher mode of being that the text evokes. Its significance is glossed in the final scene of act 5 when Cleopatra is addressed as "eastern star" (5.2.308), and Caesar describes her with "her strong toil of grace" (5.2.347) and begins the final line with "High order" (5.2.366). In the romances such moments of wonder become frankly supernatural in the manner of masque: a statue comes to life (*A Winter's Tale*), gods descend from a machine (*Pericles, Cymbeline*) and in the latter even dance. Similarly the staged masques within *The Tempest* and the elaborate procession at the end of *Henry VIII* make the cause for wonder visible. Heightened stage effects did not lead in a straight line to increased mimesis.

Nevertheless, the effect of the illusionist staging has also secularized these texts, in Jonson almost beyond recognition. The masques reveal the glory not of the king on high, but of the king on earth, although much of the glory reflected on King James derives from the implicit analogies to God, just as Rubens glorified him by seating him on clouds in the heavens on the ceiling of the Banqueting Hall of Whitehall Palace, the room in which the masques were performed. Even where the religious significance of the structure is still explicit, as in Calderón and Bidermann, both ordained priests who presumably wrote from religious conviction, heaven and its actions are represented with a worldly pomp fully comparable to that of court masque. Furthermore Counter-Reformation drama tends to celebrate not God but the institution of the church, whether in the sacrament glorified in Calderón's *autos* or in Bidermann's bureaucratic court in heaven.[21] By focusing more on the institutions of religion in the world than on individual virtue these moralities, like the court masque, are rather more secular as well as more allegorical than their sixteenth-century predecessors.

In more uniformly Catholic Spain the commercial stage could use the morality structure to explore this gap between the world and cosmic order. Thus Segismundo in *La vida es sueño* must choose both between the pleasure of revenge and the virtue of respecting his defeated father and also between the pleasure of marrying the woman he loves (Rosaura) and the virtue of marrying Princess Estrella to preserve the newly reestablished order of his world. But maintaining the order of the world is no longer congruent with possessing divine grace, which is paradoxically embodied for Segismundo in Rosaura, even though virtue requires him to renounce her. In the famous honor dramas (*El pintor de su deshonra, El médico de su honra, A secreto agravio secreta venganza, El alcalde de Zalamea*) an unwelcome lover pursues a heroine whom he still loves but also hates for having married someone else (or in *El alcalde* simply for being hidden from him). The heroines of these plays "fall" by being drawn into relations with the lovers, either by trying to justify their positions (the first three), or by rape (*El alcalde*), but only one, Doña Leonor in *A secreto agravio* actually plans to betray her husband. The villain in *El alcalde de Zalamea*, Don Alvaro, loves heroine Isabel but also wishes to destroy her—exactly the same ambivalence the various devil figures in the *autos* bring to the protagonist. Once Isabel has lost her innocence by rape she fears that her father, a wealthy peasant, will kill her, as the honor system dictates. Instead he brings his daughter's rapist to justice by setting aside the more familiar tenets of the honor code—class structure, secrecy, personal revenge. And indeed, we must not overlook the literal social problem of an excessively harsh honor code that Calderón addresses in these plays.[22] Thus Harald Weinrich asserts in passing that because classical European literature is a casuistics of honor, it automatically prefers genres related to falling (*Ehrensache Höflichkeit* 9). Like the Christ figure in the *autos*, Isabel's father cares for her gently, undergoes humiliation by begging Don Alvaro to marry her, then purifies her (by publicly punishing the recalcitrant don), and sends her to finish her life in a convent, in effect under divine protection. The less generous husbands of the other plays do murder their in the main innocent wives, but always under the guise of caring for them—Don Gutierre goes so far as the allow his wife two hours to purify her soul before he kills her beneath the sign of the cross. At the end their achievements are confirmed, with varying degrees of irony, by the king, who has opportunely arrived. If the basic plot structure is still that of morality, divine authority in the world must be ratified by the king, and the discrepancy between his judgment and that of heaven remains visible. In this respect at least the world of Calderón, court dramatist of the most rigidly Catholic court of the age, is as secular as that of Racine.

New Allegorical Idioms

Spectacle that evoked the appearance of reality did not result in more realistic characters, as a naive Aristotelian might assume. On the contrary it gave rise to flights of allegory. The lavish costuming for these spectacular dramas if anything brought character even more to the surface than in the more consistently verbal medium of, say, Shakespearean drama; and where meaning is made visible, we are in the realm of allegory.[23] Texts written for the illusionist stage elaborate the old morality technique of personification into a complex of allegorical idioms of character that make the assumed modernization of character a nonlinear development. The taxonomy below is intended to clarify five different possibilities for personification allegory that can be distinguished in these plays: vices and virtues, other personified abstractions, mythological figures, generalized types, historical and literary allusions.

VICES AND VIRTUES

The foundation remains the personified vices and virtues of the morality tradition. *Cenodoxus* features Hypocrisy, Love of Self, Conscience, and Death; Death, the Devil, Sin, Human Nature, and Mankind occur in one Calderón *auto* after another. In a Calderón *auto* typically the Devil or Sin invokes aid from one or more specific Vices like Lust, Envy, or Idolatry. Occasionally Sin herself is the attendant Vice. One also encounters institutional sins like Idolatry, Heresy, Apostasy, and even whole nations and religions (Heathendom, Islam, Synagogue), like, more tentatively, Widow Englande in Bale's *King Johan*. Calderón's Vices are less clownish than those found in English moralities, but the main character often has a clown-servant whose foolishness opens the door to the Vices: Simplicity in *La serpiente de metal*, Free Will in *Psiquis y Cupido*, Thought in *La cena del rey Baltasar*, the almond tree (associated with pleasure) in *La humildad coronada de las plantas*. Jonson seems to stray further afield, but the Vice introduces the antimasque, and usually has a more specific name— for example, the north and east winds in the *Masque of Beauty*, witches in the *Masque of Queens*, Sphinx in *Love Freed*, and so on. These names maintain at least some connection with destructive or outright evil principles. In *A Vision of Delight* the Vice is Fantasy, just as Fancy was one of the Vices in Bale's *King Johan*.

OTHER ABSTRACTIONS

The second class, like the ad hoc allegories in Mantegna's *Minerva Chasing the Vices*, consists simply of abstractions of all sorts that take on human form. Jonson offers, for example, Peace, Wonder, Delight (*Vision of Delight*), Love (*Love Freed*), Fame, Ears, Eyes, Nose (*Time Vindicated*), Euphemus ("of good omen"), and Eucleia ("fair glory") (*Love's Triumph through Callipolis*). In Calderón the human soul is anatomized into Thought, Will, Understanding, Reason, Memory, and the five senses, along with its appropriate qualities, such as Wisdom or Innocence, and the conditions of its being (World, Time, the Seasons, the Days). The soul is no longer a simple battleground for sins and virtues, but a complex body in which Reason and Understanding, Wisdom and Faith, Memory and Free Will all have roles to play. The soul also has an epistemological dimension—the five senses appear repeatedly in Calderón, and also in Jonson. Fame, Memory, Dreams appear in both, and in Bidermann as well (*Vision of Delight, El santo rey Don Fernando, Cenodoxus*). One expects a more complex notion of selfhood in the mimetic drama that begins in the seventeenth century: but, as in the Latinate tragedies, the more complex self appears initially as an assemblage of qualities with their own external existence. They are not yet represented in a single human body that obscures the relations of the parts to one another. The first function of these elaborated languages of allegory is not to deny but to adapt to a more complex notion of the self.

Similar names, though sometimes in foreign languages, occur in secular dramas as well: in Calderón's drama *La vida es sueño* characters really are what their names suggest. The king is named Basilio, from the Greek word for king. Segismundo means, from its German roots, "glorious protector," a role he grows into in the play, and, as a translingual pun, "victor over the world" (from German *siegen* and Spanish *mundo*), which identifies precisely what he achieves in the play. The *gracioso* or clown, Clarín, talks repeatedly about how his name means trumpet and he therefore cannot keep quiet (the normal problem for Calderón's figures with this name). Estrella and Rosaura mean "star" and "rosy aura," respectively, and star and rose are played on repeatedly in the love speeches. Furthermore, when she serves Estrella, Rosaura adopts the name Astraea (the goddess of justice set among the stars). The phonic and semantic resemblance to "Estrella" reflects not only that both women are the promised brides of deceitful Astolfo, but also the

potential alternatives for the ideal queen. Allegory is more than holding
its own here.

The concreteness of allegory becomes a feast for the senses; as a result, the didactic drive toward the invisible becomes ever harder to
maintain, especially for a dramatist like Calderón who served both court
and church. In *El mayor encanto amor*, based on Ovid's rendition of the
Circe episode in the *Odyssey*, he seems to ruminate on the problematic
boundary between celebrating the court and still doing justice to the
religious order that justifies its splendor. Ten years after this play was
staged on a lake in the Gran Retiro park to celebrate the new palace,
Calderón revised it as an *auto*, *Los encantos de la culpa* (1645). In the
court version Ulysses arrives with his crew at Circe's island; learning that
most of his men have fallen prey to the enchantress, he rescues them
with the aid of a magic branch given him by Iris, messenger of Juno. In
the second act Circe lures him to stay by staging a game in which each,
really in love, pretends to pretend to be in love. In the last act Ulysses'
men, frustrated that he has dallied so long with Circe, try to recall him
to his true self by calling him to arms; eventually the shade of Achilles
wakens him from his sleep and he sets off. In a rage Circe stirs up a
storm, which, however, Galatea calms. Ulysses sails off while Circe's
palace collapses, a volcano rises in its place, and nereids and tritons
dance. Circe's magical power of reading the signs of nature in earth, air,
fire, and water is understood as dangerous, indeed evil: in the later version her name is Sin. As lovers playing at being lovers, Ulysses and Circe
spend the second act reading their own meanings into nature, for example, interpreting the significance of a heron that flees from them.
Their game commits them to constant lying, and the objects of the
world have only the meaning imposed on them by the game. Nevertheless, a third of the drama is devoted to the entertainment provided by
these worldly pleasures understood as arbitrary signs. The same theme
is also developed in the comic subplot, in which a magic chest contains
jewels and gold when the first clown, Lebrel, looks in, but a nasty
duenna and dwarf whenever the second one, Clarín, approaches; the
motif suggests that the world is illusory and cannot be fixed, but again,
through a long, entertaining, worldly sequence. Calderón solves the
dilemma with two figures who fix truth in the world, Iris and Galatea,
mythological women who speak for heaven. Iris appears in act 1 as the
richly colored rainbow, but also as a sign—the "flag of peace" (*Obras
completas* 2:1513).[24] Thus natural or worldly signs sanctioned by the traditions of mythology or the Bible are dependable. Calderón amalga-
mates both figures into Iris in the *auto* version because, obviously, the
rainbow is such an important sign after the flood in Genesis. Yet, like
the extreme theatricality of the plot, her bright coloring is emphasized

in both plays: does she really justify the richness and pomp of Calderón's dramatic world as the vehicle of higher truth? The fact that Calderón, like Racine, withdrew from the pleasures of the world at age fifty, took orders, and wrote primarily only *autos* (but also more spectacles for the court), suggests that the problem continued to occupy him.

MYTHOLOGICAL FIGURES

The gap between the splendor of allegory and its abstract message is increased by the third idiom, classical mythology. The Christian equivalents of classical myth were largely set by Renaissance syncretists like Ficino to validate their enthusiasm for Plato, antiquity, and astrology.[25] A fairly standard code emerged: Pallas (Minerva) is virtue, Mercury a mediator of wisdom and grace, Diana purity and divine grace. Venus and Amor or Cupid embody both worldly and divine love—Venus Urania is the harmony of the cosmos, while Amor as divine love becomes the ultimate mediator between God and world, the double of Christ. By the end of the sixteenth century such coding was so accepted that all kinds of classical mythography, including the habit of personifying rivers and countries, could be extended to nonclassical realms without discomfort.

Jonson's mythology is a flexible idiom that pulls allegory into the concrete and empirical as easily as into spiritual realms. In *Pleasure Reconciled to Virtue*, for example, when Comus, "the god of cheer, or the belly" (*Complete Masques* 263) introduces the first antimasque of men dressed as bottles he spans the entire range from god to men to inanimate objects. Comus is obviously Gluttony, even before Hercules, fresh from defeating Antaeus, the son of earth, dismisses his "sty of vice" (ll. 93–94). Mercury, the mediator in this masque, connects Hercules' victory over Comus to that over Antaeus (ll. 163–64) and thereby extends the moral allegory: to defeat the pleasures of worldliness is to overcome the son of earth. Hercules had already chosen Virtue over Pleasure when he conquered Antaeus;[26] now Jonson attaches to it his own elaboration of the myth, in which purified Pleasure becomes the servant of Virtue. England takes its place in the classical realm under the name "Albion," as the son of Neptune in *Neptune's Triumph*. Even more remarkably, Jonson inserts England into the Oedipus myth when "Albion" becomes the answer to the riddle of the sphinx in *Love Freed*. His easy control of mythological language keeps the extension to the nonclassical realm from jarring.

But the ease can be misleading. In the less competent hands of Jonson's successor in the partnership with Inigo Jones, William Davenant, the masques wander among different idioms. His *Brittania Triumphans* (1636), for example, begins in an English village, where Action and Imposture invoke Merlin. After a series of antimasques in hell, Bellerophon arrives in the village riding on Pegasus. Merlin conjures new anti-masques as a "mock Romanza" in the world of Ariosto, then the masque proceeds to a mythological palace of Fame. It returns briefly to Britain, to conclude in the realm of mythology with a triumph of Galatea. Nothing could show more clearly the lack of hierarchy among the idioms of the court masque and the full assimilation of myth. The neoclassicist Jonson seems to have recognized the danger of this too easy assimilation, and so kept pushing his masques toward comedy. Indeed, the court preferred his *The Gypsies Metamorphosed*, with no mythology, to all his other masques (*Complete Masques* 29–32, and Orgel, *Jonsonian Masque* 71–77). Mythology does not automatically confer dignity despite the common presumption about neoclassical tragedy and opera. It is easy to assume that myth was the preferred idiom for the Renaissance and neoclassicism, but it was one of many.

Explicitly Christian writers like Calderón had to use myth more circumspectly.[27] In plays in which Heathendom and Idolatry are common Vices, it is remarkable to cast a celebration of the Eucharist in mythological terms, yet Calderón did, five times (*El divino Jasón, Psiquis y Cupido, Los encantos de la culpa, Andrómeda y Perseo, El divino Orfeo*). Reversing Christian epic, Calderón fills Christian form with classical content (but Christian meaning). Mythological figures rub shoulders with personified abstractions in the dramatis personae and in odd ways in the plots. The pleasure of these plays arises from the ingenious translations of mythical incidents into the Christian context, with generous use of Renaissance neoplatonism, for example, the moly brought to Ulysses to save his men from Circe becomes the sacrament of penitence (*Los encantos de la culpa*), and Orpheus as son of the sun is Christ the son of God (*El divino Orfeo*). Even more ingenious is the translation of the biblical myth into the classical one. Thus in *El divino Orfeo* Eurydice bites into the apple proffered her, and Envy immediately explains he will attach himself to her heels, "as the shadow of her guilt" ("Sombro siendo de su Culpa," *Obras completas* 3:1849). The same *auto* begins by enacting the Creation as the seven days and their associated works are awakened in succession by the singing of Orpheus. Despite the need for circumspection, Calderón achieves an almost magical fluidity.

Myth is legitimated as disguise or theatricality, that is to say, as allegory, to make the identity of divine works more visible. The experimental use of comic allegory to reveal the truth underlying the mimetic plot in *Twelfth Night* is now systematized. Seeking access to the heroine, Human Nature, in *El divino Orfeo*, the Prince of Darkness and Envy accost her attendant, the clown Pleasure, and pretend not to know where they are. Pleasure decides to feed them false information, a "fabula" (*Obras completas* 3:1846), by renaming the creator Orpheus and Human Nature

Eurydice and offering learned interpretations for each. But the names are not just the game of Pleasure, for the Prince of Darkness, like a skeptical commentator, is amazed at their appropriateness and explains the divine truth—the harmony of the cosmos—that underlies even pagan myths (*Obras completas* 3:1847–48). He even creates a classical name for himself under which to enter Pleasure's play of Orpheus. Similar renaming and adoption of roles to gain access to the heroine occur in *Andrómeda y Perseo* (*Obras completas* 3:1697 renaming, *Obras completas* 3:1699 role adopted) and in *Psiquis y Cupido*—

and then, in the allegory	Y pues, en la alegoría
of the concept I have explained,	de este explicado concepto,
I am Cupid and god of love,	soy Cupido y Dios de Amor,
from this moment I want	desde aquel instante quiero
you to be my Psyche.	que seas mi Psiquis. (*Obras completas* 3:352)

This self-conscious theatricality allows free access to classical myth while maintaining the proper distance from it. Pleasure serves Virtue by creating instructive plays. A Horatian fusion of profit and delight is not surprising in Jonson, the ardent classicist, but Calderón, who was considered an enemy by the neoclassicists, elaborates the same position in essentially the same terms. And in both the neoclassical element serves allegorical ends.

Myth raises the stakes in the already problematic tension between allegory and worldliness. Masques were in a very unusual sense about themselves. Some focus on the production of masque itself, such as *Christmas his Masque* or *Neptune's Triumph*, and even a very late example of the genre, when there was scarcely a court left to glorify, Goethe's *Masque of Winter* (1782), written for the minuscule court of Saxe-Weimar, has one of the maskers commenting on who is present and absent in the audience (*Aufzug des Winters*, *Gesamtausgabe* 3:1280–82). Since the most important performers in Stuart and Caroline masques were the members of the court and royal family being idealized, the audience watched not only the performance, but also the king watching the performance (cf. Orgel, *Complete Masques* 32–35 and *Illusion of Power* 9). Especially the mythological allegorical figures were understood to represent the person—queen, prince, king—playing the role or prominently watching it. Wonder fuses with natural presence rather like the double vision of the end of *Twelfth Night*. The allegories of Jonson and Jones still carried enough supernatural aura to glorify a secular referent, not so much as to become embarrassing: only slightly later, the masques Davenant produced for Charles I were already considered inappropriate and overblown. As the tradition was dying out more than a century

and a half later in Weimar, Christoph Martin Wieland and Goethe re-
signed all pretensions to celebrating in their masques anything but the
cultural achievements of their court—that is really, of the masque writers themselves (for example, Goethe's *Maskenzug, 1818* [*Gesamtausgabe*
3:1319–64]), so that the court masque collapses beneath the weight of
its own solipsism.

Calderón's more consistently religious stance, even in his spectacles
for the court, appears to reduce such difficulties but the situation is still
less than simple. His *autos* financed by the city of Madrid were normally
staged several times—before the king, before the Council of Castile, before the city council, before the different councils of state (this practice
varied), and twice to the larger public. Each performance took place before a dais or grandstand constructed for the king or the relevant dignitaries (Shergold, *A History of the Spanish Stage* 426). The public could
also watch the performances for the dignitaries, but only from the side
opposite the grandstand—thus it could see only the backs of the actors,
but had a clear view of the aristocratic spectators (Shergold, *A History of
the Spanish Stage* 452). As at the Stuart court the performance showed
the whole society to itself, but the referent of the allegory was less the
king and court than the moral cosmos. As its representative in the world,
the king participates by analogy in the divine glory revealed in the plays.
Thus the just and merciful divine figures are simultaneously an example
the populace sees being shown to its rulers, and also confirmation of the
order that gives those rulers their exalted place. It is no coincidence
that the court dramatist was also the exclusive purveyor of *autos* to the
city of Madrid from 1648 to 1681 (Shergold, *A History of the Spanish Stage*
454). Like the English masques, Calderón's *autos* thus display the court
to itself, but, because they are open to the religious order on the one
hand and to the lowest social orders on the other, they avoid the solipsism that overtakes masque. And indeed Calderón's *autos* held the stage
until 1712, when their public performance was discontinued on the
grounds that their supernatural demands were indecorous.

Generalized Type

A fourth idiom new to the allegorical tradition in the seventeenth century might best be called types. Calderón's *autos* include numerous figures designated by their social function—for example, Merchant (*La
nave del mercader*), Painter (*El pintor de su deshonra*), Shepherd (*El pastor
fido*), Infanta (*El veneno y la triaca*), Director (*El gran teatro del mundo*),
Father (*El gran mercado del mundo*). The practice is not unknown in
sixteenth-century morality, which often focused on Youth (as in *Mundus
et infans, Lusty Juventus, Wit and Science*). But here such names designate

not the human protagonist (with the exception of Infanta), but Christ or God the Father. A related example is the use of "A Voice" for Death in *El gran teatro del mundo*. While the correlation between myth and meaning was public, dependent as it was on the mythological κοινή of the age, this new phenomenon is not, for the meaning of the types is defined by the context in which they appear. Each of the examples above has a specific conceit that drives its plot, usually with a connection obvious from the title. God is the director of the theatrical troupe in *El gran teatro*, for example. Similar conceits drive the plots of the forty-five or so popular stage comedies with which Calderón began his career. They deal with intrepid young women caught between hypersensitive lovers, brothers, and fathers, all named from the small pool of conventional names like Flora, Leonora, Laura, Leander, Lelio, Fabio. The characters are types only in the most general sense, and the plays depend less on character types than on ingenious manipulation of a small number of conventional plot situations, primarily disguise, hiding people who should not be seen, or arriving home inopportunely. Like the *autos* they can be distinguished primarily by the title conceit—for example, *La dama duende* and *El galán fantasma* depend on people thinking they are seeing supernatural beings; *Casa con dos puertas, mala es de guardar* exploits an extra entrance to the heroine's chambers. The conceit is typically articulated in the last scene of the play, sometimes earlier and repeatedly. Such dramatic conceits are like the extended metaphors in the poetry of the period: they organize the disparate plot elements, whether religious events (creation, fall, redemption, Eucharist) isolated from the larger structure of biblical history or comic plot conventions. Fifteenth-century English dramatists required long cycles to cover the whole of biblical history, and then could only repeat themselves year after year. Calderón's conceits and their dependent allegories of type enable him both to relate the few essential points coherently and also to treat them over and over without repeating himself. In the process, allegory becomes more like metaphor.

Related types appear in Jonson, such as the Cook and Poet who compete in *Neptune's Triumph*. Their allegorical significance is less specific than that of Calderón's figures: they embody the real and the ideal, respectively. But in *Christmas his Masque* Jonson particularizes them: he first personifies the attributes of the Christmas feast—Misrule, Carol, Minced Pie, Gambol, and so on. If not quite social roles as in Calderón, the names are closer to that than to personified psychic capacities and, like social types, operate outside the framework of traditional morality. Their visual attributes, carriers of the allegory, are described in detail. But as he introduces them (*Complete Masques* 239–42) Christmas also maps them onto the types that inhabit Jonson's humor comedies: Carol is a "chirping boy and a kill-pot" whose real name is Kit Cobbler, and Mince Pie is "an honest cook's wife" from Scalding Alley. Jonson's revisions to *Pleasure Reconciled to Virtue* mark a decisive turn toward type in the masque. It was performed at Twelfth Night 1618 to the general dissatisfaction of the court, then restaged the following month with extensive revisions as *For the Honor of Wales*, to somewhat less dissatisfaction (*Complete Masques* 30–31; Orgel, *The Jonsonian Masque* 70–71): the mythological antimasques of Hercules and Comus were replaced by a comic scene burlesquing both the Welsh and Jonson's own failed Twelfth Night masque. Henceforth Jonson's antimasques all involve fully developed comic scenes (*Complete Masques* 32), and the speaking names of the figures in *The Gypsies Metamorphosed* (1621) bring these masques entirely into the ambience of humor comedy, a connection to be noted in terms of set as well (Orgel, *Complete Masques* 34). As Orgel points out, Jonson's revisions to *Pleasure Reconciled to Virtue* did not meet the court's objections to its shortage of dancing and spectacle. Orgel calls Jonson's masque too literary; in my terms it was too mimetic, too focused on Aristotelian coherence and psychology, and too little focused on the allegorical spectacle the court expected. As in *Troilus and Cressida* morality plot migrates naturally toward type comedy (cf. above Chapter 3).

Bidermann's *Cenodoxus* illustrates a different version of the transition from allegorical to comic types. Most of the play is standard morality, in which the title character is pulled between the forces of heaven and the Vices, Hypocrisy and Self-Love. At the climax the protagonist's guardian angel forces the devils to enact Cenodoxus's damnation in a warning dream, but to no avail; after his death Cenodoxus is tried by Christ and damned. Beside this familiar plot, however, runs a Plautine subplot, in which Cenodoxus's clever servant, Dama, drives away the parasite Mariscus. For the clever servant who manages the action appears in virtually every extant play of Plautus and of Terence, while parasites appear, for example, in Plautus's *Captivi* and *Menaechmi*. The situation is like the parallel plots in Shakespeare's comedy, but with the more mimetic material in the lower plot. The parasite suffers from the same vices that attack Cenodoxus, hypocrisy and love of self, but now as character qualities rather than as visible figures; having interiorized the Vice, Mariscus is a type such as we find in Molière. For the rest of the play the baiting of Mariscus by Dama runs parallel to that of Cenodoxus by the Vices. In the first scene Dama tricks him by appealing to his self-love: in the following scenes the Vices begin their attack on Cenodoxus by sending Self-Love to him. Dama later explains Mariscus's rage (which is really at being tricked by Dama) by saying he has been bitten by a mad dog, so that Mariscus is carried off to the madhouse, just as Cenodoxus, finally bitten by the Vices, will be carried off to hell. But Mariscus returns to flatter Cenodoxus anew. In act 3, right after Cenodoxus's warning dream, Dama unleashes a toothless bear on the sleeping Mariscus (the devils in Cenodoxus's dream are toothless in that they serve the will of heaven there). Mariscus calls for help, only to be told he is dreaming and the bear is a ghost sent to punish him, but unlike Cenodoxus, the parasite takes the warning seriously and flees from the play. Bidermann has thus assimilated the mode of Latin comedy in the subplot to the morality mode of the main plot, and thereby given to the Latin comedy an allegorical cast it previously lacked. The moralistic humor comedy of the seventeenth and eighteenth centuries arises here in the blending of classical forms with morality in what is at first a context of heightened allegory.

In *El mágico prodigioso*, a martyr play based on the legend of St. Cyprian, Calderón blends morality and comedy in similar fashion.[28] In the main—morality—plot Cypriano, who avoids paganism in his search for the unknown god, falls in love with the Christian Justina while mediating a dispute over her between two young lovers. In a version of the Faust plot[29] he offers his soul to win her, the devil appears, and Cypriano signs a pact in blood on a piece of linen. When he conjures her with the devil's power she turns into Death in his arms; Cypriano repents and becomes a Christian. When he meets Justina again in prison, she can love him in return and promise his salvation. They are martyred together, and the demon shows the cloth with the pact washed clean by martyrs' blood. But the morality component accounts for only a third of the action. There is also a mimetic plot of love intrigue involving two young men competing for Justina's love (with the devil heightening the confusion); at the center of the play she has three unwanted lovers hidden in various places and an angry father; the two young lovers cause a seemingly interminable series of duels. This plot is the Spanish descendant of Roman comedy, and the heart of Calderón's own intrigue comedies and honor tragedies, although the monotony of the duels suggests they are parodistic here. Finally, there is an actual clown subplot. Cypriano's servant Clarín also wants to make a pact and conjure a beloved, just as the servant of Faustus parodies the magic of his master in Marlowe and as Mariscus parodies Cenodoxus. When Clarín fails, he returns to the city and shares the servant-girl Livia with another servant on alternate days, instead of dueling for her as Justina's lovers do. The name Livia means lasciviousness, the sin of which Justina is falsely accused. The comedy and tone are fully comparable to the clown subplots in Shakespearean comedy.

Calderón's blending of classical and morality plots has a more specific thematic function than in *Cenodoxus*. As Cypriano becomes involved with the devil he becomes increasingly drawn into the activities and values of the mimetic love plot. After he falls in love with Justina he

changes his costume from that of scholar to gallant, and with each succeeding duel he loses status: he mediates the first as the respected elder;
he interrupts the second but plans to win its object for himself; during
the third he is off with the devil learning to force Justina to do his will
and no longer comes into question as a peacemaker. To become involved with the devil is thus to enter the mimetic plot, the comedy of the
world. In order to win free of the world Cypriano's love for Justina must
be transformed from lust, love of her body, to love just of her spiritual
qualities. The two plots thus correspond to the distinction between material and spiritual realities, world and ideal. Calderón has set the two
modes into a readable relation to one another.

Allusions

The final class of allegories in these dramas are allusions. Some are historical, such as Skelton and Scogan in Jonson's *Fortunate Isles,* some from
romance as in *Oberon* or *Prince Henry's Barriers.* Calderón's reach is
broader. Angel Valbuena Prat's classification in his edition of the *autos*
gives some idea of their range:

a) philosophical and theological
b) mythological
c) based on the Old Testament
d) inspired by the New Testament
e) occasional (for example, marriage of Philip IV, inauguration of
    Buen Retiro palace)
f) based on history or legend
g) based on apocryphal material about the Virgin. (*Obras completas*
    3:32–35)

But the specificity of Calderón's model choices is more interesting than
the range. One of his several pastoral *autos* is called *El pastor fido* and
takes Guarini's drama as its vehicle. Calderón even takes commercial
plays of his own and adapts them as *autos.* Some of his most famous
plays, like *La vida es sueño,* and *El pintor de su deshonra* reappear in this
guise. Naming in these plays ranges from abstract to particular; as in the
mythological plays, characters often have two names, the abstract name
of the morality tradition and the particular name from the text at hand.
  Calderón's images, especially, are surprisingly detailed and modern.
He knew how to make the most of traditional allegories—as, for example, in *A María el corazón,* when Sin enters in a chariot pulled by a hydra,
each of whose heads is one of the deadly sins and functions as a separate
character, or, in the same play, when the protagonist, Pilgrim, carries his

heart in his hands after the middle of the play and offers it finally at the altar of the Virgin. At the end of *El divino Orfeo* Orpheus carries Human Nature off to safety in the ship of the church, a traditional allegory. But ships can also be much more up-to-date. At the beginning of *La nave del mercader* Sin arrives as a pirate landing from a galley; her antagonist, the merchant, also arrives by ship, this time a merchant ship. Although the merchant is costumed as an Armenian, his dialogue shows that he belongs to the new class of traders who travel all over the world, old and new, for his ship was entrusted to him by the master on condition that he bring back the riches of the New World:

in the faith	en fe
that I would commit myself to earn for him	de que a granjearle me obligo
the sovereign riches	las soberanas riquezas
of a new world, in which I have heard	de un nuevo mundo, en que he oído
that among much other wealth	que entre otros muchos haberes,
there is a hidden treasure,	hay un tesoro escondido,
a precious pearl	preciosa una margarita
and fruits of infinite	y unos frutos de infinito
worth, which will return	precio, que a ciento por uno
a hundred for one, in the manner of grain;	rendirán, a fuer de trigo;
in the use of which we can	en cuyo empleo podremos
become honored and rich.	quedar honrados y ricos.

(*Obras completas* 3:1450)

The merchant is Christ, and his wealth of golden grain is to be made into the Host, evoked here in the language of discovery.[30] Even more striking are passages in which the Christ figure pulls a gun on the devil (*El veneno y la triaca, Obras completas* 3:194; *El pintor de su deshonra, Obras completas* 3:846). Insofar as this allegory exploits contemporary discourses it is more mimetic than the other idioms we have seen, for eternal truth is expressed here in the language of the temporal material world. One can encounter the same shock in seventeenth-century painting, as when Rembrandt paints biblical subjects in modern dress. In the *Holy Family* in Kassel, for example, only the title and the mysterious frame within the frame identify the family as something other than an ordinary family of the time. The mimesis does not drown out the allegory because of the larger allegorical context, represented by the interior frame in Rembrandt and by Calderón's constant references to allegory within the text, as in these lines of *El pintor de su deshonra:*

So hear henceforth what you do not know,	Pues oye desde aquí lo que no sabes,
for henceforth objects lose their reality	que desde aquí lo Real pierde el objeto
and allegory begins its conceits	y empieza lo Alegórico al concepto.
	(*Obras completas* 3:830)

The examples are too many to list. By incorporating the modern and historical world, whether as realistic detail or as familiar text, Calderón establishes a mutually illuminating and validating connection between the two. The supernatural is more accessible in signs readily appercepti-ble by the audience; but the true significance of modern reality is re-vealed when the eternal patterns implicit in it are brought to light. The wonder of Calderón's *autos* is the expansiveness of their allegorical dis-course, their effortless revelation of the mystery of the Eucharist in the disparate cultural, political, and social materials taken as the starting point—their capacity to show that all roads lead to Rome.

Aristotle and Spectacle

I began by arguing that spectacle on the Baroque stage is itself a form of neoclassicism and will now consider how it connected to Aristotelianism and Senecanism. Calderón's neoclassical critics initiated a tendency to see him as a deeply conservative, perhaps even backward, dramatist and to overlook his own reflections on his place in literary history. To be sure, the allegorical drama considered here was indeed politically con-servative. But the dramaturgy was not, as appears from Lope de Vega's "Arte nuevo de hacer comedias" of 1609 (*Obras selectas* 2:1007–11), a spirited defense of popular Spanish drama. Lope, Calderón's predeces-sor as court dramatist, not only demonstrates thorough knowledge of Aristotelianism and Vitruvianism, but turns them inside out to formu-late his own rules for success on the stage.[31] Only the ultimate triumph of Aristotelianism brands allegory as archaic and regressive.[32]

Calderón was clearly not ignorant about Aristotelianism. In *El mayor encanto amor*, for example, Clarín is transformed into a monkey but re-covers his identity by looking at himself in a mirror. In the main plot meanwhile Ulysses surrenders to Circe in act 2, then is awakened to his true identity by the ghost of Achilles in act 3. The subplot is more con-crete and allegorical than the main plot, as we have learned to expect, yet the mirror is a two-sided image. While it signifies self-reflection, it is often used in the seventeenth and eighteenth centuries to represent the activity of the artist, who imitates nature as apes imitate humans, and thus Aristotelian mimesis.[33] In Ulysses' parallel encounter with the ghost of Achilles, the emphasis lies on remembering and recovering a lost ideal, that is, on a Platonist version of action and creativity. Similarly, *La vida es sueño* begins with outright persiflage on the modality of the play in the famous image of Rosaura's horse as hippogryph:

Violent hippogryph	Hipogrifo violento
who has run races with the wind,	que corriste parejas con el viento,
where, ray without flame,	¿dónde, rayo sin llama,
bird without color, fish without scale,	pájaro sin matiz, pez sin escama,
and beast without natural instinct . . .	y bruto sin instinto natural . . .
	(*Obras completas* 2:501)

Both the hippogryph and the almost formulaic invocation of the elements through light, bird, fish, and beast are widespread in Calderón, but in their brevity here they might be understood to evoke lines much more familiar to Calderón and his audience than even to us, the opening lines of Horace's *Ars poetica*: "Supposing a painter chose to put a human head on a horse's neck, or to spread feathers of various colours over the limbs of several different creatures, or to make what in the upper part is a beautiful woman tail off into a hideous fish, could you help laughing when he showed you his efforts?" (Dorsch, *Classical Literary Criticism* 79). Calderón's hippogryph has the head of a beautiful woman because it is ridden by Rosaura, and its wild body embodies her own wild passion. Thus Calderón begins his play with the monster Horace derides as impossible for poetry and gives it thematic meaning. A few pages later Rosaura responds to Segismundo's first long speech with the Aristotelian formula, "His reasoning has evoked pity and fear in me" ("Temor y piedad en mí / sus razones han causado," *Obras completas* 2:503). But as their encounter proceeds, each is seized with amazement and wonder:[34] the vocabulary of Platonism supersedes that of Aristotle. As Rosaura then pleads for mercy with Clotaldo, Clarín turns her abstract nouns, humility and pride, into capitalized personifications, "personages who have generated and regenerated a thousand *autos sacramentales*" ("Personajes / que han movido y removido / mil autos sacramentales," *Obras completas* 2:504). Calderón seems to reserve the right to operate in all modes.

This language of dramatic form should be connected to the magnificent affirmation of doubleness with which the play ends. Rosaura appears at the end as both male and female, the outward sign of spiritual doubleness. As Rosaura the daughter of Violante (rose, love, daughter of violence) she is closely associated with passion, but as Astraea in act 2 she is the Latin star to Estrella's Spanish one, and, in Segismundo's terms, the sun from which Estrella derives her starlike qualities (*Obras completas* 2:516). Rosaura is the ideal and passion, parallel to Segismundo as man and beast (ibid.). At the end Segismundo affirms that life is dream, that the eternal and temporal must be understood as somehow superimposed. He finally decides to accept the limits of the world, that is, to renounce Rosaura-Astraea and marry Estrella, to give up the sun for the star, or, to give up the classical for the vernacular. But, since life is a dream, Estrella, the star, and the vernacular represent the other pole—Rosaura, the sun, the classical—with all the force of allegory. When the play was rewritten as an *auto*, Rosaura's role was filled by Wisdom as Christ. Even in the early 1630s, virtually from the beginning of his career, Calderón seems deliberately to have incorporated Aristotelian mimesis as an extension of his allegorical practice. While Shakespeare appeared to be experimenting with juxtapositions of various modes, Calderón has settled a generation later into a more reflected and definitive view of their relations: neoclassicism leads first to heightened allegory.

Seneca and Spectacle

If illusionist spectacle could be used to heighten morality drama without hesitation, its application to classical forms was more problematic. It worked fine for the deus ex machina, but since Aristotelians were generally hostile to the supernatural, that was not much help. The Vitruvian strand of neoclassicism was successful in infiltrating Senecan dramatic forms long before it became acceptable to Aristotelians. The last chapter showed how the narrative aspects of Seneca played into Aristotelianism. But, as has already been pointed out, Elizabethan drama, with its stronger allegiance to the allegorical tradition, readily showed onstage the violence that Seneca only described. The Elizabethan stage, however, did not have access to or embrace the full range of spectacular possibilities made available by Vitruvian neoclassicism. On the Continent, however, particularly in Spain, Catholic Germany, and the Netherlands, spectacle brought a whole new aspect of Seneca to bear: Senecan choruses became full-blown interludes (sometimes even musical), ghosts wandered the stage, long monologues were pantomimed in accompanying dumb shows, and sudden changes of atmosphere were staged as instantaneous scene changes. In Calderón and Vondel the blend is achieved so effectively that there is really no point distinguishing between religious and commercial drama for either. In Protestant Germany the issues are easier to grasp, because the strong iconoclastic element in Protestantism made all allegory more problematic.[35] Andreas Gryphius (1616–64) is a good example. Like many German intellectuals of his generation, Gryphius studied in Holland and then visited Italy before settling down as an official in his native Silesia, where his twelve plays and two translations were written as school dramas or for local private aristocratic theaters.[36] Although most of his tragedies were Senecan martyr dramas, I have chosen the one love tragedy, *Cardenio und Celinde,* as the most secular and therefore most distant from religious drama.[37]

The play is based on an Italian ghost story. Cardenio and Olympia were in love, but her family was opposed because of a series of misunderstandings, the worst of which was an uninvited visitor to her bedroom who was taken to be Cardenio. The real culprit, Lysander, admitted his guilt; and because Cardenio's letters failed to reach Olympia she acceded to her father's decision to marry her to Lysander. Feeling betrayed, Cardenio had an affair with Celinde and killed her previous lover in a duel. After summarizing these events to his confidant in the first act, Cardenio announces his intention to punish Lysander. The second act is devoted to Celinde's laments that Cardenio has abandoned her and to her plan to win him back with a magic potion for which she needs the heart of her first lover. The third act shows first Olympia telling how she has given up Cardenio and learned to love the husband given her by God, then Cardenio burning his papers and claiming to have given up all love. As Cardenio lurks outside Olympia's house late at night in act 4, waiting to attack Lysander, a veiled woman calling herself Olympia lures him away. Lysander then returns home to a warm welcome from his wife. The scene shifts to a garden, where Cardenio makes love to the veiled woman. When he asks her to unveil the garden becomes a desert and the figure a skeleton. The scene changes to a churchyard, where Celinde hesitantly approaches the grave of her dead lover. The distraught Cardenio wanders in, finds the corpse of the lover outside the grave and the terrified Celinde inside it. After she convinces him she is not another ghost he helps her out; the corpse returns to the grave, warning the two they have received a lesson from God. In the last act the two of them retell these events to Olympia and Lysander, beg their forgiveness, and retire from the world. The acts are separated by allegorical interludes labeled "Chorus."

How is this play neoclassical? Like the French neoclassicists, German Baroque dramatists wrote prefaces to their plays (and often notes as well) in which they made claims for the historical veracity of their material; this play is no exception, for Gryphius claims it is based on a true story he heard in Italy. There are two additional Aristotelian topoi in the preface: first, Gryphius worries about violating tragic decorum through the use of bourgeois characters and of a ghost from below ("Geist aus dem Grabe") instead of a deus ex machina ("Gott aus dem Gerüste," *Cardenio und Celinde* 8). Both are justified by the claim that they are true; verisimilitude here begins to shade into literal truth (assuming one believes in the literal existence of ghosts). The play itself looks typically Senecan. It is written in six-foot Alexandrine couplets imitated from the Pléïade, probably with Dutch influence, in the familiar mix of long speeches and stichomythy, and full of the familiar violent language and similes. The play observes the unities of action and time, and that of place in the looser sense of staying in the same town. The small cast, long speeches, a gruesome narration, the hero's rage and desire for revenge, the presence of ghosts, and the chorus are all typically Senecan. The strictest Aristotelian drama eschewed choruses in the seventeenth century, but Vondel typically imitated Seneca in ending each act with a chorus. German dramatists of the period often elaborated them into full-scale interludes and thus allowed allegory to thrive in a classical niche.

For despite the Senecan surface, the play is vibrantly allegorical. Consider first the cast: it consists of two couples, Cardenio/Celinde and Olympia/Lysander, a nurse/messenger figure named Tyche, various confidants, and two ghosts. "Cardenio" means in Spanish "livid" or "purple" and suggests rage, his particular sin, and of course the Senecan sin par excellence. Olympia, the object of his rage, is his former beloved who broke her troth to him in obedience to her father and is now married to Lysander. She is named for the abode of the gods. Celinde and Lysander, the new "consorts" of each are the secondary pair; both establish claims on their lovers by shady means, and their names are less obviously evocative, Lysander being an especially conventional comic name. Tyche (or Fortuna in Latin) is the goddess of chance; often depicted standing on a sphere, she signifies the instability of fortune in the world. Act 1 shows Cardenio as a fallen man, 2 shows Celinde lustfully plotting to tempt Cardenio further. Act 3 first displays Olympia as the virtuous wife of Lysander and then Cardenio, whose rage at Olympia is made visible by the fire he feeds with her letters and tokens. In act 4 the fallen man and fallen woman receive vigorous divine warnings, and the meaning of the events is rehearsed in a grand conclave of all the main characters in the last act. Like so many before him, Cardenio must choose between pleasure and virtue.

The tragedy has a remarkable amount in common with Gryphius's Plautine comedy *Horribilicribrifax* (a nonsense name for Gryphius's braggart soldier) as well as with Spanish comedy. Obvious comic motifs in *Cardenio und Celinde* are the two couples whose relationship to each other is disentangled (Olympia assumes at the end that Cardenio and Celinde will marry), doubles and disguise, men hiding in women's rooms, angry fathers, dueling. Like Don Juan Cardenio is ready to pick up any passing woman in the street, and also like him, has a terrifying encounter with a man he wrongly murdered in a churchyard. Perhaps most striking of all, despite all the language of death and the readiness of various characters to sacrifice the lives of themselves and others, the play ends with one couple happily married to each other and the other couple married to the church. Like Catholic school drama, this morality draws also on the forms of comedy.

The implications are concretely visible in the use of setting. Here the use of spectacle in its most restrained Vitruvian, classical sense enhances the allegory by making visible what in normal Senecan drama is only narrated. Acts 1, 3, and 5 take place indoors, in Cardenio's rooms or in Olympia's house, and throughout these acts characters reflect on what has already occurred and plan for the future. The first scene begins, appropriately, "So can your decision not be changed?" ("So ist der Vorsatz denn durch keine Macht zu wenden?"). Acts 2 and 4, by contrast, take place out of doors; this is the space of exposure—to sin, repentance, to tempters, and to ghosts—where things actually happen. While the indoor places are contemporary living quarters, early versions of the elaborately realistic homes in Shaw and Ibsen, the outdoor spaces are familiar from morality (and masque): the garden and the churchyard, the homes of Pleasure and Virtue. And indeed, the pleasure garden ("Lustgarten" is the term) in act 2 is Celinde's, and her goal there is to seduce Cardenio. Perhaps both names begin with C to evoke Circe, as Vices in older moralities had names beginning with the same letter. In the fourth act the use of the set is richer. It begins on the street outside Olympia's house, where Olympia's ghostly double seduces Cardenio away from his intended ambush of Lysander, and the latter is then welcomed home. The second scene shows Cardenio and the ghost in a pleasure garden: the ghost reveals its true form, a skeleton aiming an arrow at Cardenio, and the scene is transformed in an instant into a "horrible desert." As if this were not enough, in the third scene Cardenio encounters Celinde in a grave from which she has displaced an angry corpse. The transformation of the beautiful body to skeleton or corpse is popular in the Baroque; it occurs already in Calderón's Faust play, *El mágico prodigioso* of 1637, and remains popular to this day in horror film, as in Stanley Kubrick's *The Shining*; in Gryphius it still carries here its full allegorical implication—the wages of sin is Death.

More interesting yet is the tension between mimesis and allegory in these two acts. To be sure, the second act evokes Circe in her pleasure garden, but in fact Celinde has already seduced Cardenio, and in act 2 she is plotting to win him back. The real seduction is not of Cardenio, who does not appear onstage in this act, but of Celinde by Tyche, who persuades the young woman, much against her better judgment, to dig up the corpse of her first lover. Tyche operates not with the traditional blandishments of evil, but instead with the voice of reason and science as she first tries to convince Celinde not to commit suicide or to sacrifice her whole life to one faithless lover. In fact she sounds rather like the sensible maid Despina in Mozart's *Così fan tutte,* and only turns to black magic when all reasonable arguments fail. The pleasure garden is no longer Eden poisoned by a serpent, but the kind of place a woman like Celinde would normally sit. The same tension is at work in acts 4 and 5, where the ghostly Olympia is carefully juxtaposed with the real Olympia, and the latter is struck with wonder that she has been "the spirits' disguise" ("der Geister masque," 5.212). In the second half of the act Cardenio has an allegorical encounter with Death in the garden but then meets the real Celinde in a real grave with a real corpse. The second scene is hardly natural in our sense, but on a scale of bodies turning instantly into skeletons or rotting after a few months in the grave, it is certainly more mimetic than the encounter with Death in the pleasure garden. The same is true in psychological terms: the first scene in the pleasure garden could be read as the enactment of a visionary insight, such as Saul experiences on the way to Damascus, and the second as a moment of heightened imagination in which the corpse is believed to move or even speak. The difference is not categorical, but one of scale, and opens the door for further shifts. In the context allegory and classical form do not clash so much as offer choices of how to see.

In this regard the structure of representation in the play is particularly interesting. The first and last acts are strictly verbal: Cardenio narrates his experiences and reflects upon them, although the larger number of listeners in the last shows that Cardenio has entered the socioreligious order as a result of the play. In the three central acts, by contrast, the setting keeps changing and each scene has some specific allegorical meaning—the garden as place of sin, Olympia's house as the proper end of love, the fire in Cardenio's room as the result of improper love, the two supernatural warnings. In the full-blown choral interlude (rather than just spoken commentary) at the end of act 3 Time offers a man each of the seasons to wife in turn, beginning with Spring; the man keeps postponing the decision in hopes of something better and must sorrowfully make do with ugly Winter. This carpe diem allegory comes at almost the exact center of the play. Thus the play consists of two extended Senecan narrations around five allegories. Furthermore, the lengthy analysis of the action of the play in act 5 not only interprets, but even reinterprets some of these images. When Cardenio describes Celinde's siren song and lute playing in his speech at 5.365 he gives her garden in act 2 its proper meaning as a place of lust and luxury (5.367). Both he and Celinde explain at length how they have taken the divine warnings of act 4 to heart and will now retire from the world. Even more important, Olympia, who has otherwise had little to say for herself, explains in the last long speech of the play (5.401–19) that her own beautiful body is only temporary and she is really an ugly old woman, indeed a corpse. This evocation of the succeeding appearances of the seasons in the interlude after act 3 changes the meaning of that scene. It appears in act 3 to signify that one should make the best use of one's time to snatch pleasures before time carries them off. But in Olympia's restatement, one should make use of the fleeting passage of time not to take pleasure, but to prepare for eternity. The basic structure of representation in the play is the special form of allegory known as emblem; it combines visual image with interpretive description. In this play the last act offers the text to the images that have come before, and the unexpected enrichment of the significance of the interlude shows us that the allegoresis is as important in this model as the allegory.

Allegoresis and the Anxiety of Secularization

The emergence of emblem points to a new problem for allegory: as allegorical language becomes more particular and more private it risks becoming hermetic and incomprehensible. Dramatic allegory in the morality tradition was explicit—characters were named what they meant—but with the proliferation of allegorical languages in the seventeenth century, this clarity became harder to achieve. Jonson's mythological allegories depend on a common court culture conversant with the clichés of Renaissance neoplatonism. Calderón, writing for a broader audience, gives many of his figures two names. Thus Psyche is actually Faith under the name of Psyche, Andromeda Human Nature, Ulysses Man. In *El santo rey Don Fernando* (part 2) the characters have historical names (it is more of a saint's play than morality), but the sultana is also identified as Islam. The real tour de force is *La humildad coronada de las plantas*, in which the speaking characters are all trees, with the exception of two angels. Yet the thorn tree is also Jewry, the oak Heresy, the laurel Heathendom, and so on. Calderón's allegory is regularly double, with the morality cast correlated to the cast of mystery, history, myth or another text. His Vices are also typically double: the devil and a more specific Vice with an abstract name like Envy, Idolatry, or Lust. With the same plot obsessively repeated the interest centers increasingly on seeing how the specific allegory works, what its symbols represent, on tracing out the familiar truth in the welter of worldly detail. Allegorical representation becomes allegorical interpretation.

Consequently, these texts contain not only reminders to read allegorically, but also commentaries on their own meaning. Mystery plays and some very early morality plays had expositor-figures who functioned as narrators (like a Shakespearean chorus) or drew the lesson of the play.

In Calderón the interpretation is much more detailed. A few examples from *El pintor de su deshonra*: Sin explains that she cannot hide in the flowers because they signify other flowers which defeat sin, and similarly water and grain represent sacraments that will overcome her (*Obras completas* 3:832); Grace tells the painter he will understand if he turns to the allegory (*Obras completas* 3:838); the painter tosses a plank to Human Nature struggling in the water and when she comes ashore the board momentarily stops Sin from pursuing her—because of the ark painted on it, and pointed out by Sin (*Obras completas* 3:841). Later World fails to recognize the painter (Christ), who remarks, "John will tell you" (*Obras completas* 3:844, the evangelist is otherwise absent from the play). Such allegoresis is essential to masque. Jonson's *Christmas his Masque* consists primarily of explanations of the attributes and therefore identities of Christmas's children. In *Pleasure Reconciled* Comus, the belly, explains his own antimasque to potentially uncomprehending spectators: "I would have a tun now brought in to dance, and so many bottles about him. Ha! You look as if you would make a problem of this. Do you see? Do you see? a problem: why bottles? and why a tun? and why a tun? and why bottles to dance? I say that men that drink hard and serve the belly in any kind of quality . . . are living measures of drink, and can transform themselves, and do every day, to bottles or tuns when they please" (ll. 62–70). When Davenant succeeded Jonson allegoresis disappeared from the text. Instead, Davenant introduces his masques with long explanations of their allegorical program. In effect, the preface and the masque must be taken together like the text and image of emblem, so that the allegorical image does not stand alone.

Allegory has thus become emblematic. Beginning with the appearance of Andrea Alciati's *Emblematum Libellus* in 1531, emblems became a great intellectual fad.[38] An emblem in Alciati consists of three parts—a picture or hieroglyphic, a motto or inscription, and an epigram. The motto and epigram describe and interpret the picture, that is, they reveal its hidden meaning. Indeed, a single image can be diversely expounded. The dolphin curled around the shaft of an anchor, for example, can mean *festina lente* ("make haste slowly") or a prince who seeks the well-being of his subjects. Emblem developed from an interest in hieroglyphics among Renaissance neoplatonists, but the important issue here is the analogy to the development of dramatic allegory.

Allegoresis becomes necessary as even the allegorical substrate in these dramas takes on secular significance. In the honor tragedies, for example, the heroine does not fall, as she does in the moralities, but is raped (*El alcalde de Zalamea*) or murdered on the usually unjustified suspicion of adultery (*El pintor de su deshonra, El médico de su honra*). In the *auto El pintor de su deshonra* Calderón substitutes a biblical fall for the innocent suffering of the heroine; written after the secular play, it seems to correct the lack of justice in the first drama. Among the famous honor plays, only in *La devoción de la cruz* is the heroine allowed to be guilty: she flees a convent to join a lover of whom her father disapproves and who turns out to be her brother. But this is also the only honor play to have a religious, indeed, miraculous ending, as if there were otherwise a danger in reading a complex moral situation without religious allegory. Calderón replaces the explicit religious allegoresis of the *autos* with the images and mottos that serve as titles and that play a larger function than those of Shakespeare's problem comedies. Often the title falls for the first time around the middle of the play as the organizing justification or action of the hero, and the play elaborates the implications and complications of healing one's honor, for example, or of secrecy in insult and vengeance. If the plays are not openly religious, they are nevertheless specifically emblematic, the visible and textual elaborations of mottos.

One indicator of this change in allegory is the changed function of disguise. In the English moralities of the sixteenth century disguise was reserved to the Vice as the visual evidence of his hypocrisy. Disguising was also an important, but not negative, aspect of the mumming that spread in popularity through Europe in the sixteenth century and reached its apex in the Stuart and Caroline court masques of the seventeenth. It enters classicizing drama as a kind of rider onto the adaptation of Latin comedy (as in Odet de Turnèbe's *Les Contens* [ca. 1580], where everyone is in disguise).[39] By the end of the sixteenth century the heroines of Shakespeare's romantic comedies, from *Two Gentlemen of Verona* to *Cymbeline*, combine their usurpation of the clever servant role from Latin comedy with the Vice's deliberate assumption of a disguise. So thoroughly has disguise been detached from the Vice that the motif of disguise spreads to the savior as well, as in Calderón's *Andrómeda y Perseo*, *Psiquis y Cupido*, or *El pastor fido*. Sometimes the disguise is necessary to combat the disguise taken on by the fiend; in *El pastor fido* both the devil and Christ disguise themselves as shepherds. But good and evil characters basically disguise themselves for the same reason: to enter the allegorical vehicle of the play. The demon of *Andrómeda y Perseo* is explicit:

Andromeda she was called	*Andrómeda* la ha llamado
by the voice unknown	la voz de no sé qué tono
. . . .	. . . .
For this reason (because	Con esta cause (porque
as a sea monster	viéndome marino monstruo,
her disguise and my disguise	su disfraz y mi disfraz

converge one with the other,	convengan el uno al otro,
embryo of the foam	embrión de las espumas
and abortion of the waves)	y de las ondas aborto)
I went forth from here wrapped	salí a aqueste sitio envuelto
in scales, fire, fumes and dust.	en ovas, fuego, humo y polvo.

(*Obras completas* 3:1699)

So much disguise severely reduces the legibility of the world. In the moralities of the sixteenth century, all the characters except the Vice are legible in the literal sense—they are what their names say they are. But in these seventeenth-century allegories, nothing is what it seems, everything means something else. And if the world is not readily legible, separating right from wrong becomes difficult. This ethical confusion sets in with the advent of mimesis, as in *King John* and *Julius Caesar*, where phenomena no longer have a clear pointing function. But Calderón's *autos* keep the world legible despite its complexity and uncertainty. By representing the world as a series of ciphers, symbols, allegories, and all the other terms he uses, by laying out the etymologies of the characters' names, however fancifully (for example, *Andrómeda, Obras completas* 3:1697, 1699–1700; *El divino Orfeo, Obras completas* 3:1847, 1848), Calderón shows how so many different discourses—biblical, mythical, pastoral, love tragedy—all tell the same story, and hence how the world is still legible if read properly.

The illegibility of allegory clearly poses problems for the dramatic writer who, by definition, shows everything for the audience to read, and the written word is a problem from the early days of morality drama. *Magnyfycence*, in the early sixteenth century, turns on a forged letter: what guarantees the truth of documents and, by extension, of the play itself? Brutus already doubts the validity of letters thrown in at his window at the end of the sixteenth century in *Julius Caesar*, but in the seventeenth the focus shifts: Cenodoxus's guardian angel strews letters of warning for him, but the protagonist heeds neither the letters nor the warning dream staged for his benefit. Writing and even theater are true but not dependably effective. In *La cena del rey Baltasar* Calderón elaborates this version of the motif. Almost every *auto* contains a long narrative of biblical history from Genesis or Exodus; this one includes, unusually, the story of the tower of Babel. Like Cenodoxus Baltasar receives warnings to desist from his vanity and idolatry—first, in the form of documents Death gives him to read, then in a warning dream. In the final scene the hand comes and writes his doom on the wall in mysterious words—Babel to Baltasar—that can be interpreted only by the prophet Daniel. Calderón thus frames Bidermann's two incidents of reading and interpretation within biblical allusions to the Babel of human language on the one hand and the clarifying language of interpretation by God's prophets on the other. Compared to the sixteenth century the change is dramatic: even if the writing is truthful it is difficult of access, illegible to the layman.

In Calderón's secular plays the epistemological uncertainty is correspondingly greater. The most striking example is Isabel's great set piece in scene 2 of act 3 of *El alcalde de Zalamea,* where she narrates the experience of her rape to her father: she asserts repeatedly that no words can express what she must express. Yet she does find words for the unspeakable, and thereby transforms violence and disorder to the beauty of ordered language. This speech leads to her father's forgiveness (for the sin she has not committed, but that is nevertheless unpardonable in terms of the honor code) and his determined restoration of order in the social realm against apparently impossible odds. In an *auto* this would be the achievement of divine intervention; here human speech and mind force order on the world. And yet the achievement is so patently unlikely, the escape so narrow for both daughter and father, that Isabel's position seems in fact correct: what happens in this play really is beyond human comprehension. In all of these secular dramas, where knowledge is subject to reason, words and signs become extremely problematic, from the confusion of signs and behavior in *El mayor encanto amor,* Cypriano's tortured search for truth in *El mágico prodigioso,* Basilio's misreading of the stars in *La vida es sueño,* to *El alcalde de Zalamea,* where even if Isabel's language imposes order, her father and the commander of the troops have difficulty reading one another as they eat together. And in the honor tragedies (above all *El pintor de su deshonra, El médico de su honra, A secreto agravio, secreta venganza*) the hero must work in the dark and in isolation with misleading clues. Misery arises in Calderón's honor dramas from the fact that his heroes entrust themselves exclusively to their own reason—expressed by the fact that they must always work in secret. Because they are committed only to the secular they end up ignoring virtue for the sake of honor; they kill innocent women and are unable to forgive. For honor in these plays is a secular version of virtue,[40] and as such is elusive in the extreme.

If the world is so difficult to read, allegory becomes problematic. In *El gran teatro del mundo* souls are summoned to perform a play before God in which they are given roles but no scripts. Instead a prompter, the law of grace, reminds them to "do good, for God is God" ("obrar bien, que Dios es Dios," *Obras completas* 3:208). They do not have to read, only listen and obey: faith is blind, as is the neoplatonist love of the divine (Wind, *Pagan Mysteries* 53–71). This theme is explicit in *Psiquis y Cupido.* Psyche's other name is Faith, and Cupid, the Christ figure, wears a veil over his face, because Faith must be blind:

as Faith you must be blind, in believing what you see there is no merit; and so in order to earn merit, I did not want you to see me, but rather to believe blindly whatever I tell you of myself.	ciega has de ser para Fe; en creer lo que se ve, no se merece; y así por darte mérito a ti, no he querido que me veas, sino que ciega me creas, cuanto te diga de mí.

(*Obras completas* 3:355).

Cupid explains faith in typically Catholic language of obligation and merit. But the next exchange invokes the neoplatonist language of mysteries:

FAITH: Then you must speak to me in darkness? CUP: Yes, for Sacred Mysteries must be believed with closed eyes	FE: ¿Luego a oscuros me has de hablar? CUP: Sí, que Misterios Sagrados se han de creer a ojos cerrados. (*Obras completas* 3:355)

Either way, the visual, so richly emphasized in allegorical drama, is necessary only for doubting Thomases and is not the true path of salvation.[41] Here is a fundamental problem with allegory.

Something similar can be seen in Jonson. Despite his neoplatonist aesthetics and desire to arouse wonder, Jonson was engaged in a constant battle with Inigo Jones to control the proliferation of the visual. In *Pleasure Reconciled to Virtue* Pleasure is subordinated to Virtue. Jonson does not seem to associate Pleasure with vision and Virtue with hearing, but the spectacle, the satisfaction of the visual sense, does after all involve all the expense and luxury of the masque. The most important manifestation of Jonson's quarrel with Jones was his insistence on plot to order the sequence of Jones's spectacles; Davenant in fact wrote masques without plots. But Jonson's plots are the staging of the masque itself. *Neptune's Triumph*, where the action is carried by the competition of the cook and the poet, is only the most obvious example; in *Christmas his Masque* the issue is to get the child playing Cupid to say his lines. But masque is, by nature, about itself, in that all the figures explain to the audience that the occasion of the masque is the reason for their presence. When he provides a more obvious, mimetic, explanation of the masque, Jonson obscures this original justification. By emplotting the enactment of the masque in more mimetic terms, Jonson calls into question the more profound and allegorical justification implicit in all masque, and thereby betrays an anxiety similar to Calderón's about the validity of such representations.

Anxiety about the truth of what we see underlies most of the theatrical theme—perhaps the most characteristic motif of the period. How can the world, the space of the body, the physical, the material, be the vehicle to express the truth about the soul, the spiritual, the divine? The discrepancy between world and spirit has always been the problem with allegory (and with religious drama), but in the seventeenth century— under the pressure of secularization? under the pressure of its own exuberant development?—it comes to a head. The theme of drama is explored systematically in *Cenodoxus*. Through the first two acts play is deception and innocence is truth. But in act 3 Cenodoxophylax, the guardian angel, requires the devils to enact the tortures of hell for Cenodoxus so that he (temporarily) repents. Their play is deception, because the devils are only pretending, and unwillingly at that, yet it enacts the literal truth of what the devils will do, and the higher truth of what Cenodoxus ought to do, repent. But this glorification of play is immediately parodied in the scene in which Dama sets a tame bear on the parasite Mariscus. Like the devils in Cenodoxus's dream, the bear will do no harm at the moment; but he evokes the other popular activity that went on in theatrical spaces of the time, bear-baiting, not the higher truth of religion. Ultimately Bidermann closes the gap he has opened with the concept of "exemplum"—as indeed Shakespeare closes the same gap he has opened in the facade of drama with the evil theatrics of Iago when he has Othello propose himself as example at the end. But the problem is more important than the solution. As the juxtaposition at the center of Bidermann's play shows, to justify theater is to justify bear-baiting as well, to accept the secularity and worldliness of the world.

Perhaps nowhere is the theme of theater more problematic in the seventeenth century than in *Hamlet*, written the same year as *Cenodoxus*. The court of Denmark is full of deception from top to bottom, and it all expresses itself in playing roles—Claudius plays the king with all the theatrics of fanfares and cannon every time he drinks, Hamlet can't decide whether to play the prince or the madman (or whether the roles can be distinguished), Gertrude plays the loving wife (or is she now a loving wife and played this role only in her first marriage?), all the way down to Rosencrantz and Guildenstern playing the loving friends. The professional actors are an allegory—an allegoretic allegory—they render visible and interpret what is going on at all levels of this world. And at the play's center Hamlet struggles to perform an effective action and thus truly exist. Whether any of this play can be made significant, made "to be," is its question. The turn from allegory comes not from the pressure of neoclassicism and mimesis per se, but from a situation within itself, a paradox that the increased secularity of the seventeenth century had rendered no longer tolerable.

The problem of legibility dogs all the further history of dramatic allegory, and had to from the moment that dramatic allegory, like emblem, admitted the need for interpretation. For anything that requires interpretation might turn out to be uninterpretable, and its meaning could become altogether inaccessible. This is, indeed, what happened in the nineteenth century when allegory was redefined into symbol. The Romantics idealized the premodern period (which ended sometime in the Renaissance) as a time when the book of Nature was fully legible, when mysterious symbols and hieroglyphics made sense.[42] In his novel *Heinrich von Ofterdingen* of 1801 Novalis (Friedrich von Hardenberg) has his hero find his own biography in a medieval book in a cave: Heinrich recognizes himself but cannot read his own future represented in the images there. Novalis retains the sense that allegory represents some higher truth, but its location underground represents the relocation of truth from the sky to the inside of the self. It has been secularized and psychologized, and in the process rendered unreadable. The German Romantics still value allegory despite, even because of, its illegibility. Others in the period, following the lead of Goethe, substitute the term symbol for the phenomenon I have been pursuing. Two aspects of the term "symbol" relieve some of the pressure of secularization: first, a symbol is by definition incommensurable, so its illegibility ceases to be a problem. Second, a symbol has full literal existence; it is not simply the embodiment of something that exists solely in the abstract. This new description of allegory under the name "symbol" corresponds in large part to the dramatic practice we have been seeing in Calderón—a fact which Goethe implicitly recognized in his extreme enthusiasm for the Spanish dramatist. The "allegory" that Goethe and then Coleridge condemned in contrast to symbol has nothing to do with the great allegories of the seventeenth century, but refers to the debased personifications of the eighteenth. A late step in this increasing illegibility of allegory is Walter Benjamin's tragic view of allegory in *Der Ursprung des deutschen Trauerspiels*, in which he projects back onto the seventeenth century something much more exaggerated than its own anxiety—rather a full-scale mourning for the complete loss of referentiality that characterizes the twentieth-century relation to all representation, allegorical or mimetic. I will return to this crisis in Chapter 7.

Chapter 6

Opera and Dance: The Revival of Greek Tragedy

Despite all the fuss about simplicity and nature, the unbiased reader cannot overlook the fact that the Greek tragedians . . . have a much more elevated, more affected, more operatic diction than we would tolerate on our stage.

—*Wilhelm von Humboldt*[1]

Aristotelian critics of the later seventeenth and eighteenth centuries reserved their most vigorous hostility for the musical stage and have, by and large, successfully excluded opera from the purview of critics and scholars of drama. Nevertheless opera and theatrical dance were neoclassical impulses on a par with Aristotle's *Poetics* and with Vitruvius on the theater. It is well known to musicologists, but not always taken into account by historians of literature, that opera emerged in late sixteenth-century Florence as the rediscovered performance practice of Greek tragedy. Parallel discussions in France in the late sixteenth century led to ballet. Numerous other developments fed into the invention of both.[2] Musically the most important is the development of monodic singing, which was understood to express affect and thus supported the character-oriented neoclassical model. Dramatically the most important is the development of pastoral drama, which synthesized neoplatonist and Aristotelian dramaturgy with morality as the earliest example of the classical impulse apart from direct imitation of particular plays (cf. above, Chapter 3). Opera, especially, also drew from its inception on the spectacular devices of the newly recovered Vitruvian stage. It is hard to imagine a more thoroughly neoclassical pedigree. After describing the emergence of opera and ballet, this chapter analyzes first how they retained their allegorical capacity far longer than other dramatic forms, well into the nineteenth century, and second the mark their special synthesis of the different neoclassicisms left on dramatic form in the eighteenth century in terms of its psychology, formal structure, and use of the supernatural.

The Emergence of Opera and Dance

The idea for a play which would be sung rather than spoken arose from discussions among intellectuals at Florence in the late sixteenth century. Neoplatonism was in fashion, and because music was central to Platonist theories of the harmony of the cosmos, the group was especially interested in the recent emergence of monodic (as opposed to polyphonic) singing. Monody, they realized, shifted the listener's focus from the thematic meaning of the text to the expressiveness of the individual voice.[3] In the fourth book of his *De modis*, which was circulating unpublished beginning in the late 1560s, Girolamo Mei connected the new music to drama with the assertion that ancient tragedy was entirely sung; Vincenzo Galilei transmitted the idea in his *Dialogo della musica antica, et della moderna* of 1581 and connected it to discussions of Arisotle's *Poetics*.[4] Music quickly became connected to the catharsis debate. At the same time, the influence of Vitruvius had established that classical drama involved stage spectacle. Because deus ex machina and other spectacular elements were understood to be ancient, elaborate stage design readily found its place in the new model of ancient drama. The first real opera (a designation about which there is astonishingly little disagreement), *Dafne*, was performed in Florence in 1598. The libretto was by Ottavio Rinuccini, the music (no longer extant) by Jacopo Peri and Jacopo Corsi. Musical settings by Peri and Giulio Romano Caccini of Rinuccini's next opera, *Euridice* (1600, 1602), and Claudio Monteverdi's *Orfeo* (1607), the earliest opera still performed, followed soon after. As Greek tragedy reborn from neoplatonism, Aristotelianism, and the Vitruvian revival, opera was thus multiply neoclassical.

The genre spread rapidly, but its patterns settled only gradually into those familiar today. Opera was taken up in Rome by the Barberini family in the 1630s, who had it performed to large audiences, and then in Venice, where entrepreneurial rather than court performance became the norm.[5] From the numerous extant libretti of the period we know that Venetian opera already connected a written dramatic text with spectacle, dance, and music. As the century progressed, librettists progressed from mythological subjects to history, romance, pastoral, history of the Near East and novellas in their search for novelty (Rosand, *Opera in Seventeenth-Century Venice* 156). Routines became standard that go back through Spanish comedy to pastoral and ultimately Roman comedy. Since finances dictated that the expensive machinery be constantly reused, the increasing pressure to perform ever new material, the emergence of virtuoso singing and the cult of the prima donna in the latter part of the century often combined to overwhelm the coherence of the libretto and music. An evening might consist of only the most spectacular scenes of various operas, three acts of three different operas, or one opera with music by different composers in different acts. Until well into the eighteenth century libretti were recomposed for each run, even if the same composer was still responsible, and the name of the composer was less likely to be preserved than that of the librettist or the stage engineer.

Dance shares opera's neoclassical credentials. The first treatises on dance in the fifteenth century invoke neoplatonist concerns for unity, harmony, and representation of feeling in movement.[6] With the Vitruvian revival and the advent of the illusionist stage, dance became central to court performances, first at Italian courts, and then in French and English court masque, where it was both theatrical and social. Indeed, into the eighteenth century performance dance was simply social dance especially well executed, and manuals of dance made no distinction between the two.[7] The inventors of opera wanted to revive the dancing chorus along with the other aspects of Greek tragedy. In any case dance and opera flourished together because both require that a single voice lead. Indeed, so important was dance to the musical performance arts that the dances identified in the most influential of the early French treatises, Thoinot Arbeau's *Orchésographie* of 1588, dominated musical form through the eighteenth century (Kirstein, *Dance* 156). According to Wye Allanbrook, such dance meters make late eighteenth-century music "pervasively mimetic" (*Rhythmic Gesture in Mozart* 3). Discussions about the relation of music and drama in France in the late sixteenth century led, in explicit imitation of the ancient Greeks as in Italy, to the first highly elaborated ballet (Cohen on Baïf and Beaujoyeulx, *Dance as a Theatre Art* 19). With *Le Ballet des Polonais* at the court of Catherine de Medici in 1573 the primary interest lay for the first time in the dancing figures, and in 1581, in *Le Ballet comique de la Reine* Balthasar de Beaujoyeulx combined dance and drama as more or less equal partners. Furthermore, the raised stage with proscenium arch, which reached France around 1600, made dance more theatrical and dramatic (Kirstein, *Dance* 186). By 1641 dance had evidently come under Aristotelian influence as well, when the influential Michel de Saint-Hubert asserted in his *La manière de composer et de faire réussir les ballets* that audiences should be given a written narration of the performance, rather like an opera libretto, so that they could appreciate the meaning of what they saw (Cohen, *Dance as a Theatre Art* 33–34).

Musical theater spread rapidly all over Europe. Dance was refined as an independent performance art in France under the egis of Louis XIV, himself an excellent dancer, and of his superintendent of the king's music, Jean-Baptiste Lully (1632–87). In collaboration with the leading dramatists of the day—Molière, Corneille, Racine, Quinault—Lully remarried the new ballet to opera as a mimed play, rather than a suite of dances with a tenuous plot, to produce a unique form of lavish mythological opera that gave more prominence to dance, though it was denominated "tragédie en musique." Ballet in France remained closely tied to opera, even as Rameau in the eighteenth century made substantial changes to the musical nature of French opera, and indeed well into the nineteenth century. Musical theater was carried to Spain and to the courts of South Germany as early as 1618 by Italian impresarios and penetrated to Protestant Germany in the second half of the century. The first public opera house outside Italy was established as far away as Hamburg in 1678, where it thrived until 1738. In England, despite an attempt by William Davenant to pass opera off as concert music in the 1650s, opera really became established only in the early eighteenth century when Italian opera swept the London stage. Whether maintained by the court, as in France and Catholic Germany, or by a paying public, as in Venice, Hamburg, or London, opera was the dominant form of theater essentially everywhere by the early eighteenth century. In France spoken drama was sponsored in court theaters; because the patents for such theaters were restricted, virtually all other forms of drama had to involve music.[8] English theaters resisted Italian opera for some four decades after the Restoration, but nevertheless came under heavy pressure from its innovations, as adaptations of Shakespeare involving music, dance, and flying machines attest. In both Protestant and Catholic Germany its only serious competition was school drama. Opera not only took hold in Vienna in the second half of the seventeenth century, but also became part of the lavish Jesuit "imperial plays" (*ludi caesarei*) generously supported by Emperor Leopold I, which drew court and populace alike, and are typically characterized as "Gesamtkunstwerk" (Flemming, *Geschichte des Jesuitentheaters* 117). At the end of the century a permanent court opera theater was established, and by 1709 it was also considered necessary to build a public theater; under the leadership of Josef Anton Stranitzky (1676–1726) this Kärntnertor Theater was so successful with its comic translations and adaptations of the Italian court operas that it regularly drew the court nobility as well as the common populace.[9] From it developed the Viennese tradition of popular comedy and light opera that thrived into the 1930s. By the early eighteenth century, the opera house had become a major center for socializing; the opera itself often became background music for the eating, gambling, and entertaining in boxes rented by the season.[10] There were many more opera houses all over Europe in the eighteenth century than permanent theaters devoted exclusively to spoken drama. There were puppet operas and operas performed at fairs. So popular was the musical stage that theater in Hamburg floundered for decades after the opera closed before a public theater for spoken drama was established. In the eighteenth century, the theater was largely a musical affair; what had begun as the revival of tragedy became in a century popular art for the wealthy and general populace alike.

Allegory and the Emergence of *opera seria*

This preeminently neoclassical genre, rooted as it is in pastoral, has obvious links to morality and to neoplatonist allegory. Dance actually enters the dramatic tradition together with allegory. The devil was the first and most important dancer in medieval drama (Kirstein, *Dance* 77–79), the *Roman de la Rose* describes dances of allegorical figures (Kirstein, *Dance* 92), and saints' plays seem to have developed out of or attached themselves to dances, as the Saint George play did to the Morris dance (Kirstein, *Dance* 95). Sir John Davies's "Orchestra: A Poem of Dauncing" of 1596 offers a full-scale neoplatonist analysis of dance as a figure for the coherent organization of the cosmos ordered by the principle of Love itself, the generative principle of all being.[11] Social dance is an image of the cosmic dance just as earthly love is a stepping stone to love of truth; by transcending itself the poem enacts the neoplatonist dialectic. In the *Ballet comique de la Reine* Circe's magic freezes actors into statues, and thus stops the dance that represents the orderly movement of the cosmos as religious allegory modulates into neoplatonist allegory. Several early operas took moralities instead of classical myths as their plots, the earliest documented being *La sacra rappresentazione di anima e di corpo* (Sacred Play of Soul and Body) of 1600 by Emilio de' Cavalieri, who had previously composed music for *Aminta* and *Il pastor fido*. The Barberinis' operas in Rome included many on saints' lives and moralities with titles like *La vita humana* (Human Life, 1656; Murata, *Operas for the Papal Court* appendix). In Germany Georg Philipp Harsdörffer offered allegorical religious pastorals set to music as the newest in literary taste in his *Frauenzimmergesprächspiele* (Entertainments for Young Ladies) in the 1650s with titles like *Seelewig* (Eternal Soul), *Die Tugendsterne* (The Stars of Virtue, actually an allegorical ballet with machines) and *Von der Welt Eitelkeit* (On the Vanity of the World). More than a century later Mozart's first operatic commission was to set a libretto entitled *Die Schuldigkeit des ersten Gebots* (The Obligation of the First Commandment, 1767); in the following five years he set two *azioni sacre* of Pietro Metastasio, *Betulia liberata* (Judith) and the allegorical *Sogno di Scipione* (Scipio's Dream). When Gary Tomlinson asserts "that opera, through its history, has been a chief staging ground in elite Western culture for a belief in the existence of two worlds" (*Metaphysical Song* 4), the statement is grounded in these literal terms.

Strains with Aristotelianism began very early, especially in opera. The removal of dance from hall floor to proscenium stage in the early seventeenth century seems to have enhanced its mimetic effect. Watched earlier from raised seats and from galleries, the focus in dance had been on the patterns made by the movement of the dancers; watched now from one side, the bodies of the individual dancers took on new importance. But the enhanced realism did not overcome the fundamental lack of verisimilitude that attached to opera. The biggest problem in opera was the questionable realism of singing dialogue. Defenses are frequently found in prefaces to Venetian libretti (although they fall off in after the mid-seventeenth century; Rosand, *Opera in Seventeenth-Century Venice* 58), and in essays and treatises, especially in France and Germany, into the eighteenth (Strohm, *Dramma per Musica* 24; Flaherty, *Opera in the Development of German Critical Thought* esp. 39, 100). The other sore point was lack of coherence. Venetian librettists based their plots on Spanish dramas, romances, and novellas with intricate plots that could not be followed readily without assistance.[12] In the 1640s librettists were already remarking with discomfort on their distance from the prevailing Aristotelian rules, invoking Horace and Italian predecessors like Tasso, propounding questions of antiquity and modernity, sometimes blaming the apparent lack of moral purpose on Horatian pleasure and violation of the rules on music (surveyed in detail by Rosand, *Opera in Seventeenth-Century Venice* 35–58). In the early 1720s Pietro Metastasio (1698–1782) and Apostole Zeno (1668–1750) introduced a much chastened and simplified form of opera libretto that became the standard form until the 1790s and was known as *opera seria*; it was more restrained in its use of supernatural machinery and looked and sounded much more like the tragedies of Racine. The reform turned out to be only the first, as will become clear, for Aristotelians never acknowledged opera as an allied form of neoclassicism and exerted unremitting pressure into the twentieth century for opera to be more probable.

Metastasio was a fine poet and hit on an appealing formula. From the time his libretti began appearing in 1723 until the 1790s he was by far the most frequently set librettist in Europe. His most popular libretto, *Artaserse* (1730), was set more than ninety times, and more than half of the rest at least thirty times. In his classic *History of Italian Literature* in 1871 Francesco De Sanctis laid out clearly the popular nature of Metastasio's drama in two crucial respects: its rootedness in the past in its essentially pastoral nature, on the one hand, and its modern focus on transient emotions (2:835–49). While a few of his libretti are explicitly religious, most draw on ancient history for their subjects. His first success, *Didone abbandonata* (1723), set the pattern. Its plot clearly reflects Metastasio's intent to accommodate to seventeenth-century Aristotelianism. It open as Aeneas struggles to leave his beloved Dido at the command of the gods. Dido's sister, Selene, also loves Aeneas, in secret. Iarbas, king of the

Moors, arrives to woo Dido, but in disguise under the name Arbace. His confidant, Araspe, loves Selene. Dido's confidant, Osmida, resents Aeneas and supports Iarbas in hopes that Carthage will be his reward. Aeneas vacillates; Dido resists the Satanic Iarbas; Araspe woos Selene in vain. As Aeneas departs, Osmida betrays the city to Iarbas, and as the city burns, Dido hurls herself on her own funeral pyre. The stage goes up in flames; then the waters of the harbor cover the burning ruins as fire and water engage in battle. Water triumphs and the whole ends with a marine ballet and a final speech by Neptune. The morality plot (Aeneas between the pleasure of Dido and the virtue of his mission, Dido foiling Iarbas at the cost of her life) and the love plot of Racinian tragedy are both present.[13] Because opera demands generous numbers of bravura arias,[14] visuals, and dance, the resolution is more visible at the end, and the tension between the two plots is more open than in the French tragedies on which it is modeled.

The elements ultimately inherited from morality are perhaps more readily visible than the increased verisimilitude of this plot. The villains are defeated even if the protagonists end tragically, and the marine ballet at the end restores order. The many scene changes and secondary plots (though fewer than previously) raise the question of the unities. But by the standards of its predecessors *Didone* seems highly unified. Compare Joseph Anton Stranitzky's adaptation (in a manuscript dated 1724) for the public theater in Vienna of a late seventeenth-century Italian Iphigenia in Aulis plot, called *Der Tempel Dianae* (Temple of Diana). The dramatis personae begins as follows: "*Toante*, king of Taurica, in love with *Ifigenia*, princess of Aulis under the name of Alinda, in love with *Pilades*, prince of Morocco, Ifigenia's former fiancé and loyal friend of *Orestes*, prince of Aulis and lover of *Clarice*, a daughter of Toante, in love with Orestes. *Teucrus*, son of Toante, believed dead and, under the name Agenor, in love with his sister."[15] Four men in love with two women, four of six characters in disguise (the two listed plus Orestes and Pilades), and all this comes before the supporting figures and the clown plot added to the Italian original by Stranitzky. Against this background Metastasio offered a revolutionary simplification of the action and an approach to Aristotelian unity, and therewith classical verisimilitude.

More important probably than the unity, however, is the function of the arias. Metastasian operas are typically structured in short scenes of recitative followed by an aria in a specific mood. The text for the arias was brief, four to eight lines, but in performance arias were often vastly extended through repetitions and vocal ornamentation added by the singers. Their goal, after all, was to focus attention on themselves and bring the eating, conversation, games, and self-display in the boxes momentarily to a stop while they performed. For an audience that accorded the performance the level of attention often commanded (or not commanded) by television today, the unity of the plot was probably secondary; they tuned in mostly when famous singers stepped front and center to sing. The centrality of aria focused attention more on character than on plot. In this respect it was in full harmony with seventeenth-century Aristotelianism. But the music, attacked by Aristotelians for its lack of verisimilitude, was crucial. For aria developed the "ideal of dramatic identification through the means of music" (Strohm, *Dramma per Musica* 14), increasingly in the course of the century through the musical accompaniment, "which the listeners had learnt to accept as representing the innermost tones of the heart" (ibid.).[16] By 1770 it is obvious to Johann Gottfried Herder in his *Abhandlung über den Ursprung der Sprache* (Treatise on the Origin of Language) that musical tones are the expression of feeling and precede language. Only music can express the "innermost tones of the heart." Metastasian opera was modern in its time for its representation of a subject whose passions are less formulable in words because they are receding inward. Music starts to take over the function performed by the fantastic elaboration of allegorical imagery and spectacle described in the last chapter. The interior subject comes into being in European drama not directly from the influence of Aristotelianism, but through its interaction with spectacular and musical representation.

Orpheus Operas

Since Orpheus was the great singer of classical mythology, the Orpheus plot was central to the tug of war about how opera represents.[17] The following description of several Orpheus operas from the early seventeenth to early nineteenth century illustrates the irregularities of the development, beginning with the first opera still regularly performed, Monteverdi's *Orfeo* of 1607 (text by Alessandro Striggio). *Orfeo* draws on all the different forms of neoclassicism. The focus on love tragedy recalls Senecanism as it would develop in France; the splendor of its opening toccata for the entry of the prince and his train immediately evokes the courtly setting of masque; and the variety of sets, ending with the descent of Apollo and apotheosis of Orfeo, make clear the secular and modern Vitruvian element in the conception. As in pastoral, the mythical plot involves a certain minimal level of mimesis and Aristotelianism. Even without a particular Greek or Senecan model, Striggio's references to "tragedy," "pity and horror" are obviously Aristotelian, as is the deus ex machina ending. Interwoven with these mimetic elements is a large dose of neoplatonist allegory. According to the Spirit of Music the wonder evoked by the opera's music makes the listener long for heavenly music. As in Shakespeare's *King John,* eyes and light are central images: Orfeo sees the ideal mirrored in Euridice's eyes, and at the end Apollo assures him he will find her likeness in the stars. Orfeo descends into the world of darkness and blindness and may look at his beloved only when he has brought her up into the world of light. Plato's myth of the cave in the *Republic* and his account in the *Phaedrus* of the ascent of the soul through the love of beauty to the heights from which it can glimpse the truth stand behind the text. As love leads Orfeo to truth, the literal, physical Euridice can disappear and be replaced by more distant, if not more abstract representations. The same allegory of process emerged in Shakespeare also in the neoplatonist context.

Nevertheless, there is an anomaly: if Euridice is to lead Orfeo to truth why should he be punished for looking at her? The morality plot that still underlies Orfeo's doubt and loss of self-control unrolls in the familiar order happiness, fall, repentance (here doubled), and salvation. Euridice dies of a snake bite (fall) and Orfeo's descent to the underworld is a test of faith in order to redeem her. In effect he has taken her "sin" upon himself, and he repeats it in failing to obey the injunction not to look at her—"You have transgressed and are unworthy of grace," the spirit tells him ("Rott'hai la legge, e se' di grazia indegno," 4.91). Apollo chides him for his excessive grief, "Have you not learned / that no joy here below is eternal?" ("Ancor non sai / Come nulla quaggiù diletta e dura?" 5.73–74) and Orfeo is saved when he submits: "Of so great a father / I would not be a worthy son, / if I did not seek / to follow your loyal counsel" ("Ben di cotanto Padre / Sarei non degno figlio / Se non seguissi / Il tuo fedel consiglio," 5.81–84). Having repented his excesses, he receives salvation from his merciful father in heaven. Like the tragedies of the seventeenth century, *Orfeo* layers more and less mimetic neoclassical gestures over a more allegorical substructure.

The theme is expressed through a sequence of moods rather than by events. *Orfeo* begins with the hero's joy at his approaching marriage, moves in the second act to grief at the news of Euridice's death, in the third to hope and courage, in the fourth act to doubt and loss of self-control, and in the fifth from grief to joy. The emotions are all Orfeo's, and indeed there is a noticeable absence of interaction between the characters. The actions shown on stage boil down to Orfeo singing his way into Hades, Orfeo turning to look at Euridice, and Orfeo carried to heaven by Apollo. In act 3 Orfeo gains entry to Hades by singing Charon to sleep, but he also reduces himself to tears. This individuality, even self-reflexiveness, of emotion corresponds to the individuality of the monodic declaiming voice in the new dramatic recitative released from the network of polyphonic harmony. Although the minimal activity on stage is typical of allegory, it does take on a weirdly Aristotelian dimension: the central action, Orfeo's turn, is a literal peripety, precisely what one expects at the center of an Aristotelian plot. So Striggio's text repeatedly interprets itself to clarify its allegorical status—the Spirit of Music explains her presence in the prologue, for example, or Hope explains why she cannot accompany Orfeo into hell in act 3, and the chorus at the end of this act interprets the significance of Orfeo's victory; similarly in act 4 the chorus interprets Orfeo's turn back. The focus on individual and mood also makes the plot strikingly disconnected. To the extent that disjointedness suggests lack of mimesis, it also points to the allegorical nature of the text—what matters is the theme and mood, not action. The incoherence of the plot thus stems from its wealth of opportunities, the entanglement of its concern for representing passions with its allegorical basis. The embarrassment of riches will dog opera into the twentieth century.

The earliest Spanish libretto to which the music is still extant was by Calderón. He never wrote an Orpheus opera, but he did treat the myth in one of the most operatic of his *autos sacramentales, El divino Orfeo* (1663). Like Monteverdi, Calderón makes Orfeo the son of God. Orfeo marries Human Nature/Euridice and installs her in his garden, where she succumbs to the temptations of the Prince of Darkness and is stung by a serpent as she plucks the apple. The sin renders her subject to Death, who carries her across the river Lethe in his boat. Orfeo descends with his cross-shaped harp and sends her to safety in the ship of the church. The morality discourse that was obscured by the neoplatonism of Striggio (and before him the pastoralists) is more explicit here. But Calderón is also lavishly operatic. Three of the four carts (in effect movable sets) for *El divino Orfeo* called for waves with sea monsters or fish swimming in them, a favorite motif in opera; in the second scene Orfeo sings the world into being and as each day awakens the appropriate scenery comes into view. The text calls not just for inserted songs, as is common in the *autos*, but for full-fledged operatic performance with sung recitative ("cantado in estilo recitativo," *Obras completas* 3:1840).[18] Like most of the *autos* this one has an extant *loa*, or masquelike introduction in music and dance: eleven dancers enter in sequence, each with a letter signifying a particular virtue about which they sing. As they dance the letters are rearranged to spell "EUCHARISTIA," then "CITHARA IESU." They explain the anagram as follows: the myth of Orpheus is "allegorized into the universal redemption" ("alegorizado a esta / universal Redención," *Obras completas* 3:1839) and the zither or harp of Jesus is really the Cross. With *Orfeo* Calderón does not just engage myth as a form of allegory, but enriches the entire genre of religious morality with the techniques of opera. At the same time, the increased secularity and worldliness of opera requires even more elaborate allegoresis, in which the very words must be made visible and then discussed. The two forms enrich one another.

In France the development toward enhanced subjectivity was very uneven as the emphasis on dance offered other possibilities. Lully also never wrote an Orpheus opera, but in his *Alceste, ou Le triomphe d'Alcide* of 1674 Lully devotes an entire act to Alcide's (that is, Hercules') descent to fetch Alceste from the underworld after she has given up her life to save that of her husband Admète. Alcide first crosses the Styx in a comic scene in which he is too heavy for the boat; when he arrives at the court of Pluton a fete with music and dance is in progress to welcome Alceste. Alcide makes his request politely, if not pathetically, in a concise speech, receives an equally civil, concise reply that none can resist the power of love, and departs with Alceste. As is typical of Lully, the plotting is a little mechanical and proper courtly conduct takes precedence over any feelings or passions characters may experience. The focus is all on celebration of the court and its king, figured here as Alcide, through music, dance, and spectacle in the ultimate development of the masque tradition.

Yet only a decade later Marc-Antoine Charpentier's (1643–1704) *La descente d'Orphée aux enfers* (1685–86), a chamber opera in two acts, uses the same form to very different effect. The first act resumes the familiar range of possibilities:

pastoral: nymphs sing and dance with Euridice;
morality: Euridice is stung by a snake while she gathers flowers and
     her companion moralizes that "even the most fastidious cannot
     avoid the thorns when they play with flowers" ("Et les plus fines /
     Ne peuvent éviter la pointe des épines / En se jouant avec les fleurs,"
     1.1); similarly, the arrival of Orphée to witness Euridice's death in-
     stead of Monteverdi's Senecan messenger makes all significant ac-
     tion visible;
Greek tragedy: Apollo prevents Orphée's suicide;
Baroque tragedy: Orphée is cast by Apollo as the hero who is to tame
     the "tyrant of hell" ("tyran des Enfers," 1.3).

But the second act is more concerned with feeling. Orphée is greeted at the beginning of the second act not by Charon, but by a trio of famous criminals ("fameux coupables"), Ixion, Tantale, and Titye, and they beg him for pity; this looks like the hell of the morality tradition. The classical hell was, to be sure, a place where spectacular guilt was punished, but the function is not explicit in the Orpheus myth, and remains subliminal in most versions of the theme. In any case, these sinners neither expect nor receive the salvation brought to hell by Calderón's Orfeo.

Instead, they and a chorus of spirits are grateful for the temporary relief afforded by his singing. Framed by dancing at Pluton's court, Orphée's plea for Euridice's release is much elaborated over Monteverdi's and Lully's simple scenes. Instead of one plea, Orphée makes three separate ones. First, in the morality/masque mode he begs to be rewarded for his constancy ("feux constants"). When that fails he appeals to Pluton as the tyrant, arguing that even if Euridice is released now, she will eventually die and his law will be fulfilled. Pluton is moved almost to tears, and Orphée then invokes the beauty of Proserpine's eyes. While Monteverdi's neoplatonist emphasis on Euridice's eyes may haunt this reference, in the context the focus is more on the emotional identity between Pluton and Orphée—both are lovers. Love intercedes not allegorically, but psychologically. The god accedes to the request, sets his famous condition, and disappears. By making the god share human feelings, Orphée not only wins back his beloved, but makes the gods vanish altogether. The chorus then laments the departure not of their ruler, but of Orphée who has given them such relief from pain. In a final twist the trio of criminals returns to remind the chorus that even if Orphée's music has departed, the memory of it will be joy. Not only is music tied to human emotion, as in Monteverdi, but the emotion it arouses replaces the salvation brought by Calderón's Orfeo. And that salvation is not an external event, but fully internalized, the memory of the feelings he aroused. And so the phantoms dance.

But again, the development is hardly linear. In 1733 Jean-Philippe Rameau (1683–1764), the leading composer of French opera two generations after Lully, inserted an underworld scene almost as mechanical as Lully's into his *Hippolyte et Aricie*: here Thésée requests release because of his constancy to his friend Pirithoüs (who sought to abduct Proserpine!) and receives it through the intervention of Neptune (rather than Love). It seems hard to believe that Rameau's opera takes off from Racine's *Phèdre*, where Thésée's adventures in the underworld are confined to narrations, and that it was first performed ten years after Metastasio's initial success. Georg Philipp Telemann's (1681–1767) *Orpheus, oder Die wunderbare Beständigkeit der Liebe* (The Marvelous Constancy of Love, 1726, 1736), despite its title, eliminates as much of the supernatural as it can. Based on a libretto by Michel du Boullay that was first set by Louis Lully, Telemann creates a trilingual pastiche of *opera seria, tragédie lyrique,* and *Singspiel,* in which singers change languages depending upon the musical form being used. In this version the rather Senecan Queen Orasia murders Euridice out of jealousy to win Orpheus back to herself and her court. Orpheus descends to hell at the suggestion of his confidant, Eurimedes (who engages in his own modest love chase of a snippy nymph in the French style). Pluto appears as the tyrant moved to generosity despite himself.[19] After a single aria in which Opheus invokes the argument that Euridice will die and return to the underworld anyway, Pluto agrees to release her and releases all the "martyred souls" from their torment. As Orpheus departs, Pluto's servant sends the souls back to their suffering, with no hint of the memory or continuity of subject in Charpentier. By now such scenes seem distinctly archaic, yet they do not seem intended to undermine the seriousness of the larger endeavor.

To anticipate later developments: by the mid-eighteenth century it becomes harder to identify the religious or neoplatonist substrate in Orpheus operas. In Christoph Willibald Gluck's (1714–87) and Ranieri de' Calzabigi's (1714–95) *Orfeo* of 1762, Euridice is dead when the opera begins; her "fall" has disappeared. She is now a real woman rather than a mirror of the ideal, there are no gods in the underworld, and Monteverdi's allegories of Music and Hope have vanished, as has Apollo. Jove is referred to but never appears. The sole remaining allegorical figure is Amor, the longest surviving of the classical deities. Although the old structure of fall (here the loss of Euridice), testing, fall, repentance, salvation remains, its meaning is unclear. Orfeo is tested, but the issue is not his self-control nor his faith in God or in the ideal: instead, it is the strength of his love for Euridice, whom he addresses constantly as wife and spouse. In Monteverdi, Hope leads Orfeo to the gates of hell, but Calzabigi's Amor appears only after Orfeo states his intention to rescue Euridice: he is a projection of Orfeo's inner feeling rather than an independent component of the self with its own relation to the cosmos. Thus the rhetoric of the libretto undermines his allegorical existence. In act 2 Orfeo says the fire in his heart is worse than the flames of hell; since no flames of hell are shown on stage, hellfire is no longer an allegory, but a metaphor.

In exchange psychological interest is much enhanced, and now in Aristotelian terms. The point at which Orfeo looks back, the literal peripety, is much elaborated over Monteverdi and Telemann (no such scene survives in Charpentier). In the first it is motivated by a noise behind the curtain and Euridice speaks to Orfeo only after he has turned; in the second Euridice first thanks the spirits for keeping them in darkness so that they cannot see one another, but as soon as Orfeo steps out into the light (that is, leaves the spirit world) he panics that he can no longer her and turns. In Gluck the two argue from emotions that they cannot communicate to one another. Euridice thinks Orfeo no longer loves her, while Orfeo has separate knowledge of the condition stated by Amor to him alone in act 1 that he may neither look at her nor explain himself. As a result, Orfeo must argue not only with Euridice but also with himself. The psychology is more obviously mimetic.

In Gluck's successors the turning scene continues to be the focus for motivation and human-centered action. The preface to Charlotte Dorothea Biehl's *Singspiel Orpheus og Eurydike* (1786, adapted from Calzabigi and set by Johann Gottlieb Naumann [1741–1801]) expresses admiration for Calzabigi's libretto, but takes issue with the motivation for Orpheus's turn on the grounds of psychological verisimilitude: objecting to Euridice's indecorous jealousy in Gluck, Biehl substitutes a difference in Euridice's and Orpheus's understanding of the stricture laid upon them. The result is a surprisingly modern "miscommunication." In 1807 Friedrich August Kanne (1778–1833), in his grand opera *Orpheus*, opts for even more trivial realism: Euridice says "We're safe" just a moment before she steps out into the light and Orpheus turns. Monteverdi's *Orfeo* generated a sense of an interiorized subject through its disjointedness; these texts offer a more continuous, rationalist psychology to accompany the emotions represented in the music. Furthermore, one might expect that, at the height of the Enlightenment and later, Orpheus would have disappeared from the stage or, at least, recovered the tragic end of the original myth, in which Orpheus is torn to pieces by raging Maenads; but neither alternative came to pass. Neither the enhancements to verisimilitude nor the more Aristotelian plot has any impact on the end. All three persist in the happy end brought on by divine authority instantiated either in a deus ex machina—not Aristotle's preferred ending—or the lightly veiled alternative, a priest of Apollo in the opera of 1786. Kanne especially seems to go to great lengths to set off his happy ending by leading into it through the deaths of both Euridice and Orpheus, who is struck by lightning; only then does Apollo descend to rescue both. However strongly the taste for Aristotle's dramatic reversal established itself, it was unable to overcome the need to affirm cosmic order inherited from morality. Even in the late eighteenth century, the advance toward Aristotelian mimesis remains very uneven.

The outline of the general development toward personal and private relationships, psychological rather than religious categories can be readily discerned from these descriptions. But more striking is the range of opera, as it draws on all the forms of neoclassicism discussed to date. Each opera considered here draws in varying degrees on morality, neoplatonism, Seneca, visible spectacle, dance, and music. For the first century or so of its development opera frequently served and even enhanced allegorical representation, both religious and, especially in its exploitation of dance, social and political. It also performed many different social functions: public religion, public glorification of the court, celebration of the court as an esoteric unity, private and bourgeois family values. The musical aspect began as the marker of Greek performance practice and therefore of opera's claim to a classical heritage; it became, perhaps as early as Charpentier, but certainly in the eighteenth century, the carrier and sign of a modern interior subjectivity independent of the religious framework within which it began. By the 1770s music was the fundament of all emotional expression, including language. As a result no mimetic drama could do without it either, as the next chapter will show.

Opera and Enlightenment Tragedy

For the remainder of the chapter I reverse the focus to consider the impact of the musical stage, now established in its own right, on spoken drama. Opera struggled from its birth to be acknowledged as tragedy, the queen of dramatic genres for Aristotelians, and perhaps at no time more so than in the eighteenth century, when the two competed for the legitimate stage. However, the struggle obscures the true nature of eighteenth-century tragedy. French neoclassical criticism cast tragedy in strictly Aristotelian terms, but it was already hybrid in the seventeenth century and actually developed along lines very similar to opera libretto. The music, dancing, and flying machines in late seventeenth-century adaptions of Shakespeare make clear how serious drama came to be so operatic, and close analysis of Dryden and even Otway would lead to the same conclusions that follow from the comparison of tragedies by Addison and then Voltaire to *opera seria* below. I have chosen as typical examples Joseph Addison's *Cato* (1716) and Voltaire's *Olympie* (1762), whose unhappy ending seems to distinguish it sharply from opera, but the same argument could be made about essentially any serious play from the late seventeenth to the mid-eighteenth century. Opera libretto and drama are not categorically different genres in the eighteenth century; they are essentially the same thing. A separate section will address the question of the *lieto fine* (happy ending) that dogs opera, again in its relation to spoken drama.

Regarded as the model neoclassical tragedy in England and Germany, *Cato* juxtaposes the love affairs of his children to state affairs, Cato's struggle against Caesar: his two sons compete for the love of Lucia, while his daughter Marcia loves the Numidian prince Juba, apparently in vain because Cato, defender of republican virtue, refuses to marry his daughter to a king. This blank-verse drama consists of the essentially static characterization with specific moods, constant astonishing reversals, and also arialike speeches (for example, 2.6.48–57, which contains first emotional reaction then the generalizing simile) typical of Metastasio. In fact, Addison, most famous as the genial essayist and moving spirit of the *Spectator* and the *Tatler*, began his dramatic career with an opera libretto. How close *Cato* is to opera in his dramaturgy has been

masked by his obvious efforts to integrate Shakespearean themes, motifs, gestures, and even language into his correct classical forms. Thus
the play combines unity of place, dramatic opening of the doors at the
end, general avoidance of action onstage, on the one hand, with typical
Shakespearean effects like the reflective scene on Plato in act 5, the
scene in which Juba listens in on Marcia that looks at first like the tragic
misprisions typical of *Othello* (4.3), and the general rhythm of short
scenes in act 4. But Addison's *Cato* is actually less Aristotelian than
Metastasio's libretti.

Metastasio's *Catone in Utica* (1728) provides a helpful point of comparison. Like Addison's *Cato* it involves both love and political intrigue.
Cato's daughter Marzia loves her family's worst enemy, in this case Julius
Caesar, against whom there is a separate conspiracy led by the widow of
Pompey. The text ends not with death, but with the mutual regretful ac-
quiescence of the lovers to the demands of father and of state. Metastasio's original ending, in which Marzia expresses not regret at losing her
lover, but rage at him and obedience to her father's harshly expressed
commands that she should marry a man she does not love, was jeered
off the stage. Thus the revised ending was perceived as a positive resolution.[20] Addison's *Cato* has a more complex plot, for there are two young
women caught between a desired and an undesired suitor (as in
Stranitzky!)—Cato's daughter Marcia between Juba and Sempronius,
and Lucia loved by Cato's two sons. The issue is less the father's approval
or disapproval than the inappropriateness of thinking about love in
Cato's tragic circumstances and, in the case of Lucia, sowing tragic disorder in family and camp. In the manner of seventeenth-century opera
and of much of the Spanish drama from which its plots derived, the
two women end up with the right husband at the end, even though
Cato himself is dying—a comic resolution Metastasio does not permit.
Furthermore, the destruction of Sempronius, the villain who wants to
abduct Marcia, comes about through the motif of disguise, common
in the splendor of seventeenth-century morality and opera (and still
alive and well in Mozart's greatest operas, *Le nozze di Figaro* and *Don Giovanni*). In this case Sempronius disguises himself as Juba, the man Marcia really loves; Juba happens along as Sempronius slinks toward her
room and kills the villain. Recognizing only his clothes, Marcia mourns
the supposed death of her lover, and in overhearing her, Juba learns for
the first time that the woman he idolizes also loves him. Such sentimental comedy was beneath Metastasio's dignity.

With this background, I will consider Voltaire's *Olympie*, written almost
fifty years later, and more fully in the French Aristotelian tradition. The
plot is complicated. Fifteen years before the day of the play, youthful
Cassandre had been used as a tool by his father and others to murder

Alexandre, king of all Asia, and in the ensuing struggle thought he had killed Queen Statira. But unknown to Cassandre Statira survived and serves as priestess in Ephesus. Cassandre repented immediately, spared his victim's infant daughter, and has lovingly reared her as the slave Olympie. Act 1 opens in Ephesus on the wedding day of Olympie to Cassandre, now king of Macedonia. The two love one another, and Cassandre also hopes by this act to atone for his unintended crimes, even though Olympie remains ignorant of her true identity. But his putative friend, Antigone, king of part of Asia and one of the earlier - coconspirators against Alexandre, guesses Olympie's identity and desires her for himself. In act 2 Statira's duties as priestess bring her to Olympie, their hidden identities are revealed, and Statira forbids her daughter to marry Cassandre, the family's worst enemy. In act 3 Antigone persuades Statira to promise Olympie to him. In act 4 the men prepare to fight. Olympie dutifully agrees to renounce Cassandre but prefers being a priestess to marrying Antigone. Cassandre cannot persuade her to flee with him, even though she still loves him. A battle ensues, Statira mistakenly thinks Cassandre has won, and commits suicide; her last words enjoin Olympie to marry Antigone. Pressed by the lovers and the priests in act 5, Olympie promises to announce her decision at her mother's funeral. There she states her dilemma, stabs herself, and plunges onto the already-burning pyre. Cassandre stabs himself.

The play seems to follow all the rules for tragedy. Voltaire points out the most important qualities of Aristotelian drama—verisimilitude, terror, and pity—in footnotes at various points (*Oeuvres complètes* 6:151 [verisimilitude], 107 and 115 [terror and pity]). The unities of time, action, and place are conspicuously observed. The play has no subplots and takes place between morning and late afternoon on the porch of the temple in Ephesus; for a few scenes the temple doors are opened.[21] Peripety and anagnorisis, or recognition, abound:[22] friend Antigone turns rival, Statira is discovered to be alive, Olympie cannot marry Cassandre but is promised to Antigone, Statira dies unexpectedly and mistakenly (reversing the earlier peripety), and Olympie unexpectedly commits suicide; Cassandre recognizes his guilt in his first speech,[23] and Olympie recognizes her true identity in act 2. Then, as in Voltaire's earlier tragedy, *Mérope*, thunder and earthquake indicate divine displeasure as a formulaic stand-in for a deus ex machina (see *Sémiraris*, where Voltaire uses a ghost similarly but more extensively, and justifies it at length in his preface). Although the gods intervene in act 2 to initiate the process of mutual recognition by mother and daughter, they do not actually cause it: the divine sign seems simply a generic marker. A messenger reports the death of Statira at the end of act 4, and the opening doors are equally classical, since they were the only movable item on the classical stage and used by Seneca and the Greeks to great revelatory effect at the denouement. Here doors open to reveal Cassandre and Olympie making wedding vows in act 1, to reveal the secrets of the women's identities in act 3, and to reveal Olympie's heroic suicide in act 5. Peripety, anagnorisis, deus ex machina, the opening of the doors are all events that come in the second half of a proper (Aristotelian) tragedy. Peripety should come in the third act, the messenger should come at the end of the fourth act, and the rest in the denouement. But in this play they mostly come before the middle of the play; and the doors open repeatedly. It is almost as if Voltaire had a list of classical gestures to show he was playing by the rules.

Yet behind this classical facade the old morality plot organizes the action. Cassandre's fall and most of his repentance have taken place before the play begins. Now that he wants to repair his crime by restoring Olympie to the throne to which she was born, his good intentions are foiled by the plotting Vices, Antigone and Statira, who is not only a Senecan fury, but also, as a woman specifically hostile to Christian behavior, Sin, an ally often summoned to the stage at the call of the Devil in Calderón's *autos*. Voltaire has displaced the revelation of identity between mother and daughter from its more common position at the end of a romance (like Shakespeare's *Pericles*) to the second act: as in Racine, coincidence replaces the supernatural and Devil/Antigone does not have to summon assistance explicitly. Cassandre's atonement becomes increasingly the equivalent of keeping faith with Olympie; his death at her pyre is the final moment of divine justice as he avenges upon himself the crimes he has unwillingly committed against her family. Love covers for religion.

With Olympie the morality paradigm becomes more complex. On the one hand, she must choose between the good and the bad lover, as the soul must do so often in Calderón. But on the other, she must also choose between the man she loves, Cassandre the good lover, and being a priestess. The allegory is slightly weakened, in that the good lover is not Christ but the celibacy that marriage to Christ represents. Nevertheless, Cassandre reverses value from good alternative to bad one with the shift. For he now represents pleasure—what she wants—and the alternative duty or virtue, since it would be wrong to marry her father's murderer. This is actually the dilemma of Chimène in Corneille's *Cid,* and behind her, of Hercules choosing between Pleasure and Virtue in court masque. Furthermore, virtue itself has two versions tied to morality: first, Olympie tries to choose eternal celibacy as a priestess, and second, when that fails, a death that looks very much like martyrdom, for she dies keeping faith with virtue. The ending in fact looks back to plays like Calderón's *El mágico prodigioso* where the two lovers are joined in a martyr's death and their salvation is proclaimed by the Devil even as their bodies are displayed. Indeed, Voltaire asserts the play's piety to d'Alembert (cited Voltaire, *Oeuvres complètes* 6:93) and in his note to 2.2 (6:115). His note to 3.2 (6:127–30) contains such a savage attack on *Athalie* as to suggest he sought to supersede Racine even on the terrain of religious drama. These may seem odd assertions about a figure as hostile to organized religion as Voltaire, and the ironic undertones are not to be underestimated in the assertions just cited. After all, in the best of all possible worlds the purity of Olympie's and Cassandre's love for one another ought to be rewarded; it is after all tragic in the terms of the play that they cannot be united except in death. Voltaire's allusive recapitulation and proliferation of morality forms of the seventeenth century still functions, like morality drama from its beginnings, in the service of religious controversy. To be sure, it no longer seeks to validate the institutional structure of the church, as in Calderón; instead it attacks the very system from which morality derived its validity. By the mid-eighteenth century the form seems to have outlasted its meaning.

Yet the affinities to *opera seria* are striking. Indeed, this play may have been forgotten because it was more libretto than tragedy. But I selected it as a test case for the relation of tragedy to opera precisely because it was successful in its day, considered by Voltaire one of his best tragedies (6:94), and seemed on first reading the least operatic of Voltaire's plays. In his preface to *Sémiramis* Voltaire argues that Metastasio's libretti represent the closest approach in European culture to the tragedy of the ancients and, except for the sung arias, are an entirely suitable equivalent. While he may have had doubts as to whether contemporary Europe should be re-creating Greek tragedy, he does not seem to have perceived any gap between Metastasio's efforts and his own. The Hellenistic setting and romantic plot situation with obscured identities were widespread in opera before Metastasio and survived his reform intended to make opera more neoclassical and "dramatic." As in opera, the plot of *Olympie* is driven exclusively by the givens of the situation; nothing the characters do or say to one another has any effect. Antigone, supposedly Cassandre's friend, suspects him of a secret in the first scene and is thus already not his friend before the play begins. None of Cassandre's remorse or generosity to Olympie affects Statira's hate for him. Olympie is equally steadfast in her love; the new duty to hate Cassandre is simply added to her old one to love him. Although the outcome requires Olympie to choose between the lovers, we never see the process of her choice, which in fact she never makes. Tellingly, there is no stichomythic debate, because there is no back and forth. The pattern corresponds rather to *opera seria*, which shows the varying emotions of the different characters in their situations, not their development.

In fact, this play is more static than good *opera seria* because the situation is not even perceived as a fate to be resisted or even suffered. One does find fate and something close to stichomythy (it doesn't correspond to formal line divisions and is not associated with debate) in Metastasio. In that respect this play, like so much Enlightenment tragedy (especially Addison's *Cato*) is actually more archaic, that is, less classical, than Metastasio. Voltaire is also more static because he did not have to provide a range of arias to show off extremes of vocal skills. Thus the behavior and tone of the characters is predictable from the start, and indeed conforms to the normal character types of *opera seria*—Statira is the raging fury (like Cornelia in Handel's *Giulio Cesare* and Donna Elvira in *Don Giovanni*), Olympie the virtuous heroine always balances love and duty (Metastasio's *Didone abbandonata* is a more interesting version, or his Cleonice in *Demetrius*), Antigone the political villain treats love as an instrument of power (Arbace in *Didone*), and Cassandre remains constant in his love and his remorse (for all the world like Aeneas in *Didone*). Anagnorisis is thus perfunctory in this play because the issue is representation of a psychological situation, as in opera, not dynamic development through conflict between complex individuals. In effect, Enlightenment tragedy has no psychology to compete with the psychology provided by the musical space that opera allows for the representation of emotion. On the contrary, the prominence and power of opera should be understood as part of the enabling of such a psychology in tragedy.

Operatic plots pause in order to foreground performative aspects like bravura singing or elaborate spectacle. Even after Metastasio tamed the excesses of Venetian opera, *opera seria* still had formal processions, court entries, and religious rituals (for example, the stage direction for *Didone* 1.5); Mozart was still composing grand marches for such processions to the end of his career in 1791. In *Olympie* the greatest moments of truth are performative in this fashion: they are the betrothal in act 1, the single point at which Olympie articulates her state of mind to an assembled semicircle of priestesses in 5.4, and her death. Voltaire specifically emphasizes two of these moments by opening the temple doors to show a procession of priests and priestesses leading Cassandre and Olympie to the altar and their exchange of vows, and again in 5.7 to reveal Statira's funeral pyre.[24] The same gestures will still be at the heart of opera in the nineteenth century, as with the wedding procession in *Lohengrin* or the grand march in *Aïda*. Opening the doors is still a revelation, as in classical tragedy, but Voltaire has perverted its sense. It reveals the operatic moment: not the Truth per se, but the truth about the kind of play *Olympie* really is. There is no messenger in the last act, as there often is in Seneca and Racine, because the catastrophe is visible. Killing yourself or anybody else was unacceptable on the neoclassical stage, but here the cast is laboriously assembled through the fifth act for the climactic moment: all the participants and the audience witness the final deaths.[25] Olympie's suicide on the funeral pyre evokes Dido's famous similar one in Metastasio forty years earlier and the perhaps less familiar one of Eupaforice in Carl Heinrich Graun's (1703–59) *Montezuma* of 1755 (libretto by Frederick the Great), and also looks ahead to what was to become the operatic gesture par excellence.

Happiness and Happy Endings

Even as spectacular suicide emerged as a signature gesture, the happy ending—*lieto fine* is the term in opera—plagued discussions of eighteenth-century opera, where it was perceived as lacking verisimilitude, unclassical, and generally embarrassing. But it is typical not only of *opera seria*, but of most eighteenth-century tragedy as well. The usual story, in Germany at least, is that eighteenth-century tragedy was stranded in some neoclassical backwater until the rising tide of bourgeois tragedy and the Shakespeare revival, with Gotthold Ephraim Lessing (1729–81) and then Goethe as the important mediators, floated it clear. But the more complex view of neoclassicism suggests a different narrative in which the layering of dramatic traditions becomes ever more complex. Voltaire's *Olympie* shows how the underlying structure of drama had been hollowed out by the rationalist theology of the Enlightenment, and his *Candide* points to the philosophical correlative. If a rationalist God has created the best of all possible worlds, why does anything bad ever happen? *Candide* satirizes the Enlightenment tendency to theodicy, or justification of evil in a perfect world. The problem of the happy ending is in effect the formal version of theodicy. The fact that a problem normally discussed in regard to opera is just as pervasive in drama not only reflects the strong affinity of the two forms in the period, but it also suggests that the perspective gained from opera can refocus understanding of the drama.

Neoclassicism's persistent mistrust of the unhappy ending is illustrated by Lessing's joke at the beginning of the *Hamburgische Dramaturgie* (1767), his reviews of the abortive efforts to create a national theater that constitute his poetics of drama: "One spectator to another, 'But what does she die of?'—'What does she die of? Why, of the fifth act'" ("fragte ein Zuschauer seinen Nachbar: 'Aber woran stirbt sie denn?'—'Woran? Am fünften Akte,'" *Gesammelte Werke* 2:339). Neoclassical theorists in the sixteenth and seventeenth centuries were at pains to point out that Aristotle permits tragedies to end happily, yet were unhappy with the deus ex machina. In classical tragedy the unhappy end confronts the audience

with the incomprehensibility of the moral order; but the morality tradition required some kind of orderly resolution, even if the protagonist
dies at the end. For a long time the amalgamation of Platonist admiration to Aristotelian fear and pity as the emotions aroused by tragedy
covered the rift, as in Corneille's justification of martyr tragedy. With
the increasing desire to write secular drama that looked like classical
tragedy in the eighteenth century, poetic justice became ever more
prominent. This is the approach to tragedy parodied by John Gay at
the end of *The Beggar's Opera* (1728), where the beggar/author must
rewrite his ending to grant his hero a pardon and two wives. Poetic
justice could take quite abstract form—*Olympie* restores order by uniting
the lovers in death. Not only in opera (for example, *Don Giovanni*,
Gluck's two Iphigenia operas,[26] his *Orfeo*), but in much serious drama as
well (for example, Nahum Tate's adaptation of *King Lear*, which ended
with the marriage of Edgar and Cordelia and held the stage for essentially all of the century), visible divine justice remained the order of the
day, even in the classical context, into the 1790s.

In the seventeenth century martyr tragedy was already successfully secularized in relation to the absolutist state, so that moral complexities
could be unraveled by the king, who both represents and replaces divine
authority. In Corneille's *Horace* (1640), for example, the king pardons
Horace for murdering Camille on the grounds that he has served the
state. In an important variant the king could be the negative instance,
the tyrant. The tyrant model is complicated; as Walter Benjamin pointed
out, German Baroque drama brings tyrant and martyr into close proxim-
ity. The eighteenth century dealt with the ambiguity by converting the
tyrant at the last minute. Voltaire's *Alzire* (1736), considered by the more
intelligent German neoclassicists—Lessing, Mendelssohn, and Nicolai—
a model tragedy, illustrates the complexity of the model. This remarkable play begins as a morality: it opens as Don Guzman accedes to power
and his father begs him not to be a tyrant, in vain as the remainder of the
act reveals. Guzman falls into the sin of pride expressed as tyranny. The
central three acts—of love and political intrigue in which Guzman plays
a relatively minor role—are modeled on classical tragedy, with reversals,
recognitions that avert potential crimes, and Sophoclean irony. In a sudden return to morality in the last act Guzman is prevented from execut-
ing the hero and heroine when the hero stabs him. As he dies Guzman
repents and pardons the condemned hero and heroine, thereby saving
them from death, and they kneel in admiration as the generous tyrant
dies. A century earlier the audience would have seen Guzman rise to
heaven; now admiration has replaced the explicit apotheosis.

In some writers this accommodation of morality to classical form
seems quite unreflected, as in Johann Elias Schlegel's (1719–49) *Canut*

of 1746, which was recognized by all the leading neoclassicists in Germany as a model tragedy. The play ends with a moral: "Alas! Ambition, most noble of the drives, / Is nought but madness, unless controlled by brotherly love" ("Doch ach! die Ruhmbegier, der edelste der Triebe, / Ist nichts als Raserei, zähmt ihn nicht Menschenliebe," *Canut* 73). At issue is poetic justice: failure to respect the demands of brotherly love will be punished. Unfortunately, however, the ambitious figure in the play, whose name is Ulfo, is not noble at all, but a genuine villain. He rebels repeatedly against the otherwise universally loved, just, and generous King Canut, who always forgives him. Furthermore, Ulfo has stolen the sister of the king from her accepted lover by lying and then, after he married her, shamelessly admitted it. He could have requested whatever he liked from the king's kindness, but like Satan chose not to owe anything to anyone. Ulfo is a morality devil. But he can do no damage because the other characters are all too noble and humane to be led into sin. The central events of a morality play—temptation, fall, repentance—occur here only off to the side in relation to the king's sister and one of his vassals. In fact, the king's sister does everything she can to keep the king from finding out how Ulfo betrayed her. In this inverse theodicy evil has to work hard just to be recognized.

Schlegel's contemporaries seem to have overlooked the morality aspect of the play, just as Voltaire's overlooked the operatic aspects of *Olympie*, apparently because of Schlegel's Aristotelian facade—strict observance of the unities, constant discourse of fear and pity (the one is transformed into the other in the course of the play), the moral at the end. In his *Critische Dichtkunst* Johann Christoph Gottsched, doyen of German Aristotelians, requires that all tragedies illustrate a moral and goes so far as to suggest that the poet begin by choosing a moral and then invent his plot accordingly. In comparison to Voltaire's Don Guzman, Schlegel's king is far more consistent. He is not a tyrant inexplicably converted from one moment to the next, but from beginning to end a good, humane ruler. Schlegel has indubitably gained in verisimilitude, but by confusing probability with consistency he has lost coherence. If no one in the play is converted or damned, then the moral aspect loses its sense, without being replaced by anything else. The difficulty evil has in being acknowledged is symptomatic of this incoherence, which is a common problem in the otherwise so unified plays of later neoclassicists. The improbable tyrant-converted model, on the other hand, remained alive and well into the nineteenth century through German Classicism (Goethe's *Iphigenie auf Tauris* [1787], Kleist's *Prinz Friedrich von Homburg* [1812] still live from it), but is actually more familiar today from opera, as in Mozart's *Entführung aus dem Serail* (1782), where the Bassa Selim sends the hero (son of his mortal enemy) and heroine (whom the Bassa had wanted to marry) on their way with his blessing, or, indeed, *Le nozze di Figaro* (1786) or his last opera, *La Clemenza di Tito* (1791), where the emphasis has shifted, again as one might expect, from the religious import of the conversion to the question of what it means to be such a figure.

In the mid-eighteenth century the accommodation to the older tradition began to break down. Opera was easy to attack, but Lessing, for example, much as he liked Schlegel's *Canut*, was unremitting in his attacks on admiration—the basis of neoplatonist aesthetics—as a passion aroused and cultivated even by tragedy. In correspondence with Nicolai and Mendelssohn he asserted repeatedly that admiration belongs more to epic than to tragedy, and only grudgingly did he compromise with Mendelssohn's and Nicolai's faithfulness to Corneille and allow admiration to remain in their joint characterization of tragedy (*Briefwechsel über das Trauerspiel* 57, 78 and note, 81).[27] In the *Hamburgische Dramaturgie* Lessing bluntly rejects martyr tragedy as real tragedy (ch. 1 and 2; *Gesammelte Schriften* 2:336–38). Neoplatonism was not especially popular in the Enlightenment, so that it is not surprising that the Renaissance marriage of neoplatonist wonder with Aristotelianism began to unravel. As a practical example consider Georg Behrmann's adaptation of Corneille's *Horace* (1733, published 1751). Behrmann was a literary dilettante, a merchant in Hamburg whose few plays were, however, staged by Caroline Neuber, directress of the leading German troupe of the day, and sometime polemical ally of Gottsched. Corneille had himself identified the lack of unity in the plot of his own *Horace*, which combines a classical plot propelled by irreconcilable moral demands in its first three and a half acts with a Christian morality in the last act and a half, where the hero falls, is judged by the king, and finally is pardoned. In his dedication Behrmann calls attention to Corneille's self-critique and sets out to "correct" his error by eliminating the final one and a half acts. But Behrmann dismisses the tragic rage, in which he leaves his heroine, as insanity, and irons out the paradoxes of the moral situation portrayed by Corneille. Consequently, the adaptation still ends with justice done. If Behrmann has achieved neoclassical unity of plot, he has nevertheless maintained poetic justice at the end of the play, and hence failed to purge from his tragedy the influence of the religious tradition. The inconsistency is typical of the neoclassical efforts to purify the stage.

Bourgeois tragedy as it developed in Lessing, Diderot, and the German Storm and Stress movement is generally regarded as a major advance toward the modern sense of tragedy as a play with an unhappy end arising from irreconcilable conflicts (rather than moral failure).[28] Scholars of the development, and indeed critics and playwrights of the time, unanimously considered George Lillo's 1731 play *The London Merchant* the breakthrough to a new kind of tragedy for the eighteenth century. The focus in these discussions has always been on the capacity of the play to move its audience to tears and on the rejection of the neoclassical decorum of rank (for Lillo made his hero an ordinary London apprentice rather than a nobleman and made the central authority figure in the play a merchant, not a ruler). The interest in these two progressive aspects of Lillo's play has obscured the real genre of the drama. George Barnwell robs his master, kills his uncle, all for the love of a cynical seductress named Millwood, and is last seen on his way to gallows. Unlike Gay's Macheath, he is not reprieved. But in what sense is the ending tragic or unhappy? The situation from which Barnwell departs is a touching scene of repentance and embrace with Maria, his "good angel" and daughter of merchant Thorowgood, God in the play. Later in the century an additional scene had him preaching to Millwood on the way to the gallows. The structure is still that of garden-variety morality play: hero in the world—hero falls—hero repents and is saved or hero does not repent and is damned.[29] The conduct of the drama is also in the mode of morality, which starts at the beginning and proceeds linearly: basically it follows the hero through his moral descent until divine intervention, in the form of chaste Maria, marks the decisive turn in his course. Although Lillo set his play in 1588 and spiked it with allusions to Shakespeare, they are to the Bard in his most morality-like mood; the murder of the uncle, for example, plays on Macbeth's murder of Duncan. The structure is scarcely disguised by a few motifs from heroic tragedy (the friendship with Trueman and the timid love interest of Maria). On the surface bourgeois tragedy is mimetic in its representation of the middle class on the serious stage, but only on the surface.

Much the most interesting figure is Millwood, who plays the role of Satan (Blunt calls her a devil and explains why in 4.14), luring the hero to deny his (divine) master and to heap sin upon sin. When she speaks up spiritedly in her own defense one wonders momentarily if she perhaps is not Satan, but the abused woman she claims to be. Here would be a truly modern moment: in fact it is, for Millwood comes straight out of *opera seria*. She is ultimately a descendent of Circe, a first step in the secularization of Sin—female, at home in a garden, and like the Vice able to change shapes. Indeed, her transformational capacities began a tradition of extremely popular animal ballets that long outlived Circe operas, as *Die Zauberflöte* or Siegfried's bear still show.[30] Circe had a second career in eighteenth-century opera (for example, Handel, Gluck) as Armida, the sorceress in Tasso's *Gerusalemme liberata* (1581), who keeps Rinaldo from his mission in the world. Like Circe Armida is passionate and violent; her palace, too, collapses with the end of her love. But unlike Circe, Armida has resisted love until she encountered Rinaldo. As a result the tension between love and hate is directed inward, rather than outward, and opens the way to the ambivalence of Wagner's Isolde. The third popular opera heroine, Dido (in Metastasio, Purcell), detains Aeneas as Circe does Ulysses, but like Armida is sympathetically chaste, while her spectacular death by fire amid the conflagration of Carthage in Metastasio repeats the architectural collapses of the Circe and Armida finales. But now the dangerous seductress has no supernatural connection and is primarily the wronged woman whose suffering evokes sympathy. The modern ambivalence of Lillo's Millwood derives from the conflict between Sin and Dido, so to speak, between the old dramatic paradigm and the more secular, individualized, and interiorized operatic heroine emerging contemporaneously. Just a few decades later Lessing's versions of the figure were more sympathetic yet, and by the end the 1780s, Schiller's avatar, Lady Milford in *Kabale und Liebe* (1784) shared the humane political ideals of the dramatist as dramatic practice became more secular and mimetic.

Only this potential can explain why Lillo's play was so readily embraced by its neoclassicist environment, especially Lessing. The play's capacity to evoke tears apparently blinded its audiences to its archaic nature. Lessing drew on it heavily in his own first bourgeois tragedy of 1755, *Miss Sara Sampson*. Before the play begins the hero of this tragedy, Mellefont, has been seduced by a courtesan named Marwood, who now refuses to release him to his new beloved, Sara, with whom Mellefont has eloped. Lessing has made Lillo's plot, the seduction of the young man by the courtesan, into the prehistory of his own plot, the seduction of the innocent young woman by the man. On this basis he constructs a classical analytic tragedy—the entire action takes place at an inn on the day that Sara's father has found the guilty couple and is trying to forgive them and bring them home. Like an implacable, senseless Fate, Marwood prevents the happy resolution the father wants to stage. In Gluck's *Iphigénie en Aulide* (1774), which has similar tender passages between father and daughter, Calchas takes over Marwood's role. As Dido is in effect the classical model for the eighteenth-century preoccupation on the stage and in the novel for the seduced and abandoned woman, Iphigenia, another widely popular opera heroine of the period, represents the abandoned woman with a close, often ambivalent relationship with the father who dominates bourgeois tragedy for the next century. The serious operatic stage, however, would not allow this heroine to be openly bourgeois until the later nineteenth century (for example, Verdi's *Luise Millerin*): this apparent political conservatism of opera in the nineteenth century has obscured its formal innovativeness in the eighteenth.

Lessing was probably too astute not to realize that he had transformed Lillo's morality play into the exposition of his own—rather

Senecan—classical tragedy.[31] At the end the bereaved father welcomes the doctors who have arrived too late to save his daughter with the words, "If they can perform miracles let them come in." Of course, they cannot, and being only doctors, can promise her no better afterlife either. Thus Lessing marks the distance of his play from religious drama and from the *lieto fine* of opera. The structure is in effect an allegory of the historical development Lessing himself was bringing about—the renewal of tragedy and ultimate overcoming of allegorical drama by absorbing it into bourgeois tragedy in order to relegate it to the past once and for all.

Of course, Lessing did not really manage to kill off cosmic drama, not even in his own play.[32] For Sara seeks to play the role of martyr. At the opening of the fifth act she and her maid Betty discuss Sara's catastrophic encounter with Marwood in the preceding act and whose fault it was:

Isn't that so, Betty, you think [Mellefont] is innocent, too?—She is chasing him; what can he do about it? She storms, she rages, she wants to kill him. Don't you see, Betty? I'm the one who exposed him to this danger. Who else but me?—And in the end Marwood refuses to return to London without seeing me. Could he refuse her this trivial favor? After all, I have been curious to see Marwood more than once. Mellefont surely knows what curious beings we are.

(Nicht wahr, Betty, du hältst [den Mellefont] auch für unschuldig?—Sie kömmt ihm nach; was kann er dafür? Sie tobt, sie raset, sie will ihn ermorden. Siehst du, Betty? dieser Gefahr habe ich ihn ausgesetzt. Wer sonst als ich?—Und endlich will die böse Marwood mich sehen oder nicht eher nach London zurückkehren. Konnte er ihr diese Kleinigkeit abschlagen? Bin ich doch auch oft begierig gewesen, die Marwood zu sehen. Mellefont weiß wohl, daß wir neugierige Geschöpfe sind. [*Gesammelte Werke* 1:383])

In the course of these few sentences, by means of a not quite accurate summary of the situation, Sara successfully shifts the guilt from Mellefont to herself. Finally she simply asserts, "In short, it's all my fault" ("Kurz, alle Schuld ist mein," 1:384). But in the immediately following encounter between the lovers "guilt" is replaced by Aristotelian language of "fear and pity": Sara is terrified, Mellefont is afraid she may have been poisoned, and within one page we find the words "Mitleid" ("sympathy," 387), "Sympathie" (387) and "mitfühlen" ("sympathize," 388). But then, in a formulation typical for Lessing, Sara returns to the martyr model: "God must leave proven virtue in the world for a long time as an example, and only the weak virtue that would perhaps fail its too many tests does he snatch from the dangerous lists" ("Die bewährte Tugend muß Gott der Welt lange zum Beispiele lassen, und nur die schwache Tugend, die allzu vielen Prüfungen vielleicht unterliegen würde, hebt er plötzlich aus den gefährlichen Schranken," 396). The formula proven virtue, "bewährte Tugend," evokes Baroque martyr tragedy, as in Andreas Gryphius's *Catherina von Georgien, oder die bewährete Tugend* (1651). Sara claims only weak virtue; nevertheless she dies with the self-control of the stoic martyr and Mellefont acknowledges her, correctly, as a saint ("Heilige," 397). But then the formulation seems to be too much for Lessing, for it is immediately followed by Sir William's remark cited above about the miracles of doctors. The drama hesitates between traditions.

I could pursue this ambivalence further, especially in the rather arbitrary conclusions of Lessing's later plays, *Emilia Galotti* and *Nathan der Weise,* but instead I will point to vestiges of it in Goethe's problematic bourgeois tragedy *Clavigo* of 1775. Ever since a famous essay by Erich Heller, "Goethe and the Avoidance of Tragedy" (*The Disinherited Mind* 33–55), it has been a truism that Goethe avoided tragedy; but it is more accurate to acknowledge that he is rooted in a dramatic tradition much broader than tragedy. In this early play Goethe was attempting to appropriate the new fashion of mimetic play with an unhappy ending. *Clavigo* dramatizes a real incident from Beaumarchais's memoirs, in which Beaumarchais travels to Spain to assist his sister Marie, who has been jilted by the brilliant young Clavigo. It is well known how closely Goethe followed his source, often word for word in passages that had already been formulated as dialogue. Yet the most substantial scenes are the conversations between Clavigo and his friend Carlos which would have been inaccessible to Beaumarchais, even if Goethe had not invented Carlos. These invented scenes constitute a morality plot, for Carlos is at bottom a devil who encourages Clavigo in his ambition to climb ever higher at court. Like Hercules pulled between Pleasure and Virtue, Clavigo must choose between his friendship for Carlos and his promise to Marie. Beaumarchais urges Clavigo to correct his erroneous choice. Clavigo repents, returns to Marie, and receives Beaumarchais's forgiveness through the mediation of his good angel Marie (just as Barnwell is forgiven by Thorowgood through Maria's intervention). The play recaps the trajectory from morality to bourgeois drama.

But Goethe doesn't stop there. Carlos tempts Clavigo a second time, and he falls again, this time to be cured more drastically at Marie's funeral, another scene Goethe inserted into Beaumarchais's story. Scenes of conversion at the grave are frequent in Baroque drama (for example, *Cenodoxus,* Calderón's *El mágico prodigioso,* or Gryphius's *Cardenio und Celinde*), and survived happily in opera much longer, as Brünnhilde at Siegfried's funeral pyre attests. Goethe alludes to this tradition when he makes Clavigo say, "It is an enchantment, a vision of the night that terrifies me, that holds before me a mirror in which I am to acknowledge with a shudder the result of my betrayals" ("Es ist ein Zauberspiel, ein Nachtgesicht, das mich erschreckt, das mir einen Spiegel vorhält, darin ich das End meiner Verrätereien ahndungsweise erkennen soll," HA 4:303). Amid music and Baroque spectacle he repents his actions again and is yet again forgiven, this time definitively, for he dies immediately over the corpse of his repeatedly offended beloved. The ending is familiar, not only from bourgeois tragedies like Lessing's best tragedy, *Emilia Galotti* (1772), but also from Voltaire's *Olympie* and opera. In Lessing the heroine opts to have her father stab her to death rather than fall into the hands of the prince who has murdered her bridegroom; the father (standing in for Voltaire's and Goethe's lovers) doesn't stab himself, but surrenders to justice. And there is a similar operatic end of *Virginia* (1778) by Vittorio Alfieri, leading Italian dramatist of his generation. To be sure, Lessing and Alfieri have chosen the identical Roman legend for fairly obvious political reasons. But it is not only politics that determines the popularity of the motif, as Voltaire's play shows. Indeed, the double death survives in *Carmen* and, above all, *Tristan und Isolde*. The tragic end is really the *Liebestod*, which, as the highest unity of the lovers in death, has been at the heart of opera at least as early as Monteverdi's *Orfeo*, and behind which looms the reconciliation of the soul with God.[33] Goethe shows us in yet another light the deep affinity of tragedy and opera in the period, and the difficulty not of avoiding tragedy, but of achieving it.

In other respects, however, *Clavigo* points forward. The issue in *Clavigo*—as typically in the eighteenth century—is constancy in love, not constancy in virtue (see the faithful Constanze in *Entführung aus dem Serail*, where the two are synonymous, or *Cosí fan tutte*, where the men naively try to make them so); and the Beaumarchais who dispenses forgiveness is neither God nor king nor even a bourgeois father. Virtue in this play is a marriage that would stifle Clavigo's talent, and pleasure is the ambition that would foster it. Neither the reality nor the morality of the play is unambiguous. Furthermore, Carlos isn't really a devil; his warm friendship verging on homoerotic love is the fashionable friendship of eighteenth-century sentimentalism. Its closeness suggests that Carlos is not so much friend as alter ego, the projection of Clavigo's own ambition. But he is no longer a personified part of the personality, nor is he quite a Romantic *Doppelgänger*, an ambiguously projected alter ego; there is no mystery about his concrete existence. Goethe's Carlos seems truly to love Clavigo and only wants to see his own self enhanced in the mirror of his brilliant friend. This is a matter not of allegorical figures, but of modern individuals driven by internal feelings that are no longer even fully conscious. Even at the point where the drama seems most Baroque, when Clavigo meets Marie's funeral cortege, his world is entirely different, for his full speech about the magic mirror really reads as follows:

It is an enchantment, a vision of the night that terrifies me, that holds before me a mirror in which I am to acknowledge with a shudder the result of my betrayals.—There is still time! Still!—I tremble, my heart melts in horror! No! No! you shall not die. I'm coming! I'm coming!—Vanish, spirits of the night barring my way with anxious terrors— . . . Vanish!—They stand still! Ha! they turn to look at me! Woe! Woe is me! they are humans like me.—It is true—True?— Can you grasp it? She is dead.

(Es ist ein Zauberspiel, ein Nachtgesicht, das mich erschreckt, das mir einen Spiegel vorhält, darin ich das End meiner Verrätereien ahndungsweise erkennen soll. — Noch ist es Zeit! Noch! — Ich bebe, mein Herz zerfließt in Schauer! Nein! Nein! du sollst nicht sterben. Ich komme! Ich komme! — Verschwindet, Geister der Nacht, die ihr euch mit ängstlichen Schrecknissen mir in den Weg stellt — . . . Verschwindet! — Sie stehen! Ha! sie sehen sich nach mir um! Weh! Weh mir! es sind Menschen wie ich. — Es ist wahr — Wahr? — Kannst du's fassen? — Sie ist tot. [HA 4:303])

In this short speech Clavigo first envisions spirits abducting his beloved, then realizes, as the "spirits" turn to stare at him, that he is looking at a real funeral cortege. The allegorical vision is reduced to "humans like me"; the emblematic reminder of death becomes literal death. As Goethe forces his Baroque spectacular back into the bounds of mimetic dramaturgy, natural and supernatural come together: ghosts cease thereby to be allegories of cosmic order and become instead metaphors of interiority.

The Phantoms Dance

Neoclassical drama (in the broader sense that extends through the eighteenth century) is always a compromise between the forms of religious drama and Aristotelian ideals and always remains very close to opera. The mediating role of opera in the emergence of tragedy from the multiple layers of neoclassicism has been left out of Peter Szondi's compelling account of bourgeois or domestic tragedy in the eighteenth century (*Die Theorie des bürgerlichen Trauerspiels*); since the often excellent sociological and more recently feminist accounts dependent on Szondi have rested on the assumption that these texts are essentially mimetic and Aristotelian, the description offered in this chapter has particularly important implications for reading the drama of the eighteenth century. For the situation is more complicated than the view that somehow Aristotle and Shakespeare joined forces to create modern drama. To be sure, from the critical distance of the last two hundred years, Aristotle and Shakespeare are both seen as promoters of mimesis and banishers of antiquated Baroque tragedy. But it hardly looked that way to the eighteenth century, when the assessment of Shakespeare's freedom from Aristotelian rules became a touchstone of intelligence, later "genius," among critics and poets, represented successively in Voltaire's ambivalence, Lessing's admiration for Shakespeare's intuitive Aristotelianism, and the young Goethe's worship of his rule-breaking. For the generations that came of age in the 1770s and after, Shakespeare was the alternative to Aristotelianism and English culture the alternative to stodgy or (after the Revolution) dangerous French Classicism. The beginning of the nineteenth century saw a complete, "classic" translation of Shakespeare into German, and, in England, a return to staging Shakespeare in versions closer to the originals than the neoclassical adaptations of the eighteenth century. Perhaps the only thing Shakespeare and Aristotle obviously had in common then, besides stature, was that *Oedipus* and *Hamlet* shared responsibility for the great popularity of paternal ghosts on the stage. But of course ghosts were most welcome in the more operatic forms of drama. Bourgeois tragedy mimeticizes the ghostly father figure to an old man just this side of the grave who functions as a barely secularized version of God the father.

This chapter juxtaposes three alternative narratives: that opera served in effect as a laboratory in which the possibilities inherent in all the different classical revivals were explored and recombined, that it had substantial impact on the plot of spoken drama, and that the extension of mimetic representation was perceived as opposition to the operatic model. Neoclassicism was in fact at war with itself as self-styled Aristotelians tried to abolish the most varied and generative dramatic form to emerge from the classical revival. The crisis that ensued is the subject of the next chapter.

Chapter 7

The Greek Revival: German Classicism and the Recovery of Spoken Drama

> *The higher demands of poetry, which can in fact be expressed only symbolically or allegorically on stage, have become impossible for tragedy and comedy, and everything that engages the imagination at all has been redirected into opera.*
>
> —*Goethe*[1]

Europe underwent yet another wave of neoclassicism in the eighteenth century, this time a specifically Greek revival. The Greek language became routine in the school curriculum, and by midcentury classical philology was the fashionable new university discipline. The generations born after midcentury came up through the new discipline—they read some Greek, thought of classical tragedy as Greek rather than Senecan, pushed for the creation of a national verse drama on the Greek model, and regarded mythology less as an ornamental convention than as the vehicle of a hidden, perhaps subjective truth. The revival embraced not only drama, but also poetry (Pindaric ode), narrative (hexameter epic), architecture, painting (David), and the decorative arts (Wedgwood). It fed into stage culture through texts and images to result in simultaneous achievements of special note in the spoken drama of Goethe and Schiller on the Weimar stage, in the operas of Mozart, and in the pantomime dances of Jean-Georges Noverre (1727–1810).

The name "Classicism" is given to all three of these phenomena, but rarely in the same breath. Because Goethe's admiration for Mozart is well known, *Die Zauberflöte* is sometimes invoked in discussions of the ideology of humanity (*Humanität*) and education (*Bildung*) associated with German Classicism, and *Don Giovanni* is often compared with *Faust*. Discussions beginning with Mozart are rather less likely to invoke Goethe, and neither group pays much attention to Noverre and the ballet. Instead, spoken drama, opera, and ballet are largely regarded by scholars as now fully mature separate arts, and German Classicism is commonly understood to be a modified neoclassicism synthesized from the French and Shakespearean traditions, on the one hand, and from the marriage of Schiller's Kantianism with a new classical vision brought by Goethe from Italy on the other. But Noverre talks constantly about drama in his influential treatise *Lettres sur la danse, et sur les ballets* of 1760, and Mozart's librettist for *Die Zauberflöte*, Emanuel Schikaneder (1751–1812), also wrote successful spoken dramas. While Goethe and Schiller wrote five-act blank-verse dramas in elevated diction and (usually) with restricted casts, they resented Racine and Voltaire. The unmistakable French element in their plays is but a single layer in the ever more complex amalgam of dramatic forms accreting on the European stage. Mozart's libretti and even the programs for Noverre's ballets share the same complexity. All three developments are not only parallel, but they interacted with one another: read together they reveal the Greek revival working itself out in an ideology of simplicity that ultimately forced allegory to change its name to symbol.

The Greek Revival

The term Greek Revival names a style of architecture popular in the first half of the nineteenth century, but the widespread rise of interest in Greek culture actually dates back to the second half of the eighteenth century. As Greek spread in the educational system, Homer tended to replace Virgil as the foundational figure of European culture. While Pope's translation of the *Iliad* (1715–26) into heroic couplets emulated Dryden's *Aeneid*, in 1774 Goethe's Werther carried Homer in his pocket and was thus marked as a poet of the rising generation, for whom Homer shared honors with Shakespeare as the model of original genius; by the end of the century Goethe was acclaimed for his Homeric epic *Hermann und Dorothea* (1797) in dactylic hexameter set among the contemporary German bourgeoisie. Discussions of drama became more independent of Aristotle and *Oedipus* to focus on other Greek texts whose reception was not mediated by Seneca. Thus Sophocles' *Philoctetes* was prominent in the controversy begun by Lessing's *Laokoon* (1767) about decorum in Greek tragedy. The art historian Johann Joachim Winckelmann (1717–68) established that ancient culture was not homogeneous but had its own historical development. Within this trajectory Winckelmann favored Greek over Roman and early Greek over Hellenistic art. Winckelmann's dating has been superseded, but his principle of relative value remained influential into the twentieth century. Furthermore, excavations at Pompeii and Herculaneum shifted the perception of classical art from the monumental Roman architecture to the more private, almost dreamy and small-scale wall painting of the ancients. While the artifacts from

Herculaneum (from 1738) and Pompeii (from 1748) were obviously Roman, they nevertheless became representatives of a Greek style and even spawned a type of furniture known as the Athénienne (Wilton-Ely, "Neoclassicism" §1). Similarly, the revaluing of primitive Greek architecture over Roman design is mediated in Marc-Antoine Laugier's *Essai sur l'architecture* (Paris, 1753) through the image of the rustic "Vitruvian hut" illustrated in the frontispiece (Vitruvius was, of course, Roman). By the late eighteenth century more adventurous tourists, Goethe among them (a rigorous journey in his description, *Gesamtausgabe* 9:444–556), were extending the traditional grand tour beyond Rome to the older, Greek ruins of Sicily and watching the sunrise (toward Greece) from the summit of Etna: Greece was still mainly for diplomats and professional travelers but was now on the horizon as a reasonable object of longing. Lord Elgin, educated in this environment, brought the Parthenon frieze to England from Greece between 1802 and 1812.

Dance made an especially significant contribution to the accelerated shift toward the Greek Revival and all that it implied. Masque and ballet costuming in the seventeenth century, especially for women, consisted of formal court attire with an allegorical headdress to identify characters by means of elaborate attributes fastened to it. Thus Saint-Hubert (1641) emphasized that "especially the importance of having the costumes of those who represent the same thing look alike, without any difference," that "dancers be dressed in accordance with the characters they represent" and that the same applies to headdresses (Cohen, *Dance as a Theatre Art* 36 and her illustration 35). As the proscenium stage and increasing virtuosity of stage dancing shifted the focus from patterns traced on the floor to the dancer's body, costumes changed to allow first the ankles, then the body of the dancer to become visible. The French dancer Maria Sallé caused a scandal in London in 1734 by dancing in a Pygmalion pantomime "à la grecque," that is to say for the first time on the European stage "without pannier, skirt, or bodice, and with her hair down; she did not wear a single ornament on her head. Apart from her corset and petticoat she wore only a simple dress of muslin draped about her in the manner of a Greek statue," according to the London correspondent of the *Mercure de France* (cited in Kirstein, *Dance* 209). Although the stage was probably not the direct inspiration for the attitudinizing on Wedgwood's popular Jasperware with its white classical figures in graceful repose on various matte grounds, nevertheless one of the finest and most popular motifs was a line of dancing women with classical draperies fluttering about them.[2] By the 1780s Lady Emma Hamilton was performing in even more accurate costume for her husband's guests, and by the turn of the century the style affected the clothing of well-to-do women all over Europe.

The trend received both focus and impetus from the reform operas and pantomime ballets that emerged from Gluck's collaboration with the leading choreographers of the day in Vienna. In response to continued accusations of lack of verisimilitude by Aristotelians, Gluck and Calzabigi ushered in a second reform of opera with *Orfeo ed Euridice* of 1762. Shifting from the common seventeenth-century tendency to choose dramatic plots on ancient themes derived largely from Ovid, Virgil, or Roman history, they turned to the tragedies of Euripides, and followed their *Orfeo* with an *Alceste* in 1767, the preface to which (probably written by Calzabigi, though it appeared over Gluck's name) became a manifesto for the new form. Like Metastasio, their declared goal was to regularize opera to Aristotelian norms and to make it the true successor to Greek tragedy. The central slogan was simplicity. The visual elements survived in set changes, processions, and dances, but the plot and casting became simpler yet. The bravura aria was eliminated, along with the many short scenes prompted by the fixed alternation of recitative and exit aria. The resulting assimilation of recitative to melodic singing enhanced the unity of the plot. Good performance became sensitive rendition of the composer's music rather than florid ornamentation of it; in place of showy singing Gluck and his collaborators required more strenuous acting and dance. His ballet pantomimes, *Don Juan* (1761), based on Molière, and *Sémiramis* (1765), based on Voltaire, were equally important for the history of dance (Max Loppert, "Gluck 6," *Grove Music Online*, ed. L. Macy [accessed May 29, 2004], <http://www.grovemusic.com>). They were choreographed by Gasparo Angiolini (1731–1803), generally credited with the development of narrative ballet (along with Franz Hilverding [1710–68] and Noverre), and had scenarios by Calzabigi. Gluck's music preserved the simple outlines of the scenario to achieve a directness of impact new to ballet, essentially by reducing the music to theatrical essentials (ibid.).[3] The reform operas reintegrated this newly liberated ballet back into opera to make it an essential, ongoing part of the stage action, rather than ornamental numbers for which the action pauses. Given the operas' primarily Greek themes, Euripedean plots (*Alceste, Iphigénie en Aulide,* and *Iphigénie en Tauride*) and Noverre's choreography (except for *Orfeo,* which was done by Angiolini), the actors were not only clothed in the light classical drapery demanded by Noverre, but much of their dancing involved taking on attitudes and positions modeled on paintings excavated at Pompei, and also from classical statuary and vase painting. Noverre holds forth repeatedly on the natural grace and elegance of classical movement (Noverre, *Lettres sur la danse,* see for example, 259). With Gluck's reform, the music stops being ephemeral: opera and ballet achieve a new kind of permanent bond, or unity, between text and music. Aristotelian critique and the Greek revival together redefine unity to extend beyond the French rules to include Aristotle's original interest in all the media of performance.

Unifying the different media was important for spoken drama as well. Popularized by the success of Rousseau's *Pygmalion*, melodrama enjoyed a vogue from about 1780 to 1810. Sometimes designated more precisely as monodrama or duodrama, depending on the number of actors, declamation was accompanied by and often alternated with music. The libretti were primarily classical in provenance and involved tableaus similar to those in reform opera. Set design also changed in the second half of the eighteenth century: in line with the shift in classical art from Roman to Greek, sets shifted from predominantly architectural to predominantly painterly; the stage came to be viewed as a painting, in which the relation of figures to landscape or setting was important. In London this development led to spectacles even without actors, and eventually to the popularity of dioramas and panoramas in the nineteenth century (Laver on Philip James de Loutherbourg in *Drama: Its Costume and Decor* 193). In the 1790s Goethe brought this development together with the emergence of dance pantomime to develop in Weimar, where he superintended the court theater from 1791 to 1817, a characteristic style of classicized ensemble acting that favored the entire stage action as moving tableau over the individual actor.[4] The works that Goethe and Schiller created for the Weimar stage in this period form the main body of German classicist texts, and often draw explicitly on Greek drama.

Although the innovations in Weimar brought the Greek revival in spoken drama to a head, about a third of Goethe's programming in Weimar was actually musical drama—opera, operetta or *Singspiel,* and melodrama.[5] On the one hand the fact suggests that the cooperation among the arts propounded and practiced by Gluck, Noverre, and Goethe transformed Aristotelian unity into *Gesamtkunstwerk.* However, the most popular works on the Weimar stage were the operas of Mozart, particularly *Die Zauberflöte* and *Don Giovanni,* works that have remained in the repertoire associated with the name of their composer. In the wake of Gluck's reform, operas were associated consistently with the names of their composers and were classified unambiguously as music. At the same time, ballet pantomime slowly established itself as an independent genre; narrative ballets without spoken text flourished in the nineteenth century (M. Smith, *Ballet and Opera* chs. 1 and 6). Thus the Greek revival constitutes both the acme and demise of *Gesamtkunstwerk.*

Simplicity and Subjectivity

In eighteenth-century neoclassicism natural simplicity replaces decorous verisimilitude.[6] The change was central to the Greek revival. A
good example is Noverre's *Lettres sur la Danse*, which consistently uses
Aristotelian terminology,[7] in part, at least, to combat the Paris Opéra,
which obstinately perpetuated Lully's and Rameau's tradition of ballet
as interlude. The pantomimic ballet of Noverre, Hilverding, and Angiolini had an elaborated Aristotelian plot, usually that of a play already
written for the stage, even that of a Greek tragedy. Ballet thus became
the imitation of action and true to nature. But nature is more natural
than it has been; it is, Noverre tells us over and over, simple.

Although the term "simplicity" exists in a neutral or negative sense going back to the Middle Ages, it acquires a positive moral sense of "free
from artifice" only occasionally in the sixteenth century, and the meaning "free from luxury" appears only rarely before the eighteenth. With
regard to style, in the meaning "Absence or lack of elegance or polish;
in later use, freedom from ornateness or over-elaboration; plainness or
directness of an attractive kind," the *OED*'s first two citations say it all: in
1697 Dryden wrote, "The Precepts of Husbandry are not to be deliver'd
with the Simplicity of a Plow-man, but with the Address of a Poet" while
in 1783 Cowper asserted, "Simplicity is become a very rare quality in a
writer."[8] Simplicity, as a noun at least, becomes a firm positive value earlier in German culture, perhaps through Luther's use of it in his Bible
translation, which was in lower style than the standard English version.
By the mid-eighteenth century simplicity of style is associated with interiority: "with simplicity of heart goes simplicity of song" ("mit des
herzens / einfalt vereint sich die einfalt des gesanges," cited in Grimm,
Das deutsche Wörterbuch 3:173).[9] In his influential essay of 1755,
"Gedanken über die Nachahmung der griechischen Werke in der
Malerei und Bildhauerkunst," Winckelmann popularized the expression
"edle Einfalt und stille Größe" (noble simplicity and quiet grandeur) as
the foremost category for specifically ancient Greek art. Noverre trans-
lates Winckelmann into dance terms with phrases like "graces naïves"
and "pantomime noble" (Noverre, *Lettres sur la danse* 55), but in fact simplicity is associated with every positive value in Noverre's text—beauty,
elegance, and grace (274, 275, 475), nature (90, 189, 201, 221, 275, 468,
478–79), truth (201, 221, 468, 475, 482), and, finally, originality (478–79,
482). The first term in the Platonist triad of the good, the beautiful, and
the true has become the natural.

Simplicity starts to be applied to antiquity in connection with nobility
or grandeur by French critics writing about art in the 1660s (Winckelmann, *Kleine Schriften* 342, and Stammler, " 'Edle Einfalt' " esp. 368–69). It

was taken up and connected to moral feeling by Shaftesbury at the beginning of the eighteenth century, who nevertheless links it with "solemnity" (Stammler, " 'Edle Einfalt' " 369). The context was still clearly the formality and decorum of Aristotelianism. Between Shaftesbury and Winckelmann the term entered writings about opera, where "noble simplicity" appears frequently in German discussions by the 1720s (Flaherty, *Opera in the Development of German Critical Thought* 68).[10] Simplification was the watchword of both Metastasio's and Gluck's reform of opera; Gluck's preface to *Alceste* speaks of the "beauty of simplicity" (Fubini, *Music and Culture in Eighteenth-Century Europe* 365). The realm of song and dance opened simplicity to contamination from popular and primitive forms (Flaherty *Opera in the Development of German Critical Thought* 166, 214, 216, 285; Zaslaw, *The Classical Era* 5, 117, 264). By the end of the century the new neoclassical simplicity has become, at least in part through the influence of the musical stage, the reverse of neoclassical decorum.

Noverre inveighs against the complicated steps inherited from the court of Louis XIV, partly because tranquillity, the equivalent of Winckelmann's noble grandeur, is the basis of grace and harmony (Noverre, *Lettres sur la danse* 343, see also "noble et tranquille" 344, 347), even more because of the importance of representing action in ballet. One would assume action to be the equivalent of Aristotelian plot, but Noverre follows the Aristotelians of the seventeenth century in making character the primary category: he redefines action in ballet, or pantomime, as communicating emotion to the spectator (262). To express both action and character, and to be visible everywhere in the hall (388), the dancer must focus on increased use of the arms and whole body action rather than intricate footwork (264, all of letter 12). Expressive pantomime allows the dancers to capture the constantly shifting emotions of modern feeling (58, cited above). Neither the dancer nor the choreographer can depend on fixed rules and forms. If the dancer must attend to ever-shifting emotions, the choreographer must attend to ever-shifting circumstances, like the size of the theater, the qualities of the particular musical ensemble (389) or the bodies of the individual dancers (letter 11). What began as simplicity and Aristotelian plotting becomes a special complexity accommodated to a new ideal of a living nature in time.

This is the decade in which the rhetoric of the "innermost heart" became widespread. Stripped of headdress and attributes in 1734, Maria Sallé appeared only as "classical": her precise character could no longer be read from her clothes, but rather from the attitudes and movements of her body. Sallé's costume was not widely imitated right away, but by 1760 Noverre was calling for simple, light draperies (*Lettres sur la danse*

183) and attacking panniers (184–85) and emblematic costumes, especially things like windmills on the heads of the winds (203). At the same
time *Lettres sur la Danse* is full of the rhetoric of the expressive body. Ballet, Noverre says, is "conversation muette" (120)—not merely entertainment, but soul (128). Dancers are actors, and ballets are poems,
indeed—at least in aspiration—tragedies. His ideal is David Garrick,
whose acting style depended on naturally expressing the inner sensi-
bility of his characters rather than on conventional gestures (209).[11]
Dancers, too, must represent feelings—"If their gestures & physiog-
nomies are always in accord with their souls, the resulting expression
will be that of sentiment" ("Si leurs gestes & leurs physionomies sont
sans cesse d'accord avec leur ame, l'expression qui en résultera sera
celle du sentiment," 58)—and their pantomime must communicate
emotion (262). He opposes the old habit of masking the dancers, because the face is so crucial to expression (195–96) and takes issue with
choreographic notation because it does not represent facial expressions
and attitudes (365). The issue is now personal expression of some interiorized sentiment that is not immediately nameable, not one's moral nature or Senecan passions.

When Noverre wants to be Aristotelian about simplicity, he uses the
term unity. For Aristotelians unity was a matter of keeping things under
control, of maintaining decorum. Under Horace's influence it often
exerted pressure toward homogeneity, continuity, and symmetry. But
Noverre opposes ostentatious discipline: the effects of nature and simplicity can be achieved only if art is hidden (*Lettres sur la danse* 90). Costume and set design require contrast, proportion, and gradation of color:
simplicity depends not on homogeneity but on difference. "Monotone"
is a word that goes with "froid" ("cold," 21). As for symmetry: "Figures
that are symmetrical from right to left are unacceptable, in my opinion,
except for formal entries, which have no expressive character or meaning, and are there solely to give the lead dancers time to catch their
breath" ("Les figures symmétriques de la droite à la gauche, ne sont sup-
portables, selon moi, que dans les corps d'entrée, qui n'ont aucun carac-
tere d'expression, & qui ne disant rien, sont faits uniquement pour
donner le temps aux premiers danseurs de reprendre leur respiration,"
8). Symmetry is only for warm-ups or for a concluding fete with general
dancing. Although much of the treatise calls for ballet-pantomime to become the equal of tragedy, in fact Noverre treats a ballet more like a
poem than like a drama. Unity of design does not require the three Aristotelian unities of action, time, and place, but displaces them (124). The
pared-down unity of design in Racine's theater and the magnificent display of Lully's court operas fuse in a new kind of operatic totality, where
the various components work together, not independently as hitherto

(156–57). The poet must be the primary figure and must be supported by the others—the composer, ballet master, set designer, costume designer, machinist in charge of sets and lighting (158). Hence simplicity and unity eventuate in the overall control of a strong director. Such a synthesis of the arts was widely called for in the second half of the century, and always in the context of opera (Flaherty, *Opera in the Development of German Critical Thought* 199, 221, 285–86, and Fubini, *Music and Culture in Eighteenth-Century Europe* 365, 376). Simplicity leads to a totality very different from Horatian homogeneity.

In rather different fashion Denis Diderot (1713–84) also moved toward a totalizing view of the stage, as its increased visuality impelled it toward heightened mimesis. In the *Entretiens sur le Fils naturel* (1757), an aesthetic dialogue on the play of that name, Diderot identifies opera (*théâtre lyrique*) as the model for combining the visual and the vocal (*Oeuvres esthétiques* 115), and, as was typical for the period, considered opera at its best, when it was simple (121), to be the equivalent of ancient tragedy (see 167). Vocal and visual elements (poetry, music, dance, and pantomime) combine to represent individual characters (160–62). Above all, in both painting and theater, the characters must seem unaware of being observed by a spectator. As a result, mimesis is driven to the extreme: in the *Entretiens* the play under discussion is an event that actually transpired and is now being replayed in its original setting by the persons to whom it originally happened. As David Marshall describes it:

Throughout his writing about the theater Diderot remains fascinated by the possibility of a *spectacle réel* with *personnages réels*. He repeatedly rehearses moments in which actors (or characters in the place and position of actors) forget themselves and in doing so seem to forget theater. Although in the arena of acting technique he rejects the conventional belief that the best actor is the one who becomes the character he plays, Diderot remains invested (even in the *Paradoxe [sur le comédien]*) in the idea of an actor who would annihilate himself, disappear so that the character could seem to appear in his place. He returns to a dream of theater in which the actors and characters are the same, in which the characters are *personnages réels* rather than *personnages fictifs*. (Marshall, *The Surprising Effects of Sympathy* 130)

This is the ultimate realism on the stage. Yet such hypermimesis undermines itself. For the play in the *Entretiens* is performed at the request of the father at the center of the play, as he says in the "Histoire véritable de la pièce" that introduces the play, "It is not a matter of performing a play here, but of preserving the memory of an event that concerns us, and to show it just as it took place . . . We shall renew it ourselves, every year, in this house, in this room" ("Il ne s'agit point d'élever ici des tréteaux, mais de conserver la mémoire d'un événement qui nous touche, et de le rendre comme il s'est passé . . . Nous le renouvellerions nous-mêmes, tous les ans, dans cette maison, dans ce salon," Diderot, *Oeuvres complètes* 10:16, cited in Marshall, *The Surprising Effects of Sympathy* 122). In effect, this extreme reality is transformed into an annual repetition of a foundational event, a mythic ritual; drama appears to have come full circle from the medieval church and returned to the stage of mystery play before it took on the trappings of allegory. But Diderot does not do this naively. He is preoccupied in his dramatic theory, as in his novel in dramatic form *Jacques le fataliste*, with the elusive boundary between illusion and reality. In the *Entretiens* he is firm that representing the emotional reality of the characters can be achieved only by observing the Aristotelian rules, particularly the requirements of unity and liaison of scenes. These are so important, Diderot argues, that it is better to "falsify" reality in the service of "the invariable rule of dramatic verisimilitude" ("la règle invariable des vraisemblances dramatiques," *Oeuvres esthétiques* 81). Such falsification leads not necessarily to an ideal or general truth but to a simplified, clarified reality.

The result is a problem for representation. What appears on the stage is neither real nor unreal, neither true nor untrue. Reality and truth were never identical for the Aristotelian and Platonist traditions. But with the status of both called into question, their categorical difference is less obvious, and there is no longer enough distinction between them for allegory to function. Representation on the stage has reached a crisis point as the forms and the substance, representation and truth, no longer correspond. The problem applies equally to Diderot and Noverre, each driven by a vision of Aristotle and neoclassical simplicity. Diderot's leads toward a mimeticism so extreme that it ends in paradox, Noverre's to a substitution of emotion for meaning that denies meaning to formal structures. Both versions result from the conflict between a dramatic style dependent on meaning grounded in transcendence and a more secular one driven by the new simplicity grounded in an individual self. This paradox pervades the development of opera in the eighteenth century. A thoughtful musicologist like Reinhard Strohm points to the secularizing pressure of Aristotelianism on opera (*Dramma per Musica* esp. 206), and an Aristotelian of the period like Gottsched reduces Platonist wonder to pleasure and "bloßes Sinnenwerk" (mere illusion, *Critische Dichtkunst* 742–43). At the same time the elements of the marvelous at which this secularization was aimed came increasingly to be understood as representing a dream world, an inner psychology that was particularly to be valued (Flaherty, *Opera in the Development of German Critical Thought* passim and esp. 293). The crisis is visible in extreme form in Mozart's *Zauberflöte*, where the positions are recognized as reciprocal. The remainder of the chapter discusses Mozart's solution for opera and then Goethe's for spoken drama; these two figures were the most effective at creating a theatrical structure that could embrace both positions.

Mozart and Classicism

The tendency of writers and scholars to associate *Faust* with *Don Giovanni* has obscured for all but specialists how important *Die Zauberflöte* was for the following generation, and especially for Goethe. Ludwig Tieck's fairy-tale drama, *Der gestiefelte Kater* (Puss in Boots, 1797) plays on Mozart's popularity by importing elements from *Die Zauberflöte,* the more irrelevant the better, into his own play within a play, especially the set for the trials by fire and water; whenever the onstage audience gets too irritated, Mozart always cheers them up. Schiller mounts a tragic version of *Die Zauberflöte* in his *Braut von Messina* (Bride of Messina, 1803);[12] Heinrich von Kleist's *Das Käthchen von Heilbronn* (1807) is subtitled "Die Feuerprobe" (Trial by Fire) and contains in act 4 a trial of the heroine by water as well; semi-supernatural guiding figures like Tamino's three genii spook all through the plays of Zacharias Werner (1768–1823), in his day considered a dramatist of Schiller's class and now unaccountably ignored; Wagner's *Siegfried* (1876) still has its bear, magic sword, and trial by fire. Goethe thought *Die Zauberflöte* was so important that he made it the centerpiece of the Weimar repertoire, celebrated it in *Hermann und Dorothea,* used it extensively in a dramatic prologue *Was wir bringen* (1807), and worked hard on a sequel to it in the 1790s which he only gave up when he realized it was written to Mozart's already-existing music.[13] I would suggest that *Die Zauberflöte* represented for an entire generation the solution for getting past the aporias of neoclassicism and allegory to recover a viable dramatic tradition.

The crisis of representation in this opera is precisely that its plot no longer seems to make sense, because its most colorful figure, the Queen of the Night, changes valence in the middle of the libretto. First she appears as the wronged mother whose daughter has been abducted by an evil sorcerer, but abruptly in scene 15 the sorcerer turns out to be good and the Queen proves to be the real villain. For most of the nineteenth century the text was read as a quasi-dialectical Romantic allegory: a series of connected oppositions like dark and light, night and day, female and male, evil and good, enable the universe to function stably, as long as the first term remains properly subordinated to the second.[14] Then, in the early 1890s, when dialectics lost favor to positivism, Otto Jahn proposed an alternative, strictly occasional reading. In this view the opening on June 8, 1791, of Joachim Perinet's *Kaspar der Fagottist, oder: Die Zauberzither* ("Kaspar the Bassoonist, or: The Magic Zither," an adaptation of the same tale from C. M. Wieland's collection *Dschinnistan* that

Schikaneder was using for *Die Zauberflöte*) forced a sudden change in plot, in which the good Queen of the Night became an evil figure.[15] Jahn's assertion has been largely rejected on internal grounds, but the continuing discomfort with the reversal reveals the shaky status of allegory as drama becomes more mimetic.

The opera actually has an unproblematic basis in traditional allegory. Indeed, it is strikingly reminiscent of Calderón's *El mayor encanto amor*, discussed above in Chapter 5. Because of the Habsburg connection between Spain and Austria, Spanish dramas traveled readily to Vienna both with and without the names of their authors; from the early eighteenth century on there was a healthy tradition of popular drama and musical theater in Vienna based on Spanish plots.[16] Whether or not Mozart and Schikaneder knew this particular play, they had access to materials that derive from it.[17] Calderón's court spectacular is an allegory of faith based on the visit of Ulysses to Circe in Ovid, whose obvious religious import made it easy for Calderón to recast it in shortened form as a morality play. By Mozart's time even mythological allegory was archaic and had been largely superseded by, among other things, the vaguely orientalizing fairy-tale vehicle of *Die Zauberflöte*. In both texts, as in all moralities, the definition and development of humanity is a central theme, here visible in the fluid boundary between human and animal: in Calderón the clown is transformed into a monkey for part of the play, while Mozart's clown Papageno is a bird-man. Circe changes men (at least those who submit to their appetites and drink) into animals, so her island, in Calderón, is full of tame animals. *Die Zauberflöte* has a ballet of animals tamed by Tamino's flute. Furthermore the heroes of both texts must resist the temptations of the dangerous, indeed evil, female rulers of illusory realms. In both works the clown parodies the love story of the hero. Both clowns talk too much and are repeatedly punished for it. And both become tied to crones: Calderón's Clarín is "rewarded" by Circe with a duenna who appears from a treasure chest, Papagena first appears in the guise of an old woman. Clarín's duenna reveals visually for the first time the true ugliness of Circe, an ugliness which Ulysses will only later recognize. The more secular Papagena, by contrast, turns out really to be quite attractive, at least to Papageno, and they will have a large family.

Calderón's plot dramatizes the choice of virtue over pleasure. Ulysses' companions are transformed into beasts by Circe, but Ulysses rescues them with the aid of a magic twig provided by Iris: divine intervention enables man to recover his humanity. But as Ulysses tarries in Circe's domain he falls in love: man trusting to his own powers is always subject to temptation. By means of trumpet calls, the armor of Achilles, and finally the ghost of Achilles himself, Ulysses is recalled to self-reflection and resolves to depart for home, while in the adjacent comic scene Clarín looks in a mirror (concrete self-reflection) and sheds his monkey identity. In the meantime, Circe routs the army of her other lover, Arsidas, with an army of phantoms, for all the achievements of sin are but illusion. Circe calls up a storm to prevent Ulysses' departure, but Galatea calms the seas because Ulysses had earlier killed the Cyclops, murderer of Galatea's own beloved, and had thereby avenged constant love. Once again divine intervention, prompted by previous good works, comes to the aid of the repentant sinner. As Ulysses departs to the sea, Circe's palace sinks and is replaced by a fire-spewing volcano. In the tradition of masque the plot functions as a series of significant pictures.

Die Zauberflöte dramatizes the same choice. Tamino arrives in the alien realm of the Queen of the Night and it is clear by the beginning of act 2 that he must learn to distinguish light from dark and undergo moral trial. From the very beginning he requires superhuman, if not divine, assistance, for his first words are "Help me" ("Zu Hilfe"). He is delivered from a dangerous dragon by three ladies whose silver spears, echoed repeatedly in the golden flute, silver glockenspiel, and a pattern of gold and silver all through the play, elaborate the theme of divine talismans implicit in Iris's magic twig and the armor of Achilles. Like Ulysses, Tamino ignores the obvious danger of the realm he has entered (rendered visible in the poisonous serpent from which he was just rescued), and a miniature painting easily convinces him to enter the service of the Queen of the Night and fall in love with her daughter, virtually sight unseen. Here the plots diverge, for Tamino's love is not sinful, but leads, circuitously, to marriage. Instead of being recalled to virtue in a moment of self-reflection, Tamino enters the temple of Sarastro and submits to tests of his virtue that culminate in the trials by fire and water. The Queen of the Night, a late incarnation of Circe, invades the depths of Sarastro's temple, whence she is routed with thunder and lightning. She and her army are phantoms in their lack of power; they are now routed as the forces of Circe's lover were, and for the same reason— both threaten to destroy a closed artificial world. Now, however, that closed world contains not the dangerous enchantment of love, but the sacred doctrine of love generalized to love of humanity. This is the final dispersal of the Queen and her forces, and the thunder and lightning take the place of the volcano into which Circe was transformed. This moral allegory, a late and secularized descendent of European morality drama, is the traditional, underlying allegory in the opera. All readings of it as Masonic or political allegory are essentially even more secularized embroidery on this basic structure.[18]

Considered from the opposite point of view, however, with Pamina as heroine rather than as object of Tamino's interest, the story is the popular plot of abduction and seduction taken over from Richardson's novels into drama. Monostatos evokes Clarissa's Lovelace and his numerous successors in drama, Sarastro the powerful father-fixation typical of the bourgeois tragedies of Lessing and later German writers, the dilatory Tamino the half-hearted lovers of the same plays, the Queen of the Night both the typically contemptible mothers of these texts and also the virago abandoned by the dilatory lover for a new, more innocent beloved. But this mimetic plot is slightly garbled. For if *Die Zauberflöte* were a proper seduction drama, Sarastro would literally be Pamina's father, Tamino and Monostatos would fall together as the lover who carries Pamina off but cannot bring himself to marry her. Only the Queen of the Night would remain the object of the same misogynistic contempt. The seduction plot is garbled by the allegorical substrate.[19]

In response Mozart and Schikaneder undermine the allegory. First, despite its thunder and lightning, *Die Zauberflöte* lacks the most spectacular visual effects of Calderón. No Galatea floats across the waves at the end. While the last scene celebrates the initiation and marriage of Tamino and Pamina—constancy, stability, and virtue, "smooth sailing" for the future, and thus everything that Galatea represents—these values are no longer concretely personified. Even with his lion chariot Sarastro is no competition for Calderón's personifications of divine good, Iris with her rainbow and Galatea's sea chariot on a real lake; and the Queen of the Night spews only vocal pyrotechnics. Second, Schikaneder no longer works with traditional names and designations. The moral valence of Calderón's Iris, Galatea, and Circe depended on a body of mythology known to all, but the same cannot be said for Sarastro or the Queen of the Night, whose moral valence is problematic for much of the opera. Sarastro was obviously descended from Zoroastro, the kindly sorcerer in Handel's *Orlando* (1733), one of many eighteenth-century operas based on Ariosto's *Orlando furioso* (although the particular name does not derive from Ariosto). Sorcerers and sorceresses in Ariosto can be bad or good, and one rarely can tell beforehand which kind one is dealing with. Both Sarastro and the Queen of the Night belong to this indeterminate class.

Indeed, much of the problem with the opera's coherence stems from the assumption that "Queen of the Night" is a mythical designation. All modern responses to the first act depend in one way or another on that premise. But it does not stand the test of philology. A nuance—or rather, actually, a crashing guffaw—is lost on us, though inescapable for Mozart's audience. For a "Nachtkönigin" in Mozart's Vienna was a latrine-cleaner.[20] To be sure, the term occurs mostly in the masculine form ("Nachtkönig"), but it is found as a feminine in Stranitzky's collection of adaptations of Italian operas into German from 1724 (see Chapter 6). The context is telling. The clown shows off by saying to the queen: "View me from the front and smell me from behind, o beauty of beauties, queen of the night or night-queen" ("Betrachtet mich von vorn und riechet mich von hinten, Schönste aller Schönen, Königin der Nacht oder Nachtkönigin," Payer von Thurn, *Wiener Haupt- und Staatsaktionen* 2:91; also twice as a masculine with explicit reference to privies or filth, 1:58 and 95). He is dismissed with contempt. To call a woman Queen of the Night was evidently no compliment. As director and most famous member of the company at the Kärntnertor Theater, Stranitzky himself had created the role of Hans Wurst, the first of the characteristically Austrian clowns to dominate the German popular theater of the eighteenth century. A tradition of Hans Wurst comedy written by and for famous clowns leads without interruption from Stranitzky in the 1720s to clown-director-author Emanuel Schikaneder sixty years later.[21] Because Stranitzky's plays are basically translations and adaptations of operas performed at the Viennese court, they are full of motifs and gestures that recur in Mozart's *Singspiele,* such as, in *Die Zauberflöte* the central emphasis on virtue with the contrasting view of the clown, as well as more specific motifs like opening with a hero calling for help and the imposition of silence.[22] The Queen of the Night in this now unrecognized meaning is part of that large eddy in the encounter between allegory and neoclassicism.

Nevertheless, although the Queen of the Night spends the second half of the opera wandering in the "underground passages"—the sewers and drains?—of Sarastro's palace, she still maintains considerable metaphysical stature. As the source of all the weapons in the play she generates its violence, whether murder or suicide. As widow of the possessor of the great sun disk, as feminine principle in the world, and as night, she embodies the irrational forces tamed by the powers of light, wisdom, and enlightenment. Whatever Mozart and Schikaneder thought the word meant, they have maintained her mythical stature. But given the lurking scatological reference, how can any other meaning not be seriously undercut? Are her revenge arias serious, or are they not parodies of the Senecan rage arias so familiar from *opera seria?* Euphemism by nature veils its own meaning: to identify one of the moral poles in the plot with a euphemism seems to call all of the play's meanings into question.

And meaning, organized around the image black/white, is a central thematic problem in the libretto. There is no difficulty distinguishing dark from light in the opera, but their moral value is unclear, and the problem of knowing is articulated repeatedly. When Tamino is first turned away from the Temple of Wisdom and told Sarastro is its priest, he cries, "So then everything is deception!" ("So ist denn alles Heuchelei!" Mozart, *Die Zauberflöte* 31). Hypocrisy is a common vice in morality plays, but there it is always visible which figures lie and which are honest—as is still the case, for instance, in *Othello*. But in *Die Zauberflöte* the audience sees no more clearly than the characters. Tamino is soon informed that he has been deceived by a woman, a theme later elaborated by Sarastro, who speaks of the "illusions and superstition" practiced by the Queen of the Night ("Blendwerk und Aberglauben," 38). The instability derives, in turn, from the shiftiness of representation in the text. It begins with Tamino's and Papageno's difficulties understanding one another, where Papageno's total ignorance of the world reflects Tamino's own state of darkness. In the dark realm of the Queen "truth" or "knowledge" is communicated through images and signs—the painting of Pamina evokes Tamino's full-blown love, the thunder and lightning announcing the arrival of the Queen seems to confirm her divine status. But in the realm of Sarastro visual signs are problematic. The first authority figure encountered in the sunny realm of Sarastro is the black Monostatos; he turns out, however, entirely to misrepresent both the attitudes and intentions of his master, who is neither a tyrant nor even a reformed tyrant of the traditional eighteenth-century variety like Voltaire's Don Guzman or Mozart's own Bassa Selim and emperor Tito. Monostatos's slaves equate his blackness with his moral evil (24), but when Papageno matter-of-factly wonders in the next scene why people shouldn't come black as well as white, the significance of color is disrupted. Monostatos himself later pleads that, though black, he has the same need for love as anyone else—he is the same color inside—and shortly after he attributes a black outside to himself but a black inside—the intended murder of Sarastro—to the white Pamina (45, 48). When Sarastro finally says that he knows that Monostatos is as black inside as out, the final rupture has taken place: the perception of inside or moral color is an entirely separate process from that of the outside one. Instead, knowledge in Sarastro's realm is communicated in sound or language—the temples have their names inscribed over the doorways, the priests confirm Sarastro's intention to have Tamino initiated not by making a visual sign but by blowing horns, the flute and glockenspiel demonstrate their power of sound only in Sarastro's realm, even though they come from the Queen. While Papageno's enforced silence in the first scene results from his simple rudeness, in Sarastro's realm the enforced silence enhances the power of language: language must be used sparingly and carefully because it is the vehicle of truth. Thus as the play progresses from dark to light, it also progresses from nonverbal signs to language, from belief to knowledge, from outer to invisible inner, and from visual to abstract.[23] Unlike the texts of the previous century, it responds to the now familiar anxiety of secularization by deliberately moving away from allegory.

In the love relationship between Tamino and Pamina the problem of knowledge is grafted onto the question of representation. Tamino loves

Pamina from seeing her picture; Pamina loves Tamino simply from hearing Papageno report that Tamino loves her. Pamina even sings her first love duet with Papageno, who represents Tamino by proxy. A pastorale in a moderate tempo, and in the opera's central, "Masonic" key of Eb major, it is the most placid music in the opera. Oddly enough, these absurdities accord perfectly with the epistemology of the text outlined above, for Tamino sees the picture in the Queen's realm, Pamina hears the words in Sarastro's realm. So openly does the text depend on the obvious convention that an opera must have lovers that spectators rarely bother to question the "reality" or mimetic believability of the situation. But in fact, the text also precludes such questioning by calling its own mimesis into question at the crucial moment when Papageno first enters Pamina's chamber. For Papageno feels compelled to check Pamina's identity against the miniature portrait given to Tamino but now worn by his messenger. The comparison is an obvious gag, and a very old one: dark eyes, red lips, blond hair—it must be the right girl, with the possible difficulty that Pamina has hands and feet while the portrait has none. Later in the same scene Papageno then addresses Pamina as "schön's Fräuleinbild" ("lovely miss," literally: "lovely image of a miss," 28), a playful distortion of a common term for woman in eighteenth-century German, "Frauenbild." Pamina is less a mimetic reality than the image of an image. Papageno's superliteral reading of the portrait emphasizes how far this play is from truly mimetic representation.

But if this play were truly allegorical, then we would know immediately what Pamina is an image of. She would have to embody the goal of Tamino's striving, wisdom. Thus in the Corpus Christi moralities of Calderón, the hero's beloved is usually named "Grace" or some equivalent, unless the hero is Christ, in which case her name is "Humanity" or perhaps "the Soul." In an allegory the literal and figurative meanings function congruently in the plot. But in *Die Zauberflöte* Tamino's striving for wisdom, embodied in the male Sarastro, conflicts with his striving for Pamina. Tamino sends Papageno to make love in his name while he tarries at the gates to the Temple of Wisdom, and while Pamina is driven to desperation by her love for him Tamino subjects himself willingly to the trials of the priests and even, at their behest, promises to avoid and abandon her. Only when he has fully agreed to and enacted his renunciation of Pamina is she restored to him. Tamino wins wisdom, and he wins Pamina as well. But these two plots are not connected either logically or dramaturgically. Hence it would be a mistake to view Pamina as either wisdom or an allegory for wisdom: she is simply a parallel goal, not even an analogy. This radical separation of figure and meaning is inconceivable in the allegorical dramatic tradition, in which analogy implies identity.

On the one hand, then, *Die Zauberflöte* reveals a radically internalized psychology. Monostatos's blackness is confusing because the real Monostatos, as he himself claims, is his heart, inside him and invisible to the rest of us (45). Pamina judges Papageno's honesty by his "gefühlvolles Herz" (28). And when Tamino claims to be disillusioned that wisdom is the purview of Pamina's kidnapper, the priest wishes Tamino could know Sarastro's true intentions. Tamino can see nothing but the abductor; the loving foster-father can be revealed solely through verbal expression of the secret intention, the hidden self.[24] The problem of knowledge in this play follows directly from its secularized psychology. But the opera is also allegorical. It externalizes its meaning and makes it visible. How can both these assertions be true simultaneously?

It has become something of a cliché in recent decades to talk about the universality of *Die Zauberflöte* as a combining, whether blending or totalizing, of different musical discourses;[25] one might also understand the naming of the Queen of the Night as a pointed clue to the modal counterpoint or heteroglossia of the libretto.[26] Against the background of a text so ambivalent toward its own underpinnings and assumptions about how it represents, and in which its primary mode of representation is at odds with its epistemology, the anomaly of the Queen of the Night and her scatological roots makes more sense. The Queen of the Night has all the qualifications of a proper allegory: she is connected to the cosmos as the embodiment of night against day, dark against light, superstition against knowledge, evil against good. But by calling into question all the easy distinctions on which such a cosmos rests, the text acknowledges, rather than stumbles over, the fact that the cosmos is not really there any more. By making the Queen's moral significance ambiguous the opera demands that we understand simultaneously in two modes.

But this universality is, in its turn, hard to take seriously. The opera is, after all, really just a *Singspiel* with pretensions. In Stranitzsky the term "Queen of the Night" is used by the clown as an inappropriate form of address to a real queen. It would not be amiss to understand the Queen of the Night as a parody of herself. The opera calls not only meaning into question, but also the conventions of opera, of pictures, of seduction drama, of almost everything with which it comes in contact—not corrosively, but playfully. As music tames the wild beasts and wild men in *Die Zauberflöte*, parodying of course the Orpheus legend, and as the musical and playful Viola and Feste mediate between worlds in *Twelfth Night*, Mozart's and Schikaneder's playful irony allows a temporary but miraculous cohabitation of the modes. Almost forty years later, in 1828, Goethe brought about the resolution of all the conflicts in his "Novelle" of 1828 by having a small boy enter a dark enclosure playing his flute and return peacefully with a lion that had frightened all the adults, and thereby reverse the narrative's definitions of nature and art. With this salute to *Die Zauberflöte* Goethe raises Mozart's playful irony to a methodical irony of serious play, what he called in his last recorded remarks on his *Faust*, "very serious jokes" ("sehr ernste Scherze," letter to Wilhelm von Humboldt, March 17, 1832).[27]

German Classicism: Goethe

What Mozart accomplished on the operatic stage was matched by Goethe and Schiller in spoken drama. Mozart, Goethe, and Schiller are the first creators of stage works in German that have entered the world arena (followed by Wagner, Richard Strauss, and Brecht). But Goethe's accomplishment was more diverse and arguably more far-reaching than that of his close friend and sometime collaborator, and I will focus my discussion of spoken theater on Goethe. While it could be said that only three of Goethe's plays are commonly produced even in German (*Egmont, Iphigenie, Faust I*), he actually wrote more stage-worthy plays than Schiller, whose career was cut short. And while the full-length plays are mostly serious works with recuperative endings, they are in a large range of modes: *Götz von Berlichingen* (1773) is a neo-Shakespearean historical drama in prose, *Egmont* (1788) is a prose historical pageant with operatic elements (set to music by Beethoven), *Iphigenie auf Tauris* (1787) is a tight, neo-Greek work in blank verse with lyric interludes in free verse, *Torquato Tasso* (1790) is a long psychodrama entirely in blank verse. Each of these plays offers its own, uniquely crafted, response to the aporias of stage representation that had emerged in the preceding decades. I will examine several of them here, though *Faust* only briefly, since I have written extensively on it elsewhere.

Before turning to Goethe's writing for the stage, however, I want to consider the importance he attached to music and controlled movement on the stage as director of the Weimar court theater (1791–1817). Although he left the day-to-day running of the theater for long periods in the hands of his associate, Franz Kirms (1750–1826), Goethe had ultimate control of the repertoire, trained the company, conducted rehearsals for plays that especially interested him, and was even known on occasion to discipline the audience. About a third of his programming was serious spoken drama, about a third comedy, and the remaining third musical drama— opera, operetta or *Singspiel*, and melodrama. In nearby Gotha, also an innovative company located at one of the most intellectual courts in Germany, two-thirds of the performances were comedies, one-quarter operas, and only one-tenth serious dramas.[28] To be sure, most of the musical works performed in Weimar, whether designated *Singspiel* or *Oper*, had comic plots, but the balance has shifted toward music. Historians tend to focus on Goethe's introduction of Shakespeare, Calderón, and Greek tragedians into the repertoire of the modern German stage. Nevertheless, half the translated works performed on his stage were Italian (mostly operas): English works constituted only 11 percent of the translations, and Greek and Spanish works less than 3 percent each. Shakespeare's plays received on average six performances each, while Mozart works received forty-three. Goethe's programming was innovative, but biased toward musical theater.

It was Goethe who first trained German actors to speak verse. He drilled his company intensively in rhythmic declamation, and his successful production of Schiller's Wallenstein trilogy (1798–99) opened the way to blank verse as the normal language of serious drama on the nineteenth-century German stage. Goethe nurtured distinctively musical declamation among his actors, beating out the rhythm on the table with a key during reading rehearsals. In his memoirs Eduard Genast, trained by Goethe, recalls how what at first seemed mechanical gradually developed "animated movement" (*Schwung*) and he concludes rhapsodically, "It was music" ("Musik war sie zu nennen," Genast, *Aus Weimars klassischer und nachklassischer Zeit* 108). Pius Alexander Wolff, the most famous and most devoted actor trained by Goethe, describes Goethe's rehearsal technique in extended musical similes, such as the following:

The way Goethe brought a dramatic work to the stage was just like that of a conductor, and in all his rules he liked to take music as his model and use it as a comparison for all of his arrangements. In rehearsal he prepared the performance the way operas are learned. He set the tempi, the fortes and pianos, the crescendos and diminuendos, etc. and maintained them with the strictest care.

(Die Weise, wie Goethe eine dramatische Dichtung auf die Bühne brachte, war ganz die eines Kapellmeisters, und er liebte es, bei allen Regeln die er festsetzte, die Musik zum Vorbild zu nehmen, und gleichnisweise von ihr bei allen seinen Anordnungen zu sprechen. Der Vortrag wurde von ihm auf den Proben ganz in der Art geleitet, wie eine Oper eingeübt wird. Die Tempis, die Fortes und Pianos, das Crescendo und Diminuendo u.s.w. wurden von ihm bestimmt, und mit der sorgfältigsten Strenge bewacht." [Hans-Georg Böhme, *Die Weilburger Goethe-Funde* 82; see also 81])[29]

There is even a legend that Goethe conducted rehearsals with a baton (Hinck, *Goethe—Mann des Theaters* 27). Goethe himself appeals to music as the standard of reference in his discussion of recitation and declamation in his *Regeln für Schauspieler* (Rules for Actors, 1803) with formulas like "So wie in der Musik" (Goethe, *Gesamtausgabe* 15:204) and an extended simile of recitation to playing the fortepiano (*Gesamtausgabe* 15: 208–9). Spoken drama is for Goethe a form of musical performance.

In addition, Goethe focused on controlled grace of movement of the entire stage picture, in which actors were always part of a tableau. Like Noverre he draws his analogies primarily from the visual arts, but he also refers to music. The discussions of acting in Goethe's Bildungsroman *Wilhelm Meisters Lehrjahre* are illustrated with musical analogies even though the hero of that novel appears to condemn opera as a degenerate form of theater.[30] In his own discussions of the nature of drama with Schiller Goethe placed high value on opera, as theater historians if not literary scholars have recognized (Wahle, *Das Weimarer Hoftheater* 257). Noverre called for the poet to be the first among equals in the various contributors to the stage production. If Gluck temporarily appropriated that role for the composer, Goethe established that it would be above all the director. Indeed, Goethe established the model of the unified dramatic production under the control of a single director as the norm for European theater (Carlson, *Goethe and the Weimar Theater* 303). *Faust* contains as one of its prologues a conversation among the director, poet, and actor about to stage the play: Goethe in fact had performed all three functions and here he sets them in dialogue with one another and lets them come to terms. His own practice also was really a combination of roles, which only later was interpreted as the primacy of the director. But the roots of his position in opera and dance are crucial. Without Goethe, according to Michael Patterson, "the pursuit of aural and visual beauty on stage might have been confined almost exclusively to opera and the dance" (*The First German Theatre* 83). In a variant of this insight, Willi Flemming has asserted that *Faust* "conquers the machinery of the courtly theater for spoken drama" (Flemming, *Gestaltung des klassischen Theaters* 14). Flemming points astutely if not explicitly to an important issue: opera's elaborate visual realization continues the allegorical, thematic "rendering visible" of earlier theatrical spectacle. The same is true of all of the plays Goethe wrote.

But treating the spoken drama as *Gesamtkunstwerk* did not automatically save Goethe from the crisis of representation brought on by the conflict between allegorical and mimetic styles. Indeed, it brought him face to face with the issue. Those who objected to Goethe's acting style seem to show some awareness that his techniques called the newly established notions of personal subjectivity into question. Genast refers to one of Goethe's ensemble rules as "a rule that ought to be obvious to any reasonable actor focused on the whole rather than on his beloved self" ("Eine Regel, die freilich jeder vernünftige Schauspieler von selbst einhalten sollte, der nicht sein liebes Ich, sondern das Ganze im Auge hat," Genast, *Erinnerungen* 54). In 1810 F. L. W. Meyer, the biographer and disciple of the great actor Friedrich Ludwig Schröder (1744–1816), commented on a production of Schiller's *Wilhelm Tell* in Weimar: "Haide, actor of the title role has been completely submerged in this [Weimar] style and lost the ability to speak from one heart to another" ("Haide, der Darsteller der Titelrolle sei in dieser [Weimarer] Schule ganz untergegangen und habe verlernt aus dem Herzen und zum Herzen zu reden," Wahle, *Das Weimarer Hoftheater* 186–87). Goethe himself was to return ironically to this criticism in *Faust II*, where he lets the devil say, "For what is to affect the heart must come from the heart" (9685–86, "Denn es muß von Herzen gehen, / Was auf Herzen wirken soll"). These criticisms give character priority over theme, thus Aristotelianism over allegorical dramaturgy. Since Goethe was, after Rousseau, the most influential proponent in the 1770s and 1780s of an ideology of the heart—especially in his novel *Die Leiden des jungen Werther* (1774, *The Sorrows of Young Werther*) and *Götz von Berlichingen*—Meyer's objection is striking. Goethe's interest in opera, in particular his response to the achievements of Mozart and of Gluck (whose *Iphigénie en Tauride* was a major success in Weimar and supervised directly by Goethe and Schiller), evidently offered him notions about representing the self that went beyond his early enthusiasm for Shakespeare as a great dramatist of character.

As a dramatist, Goethe is of course most famous for *Faust*, a work that is sui generis, and then for his "neoclassical" plays mentioned above. In fact he actually completed some two dozen other plays, and left as well dozens of dramatic fragments. Six completed texts, all from the 1770s, were actually labeled "libretti" and were reasonably popular in their day.[31] In addition there is at least one work originally conceived as an opera but ultimately executed as a spoken drama, *Der Groß-Cophta* (1792). Furthermore, there is a corpus of thirty court masques written over the entire length of Goethe's career, as well as various allegorical theatrical prologues and the like. Since he wrote his *Singspiel* libretti in the 1770s, it is clear that musical theater belonged to his conception of drama from the beginning of his career. Considering that *Faust* is at one level an overgrown morality play, Goethe actually wrote in all the dramatic genres considered in this book.

Egmont, begun in the mid-1770s and completed in 1787, displays little specifically Greek influence. Although it works with large groups on stage, they are handled more in the manner of an opera chorus than of a Greek chorus. Indeed, Schiller accused the play of "somersaulting into opera" when the sleeping Egmont's dream, in which Freedom descends like a dea ex machina, is shown visually on stage (*Sämtliche Werke* 5:942). The play is basically concerned with answering the question, "Who is Egmont?" as characters at different social levels analyze his behavior and hidden motivations at length and in often contradictory terms. Egmont himself continually denies having secret motivations. It is the play's escape from interiority, marked by music, that so irked Schiller.[32] Two songs sung by the heroine, "Die Trommel gerühret" and "Freudvoll und leidvoll," are obviously windows into her private emotional world and thus function as arias, though more in the simple style of *Singspiel* than the virtuosity of *opera seria*. In the first and second acts citizens of Brussels chant together, "Security and calm! Order and freedom!" ("Sicherheit und Ruhe! Ordnung und Freiheit!") and later "Freedom and privileges! Privileges and freedom!" ("Freiheit und Privilegien! Privilegien und Freiheit!" HA 4:377 and 393). For the first occurrence a stage direction instructs that it should become a canon; the second lacks a stage direction: public virtue warrants the harmony of music, but demands for personal autonomy do not. The play becomes more distinctly operatic with three musical passages in act 5—Klärchen's death (a candle goes out on an empty stage as music signifies her death), Egmont's dream of Klärchen as Freedom (she appears like a dea ex machina as he describes his vision), and the victory symphony after Egmont marches out to his execution—in which the action is carried by the music and the visual effects. At the same time the drama becomes more allegorical: Klärchen passes from individual existence through death to become an abstraction. She ceases to be the individual beloved and becomes the public beloved, Freedom. Egmont similarly ceases to be Klärchen's secret lover and becomes instead the public hero with whom she originally fell in love—and the martyr who inspires the ultimate conquest of freedom for his people. By turning the characters into allegories at the end Goethe sidesteps the simmering conflict between allegory and mimesis.

Iphigenie auf Tauris, Goethe's most neoclassical play (in the common sense of the term), premiered in a prose version with Goethe in the role of Orestes in 1779, the same year as Gluck's *Iphigénie en Tauride*. The final blank-verse revision was published in 1789. Not initially popular with its audiences, by the later nineteenth century it had become the model text of German Classicism for the purity of its form and for its humane ideology. In Goethe's version Iphigenie, priestess of Diana, has persuaded King Thoas to suspend the sacrifice of strangers who arrive in Tauris; he in turn wants to marry her, but she longs to return home to resolve the curse on her family. She reveals her parentage to Thoas, who does not consider it sufficient reason not to marry her and reinstates the human sacrifices. Orestes and Pylades arrive in quest of the statue of Diana, are captured, and the revelation of identities heals Orestes of the madness caused by Furies that only he has seen. Pylades concocts a plot that Iphigenie must deceive Thoas by insisting the statue be bathed in the sea. At the last minute Iphigenie cannot bring herself to lie and reveals the plan to Thoas, begging him to free them all. Orestes returns to fetch her; she prevents a duel between her brother and the king. Orestes decides the oracle of Apollo requiring him to fetch his sister really referred to Orestes' sister, and the statue of Diana can remain in Tauris. Thoas relents and they depart civilly. The play follows Euripides in terms of plot and some obvious elements of form (like the equivalent of choral odes [esp. 4.5] and the heavily participial language that imitates Greek syntax), as well as thematically. Like most of his dramas, Euripides' *Iphigenia in Tauris* expresses considerable skepticism about Greek state religion and its moral efficacy. Goethe's version has Senecan moments: Iphigenie's first long narrative about the curse on her family summarizes the climax of Seneca's *Thyestes* and refers to the sun's chariot wandering from its course, a standard Senecan image (ll. 390–91). And it is Aristotelian. The five-act drama observes the unities of action, time, and place, operates with a restricted cast, and has virtually no action or violence on stage. Characters refer repeatedly to fear and pity. By making King Thoas a suitor for the hand of Iphigenie Goethe introduces a French-style love interest.[33] He nods further in the direction of Racine by naming Thoas's second-in-command Arkas, the name of the equivalent figure in Racine's *Iphigénie en Aulide*. Thoas also shares some of the moral insecurity of Racine's Agamemnon.

Although the plot follows Euripides relatively closely, *Iphigenie*, like other neoclassical drama, is stylized in terms of morality drama. Iphigenie begins imprisoned by a bloodthirsty tyrant, metaphorically dead, as she herself says. She is released ultimately not by Euripides' deus ex machina, but by herself persuading Thoas to be generous. Beneath this generous tyrant version of morality popular from Baroque tragedy through Metastasio and Voltaire peeps out the even older plot of atonement and salvation. Imprisonment at the beginning of a play is a Calderonian figure for being enmeshed in sin, as in *La vida es sueño*; and indeed Iphigenie first claims that she cannot marry Thoas because of her guilt by inheritance. Orestes' healing in the middle of the play occurs in a narrated dream vision of his peaceable reunion with his now forgiven ancestors in the underworld: here is the repentance central to morality, projected from the sister first onto the brother. But Pylades' plot to steal the image of Diana and escape, which Euripides but not his characters consider a heinous offense, weighs so heavily on Iphigenie's conscience in Goethe, that she finally confesses it and wins their freedom—not through deceit but through the generosity of the king, who has by now been acknowledged as her second father (2004). Here Thoas plays not only God and the generous tyrant, but also the powerful father of bourgeois drama, a form further evoked by Iphigenie's passionate devotion to

Agamemnon and her brother all the way through. Drawing as it does on so many different models, *Iphigenie* is a palimpsest of the history of European drama.

Nevertheless, no one could possibly mistake *Iphigenie* for a religious drama, for the play consistently locates divinity within the human breast. No Furies appear on stage: they are a metaphor for Orestes' own conscience. The gods are elusive, and actually a metaphor for the heart, itself a figure for the interior subject, as the most famous exchange in this regard suggests:

TH. It is not a god speaking; it is your own heart.
IPH. They speak to us only through our hearts.

(TH. Es spricht kein Gott; es spricht dein eignes Herz. / IPH. Sie reden nur durch unser Herz zu uns. [493–94; see also 740–41, 1462–63])

In Goethe's most striking departure from Euripides Orestes' living sister, Iphigenie, replaces Apollo's mythic one in the oracle (2116–17). At the emotional climax of the play Iphigenie's prayer for salvation reads: "Rescue me / And rescue your image in my soul!" ("Rettet mich / Und rettet euer Bild in meiner Seele!" 1716–17). The purity Iphigenie seeks to protect is neither sexual nor religious—it is rather her personal integrity. When Orestes says to his sister, "Let there be truth between us" ("Zwischen uns sei Wahrheit," 1080–81), what is hidden deep in the souls of each must be brought into the open and into communication. Iphigenie and her brother are concerned with their own understanding of their identities rather than with the salvation of their souls; psychology has replaced religion. The older structures of religious belief function here not as allegorical referents to a cosmic system, but as specific connections between concepts within the world, metaphors, the figure discussed at greatest length by Aristotle under the category of ornament.

Embarrassment about the happy end has dogged criticism of *Iphigenie* from early on: everyone loves to quote Goethe's comment that it was "devilishly humane" ("ganz verteufelt human," to Schiller, January 19, 1802); the problem signals the play's affinity for opera, which, as we saw in the last chapter, caused the same embarrassment. While critics still argue over how grudging Thoas's final "farewell" is, this Metastasian conclusion brought about through the clemency of the ruler was common in *opera seria*, which Goethe doubtless read extensively already as a child.[34] The scope of the cast, too, is more typical of *opera seria* (Metastasio typically calls for six roles) than of Racinian tragedy (typically seven or eight roles, but *Iphigénie* has ten); it is actually closest to the radically restricted casts of the melodramas of Georg Anton Benda (1722–95):

Ariadne auf Naxos (1774), *Medea* (1775), and *Pygmalion* (1779). Typically Metastasian are Iphigenie's constancy to her family and the image of the torrent (1506–9). After Orestes dreams of reconciliation in the underworld he brings peace back up into the world of consciousness, just as Orfeo brings back his soul's peace, his beloved Euridice, from the underworld. This time a specifically operatic plot structure has been modernized and secularized. The relapse comes about not through Orestes' error, but through Iphigenie's guilt about the plot to deceive Thoas; her desperate song of the fates at the end of act 4 corresponds to Orfeo's lament over Euridice. The secularism and modern psychology of *Iphigenie* are thus not fully mimetic; Orestes and Iphigenie, as brother and sister, are also manifestations of one identity—*the* offspring of the House of Atreus—healed in two different ways, mythologically or allegorically by dream in act 3, and through self-reflection and moral action in act 5. Brother and sister represent one another as Iphigenie also represents the goddess whose image Orestes has come to steal. This is the realm of operatic visualization.

The musical aspects of opera are equally important here. Arkas appears to function as a neoclassical confidant for both Iphigenie and Thoas, but the play begins, strikingly, with a long monologue of Iphigenie, and regularly alternates dialogue with monologue or long set pieces. Set pieces are common in French neoclassical tragedy, but monologues were normally excluded. Monologue is generally assumed to enter eighteenth-century drama through Shakespeare's influence. However, Shakespearean speeches are rarely as long as in *Iphigenie*: *Hamlet*, the longest of Shakespeare's plays, has one sixty-line monologue, one forty-eight-line narrative, and a handful of other speeches over thirty lines, whereas *Iphigenie* has one seventy-eight lines long, two over fifty, one that is forty-six, and several over thirty, all in a play 40 percent shorter than *Hamlet*. Iphigenie's opening monologue is doubtless modeled on the prologue of Euripides' play, but otherwise the extended monologues of melodrama and the elaborate arias of *opera seria* are closer to home. In *opera seria* the short text of an aria was effectively lengthened by the music and by the *da capo* structure. In spoken drama length and lyricism substitute for the amplification provided by opera's musical accompaniment. In these long speeches identity emerges, as in *opera seria*, as a sequence of postures or images. The staging intentions can be inferred from the illustration of Goethe as Orestes and reports of Goethe's stage style: during these long speeches the figures move slowly and decorously taking on appropriate attitudes and creating ever-changing tableaus, like Gluck's singers and Noverre's dancers.

An aria in *opera seria* normally consisted of three parts. The first two were in contrasting tones and/or tempi, the third repeated (*da capo* or

Figure 21. Facius, after a painting by Georg Melchior Kraus. *Corona Schröter and Goethe in Goethe's* Iphigenie auf Tauris.

"from the beginning") some or all of the first, normally with additional ornament. Iphigenie opens the play with a fifty-two-line monologue bewailing her imprisonment in Tauris. For twenty-two lines she expresses melancholy on her separation from home, for the next twelve lines, using exclamation points for the first time, resentment at the limitations imposed on female action in the world, and then at line 35 she prays to Diana and tells how the goddess brought her to Tauris, ending with an eleven-line sentence. While the third section provides new information, it returns to the tone of the first, and it ends formally by connecting the death she escaped in Aulis with her figurative death in Tauris. The next long speech (117–43), spoken by Arkas to Iphigenie, has the same tripartite pattern: for ten lines Arkas summarizes Iphigenie's great achievement in Tauris, stopping the sacrifice of strangers, then moves to the goddess's approval of her deed (128–35), then back to how much Iphigenie has improved life for all the king's subjects. Iphigenie's monologue in 4.3 moves from anxiety to memories of past happiness back to heightened anxiety, and that in 4.5 moves from anxiety to memories of her past hopes for purity back to extreme anxiety. Emotional heightening of the language functions like the ornamentation in *da capo* repetition.

Goethe elaborates the tripartite principle to scene construction. In his debate with Pylades in 2.1 Orestes progresses from melancholy to increasingly warm memories of heroic action (at 667) back to discouragement (707); in 3.1 Orestes moves from self-involvement to the great moment of truth at the play's exact center ("Zwischen uns sei Wahrheit!" 1080–81), but after Iphigenie's joyful monologue relapses to his original black mood and finally faints rather than acknowledge his sister. Iphigenie's progress in the scene seems similar at first: she moves from sad sympathy for the prisoner to extreme joy when she learns her brother is before her, and a troubled mix of joy and misery ("Glück und Elend," 1255) as she cannot convince him. But Iphigenie's is hardly a *da capo* structure, for she can never be the same after Orestes' revelation. Here Goethe goes beyond *opera seria*, where thought is suspended in aria and takes place only in recitative, to combine the two by superimposing the tripartite structure of aria onto debate. For the debate form implies that there must be an outcome, not just a repetition; the tripartite structure becomes dynamic and Goethe achieves a forward thrust that *opera seria* lacks. The scene does not achieve a resolution, but it involves heightening that goes beyond the simple arias in the first act, and it calls explicitly for a resolution when Iphigenie says at the end she cannot bear the joy and misery alone and must find Pylades. *Da capo* is underway to dialectic.

In two cases, the *opera seria* form is set aside. Thoas has a typical rage aria in 5.2 with its first section of anger at himself, and a second directed at Iphigenie. But, untypically, it lacks the *da capo* section: rage is denied

musical form, because the play drives so hard toward harmony and resolution, musically as well as socially. The higher unity of theme expels the
old *opera seria* form. Orestes' monologue in 3.2 is also not *da capo* as he
imagines that his ancestors are all reconciled in the underworld except
Tantalus himself, who yet remains in torment. The speech is uniform in
mood until the abrupt reference to Tantalus in the last five lines signals
that the central conflict of the play remains unsolved. But the famous
aria in the identical scene in Gluck's *Iphigénie en Tauride* is also not a *da
capo* aria. While Orestes sings a calm, languid melody, a nervous coun-
terfigure in the strings, recognized by all commentators as the Furies,
makes the listener aware that the central conflict has not yet been resolved, despite Orestes' assertions. Goethe and Gluck landed on exactly
parallel solutions in their efforts to modernize the psychology of opera.

Several monologues stretch the aria toward classical forms. Iphigenie's last monologue in act 1 (538–60), a prayer to Diana in four-beat ir-
regular trochees, has a loose ABA structure: praise of Diana's care for
mortals, the plea to save her from committing bloodshed (the change in
tone marked again by an exclamation point), return to the goodness
of the gods. But the speech functions more like a choral ode to mark
the break between scenes in a Greek tragedy. Other passages function
similarly, as when Iphigenie breaks into ecstatic prayer after learning
Orestes' identity, still in blank verse, to be sure, but with suddenly elevated diction. Act 4 contains two more such passages: Iphigenie begins
scene 1 with thirteen two- and three-beat largely dactylic lines of elevated generalization before embarking on her personal situation; in
scene five her heightened *da capo* monologue ends with her Pindaric
song of the fates, the closest imitation of choral ode in the play. *Iphigenie*
does not go so far as to resurrect the Greek chorus, but Goethe seems to
be casting about for an alternative.

A final group descends from the classical messenger's speech, but is
not confined to the fourth act, as in Senecan tragedy. In 1.3 Iphigenie
narrates the content of Seneca's *Thyestes* (350–96), and then of Euripides' *Iphigenia in Aulis* (400–433); Orestes summarizes Sophocles' *Electra*
in 3.1 (1003–38). None of these speeches has the *da capo* structure, and
their content acknowledges their classical provenance. In 5.3 Iphigenie
narrates an episode from the *Odyssey* (1895–1904), a general reference to
the deeds of Theseus, and then, the plot of her own play (1920–36).
With this gesture Goethe claims a place among classical dramatists. Two
other reporting speeches by Iphigenie (1841–54 and 1876–85) report
not offstage events, as is the norm for such speeches, but Iphigenie's
own feelings, her "innermost self" ("Innerstes," 1850). They also move
beyond narrative to action. Iphigenie's central speech begins, "Do only
men have to right to unprecedented deeds?" ("Hat denn zur unerhörten

Tat der Mann / Allein das Recht?" 1892–93). Her deed is to speak the truth, and thereby to free herself from her imprisonment on the island and from the family curse of always acting unjustly. Orestes healed himself of the curse in act 3 by telling Iphigenie the truth; now she heals him. Her speech act prevents violent swordplay and makes a permanent end to the barbarous sacrificial practices on the island.

The last three long speeches of Iphigenie and Orestes sum up the development as they answer Thoas's objections to a final resolution: Orestes may not be the person he claims, the statue still stands between them, and he grudges Iphigenie her departure. Iphigenie answers the first (beginning at 2064) by listing the various signs (*Zeichen*) that prove her brother's identity, Orestes the second by reinterpreting the oracle to make Iphigenie herself the holy image (*Bild*), and Iphigenie overcomes the last objection by promising to welcome visitors from Tauris and calling upon Thoas to extend his hand as a pledge (*Pfand*) of his friendship. Although no stage direction verifies the gesture, Thoas modifies his earlier dismissal, "So go" ("So geht!" 2151) into the rather more civil "Farewell" ("Lebt wohl!" 2174). The intensifying tripartite structure of representation invoked moves from sign to image to pledge (ethical action). With this the play affirms its transformation of the *da capo* structure of its early monologues into a dialectical structure in which language transcends itself to become action.

Goethe's dynamic transformation of Metastasian operatic form by means of Greek tragedy achieves for spoken drama what Mozart's music does in opera. *Iphigenie* does not, like *Egmont*, somersault into opera. Instead it returns opera to spoken drama by tying it to Greek tragedy. Goethe foregrounds the formal aspects of both opera and Greek tragedy to create a unity that nevertheless allows both kinds of drama to be visible simultaneously. The self-conscious formalism of the drama functions in the same fashion as Mozart's irony about the Queen of the Night. The result is a *Gesamtkunstwerk* in the most abstract sense of the word, in which language is the matrix that not only binds, but also constitutes, the musical and visual elements as well. Paradoxically, the achievement of the form Goethe created here was to revivify the spoken drama and definitively separate it from musical drama.[35]

Torquato Tasso (1791) and *Die natürliche Tochter* (The Natural Daughter, 1804) are increasingly rarified versions of the formal and thematic model established by *Iphigenie*. Set at the country villa of Alfonso d'Este, the elaborate symmetries of *Tasso* mirror those of both the Renaissance gardens of the Villa d'Este in Tivoli, visited by Goethe in June, 1787, and of *opera seria*. Tasso and the Princess Leonore embody drives toward the ideal, Antonio and Leonore Sanvitale those toward the real. As the poet-hero descends into madness without ever escaping the formal, enclosing garden, his dissolution is signaled by formalized symbolic outbreaks of physical and sexual violence. Such plot as the long play contains exists largely in Tasso's paranoid imagination. As Tasso must choose between the two Leonores the distinction is much harder to see than that between pleasure and virtue: they represent not moral alternatives but two ways of knowing the world that are both in effect parts of himself. The intense language and gentle, almost ritualized pageantry reveal a self that can represent itself only in gesture and language, if then, rather than in interaction with the world. Interiorized subjectivity is represented allegorically.

Die natürliche Tochter takes this radically internalized psychology further. Although its source, the *Memoirs* of Stéphanie Bourbon-Conti (1798), deals with the French Revolution, neither locale nor character names are specified. All of the action except the highly symbolic opening of a trunk takes place offstage, and the details of the intrigues that surround the heroine remain largely unclarified. At the same time, some crucial relationship between individual conduct and social order is felt, rather than shown, to be at work. Goethe intended the play to be part of a trilogy, like a Greek tragedy. Fate is a classicizing theme in both *Tasso* and *Die natürliche Tochter*, but naturalized and psychologized, and hence more in the control of the individual—one's fate (*Schicksal*) is one's character (*Charakter*). Even so, the love across class boundaries typical of bourgeois tragedy is central to both plays: Tasso loves the Princess; Eugenie, illegitimate daughter of a prince, marries a bourgeois official to save herself from exile. Scenes of symbolic stage spectacle in both evoke the dramaturgy of opera (Jane K. Brown, "Der Drang zum Gesang" 120–22). It remains unclear at the end of both plays whether the protagonist ends with hope or in despair. The almost forbidding unity of these plays synthesizes generic and historical complexity to create a superficial simplicity that Nietzsche writing half a century later would designate "Apollonian."

But *Die natürliche Tochter* also has ties to comic opera. Goethe treated another scandal at the French court, the Diamond Necklace Affair of 1785–86, in an earlier text that he originally intended to be an opera, *Der Groß-Cophta* (The Great Cophta, 1792; assertion in Genast, *Erinnerungen* 55). Even in its final form as a comedy, *Der Groß-Cophta* has an overture, musically accompanied pantomime, a substantial march rather like the entry of the priests in Mozart's *Die Zauberflöte*, and a final garden scene with lots of confused identity typical of opera back into the seventeenth century. *Die natürliche Tochter* is shaped similarly: an innocent young woman is caught in the intrigues and scandals surrounding her supposed protector at the French court when she dons a court costume above her station. Both heroines are also connected to a treasure, threatened with exile abroad or to the extreme boundary of the realm, and finally immured from the world for the foreseeable future, accompanied by a kindly but unheroic young man. Apart from the heroine Eugenie in *Die natürliche Tochter* and three servants in *Der Groß-Cophta*, neither play gives its characters names. Although *Die natürliche Tochter* purportedly adheres to severe classical simplicity, and *Der Groß-Cophta* to the conventions of Italian popular comic opera, the slight operatic comedy is actually an early version of Goethe's most sublime tragedy.[36] Furthermore, Goethe sketched two additional plays about Eugenie's return to public life but never wrote them; instead, in the same year (1803), he wrote fragments of a new play set in the sixteenth century, *Der Löwenstuhl*, about the return of a daughter of noble blood to a father who simultaneously recovers his throne. He thus continued the plot sketched out for the remainder of the trilogy, but as a sentimental German romance.[37] Its first scene, however, is in iambic trimeter, the meter of ancient tragedy.[38] Ten years later Goethe recast this new play as an opera with bizarre magical effects, like suits of armor coming to life and dancing. If *Der Groß-Cophta* is the closet first version of *Die natürliche Tochter, Der Löwenstuhl* is evidently its secret continuation, especially since in act 3 of *Faust II* Goethe does something similar: the act begins as a reproduction of Euripides' *Helen*, and ends as full-scale opera, with through-composed music, a singing chorus that was the Greek chorus of the first scene, and dance. Goethe maintains his synthesis of allegory and mimesis, representation of cosmic systems and interior selves over the length of his career with effects from ironic persiflage (dancing suits of armor) to the self-conscious formalism of an opera that enacts the origin of opera. His great insight was elaborating Mozart's irony into this more abstract playfulness of form.

Faust (*Part I* 1808, *Part II* 1832), Goethe's most substantial and sustained dramatic project, is the extreme version of this technique. Its opening "Prelude on the Stage" makes the rest of the drama a play within the play, and thereby establishes representation as the dominant activity of the work. Mephistopheles and eventually also Faust repeatedly stage plays for themselves and for others. The genre varies wildly, even in scenes that are not explicitly plays within the play: mystery play ("Night"), processional masque ("Outside the City Gate," "Walpurgis Night's Dream"), Jonsonian masque ("Carnival Masque"), opera ("Shady Grove"), melodrama (Faust's first monologue in "Night"), vaudeville ("Auerbach's Tavern"). Particular moments evoke Shakespeare, Calderón, Aeschylus, Sophocles, Euripides, Aristophanes. The backbone of Part I is formed from the popular morality plot of a scholar's pact with the devil joined to the seduction plot typical of bourgeois tragedy. The whole panoply of Baroque morality theater is invoked, however, to set an interior stage. The "Prologue in Heaven" locates Faust between God's idealizing humanity and the destructive realism embodied in Mephistopheles, rather as Tasso stands between the Princess and Antonio. By the end of Faust's Easter walk, these drives have been internalized into two souls that dwell within his breast (l. 1112). But unlike *Tasso* or *Iphigenie, Faust* is less a palimpsest than a summa: the entire evolution of the European stage is there for all to see. The object of *Faust's* allegory is no longer the cosmos, but its representation in art, which can be achieved only through the combination of extreme irony and extreme formal virtuosity.

Schiller's transition to a classical dramatic style followed in the wake of Goethe's. Although Schiller had arrived independently at blank-verse drama in *Don Carlos* (1787), he was quite hostile to operatic forms until his friendship with Goethe.[39] His dramaturgy turned both more operatic and more Greek when he returned to play writing in the mid-1790s in close collaboration with Goethe. When *Wallenstein* threatened to grow too long and complicated, Schiller divided it, in as yet only loose analogy with Greek tragedy, into a trilogy consisting of two five-act tragedies, *Die Piccolomini* (1799) and *Wallensteins Tod* (1799), and a prologue, *Wallensteins Lager* (1798). In this last Schiller follows Goethe's technique from *Egmont* more closely. Somewhat in the manner of masque, large numbers of soldiers with very small roles speak for their various masters who will appear in the following two plays. Schiller also adopted from *Egmont* the moving tableau and the use of music, both solo and chorus. *Maria Stuart* (1800) and *Die Braut von Messina* (1803) adapt the style of *Iphigenie* and *Tasso* to Schiller's more realistic dramaturgy—their tight symmetrical plots confront two modes of being associated with ideal and real embodied in rival figures. *Maria Stuart* is still reminiscent of English blank-verse drama, but *Die Braut von Messina* is stylized in more exotic traditions. Its chorus of cavaliers recreates the ancient Greek chorus for the first time on the German stage by participating in and commenting upon the action. The plot borrows heavily from Sophocles' *Oedipus Rex*, with the queen's efforts to escape the destruction of her house unwittingly bringing it about. Her long-hidden daughter, Beatrice, functions as the buried alter ego of the queen, brought to light only to destroy the two princes, who, like the queens of *Maria Stuart*, embody the opposed poles of the Schillerian personality. The subject and the rich imagery evoke the awakening interest in the dramas of Calderón. The extreme formal stylization and dependence on coincidence bring the drama very close to an opera libretto, and indeed the chorus's shifts from unrhymed to rhymed forms underscore the play's marriage of Greek tragedy and operatic romance.

Schiller's last two completed dramas, his Joan of Arc play *Die Jungfrau von Orleans* (1801) and *Wilhelm Tell* (1805), spread more toward the syncretic dramaturgy of *Faust*. Both are epic in scope, use huge casts in a variety of spaces, and engage in stage spectacle and song. Bourgeois tragedy and even Greek tragedy embrace Shakespearean style and especially opera. Johanna and Wilhelm Tell face the same kinds of moral choices as their predecessors in other Schiller plays, but these tend to be expressed more symbolically than discursively. When Johanna is attracted to the English knight Lionel and loses her moral compass, she is driven from the French court; she finds herself again in a storm straight out of *King Lear*; exposure to nature's violence reduces the self to its core. In *Wilhelm Tell* the symbolism extends to scenes with no human actors, reminiscent of the guttering candle and music on an empty stage that signify the death of Klärchen in *Egmont*. In the second act of *Wilhelm Tell*, after the representatives of the cantons have sworn their oath to resist Austrian tyranny and departed, the curtain remains open while music accompanies the sunrise. Goethe returned to this technique in the first scene of *Faust II*, where music accompanies the sunrise with only a sleeping Faust on stage.

The influence of Goethe's synthesis on the next generation appears almost schematically in two plays premiered by Goethe in Weimar, Kleist's *Der zerbrochene Krug* (The Broken Jug, 1808) and Werner's *Der vierundzwanzigste Februar* (The Twenty-Fourth of February, 1810), although the relation between them has been ignored. Kleist's comedy consists of a trial about a broken jug, which circumstances make the symbol of a girl's (Eva) broken faith to her fiancé; it develops that the judge, Adam, broke the jug and tried (unsuccessfully) to seduce Eva; the marriage is rescued, but no recompense found for the jug. The play failed in Weimar and partisans for both poets still argue about who was to blame; even so, Kleist became a pillar of the German classical canon by the late nineteenth century. Werner's play began a fad for fate dramas in Germany; it deals with the return of a son in disguise to the ancestral home, hoping to be forgiven for having killed his sister in a child's game years before. Mistaking their son for an outlaw, his impoverished parents, guilty of killing the husband's father even more years before, try to rob their son, stab him, and learn his identity only as he dies. All the traumatic events occur on the fateful date of the title. The play was a success, but Werner shortly after became a monk with strong mystical tendencies. As Kleist seemed to speak increasingly to the modern predicament, Werner was viewed more and more as a museum piece of the extreme form of Romanticism. Nevertheless, both plays are analytic dramas—indeed inversions of *Oedipus*—in blank verse and observe the unities strictly. Both contrast their core of Greek tragedy with an obvious morality structure, carried by the names in Kleist and by discussion of faith in Werner. The opposing modes are held together by irony often bitterer than Goethe's and by play even more extravagant.

In both plays marks on the body and significant objects function as leit-motifs, but the manner, and even possibility, of interpreting such signs is called into question because of the teeming miscommunications and misunderstandings. The result in both is a psychology emblematized in Baroque terms. Yet the consistent opacity and dysfunctionality of all representation drives the plays beyond Goethe's synthesis and beyond the limits of allegory.

Aftermath: Symbol and Allegory

The nature of allegory has changed. In a certain rough sense, all the allegorical structures in European drama have been psychological. The discussion began with Prudentius's psychomachia, the battle of the vices and virtues for the human soul. In the course of the seventeenth and eighteenth centuries, under the pressure of Aristotelianism what had been vices and virtues within a widely acknowledged moral system turned into feelings, expressions of an individual. Angus Fletcher astutely points out that allegory requires what he calls *kosmos*, a coherent system to which it refers. As the Christian cosmos became inscrutable in the wake of eighteenth-century skepticism, sublimated into an increasingly abstract aesthetics of design, and then transcendentalized by Kantian philosophy, there was no readily visible *kosmos* to which the allegorical tradition could still refer. In the same way, there was no longer a common belief that all people have the same feelings, or that one can know one's own, much less one another's feelings. Goethe and Mozart realized that allegory remained viable only when it was distanced in some fashion—by the bizarre irony of the Queen of the Night as latrine cleaner, or by the use of highly stylized classical form as in *Iphigenie*. This is precisely what Schiller meant when he called the Greek chorus a wall around the drama to separate it from the world (forward to *Die Braut von Messina*, *Sämtliche Werke* 2:819). In *Über die ästhetische Erziehung des Menschen* (*On the Aesthetic Education of Man*, 1794), Schiller distinguished between what he called the form drive (*Formtrieb*) and the material or content drive (*Stofftrieb*). The first he associated with reason and law and with system, the second with the physical world. The two are not identical with allegorical and mimetic representation, but they could be loosely associated with them, especially since Schiller's treatise constantly redefines and shifts its underlying oppositions. The mediator between these two drives Schiller calls the play drive (*Spieltrieb*). Play was Schiller's word for irony in the extended sense required by all allegory from Mozart and Goethe on. Similarly, nineteenth-century narrative—Trollope and Dickens are the obvious examples—tend to use allegory in their more ironic moments, and the post-Romantic narratives that have

attracted the most interest from theorists of allegory in the last few decades have been conspicuously those with very ironic narrators like Her-
man Melville's *Confidence Man.*

Goethe initially did not rename this special irony, but he did decide
that a new kind of allegory was needed, which he called "symbol." The
heart of his so-called theory of symbol is contained in three aphorisms
from the collection *Maximen und Reflexionen.*[40] The first asserts the priority of symbol over allegory:

It makes a big difference whether the poet seeks a specific correlative to an abstraction, or sees the specific in the general. From the first arises allegory, where
the specific functions only as particular case, as example of the general; but the
second is actually the nature of poetry, it expresses something specific without
considering the general or pointing to it. Whoever grasps this specific with energy gets the general along with it without even noticing, or noticing only later.

(Es ist ein großer Unterschied, ob der Dichter zum Allgemeinen das Besondere
sucht oder im Besondern das Allgemeine schaut. Aus jener entsteht Allegorie,
wo das Besondere nur als Beispiel, als Exempel des Allgemeinen gilt; die letz-
tere aber ist eigentlich die Natur der Poesie, sie spricht ein Besonderes aus,
ohne ans Allgemeine zu denken oder darauf hinzuweisen. Wer nun dieses
Besondere lebendig faßt, erhält zugleich das Allgemeine mit, ohne es gewahr zu
werden, oder erst spät. [*Maximen und Reflexionen* 279])

Symbol is not self-conscious example, as allegory is; instead its connection to the general can be unarticulated, thereby eliminating the need
for irony or convention. In its avoidance of consciousness it is closer to
metaphor than to the extended simile always implicit in allegory. The
second reads: "Allegory transforms appearances into concepts, concepts
into images, but in such manner that the concept remains limited in the
image and can be completely contained and grasped and articulated"
("Die Allegorie verwandelt die Erscheinung in einen Begriff, den Begriff
in ein Bild, doch so, daß der Begriff im Bilde immer noch begrenzt und
vollständig zu halten und zu haben und an demselben auszusprechen
sei" [*Maximen und Reflexionen* 1112]). And the third: "Symbolism transforms appearances into ideas, ideas into images, and in such fashion that
the idea in the image remains infinitely effective and ungraspable and,
even if spoken in all languages, remains ineffable" ("Die Symbolik verwandelt die Erscheinung in Idee, die Idee in ein Bild, und so, daß die
Idee im Bild immer unendlich wirksam und unerreichbar bleibt und,
selbst in allen Sprachen ausgesprochen, doch unaussprechlich bliebe"
[*Maximen und Reflexionen* 1113]). Idea (*Idee*) here is ineffable, while concept (*Begriff*) can be articulated. In this view the difference between symbol and allegory is that allegory expresses what can be conceptualized,
while symbol is necessary to address the incommensurable. Even with its

various mystical versions, Christianity is no longer convincing as a rhetoric for addressing the incommensurable elements of existence; modern science and rationality have so conceptualized the world that nothing remains ineffable. Kant reestablished the Platonist gap between the mind and truth or God; in his wake the German Romantics called for a new mythology for a postrational world. Goethe solves that problem by modernizing allegory into symbol. His crucial move is to take nature, the real world, as the visible guarantor of meaning. It is not enough that meaning should be visible on stage, but the form in which it is visible must also seem real. In other words, it must have verisimilitude. Symbol as Goethe defines it marries Aristotelian mimesis to the older concept of allegory.

From Goethe's friend, the philosopher Friedrich Schelling (1775–1854), Coleridge adapted a similar distinction in his *Biographia litteraria* and transmitted it to the English tradition. Through Goethe and Coleridge it became the established way of understanding literature in the nineteenth century, and the term allegory effectively dropped out of circulation except as denigration. Goethe is commonly taken to have rejected allegory altogether, but that position is simply incorrect. Aphorisms are by nature explicitly unsystematic and fragmentary. Without going into Goethe's skepticism about systematic theorizing, it is obviously necessary to distinguish the kind of systematic analysis in his scientific treatises from the topics treated aphoristically. In the wake of Heinz Schlaffer (*Faust Zweiter Teil* of 1981; most eloquently Jochen Hörisch in *Heads or Tails* 203–15) scholars have begun to read allegory in Goethe in Walter Benjamin's somewhat Marxist and radically modernized sense as the trope that acknowledges the tragic gap between signifier and signification. Goethe was certainly aware of the gap but was still capable of representing it allegorically, as Hörisch's elegant reading of the dismembered crucifix in *Wilhelm Meisters Wanderjahre* shows (210–12). Such Benjaminian readings reveal Goethe's prescience about the implications of industrial modernity, but a full understanding of his terminology and practice of allegory requires the broader context of drama and Aristotelianism this book attempts to provide. The result is a more flexible and dynamic interaction between symbol and allegory than disciples of Benjamin acknowledge. Thus although Goethe tended to use the term symbol for figurative language whose meaning was grounded in nature, he clearly continued to write allegorically—in his masques, theatrical prologues, poetry and especially in Part II of *Faust*, most of which was written between 1825 and 1831. He also continued to validate his allegories with ever more sophisticated and even outrageous forms of irony and self-conscious use of formal structures.

He made his final attempt to systematize his practice in an essay on Aristotle of 1827, "Afterthoughts on Aristotle's Poetics" ("Nachlese zu Aristoteles' Poetik"). Like all commentaries on Aristotle, it tells us more about its author's view of drama than of Aristotle's, but it does represent an important effort to do away, once and for all, with the conflict between Aristotelianism and allegorical practice. Goethe begins by offering his own translation for Aristotle's comprehensive definition of tragedy as the imitation of an action of a certain amplitude (6.2 1449b 24–30). His crucial departure from earlier readers is in the last clause, about catharsis, which he renders, "after a course of pity and fear makes an end by balancing these passions" ("nach einem Verlauf aber von Mitleid und Furcht mit Ausgleichung solcher Leidenschaften ihr Geschäft abschließt," HA 12:343). "Ausgleichung" is a business term relating to compensating, making the books balance. In the following paragraph Goethe reiterates that the important issues are resolution and closure when he says, "and so [tragedy] must finally complete its work on the stage by balancing, by resolving such passions" ("so müsse [die Tragödie] mit Ausgleichung, mit Versöhnung solcher Leidenschaften zuletzt auf dem Theater ihre Arbeit abschleißen," ibid.). Two paragraphs later he reiterates, "a resolution . . . is indispensable" ("eine Söhnung . . . ist unerläßlich," ibid.). Catharsis, he continues, is "this resolving closure" ("diese aussöhnende Abrundung," ibid.) required of all poetic works. Catharsis has nothing to do with the effect of emotion on characters, but simply with closure.

The next paragraph in the essay makes clear that this extreme formalism should be understood as continuous with the formalism allied to irony already identified as his solution to the crisis of representation. Goethe offers two examples of the paradigmatic theme in tragedy, human sacrifice prevented by a surrogate. The first is Abraham, the second Agamemnon in Aulis; one from the allegorical/religious tradition, one from the mimetic/classical tradition. Further he acknowledges that the final resolution pulls away from tragedy toward comedy. Indeed, he suggests, the only real difference between tragedy and comedy is that the first might sometimes end with death and the second always with marriage. Greek trilogies, he adds, were another way to make sure tragedies ended with resolution. There follows a short paragraph justifying mixed characters on the basis of the need for resolution, and then two long paragraphs disagreeing with Aristotle's position in the *Politics* that music has an effect on morals. The relative insignificance of character is striking here and clearly in opposition to the French neoclassical tradition; similarly the emphasis on music, despite the disagreement with Aristotle, calls attention to its relevance to tragedy. Taken together all these observations assimilate Aristotle's definition of tragedy to the allegorical/operatic tradition that underlies Goethe's dramaturgy.

The final section of the essay is devoted to the moral effect of tragedy. Goethe firmly denies the Horatian tradition that dominated French neoclassicism and states that tragedy has no moral effect: [the spectator] "goes home improved in no way whatsoever" ("aber um nichts gebessert nach Hause geh[t]," HA 12:345). Instead, he argues, tragedies leave the spectator "disturbed and in a vague, indefinite condition" ("in Unruhe . . . und einem vagen, unbestimmten Zustande," ibid.). The word "indefinite" ("unbestimmt") is used prominently in Schiller's *Aesthetic Education*, where it refers to the state of not being fixed by the necessity of reason or reality. The use of the Schillerian term evokes here the concept of play, Schiller's term for dealing with the tension between the allegorical and mimetic tradition. In this essay Goethe in effect repositions Aristotle as a formalist defending the radical autonomy of art. The marriage of mimesis to allegory must be confined to the realm of art.

Goethe is the last great allegorical dramatist of the European tradition. His synthesis of allegory and mimesis, opera and Greek tragedy did not survive his own death, despite this effort to ground it in Aristotle. It still depended ultimately on his own peculiar gifts as an ironist.

Chapter 8

Wagner and the Death of *Gesamtkunstwerk*

> *The danger [in Wagner] reaches its pinnacle when such music relies ever*
> *more on a completely naturalistic style of acting and gesture, not subordi-*
> *nated to any law of sculpture, that seeks only* effect, *and nothing more . . .*
> Expressivity *at all costs and music in its service, in the slavery of*
> *attitudinizing—that is the end . . .*
>
> —*Nietzsche*[1]

Nietzsche's problem in this epigraph, as anyone who reads the code inherited from Weimar Classicism will know, is that Richard Wagner
(1813–83) is not Goethe. The opposition between naturalism and law
refers to the conflict between mimesis and allegory, while "sculpture"
(Nietzsche uses the older term "Plastik") alludes to the Winckelmann-
ian view of ancient art. In the essay "Richard Wagner in Bayreuth," written before he turned against Wagner, Nietzsche accorded the composer
almost equal honors with Goethe as culture hero; in my epigraph from
"Nietzsche contra Wagner," he is Goethe's opposite. Perhaps the rhetoric is only a residuum of a critical commonplace in Germany in the
later nineteenth century—to be Goethe is right and not to be Goethe is
wrong. But implicit in such criticism is also the denial that Wagner's
practice of drama was *Gesamtkunstwerk*. (Wagner himself used the term
only in a more idealistic sense; see Borchmeyer, *Richard Wagner* 65–69.)
Nietzsche thus calls into question the view of the many Wagner enthusiasts and scholars who would claim for the *Ring* the status of the last great
dramatic allegory in European culture. Indeed I shared it myself when I
began this book. But the difficulty of deciding the referent of the allegory makes the problem clear. If Goethe was right that allegory was no
longer possible, the *Ring* is a belated artificial revival.

The same issue confronts all opera in the period. The paradigmatic
opera, *Carmen* (1875), is a case in point, for it contains a role reversal as
remarkable as that in *Die Zauberflöte* (if perhaps less remarked upon).
The novella "Carmen" of 1845 by Prosper Mérimée (1803–70) on which

it is based consists of the anthropological observations of an archeologist about Basques, gypsies, Carmen, and Don José, who tells his story to the narrator shortly before his execution. Carmen's nature is mysterious and exotic to both men: therein lies the interest of the novella. Bizet's librettist reshaped the mystery into a morality in the first act of the opera by adding the pure, innocent Micaela, so that Don José must choose between the pleasure offered by devilish Carmen and the virtue of his good angel. But in the second half the appeal of the novella comes to the fore as Carmen loses interest in her victim and ends as Don José's victim, the oppressed woman seeking her freedom. Don José presumably wants to save both their souls—or would if he were an eighteenth-century hero, but somehow salvation has gotten lost as the opera steps from allegorical structure to mimetic cultural observation. If coherence doesn't seem to matter for Bizet's splendid entertainment, it does still for the philosophically inclined Wagner. After considering the problem of coherence and allegory in *Der Ring des Nibelungen* I will look at two typical kinds of reactions to his achievement—the pursuit of pure mimeticism in Shaw, Strindberg, and Ibsen, and Hugo von Hofmannsthal's efforts to revive Baroque allegorical drama.

Wagner's *Ring* and the End of Allegory

Like Mozart and Goethe, Wagner undertook to strike a balance between music and drama to accommodate the replacement of cosmos by subject. But as a composer writing under the spell of Beethoven's *Ninth Symphony*, he added a component that altered the first: melding the operatic and symphonic modes. In his treatise *Oper und Drama* (1850–51) Wagner distinguishes between opera, in which music takes precedence over drama, and *Musikdrama*, his artwork of the future in which music will serve the word. It is necessary here to consider only two of the many musical corollaries of this position. First is the elimination of the distinction between aria or sung ensemble and recitative and, in its train, the elimination of melody in the common sense of the word and of dance.[2] Second, the distinction between leading voice and accompaniment also disappears.[3] The orchestra does not simply support the vocal line, but carries the true spirit of the work. Wagner goes earlier defenders of opera one better by claiming that music itself—not opera and not "Musikdrama"—is the inheritor of Greek tragedy (Wagner, *Oper und Drama, Dichtungen und Schriften* 7:328). Indeed, music is the heir to religion as the arts (following Hegel and Schelling) are the heirs to the church. In this vaguely neoplatonist logic music becomes the carrier of truth and truth itself; in effect music is both tenor and vehicle of allegory.

But in fact Wagner's thinking about musical drama is Aristotelian. For Wagner all good music can be made to tell a story ("Beethoven," *Dichtungen und Schriften* 9:77). Drama is, however, not text, and not words, but words in action; it is Aristotelian plot ("Beethoven," *Dichtungen und Schriften* 9:94; "Zukunftsmusik," *Dichtungen und Schriften* 8:90). Music guarantees unity: *Musikdrama* comprehends present, past, and future. The older unities of time and place become irrelevant because they are subsumed in the higher unity of feeling and understanding (*Oper und Drama, Dichtungen und Schriften* 7:335–41; cf. Borchmeyer, *Richard Wagner* 155–56). The central goal of drama is to develop character, the primary Aristotelian category since the seventeenth century.[4] However, with the hidden subconscious having displaced the soul, music alone, the vehicle of religion and dream, can express a character's inchoate feelings ("Beethoven," *Dichtungen und Schriften* 9:94; "Zukunftsmusik," *Dichtungen und Schriften* 8:46, 84–86). Expressiveness ("Ausdruck") thus becomes the highest value.[5]

Nietzsche criticizes Wagner for being too expressive. In a kinder mood Nietzsche calls Wagner a guide in the "labyrinth of the modern soul" (Nietzsche, "Der Fall Wagner," *Werke* 2:904; in a less kind mood his characters are all hysterics (ibid. 913). He also focuses too much on gesture and too little on structure; Wagner, Nietzsche sneers, makes his characters swim rather than dance (Nietzsche, *Werke* 2:1043). The difference between the two is real for Nietzsche: dancing, the element that disappeared from Wagner's operas, relates to awareness and conscious control. His most sustained attack on Wagner, "Nietzsche contra Wagner," ends with a celebration of the Greeks for what *Die Geburt der Tragödie* (*The Birth of Tragedy*) calls "Apollonian culture," their focus on surface order and control. Indeed, "Apollonian" might be understood to designate classical form and "Dionysian" its spiritual meaning, the former province of allegory. If so, *Die Geburt der Tragödie* provides a modern psychological model of neoclassicism. Wagner is too interiorized for Nietzsche the modernist, who already withdraws from the values of depth in favor of an abstract formalism. In effect, then, Nietzsche's real criticism of *Musikdrama* is that it is too naively mimetic.[6]

Wagner's mimeticism begins at the level of stage pictures designed to look as real as possible. His stage directions are, indeed, detailed and precise. He designed the Bayreuth theater to prevent distraction from the stage illusion by any element whatsoever. The stage machinery had to work smoothly, the orchestra pit was covered, the multiple proscenium arches were designed so that the stage was perfectly framed from every seat in the house, the house was dimmed for performances (a lasting innovation), and even the exit doors were designed to be invisible to the spectators from their seats.[7] Music for the interludes between scenes was based on precise measurements of the duration of set changes. In these respects Wagner drew the ultimate implications of the Vitruvian and of the eighteenth-century painterly stage; his illusions were as realistic as ever achieved in the European theater. At the same time he reduced the elaborate pageantry also driven by the Vitruvian reforms. Marches and processions, still the high point of eighteenth-century opera and even tragedy, as in Voltaire, become less common, especially in the *Ring*. Only *Götterdämmerung* has a chorus, but the stage is dark for Siegfried's funeral march, marking a distinct antipageant moment. Similarly, dance pantomime, the ultimate development of this strand in the eighteenth century and still central to nineteenth-century grand opera, is banished. No one dances in the *Ring*; when the Rhine maidens swim, the essence of their movement is separation as each lures Alberich in a different direction. But pageantry was the way society represented itself to itself; by eliminating it, Wagner's realistic stage becomes a world of isolated individuals.

Yet the text of the *Ring* is a veritable grab bag of traditional motifs from the older dramatic tradition—from morality, from opera, from Mozart, from Goethe, from Schiller. Characters are constantly falling: into sin, into love, into a faint. They descend to the depths: of the Rhine, of Nibelheim, of the forest, of Fafner's cave. They put on disguises and change their form; they tempt one another and they fall into temptation; they need to renounce, repent, atone. Supernatural figures fly through the air and descend from machines; they also rise from the depths, like Erda or Fafner. And of course, there is lots of significant fire and water. Although most come from the allegorical dramatic tradition, there are also motifs a little more individual to Wagner, like that of awakening sleepers (Erda, Brünnhilde, Hagen) or the murderous quarrel between brothers.[8]

Sometimes the motifs seem to have the same value as in earlier texts, but just as often to have the reverse value. Were Wotan not the ruler of the gods, for example, we could surely call his shady promise to give his sister-in-law Freia to the giants in return for their building him a castle, and his subsequent efforts to escape it in *Das Rheingold*, a "sin," especially as he is led into it by the lying god Loge (the devil, also marked by his association with fire). This is the original situation of the morality plot. When the dwarf Alberich steals the Rhine gold, he falls repeatedly on the slippery rocks; surely the theft is a "sin." But when Wotan takes the gold from Alberich to rescue Freia, is it also a "sin"? Yes, in that he does not right the wrong done to the Rhine maidens, but surely the power of the gold, now in the form of a ring, is better held by the gods than by the despotic Alberich. Then the giants fight over the ring and one kills the other. Again clearly a sin, but on the part of which of them?

When two operas later the young Siegfried kills the dragon Fafner and takes the ring, this is now a positive achievement, and when Siegfried is killed in his turn, his murder, although connected to his possession of the ring, has nothing to do with any guilt he incurred by killing the dragon. Fate is now decoupled from guilt. Brünnhilde makes Siegfried's death possible because he has betrayed her for Gutrune, but his fall into love with the latter was brought on by a magic potion, not by any act of will. The musical leitmotifs are best understood not as fixed signs for a single idea (fate) or object (sword) but as a network of signifiers whose meaning depends on context and particular use (Dahlhaus in Deathridge, *New Grove Wagner* 98–99); so too the motifs and images in the libretti do not constitute a moral allegory, but generate rather a labyrinth of inter- and intrapersonal relations.

In a certain sense, then, the *Ring* is an allegory of character, but in comparison to the allegory of the human understanding and its five senses in Calderón's *Los encantos de la culpa* it has lost its reference to any ethical system outside itself. In *Die Walküre* Brünnhilde disobeys her father because, as he himself says, she is his will. And she obeys his will rather than his explicit, but unwilling, orders. At the same time, this "meaning" is overwhelmed by the passion in the father-daughter relationship, partly inherited from bourgeois tragedy. Nietzsche points to the problem when he criticizes the fundamental absurdity in Wagner by saying that Wotan saved by Siegfried in the *Ring* is like God saved by a free-thinking immoralist (Nietzsche, "Der Fall Wagner," *Werke* 2:908). Like Goethe's *Iphigenie* the *Ring* often slides from dramatic action into narrative: the further the tetralogy proceeds, the more long reflective narrations it contains of its previous action, and the more it is a drama within the self.

Indeed, the *Ring* allegorizes its own turn from allegory as its structures of meaning break down. Wotan is the god of contracts; if he does not keep his promises, he will lose his power and the world will lose its guarantee of truth. In that sense he has already fallen before the cycle begins, for he has allied himself with and trusted the trickster Loge, whose name is very close to the Germanic root for "lie," modern German "Lüge." Wotan's task is to preserve the truthfulness of language, but in a world where gods can fall, the connection between signs and truth must be problematic. Hence the persistent interest in naming. In *Die Walküre* Siegmund evades telling his real name by giving a list of possible accurate names for himself: "I cannot be called Friedmund (protector of peace); I would like to be Frohwalt (bringer of happiness); but I must call myself Wehwalt" ("Friedmund darf ich nicht heißen; / Frohwalt möcht' ich wohl sein: / Doch Wehwalt muß ich mich nennen," *Ring* 81). The structure of the answer asserts that name communicates essence. Yet Hunding recognizes Siegmund as his enemy without his name, and when Siegmund and Sieglinde reveal their real names, which mark them as twins, they take the names as a prelude to union rather than a warning against incest. Similarly Wotan appears in *Siegfried* as the "wanderer." He is not really trying to hide his identity, however; the name refers to his state of exile from his godship, and reveals and hides simultaneously.

Siegfried's bear in the first scene of *Siegfried* shifts the issue to all stage representation. The dwarf Mime is terrified of it, but bears frightening cowards have been standard comedy since the Renaissance (Shakespeare had a bear chase Antigonus off the stage in *A Winter's Tale* 3.3 and a moth-eaten bear frightens cowardly Mariscus in Bidermann's *Cenodoxus* [see above, Chapter 5]) and Wagner repeats the joke with Alberich and the stagy dragon in the next act. After Siegfried kills Fafner and accidentally tastes his blood, he gains the power to hear Mime's murderous thoughts under his intended words, so that language is once again divorced from meaning. In morality plays, in Calderón, and in Shakespeare language and appearances could be deceiving, and truth resided in faith or in action. Here the model is reversed: truth resides not in Mime's actions of proffering refreshment, but in his language, which is here prevented from lying.

The most important figure of meaning in the work is prophecy, embodied in women. Wotan twice awakens Erda, the sleeping goddess Earth and mother of Brünnhilde, once in *Das Rheingold*, and again in the third act of *Siegfried*, both times for advice about the future. Erda does not like being awakened and dismisses Wotan without the information he desires. Furthermore, shortly before the second awakening, Wotan awakens the dragon Fafner, as he says to allow Alberich to recover the ring but in fact to expose his cowardice. Like Erda, Fafner has no interest in being awakened, and the ring, like the truth, remains buried. In the next scene Siegfried's horn, one of Wagner's signature instruments, awakens the dragon more successfully, and the ring is brought back into the light. And in the last scene of the opera Siegfried successfully awakens Brünnhilde. All these parallel awakenings would seem to connect the truth that Erda hides with the power of the ring and of sexuality. Presumably Wotan woke Erda one other time, when he begot Brünnhilde upon her. Does Siegfried's conquest of Brünnhilde bring anything different, however, or more of the same? What does it mean that some awakenings are openly comic and some deadly serious? Are sexuality, power, and truth the same or different? Does the gold guarded by maidens beneath the Rhine symbolize Truth guarded by Erda in the depths? Does it change value when it is guarded underground by dwarves rather than by female principles? At this point the relation among language, spectacle, and truth has become completely muddled. Thus *Götterdämmerung* begins appropriately with the unraveling of the cord by which the Norns are narrating the past and future—that is, the plot of the cycle. The thread they spin, literally the material of a "text," can no longer hold. Within the cycle the catastrophe represents the approaching end of the gods. For readers outside the text it represents the collapse of a coherent system within which cosmological signification—allegory—can exist.

Identity, like signification, is no longer guaranteed by signs. Wotan awakening Erda seems to be the conscious self seeking the unconscious. The scene climaxes in mutual denials of identity. Erda says, "Du bist—nicht, was du dich nennst!" and Wotan replies, "Du bist—nicht, was du dich wähnst" (*Ring* 224): in effect you are not what you consciously claim and you are not what you dream. From this point on, identity is unstable, or better, ineffable. Wotan wills the destruction of the gods and Siegfried breaks Wotan's spear, the sign and guarantor of his power and of cosmic law. Siegfried then wakes Brünnhilde as a mortal woman, no longer goddess (she says, "I am no longer Brünnhilde"—"Brünnhilde bin ich nicht mehr!" *Ring* 239), and the two in effect exchange identities: Brünnhilde gives Siegfried her war horse and shield, Siegfried gives her his ring of power. In *Götterdämmerung* identity is up for grabs. Hagen erases Siegfried's memory with a potion and restores it just as easily at the end. Siegfried disguises himself as Gunther to win Brünnhilde. Alberich demands an oath from the sleeping Hagen, who swears it to himself and not to his father ("Mir selbst schwör ich's," *Ring* 284). Only the ring remains constant and knowable in the relation between any of the characters, especially that of Brünnhilde and Siegfried seesawing between love and hate. The scene in which Brünnhilde recognizes the ring on Siegfried's finger (2.5) ends with characters singing simultaneously but saying opposite things. This object that destroys all relationships and should never have been given form is the only stable sign.

In the final scene the ring becomes the symbol of the cycle by returning to its own beginnings and closing the ring of the plot, as Brünnhilde casts herself upon Siegfried's funeral pyre and bequeaths the ring to the Rhine maidens. In the older allegorical system of signification this act would atone for the accumulated sins of her father, and her death by fire would be an apotheosis. Here her act brings about the end of the gods; it denies the cosmological system as it makes all the gods into transient mortals. This is the kind of formal closure Goethe celebrates in his Aristotle essay, to be sure, but Goethe's synthesis depends on rescuing the principle of order into the ineffable, the something in natural existence that remains inaccessible to human reason. Wagner locates this otherness not in nature, but within the self; once even gods are reduced to human selves, there are no ineffable truths left, but only inchoate emotions.

What possibility remains for dramatic allegory? Brünnhilde's suicide brings about the fall of the gods, but does it also signify it? Just prior to lighting the pyre she tells Wotan's waiting ravens to report what has passed on the Rhine and to summon Loge to Walhalla. "So—," she concludes, "I cast the flame into the magnificent keep of Valhalla" ("So werf ich den Brand in Walhalls prangende Burg," *Ring* 327). The emphatic "so"—whether it means "in this way" or "as a result"—and the need for the messenger ravens mark the separateness of two phenomena that must be connected by interpreting spectators. However much Wagner tried by his theatrical and architectural art to bracket the spectators out, the cycle ends with the shaken members of Gunther's court watching the conflagration of Valhalla in the final tableau. Wagner cannot escape the old play-within-the-play motif and cannot escape the seventeenth-century model of a society constituted by watching itself watch a play. But instead of Iris's rainbow, the image of worldly representation itself, the connection between the represented world and the cosmic order is made by the ravens, and the order to which they link the world is not the abiding cosmos, but its death. Brünnhilde's dramatic "so" is the firebrand that immolates allegory.

The conventional suicides at the ends of operas mark this death. Early operas typically ended with the apotheosis of the hero; the eighteenth century struggled to bring about unhappy endings in tragedy and opera; in the nineteenth it became common for serious operas to end with death, usually that of the heroine.[9] In 1723 Metastasio's *Didone abbandonata* ended with Dido's spectacular suicide leap onto her funeral pyre, followed by an elaborate stage spectacle, in which the stage was first engulfed in flames, then flooded with the rising waters of the harbor (both images of passion); it closed with a ballet of marine divinities. Suicide is a noble gesture in classical tragedy for the preservation of human dignity; here it is precisely balanced by the harmonious divinities that substitute for the older apotheosis of the morality tradition. The union of fire and water as divine harmony remained a cliché for a century,[10] as in the trials of fire and water in *Die Zauberflöte* and the elaborate marine masque that ends act 2 of *Faust II* with the joyous celebration of the marriage of fire and water, the offspring of which is Helen (that is, Beauty). A rainbow, identified as the product of fire and water, is the paradigmatic example of Goethe's new concept of symbol in the opening scene of *Faust II* (4722–27). But suicide kept its importance. *Egmont*'s Klärchen appears at the end as the goddess Freedom—after her suicide at the end of act 4. Anticipating Puccini's Tosca by a century, Schiller's Maid of Orleans jumps from the window of her English prison in the fourth act of *Die Jungfrau von Orleans* (1801). It is an operatic moment, accompanied by the French army's battle march, and Johanna cries that her soul will escape "on the wings of your battle-hymn" ("auf den Flügeln eures Kriegsgesangs," 806). Although Johanna survives the leap and leads the French troops to victory, she dies—gladly and gloriously, but also as an escape from her intolerable emotional situation—in the battle. The finale hovers ambiguously between apotheosis and suicide. Zacharias Werner ends his *Wanda, oder die Königin der Sarmaten* (1809) with the heroine, frustrated in love—like Bellini's Norma by the conflicting demands of her religion—mounting a high flaming altar and springing into the river below. The magnificent scene of ceremonial sacrifice combines suicide, apotheosis, fire, and water.[11] The final scene of Friedrich Hebbel's (1813–63) essentially realistic Nibelungen trilogy of 1855 plays before a burning building, but without water or any hint of apotheosis.[12] But Wagner still clings to the Metastasian fire-water model at the end of the *Ring*, where Brünnhilde casts herself onto the burning pyre, the stage goes up in flames, then the waters of the Rhine douse the fire and the Rhine maidens swim in to recover their ring. Nevertheless, the harmony of a final dance is replaced with the gods sitting motionless in the conflagration. Water, harmony, dance, resolution succumb in the collapse of cosmic order. The fiery end persists into the twentieth century: F. W. Murnau's film of *Faust* ends with Faust joining Margarete burning at the stake in an apotheosis of love. But in the second half of the nineteenth century only the death of the heroine remains de rigueur. She may, like Tosca, still leap, but she may also, like Butterfly, plunge a knife into her breast, like Carmen defiantly die at the hands of her lover, or, like Violetta, die decorously of tuberculosis. After Wagner, at the very latest, suicide has completely displaced apotheosis, as the classical mimetic tradition has displaced allegory.

This is not to say that there is an abrupt break in the nature of European drama. The same stage practices continued, the same conventions continued to shape plots, but the kind of perspicuous dramatic allegory that really drove the development of *Gesamtkunstwerk* was no longer viable. Although the term became current in the wake of Wagner, he did not achieve it; instead, he revealed its impossibility. Music, dance, spectacle, and spoken drama were all integrated over the centuries in the service of a particular cultural structure that no longer prevailed in the mid-nineteenth century. As psychology replaced cosmology the formal relations had to be readjusted. Wagner's appeal to conservative movements in the twentieth century may well reflect their readiness to associate *Gesamtkunstwerk* with a belief in some larger prevailing order, while his appeal to modernists reflects his new psychological power and is in accord with the ultimate ascendence of Aristotelianism and the idea that spoken drama is drama per se.

After Wagner

Of course dramas after the late nineteenth century did not cease to have meaning, but they had to devise their systems of signification anew, often in the face of structures that still presume the older one that was, like Nietzsche's God, now dead. I sketch the situation in a few landmarks of modern drama, and then in Hugo von Hofmannsthal's revivals of allegorical drama for the Salzburg Festival.

The famously detailed novelistic stage directions in George Bernard Shaw's (1856–1950) *Candida* (1898), a modern "normal" romantic comedy, guarantee its fundamentally mimetic stance. Set and characters are not only to seem real, but Shaw explains exactly how each is typical of its social stratum. Both represent by being. Gestures and tones of voice are also prescribed in detail, along with the psychological motivation that prompts them in a world of real people with real feelings. The pleasure of a Shaw play resides in the belief that its characters are just like people we know and that we can see through them as clearly as Shaw does. If this sounds rather like Molière, it should, for the play applies the techniques of neoclassical humor comedy and all the allegorical inheritance that stands behind it. It strictly observes the unities of time and place. The characters all have speaking names. Candida is mindlessly presumed by the men to be as white, shining, and innocent as her name suggests.[13] Eugene Marchbanks, her aristocratic (hence Eugene, wellborn) poetic admirer was picked up on the Embankment, and is characterized as "mad as a March hare." Her husband is James Mavor Morell, an activist Socialist preacher. Mavor, from a variant form of Mars, considers himself a conquering hero, and his last name, stressed on the first syllable, both states and ironizes his moralism. Candida's amoral, conventional father is called Burgess, the bourgeois. Morell's prim, hero-worshipping secretary, wary of the approaches of men, is named, absurdly, Proserpine, but called Prossy. To restate the plot as a morality: Morell (moral) keeps his beautiful wife Candida (purity) in the paradise of their sitting room, to which he introduces her mad admirer Marchbanks, who confronts Morell with his own fatuousness. Nevertheless Marchbanks is expelled and the garden remains innocent of the "secret in the poet's heart" referred to in the last stage direction. Yet Morell is rewarded not for his virtue, but for his lack of it, since Candida stays with her husband because, she says, he is weaker and needs her more. The work of the play is not to change Morell, but to show what lies behind the attractive hero of the opening scene, not to correct character, but simply to reveal it. The inheritance of allegory is made to serve mimesis.

Henrik Ibsen's (1828–1906) *Ghosts* (1881), a major naturalist play, is an analytic tragedy rigidly neoclassical in its observance of the unities. In this play a new orphanage, a monument to Mrs. Alving's recently deceased husband, burns the night before it was to be dedicated. All the protagonists consider the disaster appropriate, because the respected Alving was in truth a dissolute womanizer who passed on his syphilis to his son. Pastor Manders, the friend of the family, actually causes the fire, probably deliberately, having just learned of the lie he has helped to perpetuate. He does not, however, go so far as to blind himself for his previous blindness, as Oedipus did; instead Alving's son goes blind at the end from his inherited syphilis. As the representative of the traditional Christian structure, Manders is revealed by the end to be the voice of a narrow society, not that of truth or religion, and thereby undoes the morality and neoclassical tradition.

It also undoes its largely Senecan imagery of ghosts and general collapse. As elsewhere in Ibsen, Seneca's favorite image of the cosmos crashing down becomes the destruction of the house, the nineteenth-century domestic reduction of the cosmos.[14] The destroyed orphanage is never shown onstage, and by its nature cannot embody the family. So what is destroyed is not order per se, but the lying signifier of an order that did not exist. The orphanage is thus neither an allegory nor a symbol in Goethe's sense; it remains to the spectator to draw the connection between physical house and house as family. Similarly, despite the title, there are no literal ghosts in the play. They are rather Mrs. Alving's conceit, used when she overhears her son making love to the housemaid as his father had twenty years earlier. The family curse is transmitted not by ghosts or talismans, as it still was in the fate dramas (*Schicksalsdramen*) of the first half of the century,[15] but by the disease passed from father to son. The ghosts in this play are Aristotelian metaphors—rhetorical ornaments, not visible presences. The splendid sunrise after a long and difficult night at the end plays on the traditional positive ending of morality and neoclassical drama, probably with reference to the rising sun that created Goethe's symbolic rainbow at the beginning of *Faust II*. But Mrs. Alving's attempt to identify the sunrise as a symbol of hope is in vain: she recognizes that her beloved son has suddenly lost both his sight and his mind to his inherited syphilis, and that she must keep her promise to assist him in suicide. The new concept of symbol fares no better than allegory.

August Strindberg's (1849–1912) *Ghost Sonata* of 1907 appears at first more allegorical. Its dramatis personae include a vision, a dead man, and a mummy; it proceeds, at least on the surface, jumpily and illogically, like a dream. As a "chamber play" (by analogy with "chamber music") and by its title it claims a musical connection, and in fact the romantic hero and heroine are made to meet at a performance of *Die Walküre.* Yet it is closely related to *Ghosts* by both its title and its Senecanism. Strindberg uses not only the motif of ghosts, but also that of the falling house, and revenge as well. As in the *Thyestes* an old man named Hummel takes revenge on the Colonel, who seduced Hummel's fiancée years before, by exposing the crimes of his entire circle to one another; in a final twist Hummel's own crime is exposed to them. His servant twice uses the metaphor of making a house collapse for his activities, while *Die Walküre* deals with the collapse of the gods' own house. But at the beginning of the play the hero, a young student, enters from daring rescue efforts after the literal collapse of a house, and the two young people, the student and the daughter of the Colonel, are spared the searing revelations of the second act. Just as the house that really collapsed has nothing to with the metaphoric one, the ghosts wandering around have nothing to do with revenge, a strictly human activity in this play. As in Ibsen the explanatory category is human psychology, not a divine order. Furthermore, the clear difference between good and evil represented in the play is generational: young people are pure and innocent, the older generation so dreadful that innocence cannot survive. In the first scene the girl's home with its hyacinths appears to be paradise, the second scene ends with a song sung by the two isolated innocents, and by the last the paradise is a den of ghosts and the hyacinths fantastic and poisonous. As the student tells the girl about the evil in his family that corresponds to the past of her own, she collapses and dies. The play ends with music celebrating innocence, bright light, and a harp on which no one plays. But this apparent apotheosis is accompanied by the whimpers of the dying heroine. The ending of morality is invoked only to be denied. If Strindberg offers here some mystic belief in a better world outside of this one, its only manifestation is the invisible player of the harp at the end. All of its other symbols in the world, like the paradisal house and the innocent first flowers of spring, have been perverted into bearers of death. In effect, the will to allegory suffers the same fate as all innocence in the play, destruction by the pervasive evil of the world. Compared to Strindberg, Shaw's satire of the structures of allegorical drama seems innocent in its confidence in mimesis and reality, and even Ibsen's determined smashing of meaning communicates a certain confidence in human reason. Strindberg's pathetic gestures of faith suggest rather an effort to pick up the pieces of what has been irretrievably broken. He turns to a kind of meta-allegory, not to preserve the incommensurability of truth in play, like Goethe or like Kleist with his broken jug, but to agonize over its passing and perhaps force its return.

Most compelling among modern attempts to revive allegorical drama are the festival plays (*Festspiele*) that Hugo von Hofmannsthal (1874–1929), better known outside of Germany and Austria as Richard Strauss's librettist, wrote for the early days of the Salzburg Festival. At issue here are three plays: *Jedermann* (1911), an adaptation of *Everyman*; *Das Salzburger große Welttheater* (The Salzburg Great Theater of the World, 1922), an adaptation of Calderón's *auto sacramental*, *El gran teatro del mundo*; and *Der Turm* (The Tower, 1924, rewritten 1926), a tumultuous free adaptation of *La vida es sueño*. The first two were, and still are, staged outdoors before the Baroque façades of Salzburg in productions first designed by Max Reinhardt. Hofmannsthal had strong roots on the operatic stage and, with these two morality plays and a seventeenth-century commercial drama still visibly close to its morality forebears, sought to revitalize the allegorical tradition for a Europe that had lost its way in the modern world. Nevertheless, Hofmannsthal did not write from the confident position of a Calderón, who was himself a priest; he wrote as a modern, grandson of a Jew, often in the violent rhetoric of German Expressionism, trying to understand how God could create a world full of the evils recognized by Ibsen and Strindberg and experienced by Hofmannsthal's generation in all their force.

Jedermann and *Das Salzburger große Welttheater* follow their originals fairly closely, but with some telling divergences. Personified abstractions tend to be replaced with representatives of a class, or else are simply eliminated. Hofmannsthal has also substantially elaborated the plots. The additions to *Everyman* all come at the beginning, between the point at which God makes his decision to call Everyman to account and Death's arrival actually to summon him. The new elements (building a pleasure garden, resisting his mother's admonitions to Christianity, denying a beggar) are typical of other moralities but combine to give Jedermann a more individual, specific character—a wealthy man of Hofmannsthal's generation, not all that different from the spectators—in conflict with parts of the world around him. Hofmannsthal even individualizes the devil; like Mephistopheles at the end of *Faust II*, he waits for Jedermann's soul at his death and then feels cheated of his prey (see *Faust II* 11604–803). In the *Salzburger große Welttheater* Hofmannsthal devotes his energy to the Beggar, who almost begins a revolution, but then stops in a climactic moment of personal vision and withdraws to pray in the forest. The gesture is imported from the climax of *La vida es sueño*, where Segismundo does not kill his father, but exercises his free will to control himself. Hofmannsthal has mimeticized both plays by elaborating the central character and enhancing conflict, as we would expect from the development of Aristotelianism under Hegelian influence in the period.

In the process of this mimeticization, the concreteness of allegory becomes invisible. The onstage conversion involves a moment of blinding light for the Beggar, but the audience learns of it only from his narration. God is also invisible at the end of the play, when those who have played their roles well disappear into the palace, instead of ascending to the upper stage where God awaits them as in Calderón. Singing angels replace both the doctor who draws the moral at the end of *Jedermann* and Calderón's original Law of Grace in the *Salzburger große Welttheater*. The Law of Grace sings already in Calderón, but the introduction of a chorus of angels conventionalizes divine intervention in a way that denies it its supernatural weight in Hofmannsthal. Extreme theatricality stood in effectively for the supernatural in the seventeenth century and still functioned as irony for Goethe. Faust decides not to take poison on Easter morning not because of divine interference but because he hears a human chorus impersonating angels from the neighboring church. But after Wagner and after the sentimental choruses of angels at the ends of Gounod's and Berlioz's Faust operas, choruses of angels have more to do with blond/bland innocence than with divine instruction. Opera already confronted this problem by having absolute music upstage voice when it wanted to express incommensurability. In Wagner and Strauss music becomes the vehicle of the inexpressible, what used to be the supernatural but which is now a force for which there is no name. Hofmannsthal documented his crisis of language in his famous "Chandos-Brief" of 1902, the point at which he stopped writing poetry and began writing opera libretti instead. These operas typically contain moments where feelings become inexpressible and the orchestra takes over from the voices, as in the love scene in the second act of *Der Rosenkavalier*. Like the harp playing of its own accord at the end of Strindberg, the angels' singing is less revelation than a substitute for it. The age of materialism and scientific inquiry has invalidated the older abstract language of morality, even for its reviver.

Hofmannsthal repeated the struggle in *Der Turm* with greater urgency. The play takes its name, the tower, from Segismundo's prison in *La vida es sueño*, and developed out of attempts to prepare a stage version of Calderón's play. Both plays fear the Senecan collapse of Poland into chaos; Hofmannsthal's Sigismund is not, however, like Calderón's Segismundo, a human who exercises his free will to do right. Instead he is a god whose presence in the world remains invisible to all but a doctor (a scientist rather than a priest)[16] with special insight into the human soul. Calderón's women, who embodied the Platonist truth, disappear entirely from the plot. Whatever divinity exists is hidden within Sigismund, the wolf-man. At the end of the first version a mystical army of children comes to claim Sigismund's body to sanctify their new world order. In a

Shakespearean tragedy, such a compensatory gesture would restore the world to unity, if only in mourning. But here it is a desperate leap of faith, since the entire explanatory system of the play until this final moment has been not religious, but Freudian and political. As a result, the operatic trappings of the play (pageantry, background choruses, organ, an exotic army of Tartars supporting Sigismund, a gypsy scene in which Sigismund resists the phantoms, the children's army with its child king) and its visionary end ring hollow. Hofmannsthal scaled the operatic aspects back in the shorter second version and eliminated the exotica of the end to create a more mimetic ending: Sigismund is shot by the warlord rising to power from the wreckage of the aborted renewal of the world instead of having the life line of his palm slashed with a poisoned dagger by a gypsy. Allegory cannot be revived.

Hofmannsthal's early sketches for the play locate the problem with language and representation. The tower, he says, is the "center of the injustice of the world: here dreadful injustice gives birth incessantly to demons . . . Devils hover about the tower like ravens around the gallows" ("Zentrum des Weltunrechts: hier gebiert furchtbares Unrecht fortwährend Dämonen . . . Teufel umflattern den Turm wie Raben das Hochgericht," *Dramen III* 243). The passage begins with the rhetorical structure of metaphor (A = B), invokes the demons and devils of the allegorical tradition, and ends with a simile. At the center is the image of birth, that is, causation. The language thus combines allegory and the Aristotelian categories of metaphor and causality: Hofmannsthal wants to make the two modes work together. But the term "symbolic" does not carry the Goethean significance one might expect of a writer as much under the spell of the great father as Hofmannsthal; instead it is consistently psychological—for example, "he takes all the mother's actions *frightfully* symbolically" ("alles was die Mutter tut, nimmt er *furchtbar* symbolisch," *Dramen III* 244), or "a lot of symbolizing traumas" ("eine Fülle symbolisierender Traumata," *Dramen III* 249). At the same time Hofmannsthal is capable of using a phrase like "prison of the subconscious" ("Kerker des Unterbewußtseins," in the specifically Freudian sense) without connecting it to Sigismund's own tower prison. Or consider the most striking use of the term with regard to Sigismund's motivation:

in order to purge myself of the irritations of life I need a dreadful and symbolic pleasure: murder.—[Sigismund] elaborates the concept "symbolically": I must perform an action—only such a one purges me—where I forget myself *completely*; where poor Sigismund disappears and the world disappears too, and only the one who acts is there, is there and kills, kills, kills! Ecstasy!

(Um mich [der Reizen des Lebens] zu entladen brauche ich eine ungeheure und symbolische Wollust: den Mord.—[Sigismund] umschreibt den Begriff "symbolisch": ich muß eine Handlung begehen—nur eine solche entladet mich—, bei der ich mich *völlig* hingeben kann; bei der der arme Sigismund weg und die Welt auch weg ist, und nur der, der tut, der ist da, der da und tötet, tötet, tötet! Ekstase!" [*Dramen III* 246])

Hofmannsthal's "symbol" here avoids the concreteness of allegory or of Goethe's symbol; it is, instead, action—not however, creative action that produces, but destruction, erasure.

Late in the last act Sigismund calls out, presumably to the doctor who has believed in him: "Bear witness: I was there. Even if no one recognized me" ("Gebet Zeugnis: ich war da. Wenngleich mich niemand gekannt hat," *Dramen III* 381, 469). In the second version these words close the play. Their definitive position there acknowledges that the battle to manifest truth in the world has been lost, for what testimony can the spectator of Sigismund's fortunes give? "Even though no one recognized me" gives the lie to the affirmative gesture the call to bear witness implies: no interpreter steps forward to testify to the audience, as at the end of *Everyman*, and no visible apotheosis offers the play's testimony to the audience that divinity or Truth has been present. All that remains of the Baroque and operatic apotheosis is the call to the audience to believe in the transient presence of whatever it is that Sigismund represents. The burden of giving the allegorical action meaning has shifted entirely from dramatist to audience. From the fifteenth century on, at the latest, allegorical drama in Europe involved explicit allegoresis, by an interpreter or narrator, or, as in Calderón's *autos* by protagonists. As drama became ever more mimetic in the eighteenth century allegoresis depended increasingly on audience recognition of the traditional significance of conventions of plot and gesture; as a result it became less dependable. Here in Hofmannsthal all that remains of the tradition is the recognition that it was once there; the capacity of a specific dramatic tradition to unify the culture and give it meaning seems to be what Sigismund calls upon the audience to testify to at the end of *Der Turm*.

The formulation is very close to that of his friend Walter Benjamin: for him Baroque allegory incorporates within itself the abyss that tragically prevents the identity of signifier and signified required by allegory. It is a problematic description of Baroque dramatic allegory, but accurate about the problem of allegory in his contemporaries. With this shift dramatic allegory is now mourning in Benjamin's sense: it can only mark its incapacity to mean. But it has also now become like narrative allegory, where allegoresis, interpreting the allegory, has traditionally been the reader's responsibility, not the text's. It seems appropriate that Benjamin's notoriously obscure analysis should mark the end of the particular tradition of perspicuous dramatic allegory.

Coda
"This Insubstantial Pageant"

> *Believe me, sir*
> *It carries a brave form. But 'tis a spirit.*
> —*Shakespeare* (The Tempest *1.2.411–12*)

The title phrase falls in Prospero's famous set speech in *The Tempest:*

> Our revels now are ended. These our actors
> (As I foretold you) were all spirits, and
> Are melted into air, into thin air,
> And like the baseless fabric of this vision,
> The cloud-capped tow'rs, the gorgeous palaces,
> The solemn temples, the great globe itself,
> Yea, all which it inherit, shall dissolve,
> And like this insubstantial pageant faded
> Leave not a rack behind. (4.1.148–56)

Prospero's "insubstantial pageant" is an interrupted wedding masque performed by bodiless spirits summoned by the slightly more embodied spirit Ariel. The masque is an allegory that allies the marriage of Ferdinand and Miranda to the cosmic order of nature; its spirits and its meaning are simultaneously visible yet abstract. When the "real" world of the play requires Prospero to deal with Caliban's plot to overthrow him, the masque evaporates: its spirit figures give way to "real" and substantial mimetic characters—Prospero, Miranda, and Ferdinand. Here is the traditional stance of mimesis: allegory is insubstantial. And yet Prospero's swelling rhetoric in its turn subsumes the reality in the play to that of the spectator's more real world—"the great globe itself"— Shakespeare's own theater, the theater of the world, and the world. But even "the great globe itself" will dissolve, and so, in this hierarchy of mutable worlds, the insubstantial pageant of the spirits takes on the permanence of Truth and of the eternal order of the cosmos. Throughout

The Tempest Ariel stages various spirit plays; superficially delusory, they actually communicate important truths to characters and audiences who know how to read them. The spirits in the play are "brave forms," while the glittering external forms of Prospero's clothing prove empty lures for the hapless clowns, whose only spiritual support derives from the bottle. Allegory's dissolution is a sublimation that banishes not itself but mimesis.

Prospero's insubstantial-substantial truth reflects the moral structure of religious drama, as well as the moral and social context of court masque, yet in its staging, mythical content and characters, it also reflects the classicizing influence of the illusionist stage, still oddly evanescent and insubstantial. But *The Tempest* also represents the impact of Aristotelian theory with its plot unified by Prospero's stage management, its relatively restricted location, and the strict unity of time otherwise atypical for Shakespeare. Senecanism appears in the ruler's dramatic isolation on his desert island, in the constant attempts to overthrow him, and in his plan for revenge. *This* Classicism, represented also by Prospero's mutable cloud-capped towers, has remained much more memorable than the masques of his airy spirits. Classicism clothes both mimesis and allegory here: like the robes of Prospero it can seem an insubstantial shell, but also the substantial dignity of the ruler.

The Tempest embodies in summary the ambiguities and anxieties that attend the shift from allegory to mimesis through so many different kinds of neoclassicism. Like all European drama, whether Aristotelian, neoplatonist, Senecan, Vitruvian, operatic, or Greek Revival, it lives from the tension between the spiritual and the real, the allegorical and the mimetic, the insubstantial and the corporeal. In this book I have tried to show how all these different forms of classical revival interact in different fashion to create the genres we know as morality play, Elizabethan tragedy, neoclassical tragedy, court masque, Corpus Christi play, school drama, bourgeois tragedy, opera, dance pantomime, German Classicism, Naturalism, and all those other names we give to texts for stage performance.

But these oppositions are manifested not only, not even primarily, at the level of content, character and allusion, but as so often, through the formal structures we have seen organizing texts all over Western Europe from the sixteenth to the twentieth centuries, with and without music, with and without lavish sets and spectacle. Plot was the most important element of tragedy for Aristotle, and his hierarchy is validated when the Christian plot of repentance and salvation—spiritual, "insubstantial"—survives tenaciously through centuries of neo-Aristotelian focus on character from Shakespeare (as he is commonly read) through Racine, Lessing, Wagner, Ibsen, and Shaw. Only when the nineteenth century declares God dead, or at least disappeared, when the cosmos on which it depends is secularized, does its truth cease to inform and substantiate the dramatic representation of the world effectively.

Faust, Part II is the swan song of European dramatic allegory. It marks its position by a return to Shakespeare's ambiguous ruminations. In its first scene, "Anmutige Gegend" (Charming Landscape), Faust is healed from the devastations of the tragedy of Margarete, the subject of Part I, by nature spirits singing under Ariel's direction. He and his elves have two, equally important, effects upon Faust. First, they cause him to reenter the cycle of nature in time, to return to the "real" world. Second, Faust takes from this encounter a new capacity to read nature allegorically: he can now see the meaning of life, its embeddedness in the order of nature in an insubstantial rainbow caused by the reflection and refraction of sunlight in water. Goethe's Ariel follows no orders from Prospero but simply acts without the mediating mimesis of the magician plot; indeed, his name is given only in the printed speech heading. He is not a tricksy spirit being forced to heal Faust by a human mind, but a pure allegory of the order of nature. If Shakespeare has embodied himself in *The Tempest* in Prospero, Goethe keeps his distance. Yet this spectacle gives way to a carnival masque that refigures characters from *The Tempest*: Caliban is Mephistopheles, Prospero becomes Faust playing Plutus (god of wealth; all three names are synonymous), and Ariel appears as Boy-Charioteer, who is the spirit of Poetry. If in the first scene Goethe's allegories seemed purer than Shakespeare's, here the allusion to *The Tempest* keeps them from seeming arbitrary; only by connecting himself to a historical tradition of allegorical drama can Goethe still write it in the 1820s, and thereby give his pageants their proper insubstantiality, their transcendent meaning.

Goethe's focus on the insubstantial spirit in Shakespeare explains why there was a last effusion of interest in allegory as it was fading from the scene. Spirit, in German the same word as "mind" (*Geist*), became one of the code words the German Romantics set in opposition to what they perceived as the excesses of Enlightenment rationalism. In its other common philosophical formulation in the period the term was subject, as opposed to object. Aligning the spiritual with the subject, the interior self, meant that the cosmos now resided inside the self rather than outside in the universe; as a result Romantic allegory became paradoxical and soon had to give way to the term symbol, as we have seen. Nevertheless, their last-ditch effort against the complete rationalization and secularization of culture has really been the source of the terminology and categories that have made this study possible.

For the irresistible but unperformable *Faust* was stemming a tide. Before World War I, historical substance was running wild on the European stage. In the era of the great naturalists Ibsen, Chekhov, Shaw, Puccini, and Hauptmann, ever more elaborate, precisely historical illusionistic sets and costumes, stage effects, pantomime, music for mood and to emphasize emotional climaxes characterize not only opera, but all stage drama. All the paraphernalia of *Gesamtkunstwerk* were brought to bear by leading directors of the period: Henry Irving's production of *Faust* featured a sword that lit up during Faust's duel with Valentine (Booth, *Victorian Spectacular Theatre 1850–1910* 115), and Max Reinhardt rose to prominence as a master of spectacular stage effects. Now, however, the great panoply of effect was in the service not of allegory, but of mimesis. This age determines still current concepts of the "normal" on the stage; its great Shakespeare critic A. C. Bradley and his Hegelian theory of tragedy with its focus on character conflict still often prevail today. Almost simultaneously, to be sure, a reaction (that in fact embraced many naturalists themselves) developed in the exaggerated modernist formalism of "l'art pour l'art" and surrealism. Goethe's identification of Aristotle as the ultimate formalist was prescient indeed. If allegory suffered a protracted, Dickensian death from Wagner to Hofmannsthal, the same can be said of mimesis.

The lesson of Seneca is that nothing ever really dies, but remains a ghostly presence for succeeding generations. Indeed, Goethe's Faust knows this presence well and warns against it: "If spirits haunt you, continue on your way" ("Wenn Geister spuken, geh' er seinen Gang," 11450). Aristotle's categories of mimesis and the unities continue to haunt the introductions to freshman anthologies of drama and the language of reviewers to this day. And similarly, the familiar plot of morality continues its life on the stage, in melodrama, and in film, as every lover of Hollywood westerns would acknowledge. My goal is that the ghosts be recognized and their insubstantiality welcomed into our discourse rather than left to haunt its margins.

Notes

Chapter 1

1. E. H. Gombrich demonstrates the same gradual shift in the theory of visual representation from neoplatonist allegory to symbols understood in Aristotelian terms in "Icones Symbolicae." T. J. Reiss asserts a lag between neoclassical theory and practice in France in the sixteenth and early seventeenth centuries (*Toward Dramatic Illusion* 3–6), while Thomas Maresca pleads for a historicist analysis of allegory in "Saying and Meaning: Allegory and the Indefinable" 248. Neither Gombrich nor other art historians I am aware of focus on the tensions between the modes in individual texts.

2. A notable exception is Catherine Belsey's discussion of the ambiguous representation of the subject in Shakespearean tragedy, in which she sees precisely an older emblematic discourse operating side by side with a more modern discourse of the modern subject in *The Subject of Tragedy*. Belsey's argument is couched largely in social terms, mine in formal.

3. According to a private communication from Gloria Eive, it is also documentable that in Faenza in the early nineteenth century opera libretti were performed as stage dramas as an economy in times of war.

4. The term "allegory" is used repeatedly in *Faust II* by characters about one another or about themselves; see also J. K. Brown, *Goethe's* Faust: *The German Tragedy* 147–52 and below Chapter 7.

5. The greatest range is found in Quintilian's discussion of allegory in the *Institutio Oratoria*. For brief analysis of what the terms might have meant, see Philip Rollinson, *Classical Theories of Allegory and Christian Culture* 15–17. For a clear and concise history of important aspects of the term, see John MacQueen, *Allegory*. Even within the period under discussion use of the term was variable; see for example Joshua McClennen, *On the Meaning and Function of Allegory in the English Renaissance*.

6. Spenser is usually the main starting point. I have in mind here the classic studies by Edwin Honig, *Dark Conceit: The Making of Allegory*; Angus Fletcher, *Allegory: The Theory of a Symbolic Mode*; Rosamond Tuve, *Allegorical Imagery: Some Medieval Books and Their Posterity*; and Maureen Quilligan, *The Language of Allegory: Defining the Genre*. Honig to a large extent set the canon and named the topics explored and elaborated so effectively by Fletcher and later connected to modern theory by Quilligan. Tuve takes a more historical line by connecting her

phenomenology to particular transmitting texts, but at the same time identifies even more clearly than the others the relations between allegorical writing and allegorical reading. Stephen Barney's "practical reading" of allegorical texts in *Allegories of History, Allegories of Love* is also a phenomenology in this sense.

7. MacQueen points out that allegorical narrative has always depended on the interaction of allegory and mimesis, and cites Tasso to this effect at the beginning of the *Gerusalemme Liberata*: "Heroic poetry, like an animal which is formed by the conjunction of two natures, is compounded from Imitation [i.e., Aristotelian mimesis] and Allegory" (*Allegory* 65). Cf. also Tuve's insistence that reading seventeenth-century allegory still "demands a full disregard of any barriers between naturalistic and symbolical presentation of details" (*Allegorical Imagery* 200).

8. This problem dogs all discussions of allegory. Cf. Rollinson's attack on Robertson and his students for reducing all medieval allegory to Augustinian *caritas* (*Classical Theories of Allegory* x–xii). Tuve also, despite her initial distinction of moral from specifically religious allegory, increasingly reserves the term allegory for the latter sort, which is perilously close to being restricted to Christological allegories.

9. See Mitchell, *Iconology* 37, though he does not use the term "mimetic."

10. Cf. Maresca, "Saying and Meaning" 260; Mitchell, *Iconology* 41 characterizes mimesis as figural, allegory as literal.

11. I am pushing here the distinction between discourse and figure laid out by Norman Bryson in *Word and Image* 1–28, by applying it to the distinction between allegory and mimesis. The two pairs of oppositions are not identical, but the connections are suggestive.

12. But cf. both MacQueen and A. A. Parker (referred to by MacQueen) on the impact of morality play on Elizabethan drama and the emergence of the realistic novel (*Allegory* 70–73).

13. I follow here the analysis of James Hirsch in "Shakespeare and the History of Soliloquies." There have been thoughtful efforts to locate the beginnings of modern interiorized subjectivity in Shakespeare by Joel Fineman in *Shakespeare's Perjur'd Eye* and in Catherine Belsey's *Subject of Tragedy*.

14. Cf. E. H. Gombrich on Botticelli—"Botticelli's Mythologies" 64. Consider also Bryson's discussion of the blockage of allegory in seventeenth-century Dutch still life in terms of the particular tensions surrounding representation in the religious conflicts of the Dutch Reformation and Counter-Reformation (*Looking at the Overlooked* 116–21), and Mitchell's readings of different positions on iconoclasm in terms of their underlying ideologies in *Iconology* passim.

15. Anxiety like that expressed in these paintings does not seem to have arisen in Italy in the Renaissance, but it was clearly present in the Latin countries in the Counter-Reformation. But cf. Bialostocki on Giorgione's *Judith*, although Bialostocki skirts the issue of Renaissance ambivalence—"Judith: Story, Image, and Symbol" 113–31.

16. There has been virtually no scholarly discussion of the history of allegory, with the recent exception of Theresa Kelley's attempt to trace the transformation of allegory from Milton via the Romantics to postmodern allegories in *Reinventing Allegory*. Even this admirable effort is undercut by its grounding of all allegory in the historically conditioned definitions of Walter Benjamin and Paul de Man.

17. Cf. Maresca on the confusion of personification with allegory in the late seventeenth and eighteenth centuries, "Saying and Meaning" 257–60. I would

not, however, agree with Maresca's consistent denial of allegorical status to personification on the grounds of its clarity; instead I would argue for considerable historical and generic variation in the obscurity of allegory.

18. Cf. Marshall Brown's argument that even in the nineteenth century realism is always perceived only by contrast to some defined "less realistic" mode in "The Logic of Realism."

19. There is much disagreement as to the meaning of this painting—fortunately none of it relevant to our concerns—as to precisely how arcane its allegory might be, and as to its relation to the programs of the other paintings with which it was originally hung, including Mantegna's even more enigmatic Parnassus. Summarized by Christiansen, "Pallas Expelling the Vices from the Garden of Virtue."

20. In this identification I follow Seznec, *The Survival of the Pagan Gods* 5 and 109; for alternatives see Christiansen, "Pallas Expelling the Vices from the Garden of Virtue" 429. Of course Seznec's main point is that the mythological mode is an inheritance of late antiquity generously mediated by the Middle Ages; nevertheless its sudden upsurge in the Renaissance coupled to a more mimetic iconography based on classical prototypes makes it operate as a new factor in this situation.

21. Again I follow Seznec, *The Survival of the Pagan Gods*; cf. Christiansen, "Pallas Expelling the Vices from the Garden of Virtue."

22. In his magisterial *History of Literary Criticism in the Renaissance* Joseph Spingarn reserved the term (actually his term was "modern classicism") for the specifically French version of Renaissance Aristotelianism (311); in his equally magisterial *A History of Literary Criticism in the Italian Renaissance* Bernard Weinberg extends the term to the Italian sixteenth century.

Chapter 2

1. E.g.: "This gilded motley affords great sensuous pleasure and is a good example of just what it was that made Claude's landscapes so popular. It is pure pleasure, not information—landscapes graced by the presence of biblical or Ovidian figures" (Malcolm Andrews, *Landscape and Western Art* 102). Humphrey Wine's correlation of narrative texts with paintings in his 1994 exhibit, *Claude Lorrain: The Poetic Landscape*, was considered a bold gesture and aroused some irritation among newspaper reviewers precisely for its implicit assertion that Claude goes beyond "atmosphere." Michael Kitson is unwilling to consider Claude an allegorist in his review of the exhibit in *Burlington Magazine*. H. Diane Russell (*Claude Lorrain*) and Claire Pace ("'The Golden Age . . . The First and Last Days of Mankind': Claude Lorrain and Classical Pastoral") are at least willing to admit some traditional emblems and, in Pace, the relevance of the narratives is alluded to. Nevertheless, unlike Pace, I am interested not just in how the paintings evoke "the spirit of the myth concerned" (138), but in their independent statements.

2. It is now widely accepted that there is a strong allegorical—probably better called emblematic—element even to seventeenth-century Dutch genre and landscape painting, long considered exclusively faithful imitation of nature. The issue is surveyed by Jan Bialostocki in "Mere Imitation of Nature or Symbolic Image of the World?"; it is also addressed and limited in significant ways by Jan Baptist Bedaux, who finds the mimetic element now too consistently underestimated in *The Reality of Symbols* esp. 9–108.

3. A brief but cogent survey of Claude's reputation in England, "Claude and English Art" by Deborah Howard, may be found in Michael Kitson, *The Art of Claude Lorrain* 9–10. Cf. also Elizabeth Wheeler Manwaring, *Italian Landscape in Eighteenth Century England* esp. 121–66, and John Barrell on the "grammar" of landscape attributable to Claude, in *The Idea of Landscape* 6–12.

4. For a general discussion of the esteem in which Claude was still held in the early nineteenth century, see Claire Pace, "Claude the Enchanted." Intensively used by Ruskin, the Dulwich Art Gallery, the nucleus of whose collection was a gift in 1811, offers a good example of this phenomenon.

5. The comparable feature in literary neoclassicism is the focus on unity, which results in the representation of a closed unit of time and space, not the open flow of earlier drama. Cf. Marshall Brown, *Preromanticism* 201–2.

6. Claude's paintings are customarily identified by their number in the *Liber Veritatis*, Claude's own book of sketches of most of his finished paintings, often with a record of date and patron. I generally use the titles given by Röthlisberger in his invaluable catalogue of Claude's paintings, *Claude Lorrain: The Paintings*.

7. For an eloquent discussion of this topic see Kitson, *The Art of Claude Lorrain* 7–8. Cf. also Kitson, "The Seventeenth Century: Claude to Francisque Millet" esp. 19–20, and Lagerlöf, *Ideal Landscape* 9–11 and 161–84.

8. Here I follow and sharpen the reading suggested by Russell, *Claude Lorrain* 84–91, esp. 84, whose interpretation of sunrise journeys in Claude's seaports of the 1640s seems essentially correct. Cf. also Wine (*Poetic Landscape* 34–37), who cites several contemporary statements on the religious significance of nature, a tradition still drawn on by Claude's contemporary, Pedro Calderón de la Barca, in his defense of painting of 1677 (summarized by E. R. Curtius, *European Literature and the Latin Middle Ages* 561). Russell is also doubtless right in her later suggestion (*Claude Lorrain* 90) that the ship in the *Coast View with the Apostle Paul* (LV 171) is Ecclesia, the protective church; the allegory is still common in the morality plays and court spectacles of Calderón.

9. Cf. Heide Eilert on the consonance of Claude's paintings with the political and general social norms of the age in "Amor als Landschaftsmaler" 132. Eilert follows here Matthias Eberle, *Individuum und Landschaft* 184ff. On Claude's paintings as more specific representations of political status, see Rosemary Maclean, "'O gran Principe o gran Prelato': Claude's Roman Patrons and the Appeal of his Landscape Easel Paintings."

10. "Almost," because Claude was famous for having sketched from nature, but the evidence that he painted outside his studio (largely a development of the nineteenth century) is limited. The claim dates from his first biographer, Joachim Sandrart, whose brief biography is available in Röthlisberger, *Paintings* 1:47–50, with additional relevant material on 51–52.

11. Only LV 51, *Liberation of St. Peter*, the single strictly figure drawing set indoors known by Claude, has less horizon.

12. Information on Caron and the subject of this painting are taken from Jean Ehrmann, *Antoine Caron* 129–34.

13. In fact, the earliest drawing consisted only of the right hand 60 percent or so, which made the castle the end of a dark mass springing from the left edge. The latest study consisted of such a drawing with an additional sheet (which also exists in an independent version) attached to the left. See Röthlisberger, *The Claude Lorrain Album* 29, and also his *Claude Lorrain: The Drawings* 346.

14. Cf. Wine, *Poetic Landscape* 21, on landscape as "metaphor." He uses the term "metaphor" as I am using "allegory" here. Cf. also Russell's invocation of

allegory with regard to this painting as a form of rich allusiveness, *Claude Lorrain* 76. Lagerlöf, *Ideal Landscape* 143–44, 153 argues that the tiny figures enhance the grandeur and significance of nature; our explanations are not necessarily incompatible.

15. There are also three drawings of ships in storms in the LV (33, 72, 74), none of which is associated with a known painting.

16. In her thorough and thoughtful survey of Claude's use of Ovid and Virgil, Pace documents Claude's use of Anguarilla's translation of Ovid with an allegorizing commentary, "'The Golden Age . . . The First and Last Days of Mankind': Claude Lorrain and Classical Pastoral" 136 and 138.

17. Strikingly absent are Jupiter and Venus. Claude's eighteenth-century audience apparently suffered from this lack to judge from the repainting of *Acis and Galatea* (LV 141, Dresden) to add a Cupid, and of *Narcissus and Echo* (LV 77, London) to transform the clothed nymph of the spring into a reclining Venus. Jupiter has, of course, no place in pastoral; hence he appears here as a bull (Europa) and, more remarkably, in the guise of Diana in *Jupiter and Callisto* (LV 76).

18. The lyre is absent in the drawing, sometimes a sign of later overpainting. Neither Röthlisberger nor Kitson comments on this discrepancy. Apollo otherwise appears as the god of music and poetry—Claude always shows him with pipes, violin, or lyre, and three times on Mount Parnassus (LV 126, 193, 195)—and as god of prophecy—the two processions to Delphi, two paintings of Apollo and the Cumaean sibyl (LV 99, 164). Pace documents his knowledge of Mercury's gift to Apollo and its source, "'The Golden Age . . . The First and Last Days of Mankind': Claude Lorrain and Classical Pastoral" 141.

19. As for example in *The Staalmeesters* (1662, Amsterdam), where the figures appear to be on a dais and reacting to an audience outside the painting; cf. Michael Bockemühl, *Rembrandt* 60. A less subtle version of this phenomenon may be found in Rembrandt's *Ecce Homo* etchings, where Christ is displayed to the people on what looks remarkably like a seventeenth-century open-air stage: decorative figures on either side of the arch form a proscenium and spectators look on from surrounding windows, the ancestors of later theater boxes.

20. E.g., I. G. Kennedy, "Claude and Architecture," note 55, 273 and 278; followed by Helen Langdon, *Claude Lorrain* 44–45 and 136. Cf. also Röthlisberger, *Im Licht von Claude Lorrain* 57–59 on Claude and contemporary scenography, and Lagerlöf, *Ideal Landscape* 95–102, in a chapter entitled "A Stage for Life and Action" that nevertheless remains reserved about the theatrical element in Poussin, and even more so in Claude, reducing it finally to an "arena for human action" (102).

21. Cf. above note 13. In that case, as Claude worked on the subject, he literally glued a whole new landscape onto the left edge of his original sketch. It would be possible to move the palace to its expected place in the internal frame simply by rotating the plane of the painting thirty to forty degrees (receding on the right). The mass of rocks on the left would then line up properly with the trees left and right to form a closed frame (and also to close up the prospect to the left of the palace). In effect, then, the observer is displaced from the plane of the expected frame and thereby placed in a state of uncertainty analogous to Psyche's own uncertainty. This is highly self-conscious manipulation of the canvas as mimetic representation.

22. In Caron, remarkably, few of the midground figures actually watch the play in progress; most of them have their backs turned in order to watch the tournament in the left midground. It is typical of the Judeo-Christian tradition

that revelation tends to come to individuals, not to groups, and it becomes the rule as the culture is increasingly reformed and secularized.

23. Compare Lubbock ("Claude's Extras" 22) on how Claude's figures assist viewers to maintain their vantage point outside the painting.

24. The only other allegorical titles in the two volumes involve personifications, such as "Summer" or "Charity," and of two paintings by Ostade entitled "Physic" and "Law" the commentator in Boydell asserts, "These inimitable little pictures . . . are undoubtedly portraits" (*A Collection of Prints* 2:4). On Poussin: "It is conceived, that the subject is allegorical, and inculcates, that those who are in the vigor of life, ought frequently to enter into the contemplation of death; at least, we confess that this is the only explanation we can give of the picture's design, after bestowing much time and pains in endeavouring to procure a more satisfactory one" (*A Collection of Prints* 2:3).

25. The aspects Ruskin criticizes, the relation of Aeneas's hand to the arrow and the length of the arrow, both in *Landscape with Aeneas Hunting* (LV 180), are in fact much exaggerated in the engraving by Earlom from which Ruskin worked.

26. Similarly the clumsiness of medieval art serves precisely this function, *Modern Painters* 3:47 and 98.

Chapter 3

1. "Die Menschen sind nur so lange produktiv in Poesie und Kunst, als sie noch religiös sind," conversation with F. W. Riemer, July 1810, *Goethes Gespräche* 548.

2. My arguments below take for granted Madeleine Doran's *Endeavors of Art*, still the authoritative survey of Elizabethan drama in the context of neoclassicism, but where she focused on origins I seek dynamic interactions.

3. The pervasive influence of Prudentius and the most thorough description of morality are to be found in Bevington, *From Mankind to Marlowe.*

4. A long tradition going back to Tertullian, cited continually in the Middle Ages, attacked the stage (i.e., the Roman stage) as the enemy of religion and morality. Nevertheless the church was also the transmitter of all learning and hence of Roman culture, including the plays of Plautus and Terence. Their influence on the dramatic tradition is, however, only really felt in the Renaissance. Ironically enough, attacks of heretics like the Lollards (fourteenth century) and proponents of the Reformation pushed the church to defend religious drama with some energy. For detailed discussion of the emergence of English Corpus Christi cycles, see Kolve, *The Play Called Corpus Christi;* Woolf, *English Mystery Plays* 68–76; and Nelson, *The Medieval English Stage.*

5. Karl Young raises this issue in *The Drama of the Medieval Church*, in which he confines himself to texts performed in the church by clergy; Rosemary Woolf makes clear that the criteria according to which liturgical and nonliturgical drama can be distinguished are still a matter of controversy among scholars, *The English Mystery Plays* 39–41. The first play seems to emerge by the tenth century from the Easter trope, a brief cameo in the Mass elaborating the exchange between the three Maries and the angels at Christ's grave from the Gospel. It is termed "drama" rather than "trope" when it is no longer sung entirely by the choir but the roles of the women are taken by clerics and accompanied by simple gestures. In the course of the eleventh century other dramatic elements of the Holy Week celebration joined this simple structure, including, by the end of

the century, the Resurrection. Again it is difficult to mark the line between rite and drama, but in the inclusion of spectators (to the extent that the congregation is to be understood as audience and not participant) for some of the original rites, and in the transfer of their performance from the particular commemorative day, Good Friday, to another performance day, at first Easter Sunday, the actions lose some aspect of participatory commemoration and become representations more like images, less tied to a particular time and place. The emergence of a drama independent of the liturgy is also poorly understood. Liturgical drama, that is dramatic representation as part of the service, persisted into the eighteenth century in some areas, particularly at Easter. Nevertheless, it is clear that there were already dramas independent of the liturgy as early as the twelfth century.

6. Definitive accounts of these developments are Wickham, *Early English Stages*, vol. 2, for England; Shergold, *A History of the Spanish Stage* for Spain; Flemming, *Das Ordensdrama* for Germany.

7. Preaching became much more important in the fifteenth and sixteenth centuries as a vehicle for theological controversy, just as the drama did. Both draw on the same sources, the fathers and antiquity, and both address the behavior of their listeners as individuals.

8. This history has been traced by Irving Ribner, *The English History Play* 33–67. Occasional examples of personified abstractions and numerous examples of the Vice are still documented in the 1590s, not only in plays that are obvious descendants of moralities, but also in those that draw on romance or the traditions of Senecan tragedy.

9. Robortello, Castelvetro, and Scaliger are the earliest and most prominent. The development is traced by Weinberg, *A History of Literary Criticism in the Italian Renaissance*. The last important example of normative handbooks in this tradition, the fourth edition of Johann Christoph Gottsched's *Critische Dichtkunst*, appeared in Germany in 1751.

10. The venerable Butcher, *Aristotle's Theory of Poetry and Fine Art* ch. 2, is a good example.

11. Nevertheless, imitation is a matter of generally valid norms, not of the material world or of realism as the term is generally understood today, and as it was often understood by less sophisticated Aristotelians. Modern studies on the new importance of probability in the seventeenth and eighteenth centuries include Ian Hacking's *The Emergence of Probability*, Richard Newsom's *A Likely Story*, and Douglas Patey's *Probability and Literary Form*. A traditional part of our narrative about the displacement of neoclassicism by Romanticism involves, conversely, the restoration of the supernatural or the marvelous. It was a central issue in eighteenth-century German aesthetics, particularly in the controversies surrounding the admissibility of Milton to the canon, and continues to surface in titles such as Meyer Abrams's *Natural Supernaturalism*, his characterization of Romantic literature, or Wallace Jackson's *The Probable and the Marvelous*, on the transformation of English poetry in the late eighteenth century through the mediation of Milton.

12. "Tragedy and Melodrama: Speculations on Generic Form" 39–40. Ironically Heilman is trying here to distinguish the terms tragedy and melodrama on the grounds that tragedy requires plot.

13. In allegorical drama the fusion tends to be explicit—characters' names name their roles—but in allegorical narrative it often is not, so that allegory was not perceived as meeting Aristotle's standards of clarity.

14. Even interpreters trying to recover the older dramaturgy fall into this trap. James Hirsch, for example, while arguing eloquently against misreading Hamlet as a modern interior subject nevertheless criticizes D'Avenant's adaptation of *Macbeth* for stating an explicit moral at the end of the play.

15. An excellent introduction to this κοινή is to be found in Edgar Wind's *Pagan Mysteries in the Renaissance*.

16. See Orgel and Strong, *Inigo Jones* 4, for concise discussion of wonder in sixteenth-century poetics.

17. The phrase occurs at least three times in the essay (Sidney, *An Apologie for Poetrie* 10, 18, 39); cf. Wind, *Pagan Mysteries* 1–16.

18. This distinguishes my approach from that of Richard Cody in *The Landscape of the Mind*.

19. See Herrick, *Tragicomedy* 16–62. For a brief but thorough survey of the use of the term and its relatives see Guthke, *Modern Tragicomedy*, 5–19. A detailed history into the seventeenth century is to be found in Herrick.

20. The phrase occurs, for example, in Edmundo Rho's introduction to my inexpensive paperback edition and in Richard Cody, *The Landscape of the Mind* 43. Cody offers a careful reading of it as a neoplatonist allegory, 30–43.

21. Act 3, scene 2. On blind Cupid as a central motif of Renaissance neoplatonism, see Wind, *Pagan Mysteries* 53–80.

22. The scene evokes also the sacrifice of Isaac; in fact the first real pastoral drama is sometimes considered to be Agostino Beccari's *Il Sacrificio* of 1554 (Grout, *A Short History of Opera* 36).

23. Herrick, *Tragicomedy* 136–37. Herrick documents in detail the classical justifications invoked for tragicomedy, esp. 1–15, and, throughout, the unclear boundary between tragicomedy and tragedy with happy ending.

24. The dating of both plays is complex. For *King John*, see Honigmann, *King John* xliii–lviii; for *King Johan*, see Happé, *Four Morality Plays* 48–51.

25. Lady Faulconbridge has been faithless to her husband, King Richard betrayed his vassal with his wife, the Faulconbridge sons cast aspersions on the honor of their own mother, Philip of France and Austria both break their faith to Constance, Philip then breaks his to John, Hubert breaks his to John in not injuring Arthur, Lewis breaks his faith to Blanch in attacking England, the English lords betray first John then Lewis who intended to betray them, Pandulph breaks his faith to Lewis as does Melun.

26. The Bastard is knighted (i.e., has honor conferred on him) in act 1, in act 2 Blanch and Lewis join hands, in act 3 Philip drops John's hand at Pandulph's order (3.1.261–62), in act 4 Arthur falls to his death, in act 5 the crown is passed between John and Pandulph, John falls to his own death, and the Bastard kneels to Prince Henry.

27. There Philip of France has more trouble choosing to obey Pandulph, various imprisonments are shown, the Bastard is shown raiding an abbey, and John's death is depicted in more realistic detail. The standard view is that it was Shakespeare's source, but Honigmann argues that it is a bad quarto.

28. I have discussed the workings of neoplatonist allegory in Shakespeare at length in *A Midsummer Night's Dream* (J. K. Brown, "Discordia concors") and will adduce further examples below in Chapter 4. It is consistently associated with reconciliation and resolution in the comedies, and in *Troilus and Cressida*, where Platonist language is asserted to be familiar (3.3.95–102). Evidently Shakespeare's Platonist allegories were as much cliché as those taken from the morality tradition.

Chapter 4

1. "Shakespeare ist reich an wundersamen Tropen, die aus personifizierten Begriffen entstehen und uns gar nicht kleiden würden, bei ihm aber völlig am Platze sind, weil zu seiner Zeit alle Kunst von der Allegorie beherrscht wurde," *Maximen und Reflexionen* 252.

2. For a clear and accessible survey of what is known on the authorship and purpose of Seneca's plays and of their influence in England, see E. F. Watling's introduction to his translation *Seneca: Four Tragedies and Octavia* 7–39.

3. Concise discussions of the politics of Vondel's plays may be found in Aercke's introduction to *Gijsbrecht van Amstel,* esp. 17–19 and Barnouw, *Vondel* 50–82.

4. For an authoritative survey of the importance of Seneca for Racine, see Tobin, *Racine and Seneca.* Levitan's "Seneca in Racine" offers a sophisticated and thoughtful analysis of the ways in which Seneca is not Aristotelian and of Racine's struggles to deal with the tension between his Aristotelianism and his Senecanism. See also Bold's argument in response to this essay that Racine is "more Senecan than Seneca" ("The Anxiety of Senecan Influence" 431).

5. In her discussion of the undermining of moral vocabulary in Racine to create a sense of moral complexity ("The Moral Perspective in Racinian Tragedy") Mary Reilly attributes this vocabulary as coming primarily from morality play; as already suggested, it is difficult to separate morality vocabulary from that of Senecanism by the middle of the seventeenth century.

6. Cf. Lucien Goldmann's observation that *Bajazet* would end exactly like a Marivaux play if the hero's stratagem succeeded (*The Hidden God* 352).

7. On Racine as a serious historian, see Limbrick's "Racine: The Historian in the Text"; on myth and history in Racine, Delmas, "Histoire et mythe."

8. Larry Norman argues ("Racine's 'Other Eye'" 140–43) that history functions as distancing necessary for classical decorum, and that the Turkish setting of *Bajazet* substitutes spatial distance for the more common temporal otherness of history.

9. For an alternate reading of the importance of letters in *Bajazet* both as realistic aspects of life at the Turkish court and as the embodiment of the theme of problematic communication, see Michèle Longino, "*Bajazet* à la lettre."

10. Lucien Goldmann identifies an essentially religious plot, what he calls the "providential" plot, for most of the play, and argues that only Eriphile is a truly tragic figure in the classical sense (really in his own existentialist sense, *The Hidden God* 369–70). The distinction is surely right, but should be understood in more nuanced fashion.

11. It is little wonder that this plot became a staple of eighteenth-century opera. Seventeenth- and eighteenth-century opera routinely had a woman single-mindedly pursuing revenge, well surveyed by Dieter Borchmeyer in "Mozarts rasende Weiber," esp. 175–93.

12. Since the early nineteenth century our culture has preferred to regard the passage with both these solutions as the work of an interloper (Walker, "Introduction to *Iphigenia in Aulis*" 291, 294; passages assumed spurious are segregated into an appendix to the translation).

13. The denial sometimes extends to critics as well, as for example in John Campbell's "Racine's *Iphigénie,*" which insists on the fundamentally tragic nature of the play.

14. Tobin surveys the shift in popularity from Seneca to Euripides in France beginning around 1650 (*Racine and Seneca* 158–61) without particularly addressing

the pressures it created on Racine. Nevertheless the underlying tensions in his work have been effectively addressed as a thematic issue, as for example in Edward James, "Euripidean and Christian Crosscurrents in the Problematic Morality of Racine's *Phèdre*," and as a problem of character by Regine Brossmann ("*Britannicus* oder die Krise der klassischen Tragödie").

15. Sigurd Burckhardt has argued convincingly that the anachronistic references to time in the play thematize the belatedness of classical tragedy on the Elizabethan stage in "How Not to Murder Caesar," *Shakespearean Meanings* 3–21.

16. Willard Farnham provides the standard account of the geneology and importance of the term in *The Medieval Heritage of Elizabethan Tragedy*.

17. See Gordon Braden's account in *Renaissance Tragedy and the Senecan Tradition*, esp. 5–62. Betrayal was, as we saw, frequent in *King John*, but the presence of innocents, Arthur and the citizens of Angiers (2.1), both represented by Hubert, left some space, however narrow, for truth to enter the world. We recognize in retrospect the Senecan pressure on that plot as well.

18. In *Allegorical Imagery* Rosemond Tuve has demonstrated the persistence of such late medieval systems in the common reading of the sixteenth century.

19. The list of vices with associated virtues and gifts follows Tuve, *Allegorical Imagery* 77–89.

20. For a brief overview of the idea and its hegemony see John Sekora, *Luxury* 23–62. Tuve points out that the order of Luxury and Gluttony are frequently reversed in the list above. Both gluttony and lechery are forms of overindulgence, thus more closely related than they might normally seem in the modern view.

21. Diana is almost always a signpost of neoplatonizing allegory in Shakespeare. She serves the same function in *A Midsummer Night's Dream*; in *Twelfth Night* Orsino first associates Olivia with Diana, and plays as different as *Comedy of Errors* and *Pericles* find their resolution—the lost is found, what was single becomes double—in her temple. On the complex interpenetration of Diana and Venus in Renaissance allegory, see Wind, *Pagan Mysteries* 75–80.

22. It is Shakespeare's second play about avarice, for he had already written one in *The Merchant of Venice* in the mid-1590s, where Shylock's avarice is countered by Portia's counsel (no wonder she disguises herself as a lawyer) and plea for mercy.

23. T. W. Craik, in the introduction to the Arden edition, praises its mimetic strengths ("characterization, plot-construction, mood"), whose interaction enables the play to sidestep all of its obvious implausibilities (60) while Barbara Lewalski ("Thematic Patterns in *Twelfth Night*") argues for its Christian theme.

24. The argument is elaborated in greater detail in J. K. Brown, "Double Plotting in Shakespeare's Comedies," from which this section is condensed.

25. As elsewhere in the comedies, disguise has nothing to do with designs against the hero or with personal gain, nor is it the concrete correlative of deceit and hypocrisy. Viola, like so many of Shakespeare's and Calderón's heroines, claims the protection of male clothing against a hostile world, which, however, demonstrates none of its hostility to the audience. Like Rosalind in *As You Like It*, Viola seems to wear her disguise as much for fun as for protection.

26. Although Achilles is not invited to fight in it, he also doesn't want to, and confesses instead to "a woman's longing" to see Hector off the battlefield (3.3.237)—a remarkable echo of Viola's hesitation to fight.

27. I follow the *Riverside Edition* in the designation of genre.

28. That psychological drama of types derives ultimately from morality is well known to theater historians (cf. James Laver, *Drama: Its Costume and Decor* 51),

but it is important to recognize the transformation of the role of the Vice in this process.

29. In those comedies where it occurs in the "high" plot, such as *All's Well That Ends Well* or *Measure for Measure*, it is treated as a problem and must be purged.

30. As an experiment, Theodore Spencer, *Shakespeare and the Nature of Man* (New York: Macmillan, 1942), 121 (cited Bullough, *Narrative and Dramatic Sources of Shakespeare* 6:111). Shakespeare's major source, *The True Chronicle Historie of King Leir*, ends happily as Cordelia and the forces of good successfully defeat the armies of Ragan and Gonorill.

31. On Vondel's efforts to write an epic see Barnouw, *Vondel* 83–88.

32. Spitzer's essay has generated reflection on the terms "Baroque" and "classical" in relation to Racine that persists to the current day, as for example in John Lyons's "What Do We Mean When We Say 'classique'?," where "Baroque" is one of four alternatives to "classic." Levitan's tendency in "Seneca in Racine" to use the term "Baroque" as a catch-all term for anything not Aristotelian probably also reflects this heritage. It is precisely such dualist terminology that this book aims to undermine.

33. Available in the edition of Otto Beckers, *Das Spiel von den zehn Jungfrauen und das Katharinenspiel* (Hildesheim: Georg Olms, 1977); in English in Stephen K. Wright and Keith Glaeske, *Medieval German Drama: Four Plays in Translation* (Fairview, N.C.: Pegasus, 2002). I am grateful to Stephen Wright for his assistance in locating this material.

34. I have in mind here the nexus of courtliness and the development of self-constraint proposed by Norbert Elias in *The Civilizing Process*, particularly in part 4, 365–447.

35. Spanish drama is different also, but for reasons that will be discussed in the following chapter.

36. Cf. the discussion of allegory in the recognition scene between Hubert and the Bastard above, Chapter 3.

Chapter 5

1. "Wo Zufall ist, darf auch das *Wunderbare* sein, also auch im modernen Drama. Nur muß das Mythische und Idealische selbst mimisch behandelt werden," *Literary Notebooks* 24.

2. The restrictive court control over theater franchises in England, France, and Spain, as well as the involvement of the leading dramatists in all three countries in both court and commercial theaters (less in France) would suggest that categorical distinctions between courtly and commercial theater should be drawn very cautiously, and that neoclassical and "popular" theater do not align as readily with class and social milieu as generally assumed, even by so thoughtful and sensitive a reader of English and Spanish commercial theater as Walter Cohen in *Drama of a Nation*.

3. On masque as undramatic cf. Jonson, *Complete Masques* 1. It is routine among Calderón scholars to distinguish between the allegorical *autos sacramentales* (Corpus Christi dramas) and the "symbolical" secular plays.

4. The important accounts for Jonson are Stephen Orgel's *Jonsonian Masque*, and *The Illusion of Power* and his introduction to Jonson, *Complete Masques*.

5. The best general accounts are still Flemming's *Das Ordensdrama* and *Geschichte des Jesuitentheaters*.

6. The standard account of the *autos* is A. A. Parker's *The Allegorical Drama of Calderón*; on the parallels between the public theater in England and Spain in the period see Walter Cohen's *Drama of a Nation* and Fothergill-Payne, *Parallel Lives*.

7. The definitive account of staging in Spain in the period is Nicholas Shergold's *History of the Spanish Stage*.

8. The standard account of Vitruvius's influence in English is Lily B. Campbell's *Scenes and Machines*; the following discussion draws extensively on it.

9. See Shergold, *A History of the Spanish Stage* xxv–xxvi, for a compact account of the Italian tradition; Orgel, *Illusion of Power*, and Shergold figs. 9–13 for diagrams and descriptions.

10. For a concise description of the staging conditions of German school drama, see the introduction to Flemming, *Das Ordensdrama*. Generous illustrations of sets may be found in Jankovics, *Sopron Collection*.

11. But the difference must not be overemphasized: Calderón, avowedly not an Aristotelian, had to exercise his authority at court to maintain the coherence of his plots in the face of the designer's aspirations to show his wares.

12. Campbell (*Scenes and Machines* 94–95) also argues that "scaffold" should no longer be understood to refer to the morality stage in late sixteenth-century England, but the fact that such an argument must be made suggests that a transition was still underway, and even she asserts later that "the idea of a necessary relation between a change of scene and a change of place [i.e., a mimetic understanding of set] was, indeed, a late development in the history of the scenic stage" (*Scenes and Machines* 151).

13. Only the texts of the speeches have survived, so this must be surmise.

14. Although discussions of Jesuit drama were conducted in the terminology of Renaissance Aristotelianism, Flemming begins his discussion of the dramatic theory of these plays by emphasizing the concern to overwhelm the emotions of the spectator. After the first performance of *Cenodoxus* fourteen members of the court began participating in Jesuit exercises, and the lead actor entered the order. For wonder in Jonson see Orgel and Strong, introduction to *Inigo Jones* 4. In Spain, see Honig, *Calderón and the Seizures of Honor* 29–31. The most compelling analysis of the Platonist bases of Spanish golden age theories of art and literature, their transmission through the theological tradition, and their theological significance are excurses 22 and 23 in Curtius's *European Literature and the Latin Middle Ages* 547–70. So pervasive was this ethical aesthetics that it can even be traced in Calderón's use of music, see Sage, "Calderón und die Theatermusik."

15. Cf. Booth, *Victorian Spectacular Theatre*, on Victorian spectacular theater, Laver (*Drama: Its Costume and Decor* 193) on Loutherbourg and his Eidophusikon, a performance with only sets and lights, but no actors.

16. The current definitive account is to be found in Wickham's *Early English Stages*, vol. 1; cf. also Campbell, *Scenes and Machines*.

17. The *auto* is not to be mistaken for his famous commercial drama (*comedia*) of the same name. Calderón adapted several of his *comedias* as *autos*.

18. It has recently been asserted that this is an incorrect and old-fashioned reading of this text (Greer, *The Play of Power* 4–5 and 79). While Greer's reading, heavily dependent on Frederick A. de Armas's *The Return of Astraea: An Astral-Imperial Myth in Calderón*, that the play contains specific criticism of King Philip IV and his minister Olivares, may be correct within the limitations of the specific context of performance, the more general religious reading is nevertheless still demonstrably implied by the text and the only one that has made the play of any interest to succeeding generations.

19. Cf. the common shift in Jonson from belly to mind: cook to poet in *Neptune's Triumph*, Comus to Daedalus in *Pleasure Reconciled to Virtue*, Mercury to Cupid in *Lovers Made Men*, real player to role in *Christmas his Masque*.

20. *Autos* typically begin with a long narrative based on Genesis or Exodus. Other versions of the creation, for example, may be found in *El pintor de su deshonra*, *La nave del mercader*, *La humildad coronada de las plantas*; *El divino Orfeo* begins with an elaborate dramatization of the creation.

21. This is probably true for school drama in general, whose basic goal was the "glorification of the church triumphant" (Flemming, *Das Ordensdrama* 9). Cf. the anonymous *St. Franciscus Xavierus* (in Burnett, *Jesuit Plays on Japan*) in which the martyrdom of the hero consists in his inability to reach China and establish the Catholic church there.

22. On the mimetic, realistic aspects, see Dunn, "Honour and the Christian Background" 60. Cf. Ariosto's more polemical, if less tragic, critique of the same code a century earlier in *Orlando furioso*; also Jacobean revenge drama with regard to similarity of theme and mimetic technique: Calderón is considerably less Senecan, draws more on the conventions of comedy, and generally demonstrates better control of the balance between mimesis and allegory.

23. Documented in Orgel and Strong, *Inigo Jones*. Commercial companies in England at least had tended to acquire used court dress for their costumes; with the advent of masque it can only have enriched appearances.

24. The implication is articulated more explicitly in the *auto*, where Understanding says of her rainbow, "God placed it as a sign of peace" ("Dios le puso por señal / De paz," *Obras completas* 3:412). Hence Galatea appears with sirens playing music in *El mayor encanto* and their appearance evokes repeated use of "sereno" and "serenarse" ("serene" and "make serene") in their scene. They are evidently signs of peace and harmony.

25. This is a simplification of the complex process process described by Seznec in *Survival of the Pagan Gods*. For a concise presentation of the Renaissance perspective, see Wind, *Pagan Mysteries* 17–25.

26. L. 79. Apparently this victory was dramatized in production although the text presents it as over before the masque begins, see Jonson, *Complete Masques* 491n.

27. See, for example, the discussion of the "para-Christian" theology of *La estatua de Prometeo* in Ter Horst, *The Secular Plays* 12–13, and his excursus on the ambivalent relation of Christianity to classical myth, 62–67; also A. A. Parker's reservations on the doctrinal implications of myth in the secular plays in *The Mind and Art of Calderón* 340–47.

28. Initially written as a Corpus Christi play for the city of Yepes in 1637, by 1638 it was on the commercial stage, probably in the revised version published in 1663. The two and a half surviving acts of the *auto* version allow some comparisons. Although Calderón's *autos* are otherwise one-act plays, it was not unheard of for a three-act saints' play to be used at Corpus Christi. The manuscript version may be readily reconstructed from McKendrick, *El Mágico Prodigioso*.

29. Faust was known in Spain among students in Salamanca after 1560 (McKendrick, *El Mágico prodigioso* 41; Dédéyan, *Le thème de Faust dans la littérature européenne* 1:145). In the autograph manuscript of the play the heroine is called Faustina, and only changed to Justina in the published version. McKendrick calls attention to important differences between Calderón's treatment of the theme and those of Marlowe and Goethe, *El Mágico Prodigioso* 41–42. For discussion of the implications of reading it as a response to the Faust story, see J. K. Brown, "The Prosperous Wonder Worker" 57–59.

30. The pilgrim of *El veneno y la triaca* also arrives loaded with the treasure of the Orient (*Obras completas* 3:192).

31. Cf. Brüggeman, *Spanisches Theater* 1:19–22. Compare also the contradictory assertion of Abbé François Bertaut about his conversation with Calderón in 1659 that they had disputed about the rules of drama, "qu'ils ne connoissent pas en ce Pays-là, & dont ils se moquent" (cited in Brüggemann, *Spanisches Theater* 1: 39–40).

32. And in tandem with it, a larger view of history that sees allegory, because it is antimaterialist, as conservative in view of the larger progression of European culture toward first a secular, then a material worldview.

33. The classic account of the shifting implications of ape imagery in Europe is to be found in H. W. Janson, *Apes and Ape Lore*.

34. 503: "Tu voz pudo enternecerme, / tu presencia suspenderme, / y tu respeto turbarme"; "admiración" and "asombro" occur repeatedly.

35. See Franz-Josef Deiters's incisive analysis of Benjamin in this regard in *Drama im Augenblick seines Sturzes*, esp. 27–43.

36. For thorough discussion of Gryphius's plays as theater, of their staging requirements, and their performance history see Flemming, *Andreas Gryphius und die Bühne*.

37. For a good discussion of German Humanist tragedy as martyr drama see Pierre Béhar's "Nachwort" to *August Adolph von Haugwitz: Prodromus Poeticus, Oder: Poetischer Vortrab. 1684*, 103–12.

38. The seminal study for the importance of emblem in German drama of the period is Albrecht Schöne's *Emblematik und Drama im Zeitalter des Barock*. See also his extensive catalog of emblems of the period, with Arthur Henkel, *Emblemata*.

39. Disguise works differently in Latin comedy (and classical romance), where it involves the common Renaissance motif of woman disguised as young man. This latter motif, an understudied topic, seems to enter early Renaissance narrative (Boccaccio) from medieval French narrative.

40. Cf. Dunn's argument that the honor code is a "parody" of religion ("Honour and the Christian Background").

41. Cf. *Andrómeda y Perseo*, where Perseo is veiled for the same reason.

42. The view still attributed to the Renaissance by Foucault at the beginning of *The Order of Things*, 34–42.

Chapter 6

1. F. E. Ebrard, *Neue Briefe W. v. Humboldts an Schiller* (1911), 65; cited in Stammler, "'Edle Einfalt': Zur Geschichte eines kunsttheoretischen Topos" 372. Original: "ungeachtet des Geschreis von Einfachheit und Natur kann es dem unpartheiischen Leser nicht entgehn, daß die Griechischen Tragiker . . . eine viel höhere, gesuchtere, mehr opernartige Diktion haben, als wir auf unserer Bühne dulden würden."

2. A brief account in Grout, *A Short History of Opera* ch. 3, a longer account in Donington, *The Rise of Opera* 17–100, and a specifically musical and theatrical account in Pirrotta and Povoledo, *Music and Theatre from Poliziano to Monteverdi*.

3. See Katz, *Divining the Powers of Music* on secularization of musical powers, 107–10, and Tomlinson, *Metaphysical Song* ch. 2.

4. Detailed discussion of the transmission of this tradition to Rinuccini may be found in Hanning, *Of Poetry and Music's Power* 16–27.

5. On Roman opera see Hammond, *Music and Spectacle in Baroque Rome* for detailed description of all parameters, and Murata, *Operas for the Papal Court*. The most thorough study of Venetian opera is Ellen Rosand's *Opera in Seventeenth-Century Venice*, which argues that the conventions of opera as we know it were established in Venice from the 1640s to about 1690.

6. E.g., Guglielmo Ebreo: "Dancing is an action, showing outwardly the spiritual movements which must agree with those measured and perfect concords of harmony which, through our hearing and with earthly joy, descend into one intellect, there to produce sweet movements which, being thus imprisoned, as it were, in defiance of nature, endeavor to escape and reveal themselves through movement" (cited Kirstein, *Dance* 117).

7. See introductions to Hilton, *Dance of Court & Theater* and to Cohen, *Dance as a Theatre Art*.

8. See Grout, *A Short History of Opera* on placard opera and Brooks, *The Melodramatic Imagination* 62–64.

9. First established by Homeyer in *Stranitzkys Drama vom "Heiligen Nepomuck,"* and further in Payer von Thurn, introduction to *Wiener Haupt- und Staatsaktionen*. For discussion in English of the roots of Viennese Haupt- und Staatsaktion in Italian opera and a specific example, see Beare, *The German Popular Play* Atis. General accounts in Weiß, *Die Wiener Haupt- und Staatsaktionen*; Keil-Budischowsky, *Die Theater Wiens* 81–89; Urbach, *Die Wiener Komödie und ihr Publikum* 22–29; Rommel, introduction to *Die Maschinenkomödie*, which offers a condensed version of the eighteenth-century section of his authoritative history of Viennese popular comedy, *Die Alt-Wiener Volkskomödie*. A summary of the current state of the scholarship on this topic may be found in Hein, *Das Wiener Volkstheater* 9–79.

10. For basic sociological information on Italian opera in its first century, see Grout, *A Short History of Opera* ch. 13 and Rosand, *Opera in Seventeenth-Century Venice*. On the situation in Germany, see Flaherty, *Opera in the Development of German Critical Thought* 19–20.

11. The poet begins by invoking Terpsichore, the muse of dance, to narrate how Antinöus tries to persuade Penelope to forget her husband and dance with him one evening while Ulysses is away. Antinöus harnesses all the rhetoric of dancing as a basic principle of universal order, but for his own lascivious ends. When he fails to convince her, Love comes at his call and presents her with a crystal mirror. The sight of her own celestial beauty in the mirror carries the poem beyond the bounds of the world, leaving both Antinöus and Terpsichore behind; now the poet invokes Urania, muse of astronomy and divine harmony (Venus Urania is love of Truth in Plato), to tell what Penelope experiences as her mind is carried to higher spheres, but we receive at best hints as the poems ends. The poem was used by Tillyard as a touchstone for his Elizabethan world picture (*The Elizabethan World Picture* 103–8). I do not share his static reading of the dance as a simple picture of order, but offer a more nuanced reading of the neoplatonist aspects of the poem. For a more fully deconstructive reading see Marshall Brown, *Turning Points* 19–24.

12. Rosand takes the wax on the preserved printed scenarios and libretti as evidence they were read during performances, *Opera in Seventeenth-Century Venice* 288.

13. Cf. De Sanctis's analysis of the amalgam of comic and tragic elements in this plot (*History of Italian Literature* 2:841–43).

14. For good general accounts of *opera seria* and the musical demands on plot, see Strohm *Dramma per Musica* 1–29; also Grout, *A Short History of Opera* 208–57 and Smith, *The Tenth Muse* 63–100.

15. These adaptations, believed to be all by Strantitzky, are collected in Payer von Thurn, *Wiener Haupt- und Staatsaktionen*, passage quoted is from 2:4. This particular text appears to be based on Minato's *Il tempio di Diana in Taurica* of 1678 (ibid., ix). Multifarious love affairs conducted in disguise enter the tradition via Italian opera via pastoral (Beare, *The German Popular Play* Atis 10).

16. De Sanctis is already eloquent on Metastasio's importance as the key transitional figure in shifting the locus of emotion from language to melody (*History of Italian Literature* 2:850–53).

17. Cf. Rosand's survey of this theme in the seventeenth century, *Opera in Seventeenth-Century Venice* ch. 13. *Grove Music Online* lists some forty-five between 1600 and 1800.

18. There exists what Valbuena Pratt identifies as an earlier version, not published during Calderón's lifetime (the *autos* normally were published), that involved much simpler staging and much less music (Calderón, *Obras completas* 3:1820–34).

19. Pluto appears to be a comic figure, at least in the interpretation of René Jacob in his recording (Arles: harmonia mundi, 1998). Because the music and most of the text of Pluto's call-to-arms aria in 2.1 has not survived, Jacob substituted from an other Telemann opera (*Die Last-tragende Liebe oder Emma und Eginhard*) the revenge aria "Glühende Zangen, Schwert, Feuer und Rad" ("Glowing tongs, sword, fire and wheel"). In its gleeful catalog of tortures the aria anticipates the comic Osmin's famous torture aria in Mozart's *Entführung aus dem Serail.*

20. Both endings are available in Metastasio, *Tutte le opere* 1:178–89 and 1400–10. The second ending is now published as addendum, as in the 1788 edition of Metastasio's works.

21. To be sure, act 2 begins with a note that the actors will need to play on the apron of the stage in order to be heard, but from the private nature of their communications they will be understood to be actually within the temple.

22. Reversal seems to have been an appealing technique for neoclassical dramatists; one finds actually more of it in seventeenth- and eighteenth-century drama than in Greek or Roman tragedy. The extreme example is Racine's *Iphigénie en Aulide*, where Agamemnon changes his mind in almost every scene.

23. One could also argue that he recognizes at the end the futility of reparation. If the world were unremittingly tragic, that would work; but since the gods have already given an unmistakable sign earlier, Lucien Goldmann's premise of a tragic hidden god cannot apply.

24. Cf. also the opening of the play and Voltaire's specification of what should be seen through the briefly opened doors at this point (*Oeuvres complètes* 6:97). Voltaire is aware he is skating on thin ice, as his long note to 1.4 shows. There he lists all the spectacular moments, and justifies them as living pictures by pointing out how each has spectators in the play modeling the reaction of the audience. Instead, however, of acknowledging this play-within-the-play aspect, he adds a disclaimer that such spectacle is worthless in itself, and at best only enhances the poetry (6:107–8). Compare a similar defense of the crowd scene and duel in 4.3 (6:143).

25. The importance of the visual is also emphasized by the stage direction to 2.1, as discussed in note 21 above, where Voltaire says that the fact that the doors are open *signifies* that the scenes really play in the interior of the temple; also by a note of Voltaire in the same scene specifying an action only implied by the text (*Oeuvres complètes* 6:112) and by the general presence of stage directions.

26. There is much to be said on the differences between the "deus ex machina" effect at the ends of these two operas and the Euripidean model. In both these operas Diana brings about the happy end as a reward for the virtue demonstrated by the characters—duty in *Iphigénie en Aulide*, penance in *Iphigénie en Tauride*; such is never the case in Euripides.

27. When Mendelssohn defends admiration, his example sounds still very close to martyr tragedy (Lessing, *Briefwechsel über das Trauerspiel* 90).

28. E.g., Schiller, *Kabale und Liebe*. I am indebted to my colleague Brigitte Prutti for insights on the arbitrariness of the unhappy end in Lessing.

29. Scholarship on the play is remarkably reticent on this point. Clay Daniel has pointed to the fall structure in the play, but connected it to *Paradise Lost* ("The Fall of George Barnwell"); Stephen Trainor connects it to Puritan homiletics, overlooking the well-established connection between morality drama and homiletics in the sixteenth century ("Tears Abounding: The London Merchant as Puritan Tragedy"). In the most thorough evocation of the various discourses at work in *The London Merchant* Hans-Ulrich Mohr at least recognizes the morality elements in the play, but immediately dismisses them as completely deallegorized ("Lillos The London Merchant: Ein bürgerliches Trauerspiel?").

30. Even Grimmelshausen's Simplicissimus, title figure of the great German picaresque novel of 1669, finds himself dancing in such a ballet in an Orpheus opera when he goes to Paris (*Simplicissimus*, 4.3, p. 248). A search for Circe in *Grove Music Online* brings up five hundred entries, ample testimony to the popularity of the theme. Haydn staged a Circe pastiche (performance of an opera with different parts by different composers) as late as 1789.

31. For an excellent analysis of the Senecan aspects, see Barner, *Produktive Rezeption* 35–52. In any case, the story is actually more complex. The courtesan Marwood from Thomas Shadwell's *The Squire of Alsatia* has long been identified as the most likely source for Lessing's Marwood, since she too refuses to let go of a young man she has seduced after he finds an appropriate young woman to marry. The fact has no impact, however, on the essence of the argument, since Shadwell's plot is just as much of a morality as Lillo's. In either case Lessing's achievement is the same: he has transformed the allegorical form into a classicizing tragedy. Despite assertions in the last century that Lessing had never read Lillo's play, it is clear that *Miß Sara Sampson* was understood from the first—if not by Lessing, at least by his public—as an allusion to Lillo. Lessing was well informed about the British stage, and it is inconceivable that he did not know in general what was in the play, even if he had not actually read it.

32. The tension between genres described here corresponds in large measure to the tension between an older, fixed moral system and the new slippery moral bases of shifting sensibilities described by Peter Michelsen in his essay "Die Problematik der Empfindungen: Zu Lessings 'Miß Sara Sampson' " in *Der unruhige Bürger* 163–220.

33. For the classic statement of this position, see Rougemont on Wagner's *Tristan und Isolde* in *L'amour et l'occident* 192–96.

Chapter 7

1. "Man hat die höheren Forderungen der Poesie, die sich eigentlich auf dem Theater nur symbolisch oder allegorisch aussprechen können, der Tragödie und Comödie durchaus verkümmert, und alles was nur einigermaßen

die Einbildungskraft in Anspruch nimmt, in die Oper verwiesen," letter to Graf Brühl, May 1, 1815 (WA 4.25: 292).

2. For documentation on the relationship of Wedgwood ware to the Greek revival, see Carol Macht, *Classical Wedgwood Designs.*

3. Pantomime ballet, or narrative ballet, as it was also called, was essentially a dramatic genre in that it had a plot and told a story. As Marian Smith argues in *Ballet and Opera*, it remained the twin of opera through the 1840s in Paris, where it was staged at the Opéra, was accompanied by a printed libretto that included the dialogue to be mimed, was organized musically in terms of "recitative" (accompanying pantomime of specific emotions) and "aria" (dance numbers), and exploited the same musical and stage effects as contemporary operas. Only after 1850, Smith argues, was the miming aspect gradually eliminated from ballet and dance as abstract form became its central focus.

4. Goethe trained actors, often set the schedule, and directed many productions himself. He is recognized among theater historians for his role in developing the first productions entirely conceived by a single director, and also for developing one of the first companies to act as an ensemble. See Carlson, *Goethe and the Weimar Theatre*; Patterson, *The First German Theatre*; Sharpe, "Goethe and the Weimar Theatre"; and Williams, *German Actors of the Eighteenth and Nineteenth Centuries.* These analyses depend to a large extent on the memoirs of Eduard Genast, *Aus Weimars klassischer und nachklassischer Zeit.*

5. The day-to-day program of the theater under Goethe's direction is available in Burkhardt, *Das Repertoire des Weimarischen Theaters unter Goethes Leitung.* For extensive analysis of the implications of the programming, see J. K. Brown, "The Theatrical Practice of Weimar Classicism"; for analysis of the implications of Goethe's directorial technique in relation to questions of genre see J. K. Brown, "Der Drang zum Gesang."

6. For a general overview (primarily in England) see Havens, "Simplicity, a Changing Concept." For Marshall Brown simplicity is the "central literary problem of the last decades of the century" (*Preromanticism* 296).

7. In letter 3 he invokes Voltaire's *Mérope* to argue that dance should be the equivalent of Aristotelian tragedy, true to nature and with accuracy of character. Everything in the world, he says in letter 6, can be imitated by dance (82–84); like the poet the dance master can teach vice and virtue (85), for which noble figures are better suited than low ones (ibid.).

8. Havens ("Simplicity" 4, 13) argues that the value shift derives from the importance of simplicity for scientists like Newton and the Copernicans in the seventeenth century, and that the battle for simplicity as a stylistic value was fought in the Royal Society actually in the 1660s.

9. It can be in conflict with ornamental style in the seventeenth century, as in Logau's epigram:

> der worte göldner glanz hat gift zu seinem grunde
> und operment steckt drin, es schadet zum gesunde,
> es sterbt die einfalt hin, erweckt ein solches klug,
> dafür ein keuscher sinn entsatz und grauen trug. (Cited Grimm,
> *Das deutsche Wörterbuch* 3:173)

Cf. Gottsched, *Critische Dichtkunst* 736, about German *Singspiel*, "alle Dinge sind im Anfang schlecht und einfach," where "schlecht" itself probably means "schlicht," simple, unpretentious.

10. Strohm asserts that the phrase "noble simplicity" is to be found already in Raguenet's *Parallèle des Italiens et des François en ce qui regard la musique et les opéras* of 1702 (Strohm, *Dramma per musica* 23, note 53), but I find only the phrase "simplicité admirable," in his *Défense du parallèle* of 1705 (Raguenet, *Parallèle* 143).

11. Joseph Roach compares Garrick and Noverre, and positions both at the cusp of the shift from a mechanistic to a more vitalist view of the body as natural (*The Player's Passion* 91).

12. The heroine Beatrice is abducted from the convent where her mother, widow of the ruler of Messina, hides her by an unknown man who turns out to be her brother and is similar both to Sarastro and to Tamino. His twin brother functions as the equivalent of Monostatos and specifically lacks Tamino's virtues of constancy, tolerance, and discretion. Imagery of light and darkness pervades the play. Although Schiller characterizes the chorus in the play as a classical chorus it functions more like a chorus in Verdi in its participation in the action.

13. Staiger, "Goethe und Mozart" 49. Staiger analyzes the affinity at length 45–66; Robert Spaethling surveys it more extensively in *Music and Mozart*; on *Hermann und Dorothea* and *Die Zauberflöte*, see J. K. Brown, "Schiller und die Ironie von *Hermann und Dorothea*."

14. I describe the best and most general tradition of allegorizing readings, which stretches from Goethe's fragmentary sequel, *Der Zauberflöte Zweiter Teil*, to the analyses of Ernst Bloch (*Prinzip Hoffnung* 387–91 passim) and Hans-Georg Gadamer ("On the Course of Human Spiritual Development" 37–55). A more specific and limited version of this trend is to be found in the readings of the opera as a Masonic allegory, of which the most notable example is Jacques Chailley's *"La flûte enchantée," opéra maçonnique: Essai d'explication du livret et de la musique*. There has also been a tradition of readings going back as far as 1794 of the opera as political allegory and even roman à clef, described briefly in Branscombe, *Die Zauberflöte* 219–21, and more extensively by Paul Nettl in "Deutungen und Fortsetzungen der *Zauberflöte*" in Csampai, *Die Zauberflöte* 183–200. For a recent example of this tradition see Csampai's introductory essay, "Das Geheimnis der *Zauberflöte* oder die Folgen der Aufklärung" (9–40), a good example of the drivel that typifies such discussions.

15. The claim is coupled in Jahn with the assertion that not Schikaneder but an even less significant contemporary, Karl Ludwig Giesecke, was the real author of the libretto. Unimaginable amounts of time and energy have gone into perpetuating this myth by denying it; the controversy still leads a healthy existence in footnotes and textual summaries. For thorough analyses see Rommel, *Maschinenkomödie* 61–67, and Egon Komorzynski's "Entstehung der *Zauberflöte*" 149–65. For a detailed survey in English, with defense of the unity of the text, see Batley, *Preface* 105–30. Coupled with this controversy is passionate disagreement about which of the many texts evidently known to Schikaneder is to be regarded as the "real" source of the opera; in addition to the essays already cited, see Branscombe, *Die Zauberflöte* 4–34, and, most recently, Assmann, *Die Zauberflöte*.

16. The transmission is extensively documented by Sullivan in *Calderón in the German Lands and the Low Countries*.

17. Charles Rosen sees Gozzi as the determining predecessor for Mozart, particularly in *Die Zauberflöte* (*Classical Style* 318). Eighteenth-century Italian drama was heavily dependent on the Spanish plots of the preceding century and may well have been a link in the transmission to Vienna.

18. The coherence of the allegory in *Die Zauberflöte* becomes clearer when we compare it to *Kaspar der Fagottist, oder: Die Zauberzither.* Its plot is astonishingly similar to that of *Die Zauberflöte.* Prince Armidoro, while out hunting, is led to the radiant fairy Perisirime. She commissions him to rescue her daughter, who has been abducted by an evil enchanter, and gives them a magic zither, a magic ring, and a magic bassoon. As long as Armidoro and Kaspar trust in the fairy and call on her (or her assistant) in need—as long as they demonstrate proper faith—she will save them. Indeed they are all saved more by Perisirime's interference than by any great efforts of the hero, whose one deed is to steal a magic talisman from the enchanter as he sleeps. The trials, the crone, and the apparent reversals in the fairy queen and enchanter are all absent; the plot is a great deal less interesting than Schikaneder's. Allegory remains only in the way the plot structure illustrates the underlying religious premise that faith leads to salvation. So banal and saccharine had allegorical representation become in the common practice of Mozart's day.

19. For more on the mimetic aspects see the essay version of this material: J. K. Brown, "The Queen of the Night and the Crisis of Allegory" 149–52.

20. Grimm, *Deutsches Wörterbuch,* defines "Nachtkönig" as *"euphemistisch für abtritt-, cloakenräumer.* [There follows a list of examples, covering areas from Bavaria to Carinthia, and as far north as Leipzig]; der nachtkönig sol zur gewöhnlichen zeit und an den gewöhnlichen ohrten den unflath ausschütten" (13:195; "Night king, euphemism for the cleaner of sewers and latrines; . . . the night king is to dump out the filth at the usual time in the usual places"). That its scatological implications would have been appealing to Mozart seems obvious. Cf. Solomon on Mozart's enthusiasm for the carnival aspects of bawdiness (*Mozart: A Life* 356–61), which he associates explicitly with the maternal principle. The term still had negative resonance for Beethoven, who once applied it to his sister-in-law Johanna: "Tonight this Queen of the Night was at the artist's ball till 3 o'clock, not only with her intellectual but also bodily nakedness—according to rumor she can be—had—for 20 fl., o horror . . ." ("Diese Nacht ist diese Königin der Nacht bis 3 uhr auf dem Künstlerball gewesen nicht allein mit ihrer Verstandeßblöße sondern auch mit ihrer körperlichen—für 20fl., hat man sich in die Ohren gesagt, daß sie—zu haben—sei, o schrecklich . . .," to Giannatasio del Rio, February 17, 1816; *Beethovens Briefe* 92). What Beethoven meant by the term is not completely clear. Solomon assumes he meant prostitute (*Beethoven* 235), but John Burk considered it an allusion to Mozart, though without elaborating (*The Life and Works of Beethoven* 186). I am grateful to Joel Lazar for calling my attention to the Beethoven reference.

21. The name Hans Wurst for the clown occurs already in seventeenth-century German plays, but Stranitzky established the consistent persona which then remained associated with his name and that of his chosen successor Gottfried Prehauser (1699–1769). Later clowns developed other names and personae (Rommel, *Maschinenkomödie* 33). The definitive history of the Viennese tradition in the theater is Rommel's *Die Alt-Wiener Volkskomödie;* an effectively condensed version of the parts relevant to the literary-historical context of *Die Zauberflöte* is to be found in the substantial introduction to *Maschinenkomödie* already cited. A somewhat elaborated version in English may be found in Batley, *Preface.*

22. The call for help is in *Die Enthauptung des weltberühmten Wohlredners Ciceronis,* silence in *Der Großmüthige Überwinder Seiner Selbst.* The generosity of the Bassa Selim at the end of *Die Entführung aus dem Serail* is typical of *Haupt- und Staatsaktion,* as is

the confusing plot organized around the beloved in disguise found in Mozart's first operetta, *La finta giardiniera.*

23. The text conveniently overlooks the fact that words are as much signs as visual images, and that their truth value also depends on the capacity to command belief. I claim, however, only that the text has a pattern, not necessarily philosophical rigor.

24. Compare also Pamina's judgment of Papageno's honesty by his "gefühlvolles Herz," Mozart, *Die Zauberflöte* 28.

25. E.g., Charles Rosen in *The Classical Style* 317–21, with regard both to libretto and setting; Ludwig Finscher, "Mozart und die Idee eines musikalischen Universalstils," with regard to Mozart's mature style in general, and *Die Zauberflöte* in particular, 278; Ernst Bloch in "Die Zauberflöte und die Symbole von Heute" 100–103, with regard to the libretto; and Rose Subotnik, "Whose *Magic Flute?*" with regard to libretto and setting. Bakhtin has even been invoked, by Rose Subotnik, to explain in effect the layering of a postmodern deconstructive reading over an Enlightenment universalist reading of both text and music. Subotnik understands discourse, for the purposes of her argument, primarily in a political sense, and understands the different discourses diachronically. I focus rather on synchronic discourses, both present in and for the eighteenth century, and at a more abstract level than politics.

26. Such modal counterpoint indeed underlies Northrop Frye's notion of literary quality: "For while one mode constitutes the underlying tonality of a work of fiction, any or all of the other four may be simultaneously present. Much of our sense of the subtlety of great literature comes from this modal counterpoint" (*Anatomy of Criticism* 50–51). "Heteroglossia" is Bakhtin's term for the same structural phenomenon.

27. Ehrhard Bahr analyzes irony as Goethe's "methodology" in the works of his last two decades in *Die Ironie im Spätwerk Goethes.*

28. The figures (Dobritzsch, *Barocker Bühnenzauber* 52) are not weighted to account for one-act plays, but the maximum shift caused by accounting for them in Weimar was to decrease the proportion of comedies by 3 percent.

29. Small wonder that Willi Flemming refers to Goethe's emphasis on "melodische Linienführung" in *Goethes Gestaltung des klassischen Theaters* 65. Bruno Satori-Neumann also refers repeatedly to Goethe's emphasis on "tempo" in rehearsals in *Die Frühzeit des Weimarischen Hoftheaters* 264–75.

30. Book 4, chapter 14 on music and movement (HA 7:246); book 4, chapter 2 on ensemble acting and musical ensemble (ibid., 214–15); cited by Satori-Neumann, *Die Frühzeit des Weimarischen Hoftheaters* 274 and 235. On Wilhelm's condemnation of opera, see Jane K. Brown, "The Theatrical Mission of the *Lehrjahre*" 81. Smart (*Mimomania* 1–3) recurs to the misconception, although the failure to recognize Goethe's irony does not impact the usefulness of the distinction between visible and invisible music drawn from *Wilhelm Meister* for her argument about nineteenth-century opera.

31. For a thorough survey and discussion of Goethe's libretti see Waldura, "Die Singspiele."

32. For an extended reading in these terms see Jane K. Brown, "Egmonts Dämon."

33. Goethe might perhaps have encountered Thoas's love for Iphigenia in Joseph de Chancel de Lagrange's *Oreste et Pylade* of 1697, but most of the numerous Iphigenia operas of the late seventeenth to late eighteenth century had at least some love interest, as already seen with Strantizky (above, Chapter 6).

34. He was trained early in Italian, and Metastasio's works were included in the family library (Götting, "Die Bibliothek von Goethes Vater" 56).

35. The formative influence of German Classicism on the modern drama of Europe is the central thesis of Bennett's *Modern Drama and German Classicism.*

36. To be sure, it is not unusual that operas should use dramatic plots; it is, however, highly unusual for dramas to be based on the plots of operas.

37. The first fragments can be dated to 1804 on the basis of the secretary's handwriting. Not until ten years later did Goethe compose the poem "Ballade" that summarizes the plot and that he intended to include in the finished opera. He referred several times to the lengthy genesis of the opera (see commentary in HA 1:540; cf. Gräf, *Goethe über seine Dichtungen* 2.3:337–40); in "Bedeutende Fördernis durch ein einziges geistreiches Wort" he compares its long genesis to his extended engagement with the French Revolution (HA 13:39).

38. Dieter Borchmeyer correctly locates this fragment among Goethe's works that deal with the French Revolution and remarks in this context on a connection to *Die natürliche Tochter,* but he does not go far enough in my opinion. See Goethe, *Sämtliche Werke* 1.6, ed. Dieter Borchmeyer 1181–82.

39. Apart from his early hostility to the operatic aspects of *Egmont,* there is the evidence of Schiller's own *Semele: Eine lyrische Operette in zwei Szenen.* Written 1779–80, it is notable in several respects. First, it shows considerable control of the conventions of opera and has powerful dramatic language, especially by Semele. Second, it has an uncompromisingly tragic conclusion, almost as if the young Schiller intended to attack the comfortable Rococo conventions of a predecessor like Wieland, who would have loomed large on his horizon. Third, by 1789 he described the work as a grave sin against the Muses (letter to Charlotte Lengfeld, April 30, 1789, *Sämtliche Werke* 2:1292). Probably its sin was the frivolous choice of genre, but one also wonders if, as Schiller immersed himself in Kant, its sin was not also its failure to try to reconcile the ideal and the real, and thus to avoid the tragic end.

40. Goethe collected maxims for most of his adult life and published them in clusters only beginning in 1810. The standard numbering, used here, comes from the critical edition of Max Hecker, *Goethe: Maximen und Reflexionen* of 1907.

Chapter 8

1. "Die Gefahr [bei Wagner] kommt auf die Spitze, wenn sich eine solche Musik immer enger an eine ganz naturalistische, durch kein Gesetz der Plastik beherrschte Schauspielerei und Gebärdenkunst anlehnt, die *Wirkung* will, nichts mehr . . . Das *espressivo* um jeden Preis und die Musik im Dienste, in der Sklaverei der Attitüde—*das ist das Ende*" (Nietzsche, *Werke* 2:1043).

2. To be more precise, Wagner increasingly eliminates closed forms that are set off as arias or songs, except where song is the subject of discussion, as in *Die Meistersinger.* In "Zukunftsmusik" Wagner redefines "dance" to "the dramatic action" and melody to "endless melody" ("unendliche Melodie," *Dichtungen und Schriften* 8:88–93). On the endless melody see also Dahlhaus, *Wagners Konzeption des muskalischen Dramas* 45; on the complex effect on the relation of text to music of these ideas, see the section "Musikalische Prosa," ibid. 60–75.

3. For clear summaries in English of Wagner's positions see Borchmeyer, *Richard Wagner* 75–177, and Dahlhaus in Deathridge, *New Grove Wagner* 92–110.

4. Although Wagner worshipped Goethe and was deeply influenced by him, he took Schiller as his model dramatist. Indeed Schiller's dramaturgy is more Aristotelian than Goethe's, and precisely in the ways that Wagner's is, in its greater focus on character motivation and causality. On Wagner and Schiller, see Borchmeyer, *Ahasvers Wandlungen* 353–70; on Wagner and Goethe, ibid. 337–52.

5. Cf. Nietzsche's repeated attention to the centrality of this category whether he is speaking for or against Wagner (*Werke* 2:1042–43, 1050, 913, 929; 1:413).

6. Many modern critics, following Nietzsche, regard the characters in the *Ring* less as mythic figures than as rather nasty portrayals of the nineteenth-century family. It is also a commonplace that Wagner's figures have a fully developed subconscious life driven by repressed sexual concerns. In the constant references to the role of will and one's (particularly Wotan's) capacity to exercise one's will the nature of the modern self is formulated and discussed. Mary Ann Smart takes this trend to the extreme by trying to undo it, arguing that by decoupling gesture from music Wagner denied his characters independence of mind and thereby "vitality" (*Mimomania* 201–4). Dahlhaus's characterization of Wagner's shift over his career from focus on the visual to a more interiorized aesthetic (in *Die Bedeutung des Gestischen*) contradicts the argument developing here only superficially; the substitution of expressive stasis for obvious physical gesture corresponds exactly to the shift from the semiotic gestures of allegory to the realism of psychological drama where the true action is understood to be interior.

7. For a clear summary of Wagner's desired performance conditions, see Evan Baker, "Richard Wagner and His Search for the Ideal Theatrical Space."

8. Although both have some precedents in eighteenth-century opera and German Classicism—sleepers in Orlando operas and *Egmont*, the quarrel between brothers most obviously in Schiller's operatic *Braut von Messina*—both motifs derive ultimately from Ariosto's *Orlando furioso*, like so much else in European opera.

9. On the cliché about the death of the heroine, see Clément, *Opera, or, the Undoing of Women.*

10. The motif of sudden dousing of fire, especially a funeral pyre, by water from nature seems to derive ultimately from Herodotus's narration of the miraculous rescue of Croesus from death by burning at the hands of Cyrus; the rescuing cloudburst is understood to have been sent by Apollo and to signify that Croesus is a good man (Herodotus, *The Histories* 76). It appears regularly in Croesus operas, as for example Nicolo Minato's *Atis* of 1678 (Minato was Metastasio's predecessor as Viennese court poet and librettist) and Lucas von Bostel's German adaptation first performed in 1684.

11. And Heinrich von Kleist's *Käthchen von Heilbronn* (1808) almost dies by both fire and water; she is rescued from the first by an angel.

12. Hebbel says in his forward, "The goal of this tragedy was to make the dramatic treasure of the Nibelungenlied liquid [i.e., usable] for the real stage, but not . . . to sound the depths of its poetic-mythical substance" ("Der Zweck dieses Trauerspiels war, den dramatischen Schatz des Nibelungen-Liedes für die reale Bühne flüssig zu machen, nicht aber den poetisch-mythischen Gehalt . . . zu ergründen," *Werke* 2:109). Note the water imagery.

13. The reference to Voltaire's *Candide* is probably also inescapable; Candida does not share the foolish innocence of Voltaire's male hero, but her husband Morell surely does.

14. Cf. the topos of the woman as the angel of the house. Perhaps the most striking example of cosmic order figured in the cozy household is the final scene of Johann Nestroy's Viennese folk comedy *Der böse Geist Lumpazivagabundus* (1833), where the three couples on whom the play has focused are shown in their three separate apartments in the same house going about their domestic business.

15. A genre that had a substantial vogue in the second decade of the nineteenth century in Germany on the model of Zacharias Werner's *Der vierundzwanzigste Februar*. Other examples are *Der 29. Februar* (1812) and *Die Schuld* (1813) by Adolf Müllner, and Franz Grillparzer's *Die Ahnfrau* (1817).

16. The play points to this repeatedly, most explicitly on p. 467.

Works Cited

Abrams, M. H. *Natural Supernaturalism: Tradition and Revolution in Romantic Literature.* New York: Norton, 1971.

Adams, Henry Hitch, and Baxter Hathaway, eds. *Dramatic Essays of the Neoclassic Age.* New York: Columbia University Press, 1950.

Addison, Joseph. *Cato,* in *Plays of the Restoration and Eighteenth Century as they were acted at the Theatres-Royal by their Majesties' Servants.* Ed. Dougald MacMillan and Howard Mumford Jones. New York: Holt, 1931. 517–47.

Aercke, Kristiaan P., trans. *Gijsbrecht van Amstel,* by Joost van den Vondel. Ottawa: Doverhouse Editions, 1991. 9–50.

Allanbrook, Wye Jamison. *Rhythmic Gesture in Mozart:* Le Nozze di Figaro *and* Don Giovanni. Chicago: University of Chicago Press, 1983.

Andrews, Malcolm. *Landscape and Western Art.* Oxford: Oxford University Press, 1999.

Aristotle. *Poetics,* in *Classical Literary Criticism.* Trans. T. S. Dorsch. Harmondsworth: Penguin, 1965.

Assmann, Jan. *Die Zauberflöte: Oper und Mysterium.* Munich: Hanser, 2005.

Bahr, Ehrhard. *Die Ironie im Spätwerk Goethes: ". . . diese sehr ernsten Scherze . . ." Studien zum West-östlichen Divan, zu den Wanderjahren und zu Faust II.* Berlin: E. Schmidt, 1972.

Baker, Evan. "Richard Wagner and His Search for the Ideal Theatrical Space." *Opera in Context: Essays on Historical Staging from the Late Renaissance to the Time of Puccini,* ed. Mark A. Radice. Portland, Ore.: Amadeus, 1998. 241–78.

Bakhtin, M. M. *The Dialogic Imagination: Four Essays.* Trans. Caryl Emerson and Michael Holquist. Austin: University of Texas Press, 1981.

Baldwin, T. W. *Shakespere's Five-Act Structure: Shakespere's Early Plays on the Background of Renaissance Theories of Five-Act Structure from 1470.* Urbana: University of Illinois Press, 1947.

Barish, Jonas. *The Antitheatrical Prejudice.* Berkeley: University of California Press, 1981.

Barner, Wilfried. *Produktive Rezeption: Lessing und die Tragödien Senecas.* Munich: Beck, 1973.

Barney, Stephen A. *Allegories of History, Allegories of Love.* Hamden, Conn.: Archon, 1979.

Barnouw, A. J. *Vondel.* New York and London: C. Scribner's Sons, 1925.

Barrell, John. *The Idea of Landscape and the Sense of Place 1730–1840: An Approach to the Poetry of John Clare.* Cambridge: Cambridge University Press, 1972.

Batley, Edward M. *A Preface to the* Magic Flute. London: Dobson, 1969.

Beare, Mary. *The German Popular Play* Atis *and the Venetian Opera: A Study of the Conversion of Operas into Popular Plays, 1675–1722, with Special Reference to the Play* Atis. Cambridge: Cambridge University Press, 1938.

Bedaux, Jan Baptist. *The Reality of Symbols: Studies in the Iconology of Netherlandish Art 1400–1800.* 's-Gravenhage: G. Schwarz/SDU, 1990.

Beethoven, Ludwig van. *Briefe: Eine Auswahl.* Ed. Hansjürgen Schaefer. Wilhelmshaven: Heinrichhofen's, 1969.

Béhar, Pierre, ed. *August Adolph von Haugwitz: Prodromus Poeticus, Oder: Poetischer Vortrab. 1684.* Tübingen: Niemeyer, 1984.

Belsey, Catherine. *The Subject of Tragedy: Identity and Difference in Renaissance Drama.* London: Methuen, 1985.

Benjamin, Walter. *Ursprung des deutschen Trauerspiels.* Frankfurt/Main: Suhrkamp, 1963.

Bennett, Benjamin K. *Modern Drama and German Classicism: Renaissance from Lessing to Brecht.* Ithaca, N.Y.: Cornell University Press, 1979.

Bevington, David M. *From "Mankind" to Marlowe: The Growth of Structure in the Popular Drama of Tudor England.* Cambridge, Mass.: Harvard University Press, 1962.

Bialostocki, Jan. "Judith: Story, Image, and Symbol: Giorgione's Painting in the Evolution of the Theme." *The Message of Images: Studies in the History of Art.* Vienna: IRSA, 1988. 113–31.

———. "Mere Imitation of Nature or Symbolic Image of the World? Problems in the Interpretation of Dutch Painting of the XVIIth Century." *The Message of Images: Studies in the History of Art.* Vienna: IRSA, 1988. 166–80.

Bloch, Ernst. *Das Prinzip Hoffnung.* Frankfurt/Main: Suhrkamp, 1959.

———. "Die Zauberflöte und Symbole von Heute." *Verfremdungen I.* Frankfurt/Main: Suhrkamp, 1962. 97–103.

Bloom, Harold. *Shakespeare: The Invention of the Human.* New York: Riverhead, 1998.

Bockemühl, Michael. *Rembrandt: The Mystery of the Revealed Form.* Cologne: Benedikt Taschen, 1992.

Böhme, Hans-Georg. *Die Weilburger Goethe-Funde: Neues aus Theater und Schauspielkunst.* Emsdetten: H. und J. Lechte, 1950.

Bold, Stephen. "The Anxiety of Senecan Influence in Racine, or Phèdre in the Labyrinth." *Romanic Review* 92:4 (2001): 417–32.

Booth, Michael R. *Victorian Spectacular Theatre 1850–1910.* Boston: Routledge and Kegan Paul, 1981.

Borchmeyer, Dieter. "Mozarts rasende Weiber." *Mozarts Opernfiguren: Große Herren, rasende Weiber—gefährliche Liebschaften,* ed. Dieter Borchmeyer. Berne: Haupt, 1992. 167–212.

———. *Richard Wagner: Ahasvers Wandlungen.* Frankfurt: Insel, 2002.

———. *Richard Wagner: Theory and Theatre.* Trans. Stewart Spencer. Oxford: Clarendon, 1991.

Boydell, John, ed. *A Collection of Prints Engraved after the Most Capital Paintings in England.* 2 vols. London: John Boydell, 1769–72.

Braden, Gordon. *Renaissance Tragedy and the Senecan Tradition: Anger's Privilege.* New Haven, Conn.: Yale University Press, 1985.

Branscombe, Peter. *W. A. Mozart: Die Zauberflöte.* Cambridge: Cambridge University Press, 1991.

Brooks, Peter. *The Melodramatic Imagination: Balzac, Henry James, Melodrama, and the Mode of Excess.* New Haven, Conn.: Yale University Press, 1995.

Brossmann, Regine. "*Britannicus* oder die Krise der klassischen Tragödie." *Germanisch-Romanische Monatsschrift* 53:4 (2003): 387–98.

Brown, Jane K. "Der Drang zum Gesang: On Goethe's Dramatic Form." *Goethe Yearbook* 10 (2001): 115–24.

———. "Discordia concors: On the Order of *A Midsummer Night's Dream*." *Modern Language Quarterly* 48 (1987): 20–41.

———. "Double Plotting in Shakespeare's Comedies: The Case of *Twelfth Night*." *Aesthetic Illusion: Theoretical and Historical Approaches*, ed. Frederick Burwick and Walter Pape. Berlin: de Gruyter, 1990. 313–23.

———. "Egmonts Dämon: Die Erfindung des Subjekts." *Ironie und Objektivität: Aufsätze zu Goethe*. Würzburg: Königshausen und Neumann, 1999. 14–32.

———. *Goethe's* Faust: *The German Tragedy*. Ithaca, N.Y.: Cornell University Press, 1986.

———. "The Prosperous Wonder Worker: Faust in the Renaissance." *Faust through Four Centuries: Retrospect and Analysis*, ed. Peter Boerner and Sidney Johnson. Tübingen: Niemeyer, 1989. 53–64.

———. "The Queen of the Night and the Crisis of Allegory in *The Magic Flute*." *Goethe Yearbook* 8 (1996): 142–56.

———. "Schiller und die Ironie von *Hermann und Dorothea*." *Ironie und Objektivität: Aufsätze zu Goethe*. Würzburg: Königshausen und Neumann, 1999. 164–79.

———. "The Theatrical Practice of Weimar Classicism." *The Literature of Weimar Classicism*, ed. Simon Richter. Camden House History of German Literature vol. 7. Rochester: Camden House, 2005. 139–66.

Brown, Marshall. "The Logic of Realism: A Hegelian Approach." *PMLA* 96 (1981): 224–41.

———. *Preromanticism*. Stanford, Calif.: Stanford University Press, 1991.

———. *Turning Points: Essays in the History of Cultural Expressions*. Stanford, Calif.: Stanford University Press, 1997.

Brüggemann, Werner. *Spanisches Theater und deutsche Romantik*. Vol. 1. Münster: Aschendorffsche Verlagsbuchhandlung, 1964.

Bryson, Norman. *Looking at the Overlooked: Four Essays on Still Life Painting*. Cambridge, Mass.: Harvard University Press, 1990.

———. *Word and Image: French Painting of the Ancien Régime*. Cambridge: Cambridge University Press, 1981.

Bullough, Geoffrey. *Narrative and Dramatic Sources of Shakespeare*. 8 vols. London: Routledge and Kegan Paul and New York: Columbia University Press, 1957–75.

Burckhardt, Sigurd. *Shakespearean Meanings*. Princeton, N.J.: Princeton University Press, 1968.

Burk, John N. *The Life and Works of Beethoven*. New York: Modern Library, 1946.

Burkhardt, C. A. H. *Das Repertoire des Weimarischen Theaters unter Goethes Leitung, 1791–1817*. 1891. Nendeln/Liechtenstein: Kraus Reprint, 1977.

Burnett, Charles, trans. *Jesuit Plays on Japan and English Recusancy: An Essay, by Masahiro Takenaka, with Editions and Translations*. Tokyo: Renaissance Institute, 1995.

Butcher, S. H. *Aristotle's Theory of Poetry and Fine Art: With a Critical Text and Translation of the* Poetics. New York: Dover, 1951.

Calderón de la Barca, Pedro. *El Mágico Prodigioso*. Ed. Melveena McKendrick in association with A. A. Parker. Oxford: Clarendon, 1992.

———. *Obras completas*. 3 vols. Madrid: Aguilar, 1987–91.

Calderwood, James L. *Shakespearean Metadrama: The Argument of the Play in* Titus Andronicus, Love's Labour's Lost, Romeo and Juliet, A Midsummer

Night's Dream, and Richard II. Minneapolis: University of Minnesota Press, 1971.

Campbell, John. "Racine's *Iphigénie*: A 'Happy Tragedy'?" *Theatrum Mundi: Studies in Honor of Ronald W. Tobin,* ed. Claire L. Carlin and Kathleen Wine. Charlottesville, Va.: Rockwood Press, 2003. 214–21.

Campbell, Lily B. *Scenes and Machines on the English Stage during the Renaissance: A Classical Revival.* Cambridge: Cambridge University Press, 1923.

Carlson, Marvin. *Goethe and the Weimar Theatre.* Ithaca, N.Y.: Cornell University Press, 1978.

Chailley, Jacques. *"La flûte enchantée," opéra maçonnique: Essai d'explication du livret et de la musique.* Paris: R. Laffont, 1968.

Christiansen, Keith. "Pallas Expelling the Vices from the Garden of Virtue." *Andrea Mantegna,* ed. Jane Martineau. London: Thames and Hudson and Milan: Electa, 1992. 427–30.

Clément, Catherine. *Opera, or, The Undoing of Women.* Trans. Betsy Wing. Minneapolis: University of Minnesota Press, 1988.

Cody, Richard. *The Landscape of the Mind: Pastoralism and Platonic Theory in Tasso's* Aminta *and Shakespeare's Early Comedies.* Oxford: Clarendon, 1969.

Cohen, Selma Jeanne, ed. *Dance as a Theatre Art: Source Readings in Dance History from 1581 to the Present.* Princeton, N.J.: Princeton Book Company, 1992.

Cohen, Walter. *Drama of a Nation: Public Theater in Renaissance England and Spain.* Ithaca, N.Y.: Cornell University Press, 1985.

Corneille, Pierre. *Oeuvres complètes.* Paris: Seuil and Macmillan, 1963.

Craik, T. W., ed., with J. M. Lothian. *Twelfth Night.* The Arden Edition of the Works of Shakespeare. London: Methuen, 1975.

Csampai, Attila. "Das Geheimnis der *Zauberflöte* oder die Folgen der Aufklärung." *Die Zauberflöte: Texte, Materialien, Kommentare,* ed. Attila Csampai and Dietmar Holland. Reinbek: Rowohlt, 1982. 9–40.

Curtius, Ernst Robert. *European Literature and the Latin Middle Ages.* Trans. Willard R. Trask. New York: Harper and Row, 1963.

Dahlhaus, Carl. *Die Bedeutung des Gestischen in Wagners Musikdramen.* Munich: Oldenbourg, 1970.

——. *Wagners Konzeption des musikalischen Dramas.* 1971. Munich: dtv and Kassel: Bärenreiter, 1990.

Daly, Peter M. "Shakespeare and the Emblem: The Use of Evidence and Analogy in Establishing Iconographic and Emblematic Effects in the Plays." *Shakespeare and the Emblem: Studies in Renaissance Iconography and Iconology,* ed. Tibor Fabiny et al. Szeged: Department of English, Attila József University, 1984. 117–87.

Daniel, Clay. "The Fall of George Barnwell." *Restoration and 18th Century Theatre Research* 2 (1987): 26–37.

de Armas, Frederick A. *The Return of Astraea: An Astral-Imperial Myth in Calderón.* Lexington: University Press of Kentucky, 1986.

Deathridge, John, and Carl Dahlhaus. *The New Grove Wagner.* New York: Norton, 1984.

Dédéyan, Charles. *Le thème de Faust dans la littérature européenne.* Vol. 1. Paris: Lettres modernes, 1954.

Deiters, Franz-Josef. *Drama im Augenblick seines Sturzes: Zur Allegorisierung des Dramas in der Moderne: Versuche zu einer Konstitutionstheorie.* Berlin: E. Schmidt, 1999.

Delmas, Christian. "Histoire et mythe." *Racine et l'histoire,* ed. Marie-Claude Canova-Green and Alain Viala. Tübingen: Gunter Narr, 2004. 57–68.

De Sanctis, Francesco. *History of Italian Literature.* Trans. Joan Redfern. 2 vols. New York: Harcourt Brace, 1931.

Diderot, Denis. *Oeuvres esthétiques.* Paris: Garnier, 1965.

Dobritzsch, Elisabeth. *Barocker Bühnenzauber: Das Ekhof-Theater in Gotha.* Munich: Bayerische Vereinsbank, 1995.

Donington, Robert. *The Rise of Opera.* London: Faber and Faber, 1981.

Donno, Elizabeth Story, ed. *Three Renaissance Pastorals: Tasso, Guarini, Daniel.* Binghamton, N.Y.: Medieval and Renaissance Texts and Studies, 1993.

Doran, Madeleine. *Endeavors of Art: A Study of Form in Elizabethan Drama.* Madison: University of Wisconsin Press, 1954.

Dunn, P. N. "Honour and the Christian Background in Calderón." *Critical Essays on the Theatre of Calderón,* ed. Bruce W. Wardropper. New York: New York University Press, 1965. 24–60.

Eberle, Matthias. *Individuum und Landschaft: Zur Entstehung und Entwicklung der Landschaftsmalerei.* Gießen: Anabas, 1980.

Ehrmann, Jean. *Antoine Caron: Peintre des fêtes et des massacres.* Paris: Flammarion, 1986.

Eilert, Heide. "Amor als Landschaftsmaler: Goethe und die Malerei des 17. und 18. Jahrhunderts." *Pantheon* 51 (1993): 129–37.

Elias, Norbert. *The Civilizing Process: Sociogenetic and Psychogenetic Investigations.* Trans. Edmund Jephcott. Oxford: Blackwell, 2000.

Euripides. *Iphigenia in Aulis.* Trans. Charles R. Walker. *The Complete Greek Tragedies,* ed. David Grene and Richmond Lattimore. Chicago: University of Chicago Press, 1960. 4:289–387.

Farnham, Willard. *The Medieval Heritage of Elizabethan Tragedy.* 1936. New York: Barnes and Noble, 1963.

Fineman, Joel. *Shakespeare's Perjur'd Eye: The Invention of Poetic Subjectivity in the Sonnets.* Berkeley: University of California Press, 1986.

Finscher, Ludwig. "Mozart und die Idee eines musikalischen Universalstils." *Die Musik des 18. Jahrhunderts,* ed. Carl Dahlhaus. Laaber: Laaber, 1985.

Flaherty, Gloria. *Opera in the Development of German Critical Thought.* Princeton, N.J.: Princeton University Press, 1978.

Flemming, Willi. *Andreas Gryphius und die Bühne.* Halle: Niemeyer, 1921.

———. *Geschichte des Jesuitentheaters in den Landen deutscher Zunge.* Berlin: Gesellschaft für Theatergeschichte, 1923.

———. *Goethes Gestaltung des klassischen Theaters.* Cologne: H. Schaffstein, 1949.

———, ed. *Das Ordensdrama.* Leipzig: Reclam, 1930.

Fletcher, Angus. *Allegory: The Theory of a Symbolic Mode.* Ithaca, N.Y.: Cornell University Press, 1964.

Fothergill-Payne, Louise, and Peter Fothergill-Payne, eds. *Parallel Lives: Spanish and English National Drama 1580–1680.* Lewisburg, Pa.: Bucknell University Press, 1991.

Foucault, Michel. *The Order of Things: An Archeology of the Human Sciences.* New York: Vintage, 1970.

Frye, Northrop. *Anatomy of Criticism: Four Essays.* New York: Atheneum, 1966.

Fubini, Enrico. *Music and Culture in Eighteenth-Century Europe: A Source Book.* Trans. and ed. Bonnie J. Blackburn. Chicago: University of Chicago Press, 1994.

Gadamer, Hans-Georg. "On the Course of Human Spiritual Development: Studies of Goethe's Unfinished Writings." *Literature and Philosophy in Dialogue: Essays in German Literary Theory,* trans. Robert H. Paslick. Albany: State University of New York Press, 1994. 31–66.

Genast, Eduard. *Aus Weimars klassischer und nachklassischer Zeit: Erinnerungen eines alten Schauspielers*, ed. Robert Kohlrausch. Stuttgart: R. Lutz, 1904.

Goethe, Johann Wolfgang. *Gesamtausgabe der Werke und Schriften.* 22 vols. Stuttgart: Cotta, 1940–63.

———. *Goethe: Maximen und Reflexionen: Nach den Handschriften des Goethe- und Schiller-Archivs.* Ed. Max Hecker. Weimar: Goethe-Gesellschaft, 1907.

———. *Goethes Gespräche: Eine Sammlung zeitgenössischer Berichte aus seinem Umgang 2.* Ed. Flodoard Freiherrn von Biedermann and Wolfgang Herwig. Zurich: Artemis, 1969.

———. *Goethes Werke: Hamburger Ausgabe.* 14 vols. Hamburg: Wegner, 1965. Abbreviated HA.

———. *Goethes Werke: Herausgegeben im Auftrage der Großherzogin Sophie von Sachsen.* 143 vols. Weimar: Böhlau, 1887–1919. Abbreviated WA.

———. *Sämtliche Werke* I. Vol. 6. Ed. Dieter Borchmeyer. Frankfurt/Main: Deutscher Klassiker Verlag, 1993.

Goldberg, Sander M. "Going for Baroque: Seneca and the English." *Seneca in Performance*, ed. George W. M. Harrison. London: Duckworth with the Classical Press of Wales, 2000. 207–29.

Goldmann, Lucien. *The Hidden God: A Study of Tragic Vision in the* Pensées *of Pascal and the Tragedies of Racine.* Trans. Philip Thody. London: Routledge and Kegan Paul, 1964.

Gombrich, E. H. "Botticelli's Mythologies: A Study in the Neo-Platonic Symbolism of His Circle." *Symbolic Images: Studies in the Art of the Renaissance.* Oxford: Phaidon, 1978. 31–86.

———. "Icones Symbolicae." *Journal of the Warburg and Courtauld Institutes* 11 (1948): 163–92.

———. "The Renaissance Theory of Art and the Rise of Landscape." *Norm and Form: Studies in the Art of the Renaissance.* London: Phaidon, 1971. 107–21.

Götting, Franz. "Die Bibliothek von Goethes Vater." *Nassauische Annalen* 64 (1953): 23–69.

Gottsched, Johann Christoph. *Versuch einer critischen Dichtkunst.* 1751. Darmstadt: Wissenschaftliche Buchgesellschaft, 1962.

Gräf, Hans Gerhart. *Goethe über seine Dichtungen.* 9 vols. Darmstadt: Wissenschaftliche Buchgesellschaft, 1968.

Gray, Richard. *About Face: German Physiognomic Thought from Lavater to Auschwitz.* Detroit, Mich.: Wayne State University Press, 2004.

Greer, Margaret Rich. *The Play of Power: Mythological Court Dramas of Calderón de la Barca.* Princeton, N.J.: Princeton University Press, 1991.

Grimm, Jacob, and Wilhelm Grimm. *Deutsches Wörterbuch.* 16 vols. Leipzig: S. Hirzel, 1854–1960.

Grimmelshausen, Hans Jakob Christoffel. *Der abenteuerliche Simplicissimus.* 1669. Frankfurt/Main: Fischer, 1962.

Grout, Donald Jay. *A Short History of Opera.* New York: Columbia University Press, 1988.

Gryphyius, Andreas. *Cardenio und Celinde: Oder Unglücklich Verliebete.* Stuttgart: Reclam, 1968.

Guthke, Karl S. *Modern Tragicomedy: An Investigation into the Nature of the Genre.* New York: Random House, 1966.

Hacking, Ian. *The Emergence of Probability: A Philosophical Study of Early Ideas about Probability, Induction and Statistical Inference.* London: Cambridge University Press, 1975.

Hammond, Frederick. *Music and Spectacle in Baroque Rome: Barberini Patronage under Urban VIII.* New Haven, Conn.: Yale University Press, 1994.

Hanning, Barbara Russano. *Of Poetry and Music's Power: Humanism and the Creation of Opera.* Ann Arbor: UMI Research Press, 1980.

Happé, Peter, ed. *Four Morality Plays.* Harmondsworth: Penguin, 1979.

Havens, Raymond. "Simplicity, a Changing Concept." *Journal of the History of Ideas* 14 (1953): 3–32.

Hazlitt, W. Carew, ed. *A Select Collection of Old English Plays: Originally Published by Robert Dodsley in the Year 1774.* 15 vols. London: Reeves and Turner, 1874.

Hebbel, Friedrich. *Werke.* 5 vols. Ed. Gerhard Fricke, Werner Keller, and Karl Pörnbacher. Munich: Hanser, 1963–67.

Heilman, Robert. "Tragedy and Melodrama: Speculations on Generic Form." *Texas Quarterly* 3:2 (1960): 36–50.

Hein, Jürgen. *Das Wiener Volkstheater: Raimund und Nestroy.* Darmstadt: Wissenschaftliche Buchgesellschaft, 1978.

Heller, Erich. *The Disinherited Mind.* Harmondsworth: Penguin, 1961.

Henkel, Arthur, and Albrecht Schöne, eds. *Emblemata: Handbuch zur Sinnbildkunst d. XVI. u. XVII. Jh.* Stuttgart: Metzler, 1976.

Herodotus. *The Histories.* Trans. Aubrey de Sélincourt. Harmondsworth: Penguin, 1972.

Herrick, Marvin Theodore. *Tragicomedy: Its Origin and Development in Italy, France, and England.* Urbana: University of Illinois Press, 1955.

Hewitt, Bernard, ed. *The Renaissance Stage: Documents of Serlio, Sabbattini, Furttenbach.* Coral Gables: University of Miami Press, 1958.

Hilton, Wendy. *Dance of Court and Theater: The French Noble Style, 1690–1725.* Ed. Caroline Gaynor. Princeton, N.J.: Princeton Book Company, 1981.

Hinck, Walter. *Goethe—Mann des Theaters.* Göttingen: Vandenhoeck und Ruprecht, 1982.

Hirsch, James. "Shakespeare and the History of Soliloquies." *Modern Language Quarterly* 58 (1997): 1–26.

Hofmannsthal, Hugo von. *Dramen III: 1893–1927. Gesammelte Werke in zehn Einzelbänden,* ed. Bernd Schoeller and Rudolf Hirsch. Frankfurt/Main: Fischer, 1979.

Homeyer, Fritz. *Stranitzkys Drama vom "Heiligen Nepomuck" mit einem Neudruck des Textes.* Berlin: Mayer and Müller, 1907.

Honig, Edwin. *Calderón and the Seizures of Honor.* Cambridge, Mass.: Harvard University Press, 1972.

———. *Dark Conceit: The Making of Allegory.* Evanston, Ill.: Northwestern University Press, 1959.

Honigmann, E. A. J., ed. *King John.* The Arden Edition of the Works of Shakespeare. London: Methuen, 1954.

Horace. *Satires and Epistles.* Ed. Charles E. Bennett and John C. Rolfe. Boston: Allyn and Bacon, 1942.

Hörisch, Jochen. *Heads or Tails: The Poetics of Money.* Trans. Amy Horning Marschall. Detroit, Mich.: Wayne State University Press, 2000.

Jack, Ian. *Keats and the Mirror of Art.* Oxford: Clarendon, 1967.

Jackson, Wallace. *The Probable and the Marvelous: Blake, Wordsworth, and the Eighteenth-Century Critical Tradition.* Athens: University of Georgia Press, 1978.

James, Edward. "Euripidean and Christian Crosscurrents in the Problematic Morality of Racine's *Phèdre*." *Nottingham French Studies* 36:2 (1997): 1–9.

Jankovics, József, ed. *The Sopron Collection of Jesuit Stage Designs*. Budapest: Enciklopédia, 1999.

Janson, H. W. *Apes and Ape Lore in the Middle Ages and the Renaissance*. London: Warburg Institute, 1952.

Jonson, Ben. *The Complete Masques of Ben Jonson*. Ed. Stephen Orgel. New Haven, Conn.: Yale University Press, 1969.

Katz, Ruth. *Divining the Powers of Music: Aesthetic Theory and the Origins of Opera*. New York: Pendragon, 1986.

Keil-Budischowsky, Verena. *Die Theater Wiens*. Vienna: P. Zsolnay, 1983.

Kelley, Theresa M. *Reinventing Allegory*. Cambridge: Cambridge University Press, 1997.

Kennedy, I. G. "Claude and Architecture." *Journal of the Warburg and Courtauld Institutes* 35 (1972): 260–83.

Kirstein, Lincoln. *Dance: A Short History of Classic Theatrical Dancing*. Princeton, N.J.: Princeton Book Company, 1987.

Kitson, Michael. *The Art of Claude Lorrain*. London: Arts Council of Great Britain, 1969.

———. *Claude Lorrain: Liber Veritatis*. London: British Museum Publications, 1978.

———. Review of *Claude Lorrain: The Poetic Landscape*, by Humphrey Wine. *Burlington Magazine* 136 (1994): 251–53.

———. "The Seventeenth Century: Claude to Francisque Millet." *Claude to Corot: The Development of Landscape Painting in France*, ed. Alan Wintermute. New York: Colnaghi and Seattle: University of Washington Press, 1990. 11–26.

Kolve, V. A. *The Play Called Corpus Christi*. Stanford, Calif.: Stanford University Press, 1966.

Komorzynski, Egon. "Die Entstehung der *Zauberflöte*." *Die Zauberflöte: Texte, Materialien, Kommentare*, ed. Attila Csampai und Dietmar Holland. Reinbek bei Hamburg: Rowohlt, 1982. 149–65.

Lagerlöf, Margaretha Rossholm. *Ideal Landscape: Annibale Carracci, Nicolas Poussin and Claude Lorrain*. New Haven, Conn.: Yale University Press, 1990.

Langdon, Helen. *Claude Lorrain*. Oxford: Phaidon, 1989.

Laver, James. *Drama: Its Costume and Decor*. London: Studio Publications, 1951.

Lessing, Gotthold Ephraim. *Briefwechsel über das Trauerspiel*. Ed. Jochen Schulte-Sasse. Munich: Winkler, 1972.

———. *Gesammelte Werke*. Ed. Wolfgang Stammler. 2 vols. Munich: Hanser, 1959.

Levitan, William. "Seneca in Racine." *Yale French Studies* 76 (1989): 185–210.

Lewalski, Barbara K. "Thematic Patterns in *Twelfth Night*." *Shakespeare Studies* 1 (1965): 168–81.

Lillo, George. *The London Merchant*, in *Plays of the Restoration and Eighteenth Century as they were acted at the Theatres-Royal by their Majesties' Servants*. Ed. Dougald MacMillan and Howard Mumford Jones. New York: Holt, 1931. 616–45.

Limbrick, Elaine. "Racine: The Historian in the Text." *Racine et/ou le classicisme*, ed. Ronald W. Tobin. Tübingen: Gunter Narr, 2001. 195–205.

Loftis, John. *The Spanish Plays of Neoclassical England*. New Haven, Conn.: Yale University Press, 1973.

Longino, Michèle. "*Bajazet* à la lettre." *Esprit Créateur* 38:2 (1998): 49–59.

Lubbock, Tom. "Claude's Extras [What's lost if you lose the figures from those pure landscapes?]." *Modern Painters* 7 (1994): 20–22.

Lyons, John D. "What Do We Mean When We Say 'classique'?" *Racine et/ou le classicisme*, ed. Ronald W. Tobin. Tübingen: Gunter Narr, 2001. 497–505.

Macht, Carol. *Classical Wedgwood Designs: The Sources and Their Use and the Relationship of Wedgwood Jasper Ware to the Classical Revival of the Eighteenth Century.* New York: M. Barrows, 1957.

Maclean, Rosemary. " 'O gran Principe o gran Prelato': Claude's Roman Patrons and the Appeal of His Landscape Easel Paintings." *Gazette des Beaux-Arts* 126 (1995): 223–34.

MacQueen, John. *Allegory.* London: Methuen, 1970.

Manwaring, Elizabeth Wheeler. *Italian Landscape in Eighteenth Century England: A Study Chiefly of the Influence of Claude Lorrain and Salvator Rosa on English Taste 1700–1800.* New York: Oxford University Press, 1925.

Maresca, Thomas E. "Saying and Meaning: Allegory and the Indefinable." *Bulletin of Research in the Humanities* 83 (1980): 248–61.

Marshall, David. *The Surprising Effects of Sympathy: Marivaux, Diderot, Rousseau, and Mary Shelley.* Chicago: University of Chicago Press, 1988.

McClennen, Joshua. *On the Meaning and Function of Allegory in the English Renaissance.* Ann Arbor: University of Michigan Press, 1947.

Metastasio, Pietro. *Three Melodramas.* Trans. Joseph G. Fucilla. Lexington: University Press of Kentucky, 1981.

———. *Tutte le opere.* Ed. Bruno Brunelli. 5 vols. Milan: Mondadori, 1947.

Michelsen, Peter. *Der unruhige Bürger: Studien zu Lessing und zur Literatur des achtzehnten Jahrhunderts.* Würzburg: Königshausen und Neumann, 1990.

Mitchell, W. J. T. *Iconology: Image, Text, Ideology.* Chicago: University of Chicago Press, 1986.

Mohr, Hans-Ulrich. "Lillos *The London Merchant*: Ein bürgerliches Trauerspiel?" *Germanisch-Romanische Monatsschrift* 36 (1986): 267–88.

Mozart, Wolfgang Amadeus, and Emanuel Schikaneder. *Die Zauberflöte.* Stuttgart: Reclam, 1973.

Murata, Margaret. *Operas for the Papal Court, 1631–1668.* Ann Arbor: UMI Research Press, 1981.

Nabokov, Vladimir. *Pnin.* New York: Avon, 1969.

Nelson, Alan H. *The Medieval English Stage: Corpus Christi Pageants and Plays.* Chicago: University of Chicago Press, 1974.

Nettl, Paul. "Deutungen und Fortsetzungen der *Zauberflöte.*" *Die Zauberflöte: Texte, Materialien, Kommentare,* ed. Attila Csampai und Dietmar Holland. Reinbek: Rowohlt, 1982. 183–200.

Newsom, Robert. *A Likely Story: Probability and Play in Fiction.* New Brunswick, N.J.: Rutgers University Press, 1988.

Nietzsche, Friedrich. *Werke.* Ed. Karl Schlechta. 3 vols. Munich: Hanser, 1966.

Norman, Larry F. "Racine's 'Other Eye': History, Nature, and Decorum from Ancient to Modern." *Racine et/ou le classicisme,* ed. Ronald W. Tobin. Tübingen: Gunter Narr, 2001. 139–50.

Noverre, Jean-Georges. *Lettres sur la danse, et sur les ballets.* 1760. New York: Broude, 1967.

Orgel, Stephen. *The Illusion of Power: Political Theater in the English Renaissance.* Berkeley: University of California Press, 1975.

———. *The Jonsonian Masque.* New York: Columbia University Press, 1981.

Orgel, Stephen, and Roy Strong. *Inigo Jones: The Theatre of the Stuart Court.* London: Sotheby Parke Bernet and Berkeley: University of California Press, 1973.

Pace, Claire. "Claude the Enchanted: Interpretations of Claude in England in the Earlier Nineteenth Century." *Burlington Magazine* 111 (1969): 733–40.

————. "'The Golden Age . . . The First and Last Days of Mankind': Claude Lorrain and Classical Pastoral, with Special Emphasis on Themes from Ovid's *Metamorphoses*." *Artibus et Historiae* 23 (2002): 127–56.

Panofsky, Erwin. *Idea: A Concept in Art Theory*. Trans. Joseph J. S. Peake. New York: Harper, 1968.

Parker, A. A. *The Allegorical Drama of Calderón: An Introduction to the Autos Sacramentales*. Oxford: Dolphin, 1943.

————. *The Mind and Art of Calderón: Essays on the Comedias*. Ed. Deborah Kong. Cambridge: Cambridge University Press, 1988.

Patey, Douglas Lane. *Probability and Literary Form: Philosophic Theory and Literary Practice in the Augustan Age*. Cambridge: Cambridge University Press, 1984.

Patterson, Michael. *The First German Theatre: Schiller, Goethe, Kleist and Büchner in Performance*. New York: Routledge, 1990.

Paulson, Ronald. *Literary Landscape: Turner and Constable*. New Haven, Conn.: Yale University Press, 1982.

Payer von Thurn, Rudolf, ed. *Wiener Haupt- und Staatsaktionen*. 2 vols. 1908–10. Nendeln/Liechtenstein: Kraus Reprint, 1975.

Pirrotta, Nino, and Elena Povoledo. *Music and Theatre from Poliziano to Monteverdi*. Trans. Karen Eales. Cambridge: Cambridge University Press, 1982.

Quilligan, Maureen. *The Language of Allegory: Defining the Genre*. Ithaca, N.Y.: Cornell University Press, 1979.

Racine, Jean. *Oeuvres complètes*. Vol. 1. Ed. Raymond Picard. Paris: Gallimard, 1950.

Raguenet, François. *Parallèle des Italiens et des Français en ce qui regarde la musique et les opéras* and *Défense du Parallèle des Italiens et des Français en ce qui regarde la musique et les opéras*. 1702 and 1705. Geneva: Minkoff Reprint, 1976.

Reilly, Mary. "The Moral Perspective in Racinian Tragedy." *Neophilogus* 88 (2004): 33–41.

Reiss, T. J. *Toward Dramatic Illusion: Theatrical Technique and Meaning from Hardy to Horace*. New Haven, Conn.: Yale University Press, 1971.

Reynolds, Sir Joshua. *Discourses on Art*. London: Collier, 1966.

Ribner, Irving. *The English History Play in the Age of Shakespeare*. Princeton, N.J.: Princeton University Press, 1957.

————, ed. *King John*. The Pelican Shakespeare. Baltimore: Penguin, 1962.

Roach, Joseph R. *The Player's Passion: Studies in the Science of Acting*. Newark: University of Delaware Press, 1985.

Rollinson, Philip. *Classical Theories of Allegory and Christian Culture*. Pittsburgh, Pa.: Duquesne University Press; London: Harvester, 1981.

Rommel, Otto. *Die Alt-Wiener Volkskomödie: Ihre Geschichte vom barocken Welt-Theater bis zum Tode Nestroys*. Vienna: A. Schroll, 1952.

————. *Die Maschinenkomödie*. Leipzig: Reclam, 1935.

Rosand, Ellen. *Opera in Seventeenth-Century Venice: The Creation of a Genre*. Berkeley: University of California Press, 1991.

Rosen, Charles. *The Classical Style: Haydn, Mozart, Beethoven*. New York: Norton, 1972.

Röthlisberger, Marcel. *The Claude Lorrain Album in the Norton Simon, Inc. Museum of Art*. Los Angeles: Los Angeles County Museum of Art, 1971.

————. *Claude Lorrain: The Drawings*. 2 vols. Berkeley: University of California Press, 1968.

————. *Claude Lorrain: The Paintings*. 2 vols. New York: Hacker Art Books, 1979.

————. "Das Enigma der überlängerten Figuren in Claudes Spätwerk." *Nicholas Poussin Claude Lorrain: Zu den Bildern im Städel*, ed. Michael Maek-Gérard.

Frankfurt/Main: Städtische Galerie im Städelschen Kunstinstitut, 1988. 92–100.

———. *Im Licht von Claude Lorrain: Lanschaftsmalerei aus drei Jahrhunderten.* Munich: Hirmer, 1983.

Röthlisberger, Marcel, and Doretta Cecchi. *Tout l'oeuvre peint de Claude Lorrain,* Paris: Flammarion, 1977.

Rougemont, Denis de. *L'amour et l'occident.* 1939. Paris: Union générale d'éditions, 1962.

Ruskin, John. *Modern Painters.* 5 vols. New York: Wiley, 1886.

Russell, H. Diane. *Claude Lorrain. 1600–1682.* New York and Washington: George Braziller and National Gallery of Art, 1982.

Sage, Jack. "Calderón und die Theatermusik." *Calderón de la Barca,* ed. Hans Flasche. Darmstadt: Wissenschaftliche Buchgesellschaft, 1971. 291–320.

Satori-Neumann, Bruno. *Die Frühzeit des Weimarischen Hoftheaters unter Goethes Leitung (1791 bis 1798).* Berlin: Gesellschaft für Theatergeschichte, 1922.

Schiller, Friedrich. *Sämtliche Werke.* 5 vols. Ed. Gerhard Fricke and Herbert G. Göpfert. Munich: Hanser, 1960.

Schlaffer, Heinz. *Faust Zweiter Teil: Die Allegorie des 19. Jahrhunderts.* Stuttgart: Metzler, 1981.

Schlegel, Friedrich. *Literary Notebooks: 1797–1801.* Ed. Hans Eichner. London: Athlone, 1957.

Schlegel, Johann Elias. *Canut: Ein Trauerspiel.* Stuttgart: Reclam, 1967.

Schöne, Albrecht. *Emblematik und Drama im Zeitalter des Barock.* Munich: Beck, 1964.

Sekora, John. *Luxury: The Concept in Western Thought, Eden to Smollett.* Baltimore: Johns Hopkins University Press, 1977.

Seneca, Lucius Annaeus. *Seneca: Four Tragedies and Octavia.* Trans. E. F. Watling. Harmondsworth: Penguin, 1966.

Seznec, Jean. *The Survival of the Pagan Gods: The Mythological Tradition and Its Place in Renaissance Humanism and Art.* Trans. Barbara F. Sessions. Princeton, N.J.: Princeton University Press, 1972.

Shakespeare, William. *The Riverside Shakespeare.* Ed. G. Blakemore Evans. Boston: Houghton Mifflin, 1974.

Sharpe, Lesley. "Goethe and the Weimar Theatre." *The Cambridge Companion to Goethe,* ed. Lesley Sharpe. Cambridge: Cambridge University Press, 2002. 116–28.

Shergold, N. D. *A History of the Spanish Stage from Medieval Times to the End of the Seventeenth Century.* Oxford: Clarendon, 1967.

Sidney, Sir Philip. *An Apologie for Poetrie.* Ed. Evelyn S. Shuckburgh. Cambridge: Cambridge University Press, 1951.

Smart, Mary Ann. *Mimomania: Music and Gesture in Nineteenth-Century Opera.* Berkeley: University of California Press, 2004.

Smith, Marion. *Ballet and Opera in the Age of* Giselle. Princeton, N.J.: Princeton University Press, 2000.

Smith, Patrick J. *The Tenth Muse: A Historical Study of the Opera Libretto.* New York: Knopf, 1970.

Solomon, Maynard. *Beethoven.* New York: Schirmer, 1977.

———. *Mozart: A Life.* New York: Harper-Collins, 1995.

Spaethling, Robert. *Music and Mozart in the Life of Goethe.* Columbia, S.C.: Camden House, 1987.

Spingarn, J. E. *A History of Literary Criticism in the Renaissance.* New York: Columbia University Press, 1924.

Spitzer, Leo. "The 'Récit de Théramène,'" in *Linguistics and Literary History: Essays in Stylistics*. Princeton, N.J.: Princeton University Press, 1967. 87–134.

Staiger, Emil. "Goethe und Mozart." *Musik und Dichtung*. Zurich: Atlantis, 1966. 45–66.

Stammler, Wolfgang. "'Edle Einfalt': Zur Geschichte eines kunsttheoretischen Topos." *Worte und Werte: Bruno Markwardt zum 60. Geburtstag*, ed. Gustav Erdmann and Alfons Eichstaedt. Berlin: De Gruyter, 1961. 359–82.

Strohm, Reinhard. *Dramma per Musica: Italian Opera Seria of the Eighteenth Century*. New Haven, Conn.: Yale University Press, 1997.

Subotnik, Rose Rosengard. "Whose *Magic Flute?* Intimations of Reality at the Gates of Enlightenment." *Nineteenth-Century Music* 15 (1991): 132–50.

Sullivan, Henry W. *Calderón in the German Lands and the Low Countries: His Reception and Influence, 1654–1980*. Cambridge: Cambridge University Press, 1983.

Szarota, Elida Maria. *Das Jesuitendrama im deutschen Sprachgebiet*. 4 vols. Munich: Fink, 1979.

———. *Künstler, Grübler und Rebellen: Studien zum europäischen Märtyrerdrama des 17. Jahrhunderts*. Berne: Francke, 1967.

Szondi, Peter. *Die Theorie des bürgerlichen Trauerspiels im 18. Jahrhundert*. Ed. Gert Mattenklott. Frankfurt/Main: Suhrkamp, 1973.

Tasso, Torquato. *Aminta*. Ed. Luigi Fassò. Florence: Sansoni, 1967.

Ter Horst, Robert. *Calderón: The Secular Plays*. Lexington: University Press of Kentucky, 1982.

Tillyard, E. M. *The Elizabethan World Picture*. 1944. New York: Vintage, n.d.

Tobin, Ronald W. *Racine and Seneca*. Chapel Hill: University of North Carolina Press, 1971.

Tomlinson, Gary. *Metaphysical Song: An Essay on Opera*. Princeton, N.J.: Princeton University Press, 1999.

Trainor, Stephen L., Jr. "Tears Abounding: *The London Merchant* as Puritan Tragedy." *SEL: Studies in English Literature 1500–1900* 18 (1978): 509–21.

Tuve, Rosemond. *Allegorical Imagery: Some Medieval Books and Their Posterity*. Princeton, N.J.: Princeton University Press, 1977.

Urbach, Reinhard. *Die Wiener Komödie und ihr Publikum: Stranitzky und die Folgen*. Vienna: Jugend und Volk, 1973.

Védier, Georges. *Origine et évolution de la dramaturgie néo-classique: L'influence des arts plastiques en Italie et en France: Le rideau, la mise en scène et les trois unités*. Paris: Presses universitaires de France, 1955.

Vega, Lope de. *Obras selectas*. 3 vols. Madrid: Aguilar, 1991.

Voltaire (François-Marie Arouet). *Oeuvres complètes*. Vol. 6. Paris: Garnier, 1877.

Vondel, Joost van den. *Volledige Dichtwerken en oorspronkelijk Proza*. Ed. Albert Verwey. Amsterdam: H. J. W. Becht, 1937.

Wagner, Richard. *Dichtungen und Schriften*. 10 vols. Ed. Dieter Borchmeyer. Frankfurt/Main: Insel, 1983.

———. *The Ring of the Nibelung: German Text with an English Translation*. Trans. Andrew Porter. New York: Norton, 1977.

Wahle, Julius. *Das Weimarer Hoftheater unter Goethes Leitung*. Weimar: Goethe-Gesellschaft, 1892.

Waldura, Markus. "Die Singspiele." *Goethe Handbuch* 2. Ed. Theo Buck. Stuttgart: Metzler, 1997. 173–94.

Weimann, Robert. *Shakespeare and the Popular Tradition in the Theater: Studies in the Social Dimension of Dramatic Form and Function*. Ed. Robert Schwartz. Baltimore: Johns Hopkins University Press, 1978.

Weinberg, Bernard. *A History of Literary Criticism in the Italian Renaissance*. Vol. 1. Chicago: University of Chicago Press, 1961.

Weinrich, Harald. *Ehrensache Höflichkeit*. Augsburg: Universität Augsburg, 1996.

Weiß, Karl. *Die Wiener Haupt- und Staatsaktionen*. Vienna: Carl Gerold, 1854.

Wickham, Glynne. *Early English Stages 1300–1660*. 3 vols. London: Routledge and Kegan Paul; New York: Columbia University Press, 1959–81.

Williams, Simon. *German Actors of the Eighteenth and Nineteenth Centuries: Idealism, Romanticism, and Realism*. Westport, Conn.: Greenwood, 1985.

Wilson, Edward M., and Duncan Moir. *The Golden Age Drama 1492–1700*. London: Benn, 1971.

Wilton-Ely, John. "Neo-classicism." Grove Art Online. Oxford University Press, [July 30, 2005], http://www.groveart.com/.

Winckelmann, Johann Joachim. *Kleine Schriften, Vorreden, Entwürfe*. Ed. Walther Rehm. Berlin: De Gruyter, 1968.

Wind, Edgar. *Pagan Mysteries in the Renaissance*. New York: Norton, 1968.

Wine, Humphrey. *Claude: The Poetic Landscape*. London: National Gallery Publications, 1994.

Wittkower, Rudolf, and Margot Wittkower. *Born under Saturn: The Character and Conduct of Artists: A Documented History from Antiquity to the French Revolution*. New York: Norton, 1969.

Woolf, Rosemary. *The English Mystery Plays*. Berkeley: University of California Press, 1972.

Yates, Frances Amelia. *Giordano Bruno and the Hermetic Tradition*. Chicago: University of Chicago Press, 1964.

Young, Karl. *The Drama of the Medieval Church*. 2 vols. Oxford: Clarendon, 1967.

Zaslaw, Neal, ed. *The Classical Era: From the 1740s to the End of the 18th Century*. London: Macmillan, 1989.

Index

DATE DUE
